Family History in the Middle East

SUNY Series in the Social and
Economic History of the Middle East
Donald Quataert, Editor

Family History
in the
Middle East

Household, Property, and Gender

Edited by
Beshara Doumani

State University of New York Press

Published by
State University of New York Press, Albany

Cover etching and design by Marwan, 1999

For information, address State University of New York Press,
90 State Street, Suite 700, Albany, N.Y., 12207

Production by Diane Ganeles
Marketing by Michael Campochiaro

Library of Congress Cataloging-in-Publication Data

Family history in the Middle East: Household, property, and gender / Beshara
    Doumani, editor.
        p. cm. — (SUNY series in the social and economic history of the Middle East)
    Includes bibliographical references and index.
    ISBN 0-7914-5679-X (alk. paper) — ISBN 0-7914-5680-3 (pbk. : alk. paper)
        1. Family—Middle East—History. 2. Domestic relations (Islamic law)—Middle
East—History. 3. Middle East—Social conditions. 4. Middle East—History I. Doumani,
Beshara, 1957 – II. Series.

HQ663.3 .F36 2003
306.85'0956—dc21   2002067043

10 9 8 7 6 5 4 3 2 1

For Issmat, Tala, and Yara

Contents

Note on Transliteration and Pronounciation

Turkish and Arabic terms are translated according to the system of the *International Journal of Middle East Studies*. Wherever possible, English terms were used in order to make the text more accessible. All diacritical marks for Arabic terms were omitted except for the *ayn* (ʿ) and hamza (ʾ), and these were used only when they occur in the middle of the word or name. Below is a guide for the pronunciation of Turkish words.

Guide to Pronounciation of Turkish Words

C, c = "j" as in juice

Ç, ç = "ch" as in cheek

Ğ, ğ = soft "g", hardly pronounced

ı   = without a dot, pronounced like the first syllable of "earnest"

İ, i = with a dot, between "in" and "eel"

Ö, ö = as in the umlaut ö in German

Ş, ş = as in "sheet"

Ü, ü = as in the umlat ü in German

ˆ = used to denote a lengthened vowel (a, i, and u) or to palatize a preceeding g, k, or l

After Cornell H. Fleischer, *Bureaucrat and Intellectual in the Ottoman Empire: The Historian Mustafa Âli (1541–1600).* Princeton, 1986, xvi.

List of Tables and Figures

1

Introduction

Beshara Doumani

As a nexus of interest and emotion on the cellular level of social organization, and as a key referential grid for the social imaginary, family is everywhere.[1] It can be studied as a structure, a process, a cultural construct, and as a discourse. The considerable literature on history of the family in Europe and the United States published over the past four decades, which pushed out in all four directions, has produced fascinating and largely unexpected results and has deeply influenced research agendas in a variety of disciplines.[2] In Middle Eastern Studies one cannot yet speak of family history as a distinct and established field of inquiry, but it is increasingly becoming a strategic site of analysis.[3] This anthology is simultaneously a product of this increasing interest and an introduction to exciting new possibilities for rethinking Middle East Studies.

Family history is a strategic site of analysis, because it demands careful attention to the interplay between micro and macro processes of change, and invites the building of conceptual bridges between materialist and discursive frameworks of analysis: two key challenges currently facing most scholars, especially social and cultural historians. The articles in this anthology are useful precisely because they grapple with the issues raised by these challenges on the level of praxis: i.e., through archival research and/or field work focused on specific times, places, and social groups.

Family history is also an ideal intellectual space for cross-disciplinary conversations, a fertile ground for the emergence of new lines of inquiry. In addition to historians, this anthology brings together scholars from the disciplines of anthropology and demography who are committed to a critical perspective on family, household, and kinship as historically contingent units of analysis. The purpose is neither to provide a schematic overview of the rich diversity of family life in the Middle East nor to present an orderly historical account of change over time. It is much too early for that and, in any case, it is not clear that such a project is desirable, as it might valorize the very assumptions that historians of the family are fond of challenging. Rather, the aim is to provide a cross section of the various thematics, theoretical approaches, methodological issues, and sources currently being explored.

The very centrality of the family also makes it a slippery concept. The flexibility and fluidity of family forms as well as the diversity of household structures within a single setting, not to mention across time and space, wreak havoc with attempts at taxonomies and large-scale generalizations (whether about epochs, regions, or cultures). In addition, the wide range of sources and questions that can be brought to bear on family life means that family can easily be (and has been) used as a convenient vehicle for pursuing different visions and approaches to history and social analysis in general.[4] The articles in this anthology reflect these differences and uncertainties, all the more so considering that most of the authors did not begin their careers with a focus on family history. Hence, their tentative move in this direction carries with it theoretical baggage and topical concerns developed for other purposes. By the same token, however, the flexibility, diversity, and dynamism of family life can be liberating for those who want to explore alternative ways of recovering the past. They allow historians to follow the complex juxtaposition of different rhythms of time— individual time, family time, historical time— and make possible a much-needed nonlinear non-Eurocentric approach to history: that is, an approach that does not assume an inexorable movement forward towards a Western model of "modernity."[5]

Finally, family history directly interfaces with the three major prestige zones that have dominated intellectual production in Middle East Studies over the past two generations: Islam, gender, and modernity.[6] In all three, notions of family and household are omnipresent, but they remain in the background and float in and out between the lines in the form of assumptions that privilege some arguments and silence others. The very structure of this anthology makes the point that there is a need for a critical reassessment of scholarship in these three prestige zones in light of historically grounded studies on family life.

The Middle East contains diverse regions with long and rich histories.[7] This anthology remains within the bounds of the early modern and modern periods (the seventeenth century to the twentieth), and of the Arab heartlands of the Ottoman Empire –Greater Syria and Egypt— as well as Iran. Those readers familiar with the literature on European family history will immediately notice that the basic approaches discussed by Anderson (1980)—demographic, sentiments, and household economics—are represented here. For example, two of the studies utilize family reconstitution techniques to analyze census data for large urban populations (Cairo and Damascus). Two other articles deal with the political economy of households on the village level as a way to get at the historical evolution of marriage and property devolution strategies. Still another examines the meanings of gold jewelry in relations between spouses and between women and their natal kin. Most of the contributions, however, do not fit neatly into these three basic approaches.[8] This is a healthy sign, for the growing interest in family history in Middle East Studies, while mindful of the literature on this topic generated in the United States and Europe, is taking place within a historically specific set of intellectual trajectories and relies on different types of sources. The contributions to this volume must be seen in light of these two larger contexts.

Invoking the Family

Family is frequently invoked, but is rarely historicized. In public debates, society is family writ large—that is, family is deployed as a metaphor. Aside from the closely related concept of "woman," family is the most commonly used trope for communicating visions of the past and hopes for the future or, put differently, for expressing ideological positions about how society has been organized and how it should be properly ordered.[9] In this particular lineage in the use of the word, family is packed with meanings but emptied of historical substance. Consequently, it is talked about in monolithic terms—as evident by the prefixes Arab, Muslim, or Mediterranean—and framed monochromatically as either traditional or modern.

In scholarly writings, a long-standing and pervasive notion is that Middle Eastern societies are family-based, the implication being that modernity constitutes a leap forward to societies based on the individual.[10] While this may sound similar to the position that society is family writ large, it actually involves a move in the opposite direction: a detailed inquiry about the contemporary place of family and, especially, kinship in society. The development of this second lineage in discourses about the family began with ethnographers and anthropologists. Their writings provided the first and most detailed descriptions of social practices and cultural norms in specific locales, usually from the perspective that these are expressions of two ordering principles: family and religion.[11] Family is also a primary concern for sociologists, economists, demographers, and political scientists anxious about trajectories of future developments in the region. Using new tools developed in their respective disciplines (such as surveys and statistical techniques), they linked studies of family relations and household structures to the issues of the day: modernization, political mobilization, and economic development. Unlike ethnographers and anthropologists, however, their main focus was on large urban populations, especially in the coastal cosmopolitan cities where they expected to find the greatest changes as a result of the intensive encounter with European culture and economy.[12]

In both popular and scholarly discourses, the assumption that a monolithic traditional family type constituted the bedrock of Middle Eastern societies for centuries and the pervasiveness of a master narrative of linear evolution from primitive extended group to modern nuclear family help explain the lack of interest in family history. This is not, by the way, a phenomenon peculiar to Middle East Studies. The same situation obtains in South Asian and Chinese studies.[13] In all three cases, a traditional family type was invented in the nineteenth century—the Joint-Hindu family, the extended Chinese family, and the patriarchal Middle East family—and much ink was spilt over its ills or advantages as well as about how its inevitable transformation ought to be managed.[14] In all three regions, moreover, the most insightful writings about family life—whether of affective ties, conflicting interests between family members, relations between kin, and the role of family in society—have been those of novelists. Naguib Mahfouz's trilogy (*Palace Walk*, *Palace of Desire*, and *Sugar Street*) is a classic example. Indeed, one is hard pressed to think of any novel published over the past century in which family was not a central concern. But even in this realm, and despite the great sensitivity and complexity in the way the family is dealt with, most narratives mulled over the problems of intensifying social fissures and conflicting loyalties as ideas about conjugal love, more democratic relations between parents and children, individuation, and other dimensions of the stereotypical modern family began to loosen the grip of the traditional patriarchal household.

Historicizing the Family

It is not a coincidence that family history as a field of study came into its own in the 1970s, for that is precisely when the larger enterprise of social history was at the peak of self-confidence and influence in the

Western academy. By then, increasingly sophisticated quantitative and qualitative methodologies, mostly borrowed from sociology and economics but also drawing on theoretical debates in anthropology and comparative literature, were already being used with stunning effectiveness to recover the history of ordinary people and marginalized groups—workers, peasants, women, slaves—in stark contrast to the hitherto myopic and often politically conservative focus on elites and their institutions. With (perhaps unjustified) optimism, social historians took on the notoriously difficult concepts of family and household and waded neck-deep in massive, yet diverse and uneven, archival sources. Their goal: to explore the connections between Europe's transition to modernity (the rise of the modern state, capitalism, industrialization, and the like) and the inner workings of social life on the micro level, the latter seen as both a reflection of and an agent in shaping the Big Picture.

The early findings were as startling as they were unexpected. The nuclear family is not a product of the industrial revolution; it predominated long before. The processes of modernity did not lead to the destruction of the extended family in industrial cities; rather, they led to an increase in co-residence with extended kin. The age of marriage prior to industrialization was late, not early as commonly believed. Family size was small, not large; and mobility was substantial, not limited.[15] Kinship relations became more, not less, important in the nineteenth century, and were cemented by sharply increased rates of repeated endogamous marriages, especially between cross-cousins.[16] These are but some of the findings that propelled family history into a major field of inquiry and laid to rest grand theories about family in the past and about the impact of modernization.

Most of the above findings were distilled through family reconstitution techniques applied to masses of hitherto untapped sources, such as parish registers, that allow for in-depth analysis over long periods of time.[17] These techniques were developed by French historical demographers in the mid-1950s and used extensively by the Cambridge Group for the History of Population and Social Structure, established in 1964. Arguments still rage about the interpretations and the generalizability of these findings, not to mention the Eurocentric questions that drive them. But two things are clear: pervasive myths about linear evolution are now replaced by a large and ever-growing data base amenable to comparative analysis; and, for the first time, the discussion is about the family life of the mass of ordinary people, not just elite groups.

Middle East Studies seems to be at a disadvantage here in terms of sources, especially when it comes to the demography and political economy of households. There are no archives that come close to what is available in some parts of Europe, especially England, France, and southern Germany. True, the Ottoman state had a love affair with paper, and its bureaucracies produced massive amounts of documents, but its far-flung territories and its pragmatic policy of rule through local intermediaries—the latter of which endowed it with flexibility and, by any measure, amazing longevity—ruled out for the most part the kind of minutely detailed surveillance used to construct an official memory by states and principalities in some European regions. This is especially true for tribal areas, villages, and provincial towns. To take one example: census counts that use the individual as the basic statistical unit were not conducted by the central Ottoman government until the end of the nineteenth century. Prior to that time, periodic cadastral surveys based on the household as the statistical unit were carried out, but there are huge gaps over the centuries. With the exception of Egypt, we know of no consistent or comprehensive sources that allow for comparative analysis within the empire, much less with other regions prior to 1885.[18]

Family and Household

In this context, the 1848 census carried out in Cairo—which is based on the individual as the statistical unit of analysis, and which provides our first opportunity to make generalizations about an entire urban population, not just its elites—takes on a special significance. In his contribution to this volume, Philippe Fargues, a French historical demographer, presents the findings of an analysis based on family reconstitution of this census. He makes three fundamental points. First, in terms of residential living the nuclear (or conjugal) family household predominated over every other form. In addition, female-headed households constituted a significant part (15.9 percent) of the total number of households. Second, and more important, he shows that the most salient feature of the typical family in the largest Arab city at the time was extreme volatility. Short life-spans, high rates of infant and child mortality, and the dislocations caused by a state that faced a manpower shortage in its military, agricultural, and industrial projects —all brought about a high degree of mobility and a rapid rotation in the life cycle of individuals. For example, 70 percent of boys between 10 and 14 were separated from their parents either because both father and mother had already died or because these boys had already left home. Prior to the age of 10, it was not unusual for at least one of the parents to be dead, and to know one's grandfather or grandmother was rare. This placed severe restrictions on the extent and depth of

relations within the conjugal family and drastically reduced the incidence of large, extended families.[19] Third, he argues that the individual was not dissolved in kinship as commonly assumed. Rather,
she or he existed, often precariously, in rapidly changing sets of
domestic contexts that intimately involved both kin and non-kin. All
of this is made more complicated by the fact that the experiences of
each individual in terms of household composition, residential location, marriage age, fertility, education, and so on differed widely
depending on sex, class, occupation, religious sect, and a number of
other factors.

Can one generalize the demographic patterns of one city to another within the Ottoman domains, or was each city or region unique?
Tomoki Okawara shows that the latter may be true. In a painstaking
quantitative analysis of household structures in late-Ottoman Damascus, he compares his findings to those of Alan Duben and Cem
Behar, who published the first book on family history in Middle East
Studies, *Istanbul Households: Marriage, Family, and Fertility, 1880–1940*.
Following the example and methods of the Cambridge Group, Duben
and Behar undertook a quantitative analysis of the rich censuses of
1885 and 1907, which provided for the first time substantial information on every individual, not just general information about households. They also drew on the ideas and methods of Philippe Ariès and
other icons of the sentiments approach to family history in order to
put flesh on the bones of the census. Newspapers, magazines, novels,
biographies, and private letters, as well as "retrospective interviews,"
were used to discuss values, meanings, and affective relations within
households.[20] Their conclusions (minus the nuances): the median family form was the simple conjugal household, average household size
was small, fertility rates declined, marriage age was already late for
men and became later for women, and family planning was practiced.
This led them to argue that Istanbul was unique within the Ottoman
Empire, and did not even belong to the rest of Anatolia.[21]

Based on the same 1907 census, but centering on the city of Damascus, Okawara's analysis presents a rather different picture: the
typical Damascene household was large in size and complex in structure. This is reflected in and is perhaps an outcome of the high proportion of multiple-family residences, the sheer size of the pervasive
Damascene courtyard-house, the relatively high rate of polygyny, and
the multigenerational character of households. Okawara is quick to
point out that his empirical description of household structures at one
point in time raises more questions than it answers. He calls for further research on demographic issues (such as fertility rates and marriage patterns) and on the specific historical context of Ottoman

Damascus. At some point, in other words, the statistically based categories of historical demography have to be connected to specific families and social groups whose history can be traced over the long term.

In this respect, elite groups left far more traces for the historian to follow, allowing for a wider range of stories. Mary Ann Fay's discussion of the transformation of elite Egyptian households from large and complex structures in the late eighteenth century to ones in which the values (if not necessarily the practices) of simple nuclear family forms prevailed by the early twentieth century is the mirror opposite of Fargues's and Okawara's projects. Hers is a story about process and agency rather than structure and form. Instead of reconstituting a general picture about family life from an immense database of an entire urban population at one point in time, she follows the transformations in the political economy of the upper crust of Egyptian society over the course of two centuries. The question that Fay outlines a tentative answer for is this: Why did elite Egyptian women, especially those like Huda Sha'rawi who were instrumental to the creation of the first feminist movement in the modern Arab world at the turn of the twentieth century, become champions of what she calls the "Western-style" nuclear family?

Fay begins by dismissing as teleological the two approaches she sees as pervasive in studies of the women's movements in Egypt: modernization and Westernization. The first posits that Egypt's incorporation into the European-dominated world economy naturally leads to the rise of a nuclear family, while the latter privileges a process of cultural borrowing by an elite heavily influenced by European models of family life. Fay suggests an alternative explanation that endows elite women with a form of historical agency. Simply put, she argues that elite women in the eighteenth century enjoyed significant social and economic power as well as autonomy and influence within ruling Mamluk households that operated in a decentralized political environment. The rise of a modern centralized state broke the back of these households and replaced them with a modern army and a bureaucracy. Consequently, this diminished the status and power of elite women, cut off their access to economic enterprises, and undermined their influence over, as well as the importance of, the marriage strategies that had long been central to the solidarity of these households. She then sketches out a biography of Huda Sha'rawi to suggest that she and women like her began to valorize the conjugal family in order to strengthen their position within the household, to carve out a role in public political life, and to gain access to education and work. The merits of this argument remain to be tested. As Fay notes, we do not have as yet a systematic study of the social history of elite Egyptian women in the nineteenth century. Still, Fay's approach may add an important historical dimension to gender studies in the Middle East, in that she makes a direct connection between the political economy and spatial organization of the household as a unit of analysis, on the one hand, and the particular fields of experience of women within these households, on the other.

Family, Gender, and Property

Until fairly recently, the relationship between family history and gender studies has oscillated between tension and estrangement.[22] It is only fitting, perhaps, that marriage, more than any other issue, dominates the growing number of works that seek to integrate these two approaches. All three articles in this section explicitly take marriage as a point of departure for analyzing the relationship between gender and property within the context of a long-term perspective on family and kinship. The different approaches and methodologies employed point, at the same time, to the rich possibilities for pushing family history and gender studies towards a mutually gratifying embrace.

Erika Friedl brings to bear thirty-five years of ethnographic research among the Boir Ahmadi, a tribal Luri-speaking Shi'ite people in the southern Zagros Mountains in Iran, in a sweeping account of changes in marriage strategies in a single village, Deh Koh, over a period of 110 years (1880–1990). Hers is a materialist approach that is concerned with and persuasively argues for a direct connection between changes in marital customs and relations—such as wedding ceremonies, bride-price, expectations the bride and the groom have of each other, parental influence in the choice of partners, and the division of labor within the household (and with it, gender identity)—to changes in forms of property holding, in relations of economic production, and in political struggles both within the village and between it and the state over control of the surplus. This richly detailed study transports the reader into the inner world of Deh Koh and shows the myriad of ways that both the ideology and praxis of marriage were fundamentally transformed by the 1960s, when most of its residents became small landowners and wage laborers.

The relationship between marriage strategies and property is inextricable, especially if one is concerned not only about larger economic forces, but also with inheritance practices, bridal gifts, and the reproduction of family relations in general. The literature on these issues is substantial in Middle East Studies, but the article by Martha Mundy and Richard Saumarez Smith on peasant households in a Jordanian village from 1880 to 1940 raises the bar for standards of empirical depth and theoretical rigor. On the surface, theirs is a study of the place of *mahr* (the dower) in social exchanges within a network of kin and between households over time. The idea is to tease out the differences and reveal the connections between legal prescriptions, registration procedures by the state, and actual practices of property devolution. But this only opens the door to a series of arguments on two levels. The first is a theoretical intervention that engages Lévi-Strauss's structuralist model about the exchange of brides. Mundy and Smith use a formidable array of sources—oral history, Islamic and civil court records, Ottoman *tapu* and *nufus* records, and documents from the Mandate cadastre of the Emirate of TransJordan—to reconstruct three case studies of exchanges, which demonstrate how brides permit the economic individuation of the groom by producing not only objects, but also persons; hence, the futility of separating the two in social analysis of the household. The second level is a historical discussion based on the premise that, as Mundy and Smith put it, "Between the abstract categories of law and the concrete practices of property and gender stand living persons." They show that historical time, in itself a collision and interaction between three histories—accidents of demography, family property transmission strategies, and endowment of marital alliances—did not always mesh with individual time and archival time. This led to forms of agency characterized by plurality and tension, as women's claims to properties that both state law and their marriage contracts promised them were pursued with greater assertiveness.

Annelies Moors also writes about the relationship between marriage and property through the lens of bridal gifts—in this case, gold jewelry. Like Mundy and Smith, she uses archival and oral sources that span a long period of time (1920-90) in order to problematize the issue of agency and to explore the ways that woman, property, family, and kinship are constructed through social exchanges. In a similar vein, she argues that studies of inheritance practices and family reproduction strategies must distinguish between different forms of property as well as the changing meanings of a specific form of property over time. Thus positioned at the crossroads of women's history and family history, this article investigates at which moments, in what contexts, and under which conditions men and women identify with, construct, and contest the meanings of family. In a fascinating narrative, Moors argues that the changing preferences for styles of gold jewelry (*baladi*, Italian, and Gulf) speak volumes about differences between women depending on class and location (rural or urban), as well as about notions of love, the nature of the relationship between husband and wife, and the economic strategies of women. She concludes that although there was considerable change in marriage arrangements and in the meanings ascribed to gold jewelry, the inheritance strategies of women remained by and large the same. This is especially true in the ways that women often exercised their agency by refraining from claiming their legal inheritance in favor of their brothers. As Moors points out, this provides them with more negotiating space within their natal families and, with the growing emphasis on conjugality, partially balances their dependence on husbands who were increasingly becoming the sole bread winners.

Family and the Praxis of Islamic Law

It is not a coincidence that all three articles in the section on family and gender are by anthropologists. After all, these topics have been a key concern of this discipline before most historians took them seriously. But there is another reason: to integrate gender studies into family history or vice versa requires greater emphasis on relations between family members and a partial move away from family or household as an indivisible unit of analysis. The often conflicting inner world of family life and the differential positioning of family members within a single household acquires as much or greater significance than a focus on household structures with a view to building a taxonomy of family types that are then plugged into some larger social process evolving in linear time.[23] This is especially true if one views family as both the crucible for and the product of the social constructions of kinship, property, and sexual difference.

Getting a sense of the inner world is not easy for historians who study pre-twentieth-century societies. Oral interviews and field observations are severely limited if not impossible. In addition, and unlike the situation in Europe and the United States, there is precious little by way of memoirs, private correspondences, novels, paintings, and other types of sources that lend themselves to this kind of analysis prior to the mid-nineteenth century. Needless to say, the sources become even more drastically limited the farther back one goes in time. There are other sources, to be sure, but they have yet to be systematically interrogated. These include biographical dictionaries; compilations of legal responsa (fatwas) by legal experts (muftis); manuscripts on law, theology, history, and other matters by local religious scholars; private family papers; objects of material culture; and the built environment of houses, markets, mosques, baths, streets, and other types of structures, some of which date to the Mamluk era and even before.

Still, the records of Islamic courts, which operated in all the major cities and provincial towns, have become recognized as the richest

archival resource for the social and cultural history in general and
family history in particular for most regions in the Middle East and
North Africa during the Ottoman era. As the key state institution in
charge of matters relating to personal status and property and as a
public records office of sorts, the Islamic court was resorted to on a
daily basis by countless numbers of Ottoman subjects: rich and poor,
men and women, young and old, Muslim and non-Muslim, powerful
and weak, and everything in between. There they registered the purchase and sale of property; the endowment of *waqfs*; and the particulars of marriage contracts, divorces, probate inventories, commercial
dealings, custody of children, and so on. The court also adjudicated in
civil and criminal lawsuits and made official legal settlements of all
kinds, such as the division of properties and payments of debts. This
is but a sampling of what can be a daily record of a massive interaction between people and the principal legal arena for negotiating property access rights, public morality, kinship relations, and lines of authority
both within and between (mostly propertied) urban families.

Historians have latched onto the Islamic records in a feeding frenzy
since the 1970s, but the harder they have tried to squeeze them for
content, the more aware they have become of the tremendous methodological difficulties involved. One set of problems is largely technical: the records are massive, yet they are fragmented in terms of
structure and time periods covered; moreover, they are geographi-
cally scattered, unindexed, and often in a state of confusion. As of yet,
we do not have a firm grasp of a comparative topography of these
records: i.e., the types of cases registered, the way such cases are summarized, the procedures followed, the personnel involved, and the
social groups represented, to mention but a few variables. This is to
say nothing of two other larger problems. First is the angst and nail-
biting sweeping the academy when it comes to the issues of form and
content, text and context, structure and agency. An anthropology of
archives that focuses primarily on literary analysis is slowly emerging
and poses a serious challenge to the work of most social historians.[24]
Second, legal history in the full sense of the word is just beginning to
breach the fortresses of Islamic Studies. The social history of the production of legal norms, studies of specific groups of religious scholars
over time, and intellectual history on both the popular and elite levels
still have a long way to go.[25] Consequently, historians who rely on
court records as a primary source often have to operate in a dimly lit
world, especially if they focus on provincial towns, the histories of
which have yet to be systematically investigated.

The significance of the three articles on family and the Islamic
court lies in their tentative attempts to address these theoretical

and methodological challenges through specific case studies. Iris Agmon takes on the problems posed by the fact that the court cases that the historian reads are usually paragraph-long summaries of what could be several documented court sessions. As far as we know, pre-summary documents were not officially kept (if they did exist) prior to administrative changes by the central Ottoman state in the 1870s. Agmon, who found records of protocol sessions in the courts of Haifa and Jaffa in Palestine dating to the late nineteenth century, tracks the changes in the process of document production over time (diachronically) and between the two courts (synchronically) and compares them to the summaries. She argues that the new procedures led to an intensification of the encounter between individuals and the court and provided greater scope for that institution to inscribe a legal notion of family. Through a gripping case study of several lawsuits between an estranged couple, Agmon skillfully elucidates the critical role of the court in mediating family relations and the possibilities of agency (especially for women). She does this by following how litigants negotiated court procedures, faced a new breed of judges, and dealt with a growing group of professional lawyers—all in the context of unprecedented intervention in domestic life by a centralizing state and the rapid demographic change and integration of these two cities into the world economy.

As previously mentioned, using court records demands at least a double reading. Historians can scour the contents of cases for information about specific individuals, families, social groups, events, and practices of daily life. At the same time, they need to consider the narrative patterns of the stories likely to be discursively authorized by the Islamic court records as a specific kind of archive. In my comparative analysis of lawsuits between kin litigated in the Islamic courts of Nablus (Palestine) and Tripoli (Lebanon) during the early eighteenth and the first two thirds of the nineteenth century, I attempt such a double reading in order to understand the mutually constitutive relationship between kin and court. On the one hand, kin partially defined the role of the court as a social institution, shaped its archives, and influenced the praxis of Islamic law by resorting to it in great numbers as a forum to enact, among other things, legally sophisticated property devolution strategies. On the other hand, the discursive structures of Islamic legal norms, the legal procedures of a state-sanctioned institution, and the active authority of the judge set the parameters and the ground rules for negotiations between kin. By applying two methodologies of scale: a micro analysis of two sets of lawsuits between kin, and a macro analysis of the changing patterns in lawsuits over time and across space, I make some tentative generalizations about how a textual memory is constructed and about the ways in the which the Islamic court is used as an arena for the reconfiguration of family relations and household structures.

Through a case study of a single lawsuit in seventeenth-century Tripoli, Heather Ferguson examines notions of family and personhood in legal discourses. Hers is essentially a methodological intervention on how one can read and deploy historical documents in constructing narratives about the past. Ferguson throws down the gauntlet to conventional readings of court documents as expressions of social reality and draws on theories of practice and performance to argue for a three-tiered analysis that synthesizes text, context, and the labor of the historian. First, there is the key moment of litigation, which can be understood as a cultural performance that both reproduces and transforms communities and persons. Second, there is the moment of writing the summary document by the court, which can be analyzed as a process or specific structure of ideological production that has its own local history. Third, there are the ways in which the very deployment or reading of documents by historians becomes part of the document's own history or field of production. This multidimensional approach reinforces the call for a relational understanding of concepts such as family, household, and property that are often naturalized in social analysis and engages wider theoretical debates in other fields of study.

Family as a Discourse

The pervasive use of "woman" and "family" as tropes in discourses about modernity and the role of the state in society has attracted increasing attention by historians, especially those interested in family as both a cultural ideal and a lived reality. This requires combining discursive and materialist modes of analysis. Ken Cuno employs precisely such a methodology to show that the apparent switch by the khedival household in nineteenth-century Egypt from concubinage and harem life to monogamy, companionate marriage, and a public role for women was riddled with ambiguities. He argues that this transition was not the result of changing attitudes precipitated by Westernization, as has long been assumed, and that there is no foundation for the view that the khedival household, by consciously embodying the ideals of modern family life, had any significant influence on modes of domesticity among the Egyptian middle and upper classes. Rather, the very public switch, if one can call it that, must be seen as but one dynastic strategy of reproduction in the larger contexts of the political culture of the Ottoman ruling classes, as well as in the specific Egyptian context of internal power struggles within the household, economic changes (especially the bankruptcy of 1875), and the British occupation of 1882. The ambiguity is generated by the fact that the pronouncements, public rituals, and media campaigns of the khedival household about its modern family goals were expressed in two different registers: one targeting Western powers and observers and the other geared towards local public opinion. To complicate matters further, the former were mired in a terrible misunderstanding of the actual operations of the khedival household due to their own pervasive discourses on the harem and slavery. Thus, Europeans considered this switch a significant departure. As to local public opinion, the Egyptian press, with the blessing of the khedives, cast it in terms of closer adherence to traditional Muslim family values. This, in turn, was not a cost-free message, as the actual private behavior of the khedives lived up to neither image.

Akram Khater adds the Lebanese case to the growing literature on women and the family as metaphors in debates on modernity at the turn of the twentieth century, but with two twists. First, he follows contemporary discussions in the press about marriage, the proper role of women, and attitudes towards raising children not in Lebanon itself, but among immigrants from Mount Lebanon in the United States. On one level, he argues that their experience with "modernity" did not lead to predictable conclusions as to what constitutes an ideal family and that the changes in family structures cannot be easily plotted on linear continuums of public to private and of extended to nuclear. On another level, he shows that their vigorous discussions were carried out in the context of and were influenced by an ongoing discourse in the United States itself about how immigrants must become assimilated into the cultural ideal of a white Anglo-Saxon middle class. The second twist is a methodological intervention about what it means to write a "history" of family when the reality of individual lives is much too messy and diverse to fit into neat analytical boxes of ideal family types. This mirrors the obvious disconnect between the ideals articulated in newspapers and the actual experiences of daily life, such as those of thousands of Lebanese women who fanned out all over the United States on their own, peddling wares from house to house and from one small town to another.

Thinking Family History

The articles in this anthology suggest some possible approaches for the study of family history in the Middle East and indicate both the potential and limitations of available sources. Those that emphasize structural demographic analysis disabuse us of the notion that there is some universal traditional family form. Rather, they suggest that there was a broad range of family arrangements, both within a single urban center and between them. This is but the tip of the iceberg. Reconstituting family history from the mountains of largely untapped quantitative data available for cities, towns, and villages since the 1500s is a daunting but essential task. Another challenge is to produce indepth case studies of specific families and social groups over long periods of time in order to make linkages between family life and the changing political economies, cultural dynamics, and intellectual environments of the various regions in the Middle East. Only when substantial progress has been made on both fronts will we be able to make some useful generalizations about significant changes in the history of family life over the past few ceturies.

It is no surprise that most of the articles in this anthology are concerned with the issues of women, gender, and property. In Europe and the United States, family history and gender studies developed fairly independently of each other, and each constitutes a major field in its own right. In Middle East Studies, the field of family history, insofar as it exists, developed at the margins of the much larger and already well established fields of women's history and gender studies. This is why the overriding concern in these articles, regardless of approach, is with the possibilities and strategies of agency. What they show is that family is a fluid amalgam of different fields of experience for differently situated members, and that there is room for a variety of strategies by women, some of which maybe be counterintuitive, but not any less effective. Especially revealing in this regard is the complex relationship between gender and property, both of which can be shown to be socially constructed and mutually constitutive. Indeed, the most significant contribution of family history might very well be the fact that it is best situated to analyze the kinship/gender/property matrix as a complex whole that can only be disaggregated at our peril.

It is not easy to focus on complex wholes. Indeed, researching and writing on family history is a bit like taking a journey into the center of the galaxy: the closer one gets to the event horizon of the enormous black hole around which everything revolves, the more difficult it is to use conventional categories of knowledge to make generalizations about how our world is reproduced and transformed in historical time. This generates ambiguities, tensions, and dilemmas that cannot be resolved through attempts at definitional clarity or stable taxonomies. Rather, the reward lies precisely in the messiness of family history and its conduciveness to the formulation of questions that can enrich and build bridges between approaches, disciplinès, and areas of study—not to efface, resolve, or essentialize difference.

Notes

All of the contributors to this anthology, with the exceptions of Philippe Fargues and Heather Ferguson, presented papers at an international conference, "Family History in Middle Eastern Studies," held at the University of California, Berkeley, 7–9 April, 2000. The Center for Middle Eastern Studies, the Al-Falah Program, the Andrew Mellon Foundation, the Department of History, and the Townsend Center for the Humanities funded this conference. Heather Ferguson and Adrian McIntyre helped with the logistics. Soraya Altorki, Tulay Artan, Jamila Bargach, Beth Baron, Donald Cole, Colette Establet, Mary Hegland, Suad Joseph, Lilia Labidi, David Powers, Martina Reiker, James Reilly, and Sylvia Vatuk also presented important papers based on original research. Unfortunately, and primarily for reasons of limited space, these papers could not be included in this volume. The comparative and theoretical comments by David Sabean, Barbara Ramusack, Linda Lewin, Carol Stack and Cynthia Nelson—who acted as discussants of the various panels—sharpened the focus of the final product. Martin Garstecki, Mitch Cohen, and Christian Schmitz of the Fellow Services Department at the Wissenschaftskolleg zu Berlin helped with manuscript preparation. Heather Ferguson proofread the galleys and Alan Mikhail prepared the index. My dear friend, Marwan, donated the cover artwork and design.

1. For a discussion of the terms "interest" (material, objective) and "emotion" (subjective, sentiments) in the study of family history, see Medick and Sabean 1984. I use the term "referential grid" to emphasize the importance of family as not only a site of praxis, but also as a powerful idea that carries within it the matrix of expectations, rules, obligations, and rights implied in religious, political, legal, ethical, and moral discourses.

2. For general literature reviews see Anderson 1980, and Hareven 1991a. For reflections by prominent family historians and anthropologists, see Hareven 1987 and Netting et al. 1984, respectively. For more specialized reviews see, for example, Yanagisako 1979; Stone 1981; Medick and Sabean 1984; Kertzer 1984; Censer 1991; Rudolph 1992; Faubion 1996; and Bradbury 2000.

3. If the topic is characterized as the study of how and why family forms and/or household structures change over time, scholars of the region cannot claim more than two monographs, both published in the past decade: Duben and Behar 1991 and Meriwether 1999. Of course, there are a number of published articles on family history, as well as a large related literature on kinship, women, gender, Islamic family law, families in politics, and so on. For a few examples of recent scholarship see Green 1981; Schilcher 1985; Fathi 1985; Ortayli 1985; Atran 1986; Mundy 1988, 1995; Gerber 1989; Fernea 1985, 1995; Hathaway 1995; Hatem 1986; Keddie and Baron 1991; Ferchiou 1992; Tucker 1993, 1998; Powers 1993a, 1993b, 1994; Mir-Hosseini 1993; Cuno 1995; Moors 1995, 1998a; Marsot 1995; Sonbol 1996b; Hanna 1998; and Doumani 1998.

4. Anderson 1980, 2–3.

5. Hareven (1991a) outlines the main arguments.

6. For the theoretical significance of prestige zones, see Appadurai (1986). Lila Abu-Lughod builds upon his insight in her review of anthropological literature on the Middle East (1990, 93).

7. Needless to say, "Middle East" is a constructed term that carries a great deal of unwelcome baggage. It is used here purely for convenience.

8. These approaches have become increasingly integrated over the past two decades. Duben and Behar 1991 is one example. The growing influence of gender analysis in family history and vice versa is another. See Anderson 1980, Yanagisako 1987, and Censer 1991.

9. For an insightful analysis see Cole 1981. The debates around women and the family as tropes for modernity became a worldwide phenomenon by the turn of the twentieth century and are intimately connected to the rise of the mass print media. An extensive literature on this topic has emerged over the past two decades. The articles in this anthology by Fay, Cuno, and Khater cite some of the key works.

10. This formulation can be attributed to Le Play's writings in the nineteenth century, which had a profound influence on social analysis in general and views about the family in particular. See Le Play 1982, 76–80.

11. During the nineteenth and early twentieth centuries, ethnographers, driven by a curiosity about what makes the Orient different from the Occident, and convinced that the unchanging essence of the Other is best preserved among groups that had the least contact with the modern world, fanned out into villages, country towns, and nomadic areas. The cultural norms they claimed to be the building blocks of Middle Eastern societies often tell us far more about their worldview than about the people they observed (for example, see Mitchell 1990), although some were very insightful (see, for example, the work of Hilma Granqvist 1931). In any case, the influence of their generalizations was considerable. It was at that moment that traditional society was born and, simultaneously, "scientifically" fixed in a state of stasis. According to Lila Abu-Lughod (1990), the dominant prestige zone in anthropological works on the Middle East is the study of patrilineal kinship (segmentation), mostly among peasants and tribal groups. In these two senses that concern us—the focus on kinship relations (whether as a lived reality or cultural ideal) and on "exotic" locales (hence, the preponderant number of works on Morocco and Yemen)—one can see a direct line of continuity with earlier studies. For a chronological sampling of ethnographic and anthropological works on the family, see Lane [1842] 1978; Jaussen 1927; Chatila 1934; Barth 1954; Beck 1957; Rosenfeld 1958, 1968a, 1968b, 1976; Antoun 1967; Hilal 1970; Khuri 1970; Peristiany 1976; Green 1981; Rugh 1984, 1997; Fernea 1985, 1995; Atran 1986; Brink 1987; Holy 1989; Khalaf 1981; Young and Shami 1993; Moors 1995; Mundy 1988, 1995; and Inhorn 1996.

12. For a small sample of works by sociologists and political scientists, see Daghestani 1932, 1953; Farsoun 1970; Prothro and Diab 1974; Springborg

1982; Barakat 1985; Kandiyoti 1985; Erder 1985; Ata 1986; Hatem 1986; and Singerman and Hoofdar 1996.

13. Until recently, only a handful of articles on these three regions appeared in the two major periodicals concerned with family history (*Journal of Family History* and *History of the Family: An International Quarterly*). A recent Ph.D. thesis argues that a historiography of the family in South Asia does not exist (Hodges 1999, 5–6). I thank Barbara Ramusack for sharing this reference with me. For a sampling of works on family in South Asian studies see Shah (1974, 1998); Kolenda 1996, (originally published 1968); Minault 1981, Gray and Mearns 1989, Vatuk 1990, and Uberoi 1993. For China, see Baker 1979; Chao 1983; and Johnson 1983.

14. An insightful attempt to deal with this issue within its own frame of reference is Sharabi 1988.

15. Hareven 1991, Anderson 1980.

16. Sabean 1998.

17. For an overview, see Plakans 1984.

18. Duben and Behar 1991, 15–16. It is certainly possible that new sources will be discovered and, more important, that new techniques will be developed to deal with the specific character of existing archives. In any case, the potential of available sources is enormous and just beginning to be tapped in a systematic manner.

19. This preliminary portrait very much fits the description of Le Play's third form of ideal family type, which he described in the mid-nineteenth century as typical of urban manufacturing areas in Europe. Le Play 1982, 79–80.

20. Duben and Behar 1991, 15–22.

21. Ibid., 239-48.

22. Louise Tilly 1987 set out the problem. For a sophisticated effort to integrate kinship and gender analysis see Sabean 1998. For the Middle East, see the anthologies by Keddie and Baron 1991 and by Sonbol 1996b.

23. For an insightful discussion of this issue, see Sabean 1990, 97–101.

24. See Messick 1993, 1995; and Qattan 1994, 1996. See also the article by Ferguson in this anthology.

25. See Johansen 1996, 1999; and Hallaq 1998.

I

Family and Household

2

Family and Household in Mid-Nineteenth-Century Cairo

Philippe Fargues

The most salient characteristic of the family in mid-nineteenth-century Cairo, the largest Arab city, was extreme instability. Indeed, physical survival was precarious for everyone, primarily because the newly instituted measures of public hygiene were still too recent to bring about any effective social regulation of mortality. One individual out of two died at such a young age that his or her only experience was that of a childhood, and often a short one, amid his or her family of birth. Due to the high infant and child mortality, siblings formed the most ephemeral grouping. Due to the high adult mortality, two generations overlapped for only a short time. It was not the norm to enjoy the company of both parents for a long period of time, and it was even rarer to have surviving grandparents. In contrast to this instability, the family operated within a rigid social order that based its stability on the organization of families by trades and religious communities. By the mid-nineteenth century, however, strong forces of renewal were emerging in Cairo and challenging the old order. After several decades of demographic stagnation and possibly decay as a result of intense labor mobilization for compulsory public service outside Cairo, conscription in the military, and plague epidemics, population growth witnessed an upturn. This was in large part due to immigrants recently attracted to the city by the emergence of large industries and the resumption of trade.[1]

The unpublished population census of 1848 reveals this transition towards modernity. This census deserves special mention, since it marks a turning point in the political history of statistics in Egypt.[2] Generally speaking, this census does not take the Ottoman census of Anatolia and Rumelia (1831) as a model, but instead seems to follow the population censuses concurrently undertaken in Western Europe, notably in France, a country to which Muhammad Ali was resolutely open and where his administration regularly sent students for training. Specifically, the Ottoman registers of 1831 were geared towards fiscal and military objectives.[3] In these registers, Muslims, who were susceptible to be enrolled in the military, were classified according to conscription criteria: age group and health status (absence/presence of a disability). Meanwhile, Christians, who were not admitted in the army but were subject to a poll tax, were classified differently, according to criteria of wealth. Since conscription was reserved for males and taxation was applied to households (normally headed by men), only adult men were recorded in Ottoman registers.[4] Women and children did not matter for the military or the fiscal administration; consequently, they were not counted.

In the Egyptian census of 1848, it was the individual who became the statistical unit. The administration in charge of the census was guided less by taxation or conscription purposes and more by the objective of making a comprehensive account of what today would be named the "human resources" of the country, the capital upon which the government would be able to build a national economy. For the first time, not only potential conscripts or taxpayers, but all individuals residing in Egypt were recorded: women as well as men, children as well as adults, slaves as well as free persons, Egyptian citizens as well as foreign residents. Also for the first time, particular attention was paid to the record of individuals' economic activities—such as detailed information on occupation, place of activity, employment status (employed/unemployed), and the number of young students (*bi-l-kuttab*). From this point of view, the census of 1848 was modern. However, it remained archaic in the use the government made of it. As a matter of fact, registers were kept in their original form—a nominal list of households and of individuals within each household, closely reflecting the visible structure of the society. They were never transformed into a statistical map of abstract groups, such as an age pyramid or categories of a professional classification.[5]

The Source[6]

Muhammad Ali's household and population census of 1848 offers the oldest comprehensive statistical source covering all the inhabitants of

Egypt. It was based, at one and the same time, on an Ottoman accounting tradition and on a modern knowledge newly acquired in the West. When the Ottomans conquered new lands, they would rapidly take count of its material and human resources.[7] In the case of Egypt, as early as the sixteenth century, fiscal and land registers held lists of households, although they seem less elaborated than those found in Anatolia and Syria. The documents of the 1848 Egyptian census are different in nature from these primitive registers, since the statistical unit is not the household but each individual within it, and a systematic record of a set of individual variables is detailed. Such an initiative reflects the endogenous development of an Egyptian state apparatus breaking away from the Ottoman imperial mold that heretofore constrained it. Furthermore, nineteenth-century Egypt came in contact autonomously with foreign administrations and intellectual circles likely to offer it more advanced models of the design of statistical surveys. The educational missions sent to France and England may account for the adoption and adaptation of the techniques, perhaps even for the spirit, of European statistical practices.[8]

However, this statistical operation did not lead to the creation of a full statistical apparatus. The data collection covered the whole country, but the processing remained summary and incomplete.[9] Only a few total population figures for large administrative divisions appeared in the Official Journal. Some partial tables were also produced in the registers themselves, but never published.[10] In addition, the civil registration that Muhammad Ali's administration (1838) made mandatory could not help updating the census, since the official notification of births and deaths was only workable in large urban centers and in small towns, without reaching either comprehensiveness or regularity. The administration thus later undertook updates of the 1848 census in certain localities, probably by direct survey. The collection of registers—which is almost entirely preserved and available for consultation to this day at Dar al-Watha'iq, the National Archives in Cairo—in fact includes registers dated ten years later, indicating on the list of 1848 the changes that had occurred in the composition of households, births, deaths, and migrations of the previous decade.

Despite the lack of a full apparatus, this census marks the birth of a statistical practice. Muhammad Ali's successors would carry on the task by undertaking a second census twenty years later (1868) and then by setting up an office for statistics (1870). The 1848 census was a political operation. By granting Egypt independence in its administrative justice, the 1841 Firman by the central Ottoman government reshaped the relations between province and empire. Though the Egyptian state thereby gained its autonomy, it also saw political and geographical boundaries being imposed upon itself. The 1848 census reflected both the redefinition of Egypt's external relations and the acknowledgment of its sovereignty within its borders. The categories it used clearly confirm this change: the first criterion used to break down the population distinguished between individuals under Egyptian jurisdiction (*dakhila al-hukuma*, "subjects of the government," which became "local subjects" in the following censuses until 1917) and those who remained beyond its authority (*kharija al-hukuma*, "non-subjects of the government," "foreigners" in the following censuses), among whom the Turks were numbered.

Each locality and, in the case of cities, each district (*qism*) had its own register or set of registers. Each register appeared as a survey of buildings, residential or not, inhabited or vacant. Within each of the inhabited buildings, a survey of the households themselves was noted. This allows an analysis of household and population patterns.

The variables related to households are few in number. The ownership status is recorded everywhere. Coming under the rule of law, it is of four types: individual property, collective property held in common, inheritance, and endowments. In the cities, the type of building is also specified. The description of the building, based on common use rather than documents, is very detailed: in Cairo and Alexandria, sixty-four types have been identified, from the basic shack (*ishash*) to the collective building (*rab*). Nothing is recorded on the state of the dwelling, on its size, or on its furnishings. Thus, the interest shown towards housing probably reflects a concern for making an inventory of the patrimony rather than that of the individuals' living conditions.

Variables related to individuals are more numerous. The systematic recording of a standard set of individual variables is indeed the real novelty of this census and its main wealth for the historian. The Egyptian registers of 1848 are not coded like the questionnaires of modern censuses. Individual characteristics are all written in full words. They provide a finer and more flexible description of the individual situation than any classification preset by the state administration.[11] Seven variables appear systematically while a few others appear only occasionally. The seven variables are:

- The sex of the individual: this variable is always indicated and is the key for the whole recording process. All the males are listed first with their own characteristics, and then all the females.

- Kinship relation: the list of the individuals of a household always includes an individual of reference, generally placed at the top of the list, in relation to whom all the others are positioned. Let us name this individual "head of household." The relations with the head of household are recorded with all the accuracy provided by the Arabic language, which makes it possible to describe them according to basic categories such as relationship through marriage, descent, ancestry, and laterality. Individuals unrelated to the head of household are described according first to their position in the household and then to possible family ties among themselves.

- Age: for the men, age is noted in years.[12] In Cairo and Alexandria, women are simply split into two groups: "children" (below 10) and "adults" (above 10).

- Legal status: freeman or slave.[13]

- Nationality: the census includes this concept (with the same term used today, ginsiyya). It basically serves to distinguish between nationals and foreigners, but the distinctions made do not fit well with the modern definition of nationality. The Egyptian subjects are most frequently recorded as "son of an Arab,"[14] but also as fallah (peasant), qibti (Copt), or as barabra (Nubian), which applies both to Egyptian Nubia and Sudan under Egyptian domination. Foreigners are broken down by region or country.

- Religion: Muslims, Jews, Copts, and other Christians (often with reference to a particular sect or rite).

- Origin: under the label of iqlim (province), it refers to a geographical origin, real or constructed. It is not necessarily the birthplace of the individual: within the same household, the children systematically inherit the origin of their father, but the wife does not get that of her husband.

Economic activity is described with a degree of detail that depends on occupation. The details are particularly numerous for state employees such as civil servants and factory or arsenal workers. A total of 1,537 different designations of the economic activity have been found in the Cairo sample alone. Nonsystematic records of certain individual characteristics are also found, for example: marital status for widowed or divorced women heads of household, disabilities, polygamy, and so on.

We analyzed the census of 1848 through a sampling procedure.[15] The sample size was set at approximately eighty thousand people out of a total of 4.5 million inhabitants. The country was divided into twenty-nine strata: each of the ten districts of Cairo and the five of

Alexandria, the city of Damietta (the third-largest city of Egypt at the time), and each of the thirteen provinces making up the rest of the country. In each strata, a sample was taken with its own sampling fraction. The Cairo subsample contains 20,163 individuals, representing the 256,679 inhabitants of the city in 1848.

For the purposes of this article, we make use of two variables systematically recorded for each individual: the detailed address (district, street, number) and the kinship relation to the head of household. The first variable makes it possible to study the social geography of the city at the finest possible level by answering questions such as: who lives where, next to whom, apart from whom? The second variable, combined with others (such as age, sex, marital status, place of origin, etc.), makes it possible to reconstruct the stages of the life cycle. Together, they allow us to capture some aspects of family life related to space and time.

Rigidity of the Social Environment of the Family

According to the views of the prestigious reformer Ali Pasha Mubarak as well as those of numerous Orientalists, the classical Arab city reflects a systematic arrangement of the social and political order. The compartmentalization of the districts and the related clustering of the population would basically echo the division of the society into primary social groups. Indeed, until the end of the nineteenth century, maps of large Arab cities, from Fes to Aleppo and from Tunis to Cairo, display the same configuration, which seems specific to the region. The neighborhoods, each of them containing housing and trade units closely interwoven, take the form of compact and dense blocks that are next to each other but not directly connected. Each district is penetrated by a long and sinuous path (always a dead-end alley), which serves all houses and workshops inside the district. The dead-end alley itself starts from one of the rare open streets that channel traffic and lead to places of moral and political control of the city, the great mosque and the citadel. The place of sociability would be the dead-end alley, not the busy open street.

Similarly, the population would be segmented into religious communities, guilds, or even groups whose members were linked by a common geographic origin, these markers often overlapping with each other. Such mechanisms as communal endogamy or transmission of professional skills within the family would provide these basic groupings a kind of autonomous social existence, the interaction of the group with the rest of the society being limited to the division of labor between groups and to their common subjection to the same political authority. The family, as the primary social unit, would be a necessary relay between individuals and the larger society. The individual would exist as such only within the family.

This schematic vision is challenged by the population census of 1848. The tables that we have been able to draw from this census reflect a transition: while the lines of collective identities—religious communities, trades, and provinces of origin, but also socioeconomic positions—continue to structure the space, individuals are less and less reducible to the groups they belong to. Their existence comprises several periods during which they live alone, possibly not free and independent, but without a family to mediate their relation to the society and the state. One witnesses the passing from an archaic society, segmented into vast groups of which the elementary unit is itself a group—the enlarged family—to the more complex arrangements of modern cities, in which the individual moves from one group to the other according to life phases or even to moments of the day.

Community and Spacial Patterns

Like most large Arab cities at the time, the population of Cairo included a variety of religious groups. In addition, movements of persons between the different provinces of the Ottoman Empire had brought about a variety of "nationalities" (ginsiyya), a concept already used by the Egyptian administration even though it had not yet received its legal definition.[17] The community, defined by the fact of sharing a religion and a nationality, was probably the most important marker of collective identities for various minorities, but not for the vast majority of Cairo inhabitants who were Muslim Egyptians. They represented 89 percent of the total population, and there was not a single district that did not comprise at least a small number of Muslim Egyptians, including Mari Girgis, a block predominantly composed of churches and convents in the heart of the Coptic Old Cairo. But, reciprocally, there are not many districts in which Muslim Egyptians are the only inhabitants to be found.[18] In fact, Muslim Egyptians formed the fabric in which the other communities were integrated, each of them in its own way.

The Copts, an Egyptian community par excellence who gave the country its name in every language except Arabic, constituted 3.5 percent of Cairo's inhabitants.[19] They were mainly grouped in two places, very distant from one another: Old Cairo, a district located in the periphery of the city since the foundation of Cairo by the Fatimids; and, in the heart of the city, the districts of Abdin, Muski, and, above all, Harat al-Nasara, the "Christian quarter," where more than one-third of all Copts of the city were concentrated. In this district, the Copts possessed their patriarchate but not a single church, so that they had to necessarily leave their place of residence in order to practice their religion, a sign that, despite their concentration, they did not at all form a ghetto. On the contrary, it was Harat al-Nasara's professional homogeneity that gave this quarter its specific identity: in this district, more than four out of ten Copts were clerks or public writers, a specialty largely kept in their community since the period of the mass conversions to Islam under the Mamluks. This specialty integrated the Copts into the larger society: public writers were a particular but indispensable link between the population, predominantly illiterate at that time, and the state.

By contrast, the spacial configuration of the Egyptian Jewish community (0.6 percent of Cairo's population) resembled that of a ghetto. The vast majority of them (87 percent) resided in two tiny and contiguous districts, one of them bearing their name (Harat al-Yahud, where 97 percent of the inhabitants were Jews) and containing all the Jewish schools and synagogues of Cairo. In other words, it is likely that the entire Jewish population of Cairo could limit their daily life to this handful of dead-end alleys, where they met almost no Muslims,[20] with the exception of participation in the financial transaction in which they were specialized (158 out of 447 moneychangers [*sarraf*] in the city were Jews).

The other communities originated from the other provinces of the Ottoman Empire and were not placed under Egyptian jurisdiction. Turks, all of them Muslim, constituted the largest non-Egyptian community (3.6 percent of Cairo's population). Although scattered throughout the city, they were mainly found in the commercial districts (for example, 63 percent of the merchants residing in Gamaliyya were Turks) as well as in the upper classes' residential places, such as Abdin, where two-thirds of the Turks either belonged to the army or lived as rent collectors. As for the Christian communities that hailed from outside Egypt, the Syrians and the Greek Orthodox illustrate two different models of integration. The former lived in districts where Christians of other sects were concentrated, while the latter lived next to Muslims. Indeed, the Greek Orthodox in Cairo as well as in all other large Arab cities depended upon the far distant Phanar of Istanbul, and their *millet* has an age-old experience of coexistence with its Muslim environment.

The Maghrebians, all residing in the vicinity of al-Azhar, represent a third type of grouping on the basis of origin. Despite the variety of their professions, people originating from Morocco (at that time, an independent country), Tunisia and Cyrenaica (both Ottoman), or Algeria (lately under French rule) were found next to each other.

Other collective lines were drawn by socioeconomic status and living conditions. There were not many neighborhoods entirely poor or entirely rich, but a large majority of mixed neighborhoods, which gives the impression that people themselves, whether poor or rich, tended to be mixed with each other.[21] However, if one considers more closely the city map, street by street, one loses this impression of mixing. Enclosed huts (hawsh: 14.4 percent of all housing units) and scattered slums (ishash: 4.3 percent), where the poor lived, almost never adjoined rich houses. The wealthy stayed in the streets adjacent to their residences and engaged only with the people whose services they depended on for their daily life: donkey-drivers, carters, porters, water carriers, peddlers, and all sorts of craftsmen and service workers living in nearby slums separated by only one block from their wealthy patrons. The rich accommodated only their servants and slaves. The servants head the list of occupations.[22] Public writers and administrative personnel were the largest employers of servants (with fifty servants per one hundred households). For craftsmen and traders (shopkeepers?), who represent the majority in Cairo,[23] the servant, khaddam, is most often at the same time a work assistant.

In this society still deeply stamped with collective identities, some signs of individualization are already discernible. The birth of a wage-earning class is one of them. Opening textile manufactures in the districts of Sayyida Zaynab and Bulaq, the state had given birth to a class of industry workers. Representing 4.2 percent of the active population, this class was not yet very numerous in comparison with the huge mass of self-employed craftsmen and traders, with their crowd of apprentices and family helps, but the wage relation between individuals and the state had been truly born. It was during this very short period that modern wage earners coexisted with one of the most archaic forms of work, slavery, which was even about to recommence for a decade or two during the cotton boom decade before its official abolition in 1877.[24] In the population registers of 1848, 5,921 slaves were found in Cairo, which is 2.5 percent of the residing population. Most of the slaves were concubines, although a few boys, generally employed as servants, were numbered among slaves.[25] Merchants were the largest owners of slaves (with 141 slaves for 100 households) and among them, slave merchants (gallab al-abid) who easily joined a personal to a professional use of their merchandise. Turks and Maghrebians owned greater numbers of slaves than Egyptians and, among the latter, the Jews, followed by the Copts, possessed more slaves than the Muslims.[26] Muslim owners declared their slaves as concubines, while Christians and Jews registered theirs simply as slaves, perhaps in order not to contradict their religion, which prohibits concubinage.

Table 1. Number of Slaves and Servants per Household according to the Head's Profession in Cairo in 1848

Profession of the head of household	Average number (per 1000 households)		
	Slaves	Servants	Total
Traders	846	402	1249
Directors of financial administrations	312	562	874
Writers, clerks	306	505	811
Teachers	151	652	803
Engineers	525	240	764
Waqf managers, neighborhood shaykhs	89	453	542
Physicians	96	390	486
Services and administration employees	138	317	455
Others	144	309	486
Craftsmen and laborers: mineral and chemistry	75	305	380
Merchants of consumption goods	111	238	349
Merchants of intermediary goods	73	254	327
Technicians	0	302	302
Military	82	160	242
Servants	54	187	241
Craftsmen and laborers: food trade	32	185	217
Craftsmen and laborers: textiles and leather	42	141	183
Azharis, faqihs, imans, priests or rabbis	19	147	166
Guards, messengers	13	140	153
Poets, singers, musicians	0	151	151
Craftsmen and laborers: metals	32	117	149
Craftsmen and laborers: wood	52	93	145
Muezzins and other cult employees	24	117	142
Boatmen	120	8	128
Fishermen	0	127	127
Breeders	0	118	118
Porters, packers	0	106	106
Donkey-drivers, camel drivers, carters	0	94	94
Gardeners	0	80	80
Other craftsmen and laborers	0	70	70
Craftsmen and laborers: construction	0	60	60
Water carriers, barbers, ironers	5	54	59
Bonesetters, midwifes, nurses	0	0	0
Koranic schoolmasters	0	0	0
Peasants, farmers	0	0	0
Stableboys, grooms	0	0	0
Average	87	181	268

A clear sign of the transition to modernity is the particular mode of coexistence between the religious and the secular, which was imprinted on the social geography of the city. We find two groups of well-read professionals who played distinct roles. The first group was made up of religious men (*azharis* and *faqihs* for Muslims; priests for Christians and rabbis for Jews) who assumed the moral control over the society, and the second group was composed of clerks (public writers, accountants, shaykhs, sworn weighers—persons who were entitled under oath to weigh various goods—secretaries, money changers, etc.) who carried out the administrative management of the society by mediating between public authorities and individuals, the vast majority of whom were illiterate. These two groups have rather similar demographic weights, the religious representing 6.9 percent of the total active population and the clerks 6.4 percent. Both resided mainly in the central districts of the city, next to its important institutions, religious or administrative, and amid the well-to-do classes among whom they had their patrons. Not a single religious person or clerk is recorded in the poorest districts, which were thus condemned to illiteracy.

If the two groups lived in the same districts, they did not mix with each other. No clerk is recorded in the dead ends where religious functionaries lived, and vice versa. Such a residential separation partially reflects that of the religious communities, since most of the secretaries and public writers were Coptic and most of the moneychangers were Jewish, while the vast majority of men of religion were Muslim. But the separation also reflects the fact that religious and secular functions repelled each other. It is significant that the main concentration of Muslim public writers, secretaries, and clerks formed an enclave in Harat al-Nasara, the neighborhood of their Christian counterparts, instead of in al-Azhar, the district where Muslim men of religion were concentrated. Sharing the same profession thus seems more important than religious affiliation in determining the place of residence of those who occupied secular functions.

In 1848, the education of children was mostly by men of religion, and schools were themselves managed by religious foundations. The civil teacher and the public school were recent innovations not yet visible in the statistics.[27] The population census of 1848, in which students of religious schools were carefully recorded (*bi-l-kuttab*) thus provides at the same time the first figures on the schooled population and the last picture of an archaic order.[28] In 1848, students were found in almost all the districts of the city, a fact that reveals a dense network of schools. Reflecting a city still segmented by communities, a given school consisted of children of the same religion. Among boys from 5 to 14 years of age, school enrollment rates reached 34 percent for the Muslims, 50 percent for the Copts, 77 percent for Christians of other rites, and 100 percent for the Jews. Inequalities of opportunity for education between religious communities resulted from a strong social selection. Indeed, the profession of one's father often determined the probability of attending school. Engineers had a 100 percent school enrollment rate for their sons, teachers 73 percent, clerks 63 percent, and men of religion 57 percent. Together, they formed a sort of intellectual class that seemed to consider school a necessary step for their children. Other classes that held greater economic power were less present in the neighborhood schools—only 48 percent of the sons of merchants *(s. tajir)* were schooled, for example—possibly because they more often used private tutors for their sons, a fact that cannot be documented by census-type data. At the bottom of the social ladder, the exclusion from the education system was absolute, with representatives of many trades never enrolling their children in school.

Instability of the Family Life Cycle[29]

The census of 1848 makes it possible to locate the "critical points"[30] in the life history of individuals: their departure from the family to which they were born, their marriage, the birth of their children, the departure of their children, and sometimes their residence at old age with one of these children.[31] Since all these events happen a limited number of times—some of them only once—in the life of a given individual, the study of the life cycle is necessarily statistical. Taking into account a great number of individuals, what is reconstructed is not a particular family that existed, but an average. It is a model rather than an actual situation. It is also a normal family, since it represents the whole population, not only a given segment of the society. From this point of view, the population census radically differs from most other sources that are selective according to the social position—for example, the registers of deeds that only record people having property to transfer.[32] It is, rather, a source for a comprehensive account of all individuals, in which everyone has the same weight regardless of social condition. The registers of the population census are, in fact, the only source containing each of the four and a half million individuals living in Egypt at the time.[33]

Childhood

The first stage of life, which the child spends with his parents, does not last very long. It is only before 10 years of age that living with at

Table 2. School Enrollment Rate of Boys, according to the Profession of the Father in Cairo in 1848

Profession of the father	School enrollment rate of boys (%)
Engineers	100.0
Teachers	72.9
Writers, clerks	63.0
Azharis, faqihs, imams, priests, or rabbis	56.7
Waqf managers, neighborhood shaykhs	54.4
Servants	52.8
Traders	48.5
Physicians	47.4
Craftsmen and laborers: food trade	46.7
Service and administration employees	45.9
Military	44.5
Merchants of consumption goods	44.1
Water carriers, barbers, ironers	41.8
Merchants of intermediary goods	39.8
Breeders	37.3
Inactive	34.7
Guards, messengers	33.8
Porters, packers	31.4
Craftsmen and laborers: mineral and chemistry	30.3
Profession not specified or unclean	28.7
Craftsmen and laborers: textiles and leather	28.6
Donkey-drivers, camel drivers, carters	28.5
Craftsmen and laborers: metals	28.4
Craftsmen and laborers: wood	28.2
Muezzins and other such employees	27.1
Craftsmen and laborers: construction	25.7
Directors of financial administrations	9.4
Gardners	9.2
Boatmen	4.4
Poets, singers, musicians	0.0
Technicians	0.0
Bonesetters, midwifes, nurses	0.0
Koranic schoolmasters	0.0
Stableboys, grooms	0.0
Fishermen	0.0
Other craftsmen and laborers	0.0
Average	36.5

least one parent was the norm (87.6 percent of the boys, 86.7 percent of the girls). When the father was present, he was recorded as the head of household. When the mother lived alone with her children, whether she was widowed or divorced, her eldest son was the one who received the status of head of household. In this respect, the census record conforms to the legal rule that left the children in the care of the mother until 15 years of age, without giving her their guardianship. A widow or a divorced woman established with her children was recorded as head of household only if all her children were daughters. However, in this case, it was more common for a woman to reside in the household of a relative, such as one or both of her own parents, a brother, or a sister.

Most children were still very young when separated from their mother and father, either because of the death of both parents, or by the child's departure from his or her home.[34] At 10–14 years of age, 70 percent of boys already lived outside their family residence. This number increases to 77 percent for those 15–19 years of age. Half of those who left their family residence did so in order to join a public collectivity: boarding schools, barracks, or work sites run by the state. At the end of the reign of Muhammad Ali, the most common reason for leaving one's family residence was for the purposes of enrolling in a public institution, whether by requisition of the state or by choice of the family. That is, it was an act of protocitizenship that led to emancipation from the family. Military conscription, which during the reign of Muhammad Ali replaced the system of mercenaries formerly used, meant that young men were conscripted in cities as well as in villages. The mobilization of workforces through the "corvée," in contrast, was restricted to the peasants *(fellahin)*.[35]

Table 3. Departure from the Family of Origin in Cairo in 1848

Age group	Percentage of men residing apart from their family of origin
0–4	3.1
5–9	18.6
10–14	70.3
15–19	77.2
20–24	84.0
25–29	78.9
30–34	84.5
35–39	89.0
40–44	92.1
45–49	94.4
50 & +	93.5

Children did not all share the same destiny. Some of them were left very young without their father and mother, long before the age of enrollment in public institutions. Starting from the very beginning of their existence, boys could be found residing out of their family of birth, either as orphans or as children placed by their parents with a foreigner, and sometimes they were fugitives.[36] In 37 percent of the cases, children under 10 living without their father and mother resided with relatives: a brother or a sister, sometimes an uncle or an aunt, even a first cousin, generally on the father's side. More frequently (58 percent), these children were housed by nonrelatives. Slaves were not rare among them (11 percent), and one finds also very young servants. In addition, there were also children actually alone, recorded as heads of household. The registers tell enough about their situation to describe the precariousness of their existence. In a dwelling *(manzil)* of Abdin, a boy of 7 is recorded as a cobbler and lives alone; in Darb al-Ahmar, a boy of 6 years is found, equally alone but without profession; in a *takiyya* of Qaysun, a stonecutter of 7 years; in a mill of Bulaq, a boy of 4 years of age; in Gamamiz, two brothers aged 7 and 5, clothessellers, formed a household together; two other brothers, ironsmiths of 9 and 7, lived alone in a *hawsh* of Khalifa; and so on. Perhaps less destitute was the situation of a nine-year-old *faqih*, living alone with his servant of 19 in an *isha* of Misr el-Qadima (Old Cairo).[37]

Even before 10, there was some difference between the situation of boys and girls. The proportion living outside their own family was very similar (8 and 9 percent of boys and girls, respectively), but their position in the household that hosted them differed. There were no heads of household among the girls, but already a significant proportion of wives: 5 percent of the orphan girls are recorded at the same time as "children" (that is, below 10) and married.[38]

The kinship relation between a child without his/her father and mother and the person with whom he/she lived varied according to sex. There were more brothers than sisters of the head of household, as if an elder was more willing to take a brother under his protection, as an apprentice for example, than a sister, whom he would rather have placed elsewhere. More girls than boys are recorded as children of a previous marriage of the wife, since the custom dictated that boys should be left with their father. Finally, more girls than boys resided with persons not related to them, who often employed them as servants.

Household Structures

The scattering of the population into small residential units, nuclear families, isolated individuals, or groups of unrelated men sharing a house and a trade characterized Cairo in the mid-nineteenth century. An average household comprised only 3.54 persons, a very modest size for the time; 70 percent of households consisted of a single nucleus, i.e., an individual who lived alone[39] or a married couple, possibly with their unmarried children. The remaining 30 percent were more or less complex households, made up of more than one nucleus, related or not to the head of the household.[40]

This stands in contrast to villages and rural areas still dominated by large, multinuclear households. In Cairo almost every man, provided that he survived long enough, founded a household and established independent living arrangements.[41] The concept of "household," as it is used in modern statistics, is obviously an anachronism when used to name a group of persons sharing a dwelling in nineteenth-century Egypt. However, the fact that the administration of the census had identified such groupings as placed under the authority of a single person, the one who gave his/her name to the dwelling unit in the registers, is probably a sign that in becoming head of household, one acceded to a collective responsibility toward the other members of the household and toward the state administration, which held him accountable for them.

Men become heads of household at the age of 20.7 years on average. Some of them attained this status very young (3 percent under 15 years of age).[42] Half of these young heads of household were simply the oldest of a group of siblings living with their divorced or widowed mother or father's cowife—all of whom the administration would not easily consider head of the household. A few were boys who had been separated very young from their father and mother, and they are recorded as heads of household simply because they were the only males in households composed of female relatives who were raising them. All others were men still very young but responsible for themselves. But for the majority, it was between 15 and 20 that this passage took place. At this age, it was more common for a young man to be a head of household (43.8 percent) than to still live in his father's house (26.0 percent).[43] The presence of the mother in the son's household became increasingly rare, a sign of the independent establishment of the son.[44] The foundation of a separate family usually followed the establishment of independent living arrangements, but sometimes long after. At 15–19 years, 28.9 percent of heads of household lived neither with their mother nor with a wife or a child. Some 19.4 and 14.5 percent were still in this situation at 20–24 and 25–29 years respectively. By the age of 40, almost all men were responsible for a household. Only 7 percent of men aged 40 and above resided in a household that did not bear their name: these were servants housed by their master, sometimes with their children, and a few old men who had joined the household of one of their sons.[45]

The typical destiny of women was completely different. Leaving the house of their father for that of their husband, they did not have the transition period during which young men moved away from their family without starting their own. Unlike men, for whom the foundation of a household opened an era of family responsibility, women established themselves apart only when they were widowed, divorced, or neglected to the benefit of a younger cowife. Women registered as heads of household are in significant numbers: 10,659, that is 12.8 percent of all women above 10 years; 15.9 percent of all Cairo households were headed by women, all of them widows, divorcees, or concubines. Half of them lived alone and the other half with their children. To these women considered heads of household must be added those mentioned above, whose sons are recorded as heads of households even though they were aged less than 15 years, simply because the census administration did not acknowledge these women as responsible for the children who were actually in their charge. In total, 13.6 percent of women aged over 10 headed a household.

Marriage and Fertility

Marriage seems to have been less an issue of choice than a religious duty. Still, marriage remained subject to the whims of fate. Not every one could fulfill the conditions for marrying and find a suitable mate at the same moment in life. The mean age of men at first marriage was 20.1 years. Marriage of minors was statistically very rare, even though it was legal and attested to in court records.[46] Age of men at marriage was influenced by their profession. For example, marriage was usually delayed by a long duration of training or apprenticeship, by the high mobility particular to certain trades, which prevented workers from meeting the appropriate bride from the necessary social level, or by a profession requiring the accumulation of capital, which conflicted with the need to save for the bride-price. Marriage was thus late among skilled workers trained on the job, such as leather craftsmen (saddlers, cobblers, or tanners) or metal craftsmen (casters and smiths), as well as men of religion (*azharis* and *faqihs*) who had to wait until the end of their studies, which were sometimes very long, or merchants of grain, tobacco, and spices, who frequently traveled from Cairo to Asyut, the city of their origin.

By contrast, marriage was early among independent workers whose occupations did not require the mobilizing of significant capital, such as servants, cooks, water carriers, ass-drivers, carters, grooms, and vegetable sellers. Men also got married early in particular crafts, such as those related to bread production, from the miller to the worker of the neighborhood oven *(farran)* and the baker *(khabbaz)*. None of these trades required any mobility, and they put individuals at the very beginning of their adult life in the neighborhood or family networks within which they would probably marry. The wife's contribution to such trades would be an additional incentive for early marriage. Unfortunately, the census does not mention the economic activity of women: like all women except servants, the wives of millers and bakers are registered without mention of their participation in the husband's trade.[47] The fact that women's economic activity has no place in the 1848 registers can be interpreted in several ways. For instance, it could be a sign that husband and wife usually had the same occupation; in that case, the profession recorded for the man would designate the occupation of both spouses. It could also be a gender bias in the perception of economic activities, since registers were recorded by men (the census agents) according to information provided by other men (the heads of households).[48]

In mid-nineteenth-century Cairo, everyone seems to have married within his or her religious community. At least, husband and wife were systematically registered under the same religion, a situation that does not exclude cases of conversions prior to the marriage.[49] If the city favored communities living side by side, at the same time it prevented their intermingling: the separation that has been observed for places of residence and even professions is all the more true when one comes to marriage rules. However, while one married within one's own community, one did so according to age patterns common to all communities: the age at first marriage does not vary according to this primary social marker. The only exception is that of Christians originating from the Ottoman Empire, whether Orthodox or Catholic, who married later than both Copts and Muslims.[50] It is probably their particular social characteristics that explain their late marriage: Ottoman Christians had a longer than average schooling for boys and were frequently engaged in professions requiring a longer period of training. But it is also likely that the small size of these communities may have itself impeded marriage in more than one case. For there to be a marriage, in fact, the community within which one must marry must include the appropriate spouse. Syrian Catholics, Armenian Orthodox, Greek Orthodox, and Syrian Muslims were communities comprising only about one thousand persons each, which meant only a narrow marriage market. All of these groups were subject to a rule of religious endogamy. However, the same rule does not produce the same constraints. In the first three communities, religious endogamy, among Eastern Christians often an endogamy of rite, limited the number of potential candidates to very small numbers, but it opened up the fourth to the entire community of Muslims, regardless of whether they were of Syrian origin, Turks, or Egyptians.

The experience of women substantially differed from that of men. The asymmetry of figures is striking: 67,640 women never married, as compared to 49,760 men. It is not polygyny that explains such a huge difference, since only 2.7 percent of married men are recorded with two or more cowives in their household, with a maximum of 3.1 percent at 40–44 years.[51] Rather, it is the existence of large numbers of women living without a husband in their household, although their marriage is attested by the presence of a child: 18,988 women fit into this category, against 2,390 men. Such an asymmetry is linked by simple arithmetic to three possible inequalities between the sexes: the age at first marriage, the way this first marriage ended, and the probability of remarriage.[52] The first marriage was as universal for women as it was for men, but it happened much earlier: at 13.8 years on average. This age gap of 6.3 years between spouses at first marriage affected their subsequent marital mobility. Because, on average, girls were married 6.3 years younger than boys, there was a surplus of marriageable females on the age pyramid.[53] As a consequence, a number of them would conclude their first marriage with a man who had already been married: either divorced or widowed. When they themselves became divorced or widowed, they found only with difficulty a man available for remarriage.[54] The combination of equally universal marriage for both sexes with a wide age gap implies a higher marital mobility for men than women, which in turn explains the large number of unmarried women found without a husband in the registers.

The first child was born on average 2.6 years after the first marriage. The typical age of a new father was 23 years, compared to 16 years for the mother. During their whole life, an average couple produced six to ten children, depending on social class and the particulars of each community. The average number of children actually residing in households was much less than one would have expected with such a high fertility rate. The explanation lies in children's mortality and mobility, which varied according to religious community, place of origin, and the profession of the parents, thus determining the diversity of family situations. Muslims found themselves childless more often than Copts, Ottoman Christians, or Jews. Here the rules of personal status seem to be at play, for divorce existed only for Muslims, who seem to have made a frequent use of it at this time. But the individual's relationship with the state and his place in the social hierarchy also played a significant part. Only Muslims were subject to military obligations, which often separated men from their families. Only Muslim families appear to have been relegated in large number to the bottom of the social stratification, where children were exposed to the highest mortality rates.[55]

Living Arrangements

Whatever the religion, it was the father's profession that largely determined where the children resided.[56] Living without children was an exceptional situation for those who practiced professions requiring stable establishment in the city or trades that the father taught his sons on the job, as was the case for craftsmen such as tanners, dressmakers and tailors, saddlers, millers, casters and blacksmiths, perfumers, and fabric sellers. It was also the case for the most modest professions, such as servants, porters, water carriers, and gardeners. By contrast, not having a single child at home was the most frequent situation among a mobile population located higher in the social hierarchy, such as wholesale traders and merchants of grain, tobacco, and spices, as well as for the men of religion, whose presence in Cairo was motivated by a temporary, although long, period of study at the great mosque of al-Azhar. Azharis, 27 percent of whom lived alone, rarely had children in their household. In contrast, faqihs, who formed a religious class more dispersed among the population, lived in families similar to those of their neighbors. Finally, doormen, and especially doorkeepers, usually did not reside with children in their household, since their living conditions often precluded housing a family.

Table 4. Percentage of Men Residing with at Least One of Their Children, According to Origin, Religion, and Profession in Cairo in 1848

Group of population	Percentage
Origin	
Cairo	74.1
Other	54.0
Religion	
Muslims	60.9
Copts	73.8
Other Christians	70.1
Jews	85.7

(continued)

Table 4. Percentage of Men Residing with at Least One of Their Children, According to Origin, Religion, and Profession in Cairo in 1848 *(continued)*

Profession (men aged 25–34 years)	
tanner	10.0
gunpowder manufacturer	14.5
street porter	14.8
tailor	15.3
gardener	19.9
miller	22.6
saddler	24.8
merchant of perfume and salt	26.2
water carrier	26.2
official weigher	27.0
industry worker	27.8
whitewash maker, plasterer	27.8
caster, maker of weigh	27.9
ironmonger	28.2
cloth merchant	28.8
smith	29.1
sawyer, caulker, ship carpenter	31.2
mason, laborer	31.2
mule driver, camel driver, carter	31.5
porter	31.7
lace maker	32.2
greengrocer	32.4
moneychanger	32.6
groom	32.9
public writer, copying clerk	35.6
weaver	36.3
military man	39.9
cook	40.8
profession undetermined	42.9
servant	45.0
cobbler, shoemaker	45.6
industry weaver	49.2
faqih	51.2
coffee maker, cupbearer	51.5
grain, tobacco, and spice merchant	51.9
boatman, barge driver	52.2
doorman	53.3
merchant *(tajir)*	53.5
fruit seller	56.3
unemployed	59.0
bread maker *(khabbaz)*	63.0
azhair	64.8
no profession	65.4
guardian, eunuch	74.6

While early separation of children from their parents was the rule, certain professions, specifically those passed on from fathers to sons, favored keeping boys with their fathers until later in life. These are, first of all, craft industries, which either required capital that the craftsman made profitable by sharing it, or required technical knowledge that took a long time to pass on. Thus, one-third of slaughterhouse butchers had in their own household at least one son who was himself a slaughterhouse butcher. The same was true for tanners, woodworkers, and carpenters, as well as for most stone crafts, though in a smaller proportion. The same motives probably explain fathers' residential and professional association with their sons in certain nonartisanal professions, such as that of boatman, where capital was shared, or that of public writer, in which the father passed education and clients on to his sons at the same time. However, when all the professions are considered together, such an association of profession and residence is rare (7.9 percent of men), both because the family had typically become nuclear and because the rapid evolution of professional specializations in mid-nineteenth-century Cairo limited the capacity of a generation to transmit to the next generation the professional skills the latter would need.

Household configurations that characterize Cairo in 1848 demonstrate the weakness of the well-accepted rationalist argument that the domestic economy can explain the high birthrates of the past, when the child would rapidly become a source of revenue for his parents. Inhabitants of the city, in this period, probably did not procreate numerous children in order to ensure free manpower for the household, nor to increase its money income: boys usually left the household very early, and even if they stayed, they rarely shared their father's trade. Instead, it is the situation of women whose husbands had passed away or remarried that may help us understand one of the benefits of high fertility. In the population of 60 years and above, only 6 percent of the women were still living with a husband. The others were either single (35 percent) or living with a relative, who was their son in 29 percent of cases. After the father and husband, the son was the third and last man of their lives. This state of affairs gives more weight to another rationalist argument, according to which the procreation of numerous children serves as a woman's strategy to secure her position in old age. Along this line, one can interpret as a sign of the value of a son the fact that boys living with their mother alone, either divorced or widowed, were the most schooled of their neighborhood.[57] If the diffusion of schooling is considered a factor of progress for the whole society, the female strategy that, as early as 1848, consisted in counting on the education of boys could well have been a driving force of progress.

Conclusion

The writing of social history is based on relics left by institutions or individuals. Built structures, recorded deeds, or chronicles—all of these traces reveal only a part of what the complex society really was: the resistance of monuments to the passing of time, the recording of inheritances, or the perspective of the writer reflecting his time are often filters focusing on the elite rather than on the common people, on the institutional framework rather than on the life of ordinary individuals. Processing a comprehensive census that gives the same weight to every individual, whatever his social condition, sex, legal status, or age, may complete the picture. Beyond the divisions instituted by the community or the guild, more universal lines divide the society and organize the lives of families and individuals. In particular, the boundaries of poverty and wealth, both clearly visible in the geography of the city, mark a segregation probably more ordinary and less specific to Cairo; the different groups of society were very intertwined.

The contrast between the rigidity of the city social map, showing families each at its right place ascribed by community, trade, and social condition on one hand, and the rapidity of changes over the family life cycle on the other hand, presents us with a paradox: the family is as stable as an institution as it is ephemeral as a grouping. The universality of its founding act, marriage, confirms the force of the rules. But the unit effectively created through marriage proves extremely volatile. This volatility is due in part to nature, if extremely high mortality that entails a rapid turnover of individuals living together in the same given place at a given moment of time can be called natural. Volatility was also due to the social order, which quickly redistributed individuals outside the group of relatives in whose midst they were born. The predominance of the nuclear family over every other kind of household, the high proportion of individuals living alone (such as immigrant workers, widowed or divorced women, and even young children seemingly relying on themselves), or the broad scale at which the public authorities drew on young men are all signs that individuals were not dissolved into kinship relations and that they were in direct contact with the larger and anonymous society. The existence of rather long periods during which they resided alone or with persons unrelated to them contrasted with the idea that the demographic and economic constraints of the time could strengthen extended-family solidarity. Such traits probably characterized the urban condition. Were things this way for a long time, or are we observing a transition toward the establishment of a new relationship between individuals and their kin? The administration could have acknowledged this evolution by conducting for the first time in Egypt a census recognizing the individual. By identifying households, in which kinship relations situate each individual, it certainly consecrated the family as the fundamental social unit. But at the same time it recognized the family's complexity; that is, the fact that each family had its own composition, varying from one to another, and so is not reducible to a single unit, embodied in its head, who would be accountable for all and acting as an intermediary between the person and the public authority.

Notes

1. J. Abu-Lughod 1971; Baer 1969; Chaichian 1988; Raymond 1993.

2. Abd al-Hakim 1968; Alleaume and Fargues 1998a; Reimer 1996; Shu'aysha 1984.

3. Karpat 1985.

4. Doumani 1994.

5. These abstract classifications make their first appearance in the processing of the population census of 1917, directed by the British administrator J. I. Craig (Owen 1996).

6. This section borrows from Alleaume and Fargues 1998a.

7. Barkan 1978; Bakhit 1982.

8. The presence of Gallicisms in certain terms denoting profession (such as *khudari nashif*, the literal translation of "merchant of dry vegetables" while Arabic already has its own term: *allaf*) may signal either the presence of French technicians or the use of imported nomenclatures.

9. At the top of each page, one systematically finds the cumulated total of the preceding pages, by category of population. At the end of each register, three summary tables are found: by professional activity, by nationality, and by religion, each of these variables being cross-referenced with gender and age. These summaries probably served to control the successive counts; in any case, they indicate that the data processing of the census had been initiated. But this processing does not go beyond the basic cross-tabulation of these three variables, nor beyond the disaggregated level of the localities.

10. The publication of the collected data, which was to put an end to the tradition of secrecy surrounding the state's activities, came much later, with the census of 1882 carried out on the eve of the British occupation.

11. Of course, the historian is not totally free from the official representations of the society, since the way the collected data were first given by the surveyed individuals and then recorded in registers already implies a certain categorization of society.

12. One finds the classic attraction towards numbers ending in 0 and 5. Since age refers to the coming birthday and not to the last one (between birth and the first birthday, one is considered one year old, and so forth) it figures on age pyramids as an attraction towards numbers ending in 9 and 4. This attraction does not appear below the age of 10, which means that the recording of young children was very careful.

13. Slavery was abolished by law, if not in practice, during the rule of Ismail (1877), so that the 1848 Egyptian census is probably the only quantifying source on this phenomenon, marking both the birth and death of a statistical category.

14. *Abna al-arab*, which cannot be mistaken for *urban*, which refers in these registers to the Arab tribes.

15. The research was carried out between 1995 and 1998 by CEDEJ, the French Center for Economic, Social, and Legal Studies established in Cairo, in collaboration with a team of Ph.D. students at Cairo University.

16. Alleaume and Fargues 1998a.

17. Egyptian nationality would not be legally defined until 1929; that of the other Ottoman provinces, only after the end of the British and French mandates. For the processing of this variable of the 1848 census, see Alleaume and Fargues 1998a.

18. Forty-four *shiyakhas* out of 160 have a homogenous Muslim Egyptian population.

19. During the twentieth century, the proportion of Copts in Cairo would increase as a result of migrations from Upper Egypt (Copts represented 8.6 per cent of Cairo governorate inhabitants in the census of 1996). At the same time, their proportion would decrease in the whole country, because of an earlier decrease of the birthrate, a higher rate of emigration abroad, and a number of conversions to Islam on the occasion of marriage or divorce.

20. Muslims constitute 20 and 2 percent, respectively, of the districts of Hawsh al-Suf and Harat al-Yahud.

21. Living conditions are not recorded as such in the census of 1848, but the type of housing is mentioned. Here, we consider as "poor" those dwelling units recorded as follows: enclosure, hut, garden, orchard, tent, cattle pen, waterwheel, grave, tomb, shelter, ruin, homeless.

22. Of the economically active population, 9.7 percent were servants.

23. Artisans of production, artisans of services, and traders represent respectively 36.2, 12.2, and 11.8 percent of Cairo's active population, i.e., a total of 60.2 percent.

24. Toledano 1998.

25. During the 1840s, Egypt imported some five thousand slaves annually, mainly from Abyssinia and the Caucuses. During the following decade, their annual number fell to thirty-five hundred, but it would reach a maximum of ten thousand slaves a year later, in the 1860s.

26. Among Muslims, 76 percent of slaves were women; among Christians, 91 percent; and among Jews, 86 percent.

27. Delanoue (1982) gives 120,000 and 5,000 students enrolled in religious schools (kuttab) and public schools (madaris ahliyya), respectively.

28. Alleaume and Fargues 1998b.

29. This section and the conclusion are taken from Fargues 2000.

30. Lansing and Kish 1957.

31. Fargues 2000.

32. These selective sources have been privileged so far in the writing of urban social history (Tucker 1993; Marsot 1995).

33. Boinet 1886.

34. The departure from the parents' home was not early for everyone. At no age did the proportion of men living with at least one of their two parents become negligible. Above 40 years, it still reached 6 percent. These were mainly men housing one of their two parents, typically their widowed or divorced mother.

35. Marsot 1984; Toledano 1990.

36. Together, these three categories represent 3.1 percent of boys at 0–4 years and 18.6 percent at 5–9 years.

37. Several cases pertain to the way registers were filled and do not necessarily reveal poverty. A boy was generally recorded as head of household as soon as he was the only male of the household, however young he might have been.

38. Very early marriages nevertheless remained rare, since married girls represent only 0.4 percent of girls below 10 years of age.

39. Individuals living alone represented 16.5 percent of households, or 4.7 percent of the whole of Cairo inhabitants in 1848.

40. Complex households comprise either father or mother of the head of household, brothers or sisters, sons or sometimes married daughters accompanied by their own children, and so on. Unrelated individuals are mostly servants and slaves.

41. What is meant here by household, a modern term not used in the census of 1848, is the group of persons, related or not, who live together in the same house and are registered as a single unit. The list of such persons is organized around an individual, generally placed at the top of the entry, who gives his name to the unit and to whom all individuals are set in relation. The relationship between each of the other individuals and this central person is described by the elementary categories of kinship (wife or husband, son or daughter, father or mother, brother or sister), by certain categories not pertaining to kinship (servant, slave), or by any combination of the two.

42. Men under 15 years represented 1,388 out of 46,192 heads of households. Half of them were 14 years old.

43. The other situations are more complex: living in the household of another relative (16.1 percent of boys at 15–19 years) or in that of a nonrelative (14.1 percent), which is another form of autonomy from the family of birth.

44. At 15–19 years, 31.5 percent of male heads of household still resided with their mother, who was widowed or divorced, or whose husband was a polygynous man living elsewhere; at 20–24 years, 19.5 percent; and at 25–29 years, 13.8 percent.

45. A total of 321 cases, half of which were men aged 75 or above.

46. Sonbol 1996a.

47. Only 3,616 females are recorded with a profession, against 70,832 men. For 2,989 of these women, the profession is servant. There is no trace in this census of the textile-worker women mentioned by Marsot (1995), nor of the other female urban trades described by Tucker (1985).

48. The underestimation of women's productive contribution is not a bias peculiar to the census of 1848. The same bias is found in all subsequent censuses until the present day (Anker 1995).

49. Out of 48,241 couples, only forty cases of denominational intermarriage are found, all involving a Muslim man and a Coptic woman.

50. At 20–24 years, only 30 percent of the Ottoman Christian men were married, against 73 percent of the Copts and 80 percent of the Muslims.

51. This proportion underestimates actual polygyny, since not all polygynous men resided with all their wives together in the same household.

52. The arithmetic of this asymmetry in the marriage market was modeled in general terms by Ryder 1987.

53. Without sex differences in migration patterns under the conditions of mortality prevailing at that time, the number of females aged 13.8 was about 15 percent higher than the number of males aged 20.

54. At an earlier time (seventeenth century), the shari'a court records mentioned numerous cases of women's remarriage (Abd al-Rahim 1996). Did

the situation of the women actually change, or does the census give a different picture of the society because it covers all individuals without selectivity, regardless of social conditions?

55. Alleaume and Fargues 1998b.

56. The proportion of men without children was extremely variable by profession: it ranged from 10 to 75 percent at 25–34 years.

57. In the districts of Abdin and Ezbekiyya, the average school enrollment rate among Muslim boys aged 6 to 14 years was 35 percent, but it reached 59 percent for households headed by a woman.

3

Size and Structure of Damascus Households in the Late Ottoman Period as Compared with Istanbul Households

Tomoki Okawara

Introduction

For a long time, the social reality of family and household in the Ottoman Empire has been obscured as if by a heavy fog. This fog was somewhat broken up in the 1950s and 1960s by Ömer Lutfi Barkan and other historians, who started to use tax registers *(tahrir defterleri)* and the other documents in the field of demographic study. These scholars, mainly concerned with the study of social and economic issues, tried to determine mean household size as a coefficient, in order to estimate total population and analyze the demographic situation of the empire. Barkan's demographic study of the *hane* ("household" according to him) of the sixteenth century has stimulated discussion among scholars.[1] However, the meaning of *hane* is a point that needs to be clarified.

A more important question remains: What was household composition in the Ottoman Empire? Studies based on tax registers could not frame a clear answer, because tax registers do not contain any information about household structure, age, or sex ratio. This kind of register normally recorded only the names of male taxpayers according to their marital status (married or single), data insufficient to reconstruct household composition.[2]

Thus, while the Cambridge Group for the History of Population and Social Structure, led by Peter Laslett, began in the 1960s to make radical innovations in the field of European family history, Ottoman family history could not make any contribution to their discussions. The few exceptions were the case studies of Serbia under the Ottoman rule, where multiple-family households (two or more kin-linked conjugal family units), called *zadrugha*, were typical, which attracted attention from scholars of the Cambridge Group.[3] In simplified terms, their studies divided the Ottoman realm into two regions: European Turkey (the Balkans) and Asiatic Turkey (Anatolia and Arab lands).

Laslett classified all households in traditional Europe into four regions according to domestic group organization as "west," "west/central or middle," "Mediterranean," and "east."[4] He then observed these four sets of tendencies in domestic group organization in accordance with four major criteria: "occasion and method of domestic group formation," "procreational and demographic criteria," "criteria of kin composition of groups," and "criteria of organization of work and welfare."[5] In his view, the "east" region was east of a line of demarcation running from Leningrad (St. Petersburg) to Trieste, and one of its distinguishing characteristics was a "very high" rate of multiple-family households. For example, Krasnoe Sobakino in Russia in 1849, with four-fifths of its households multiple in composition, contrasted markedly with the "west" region cases such as Elmdon in England in 1861, with nearly three-quarters of its households simple family (conjugal family unit only). We cannot elaborate further here, but the "Mediterranean" type is relatively near to "east," and the "west/central or middle" type is relatively near to "west." Laslett classified households in the Balkans under Ottoman rule as "east" together with Russian households. However, households in Anatolia and Arab lands have never been studied carefully. What were the household composition tendencies there? Should the households be classified as "east" or "Mediterranean," or did they show other tendencies?

The 1990s marked a new start for Ottoman family and household history that began to answer this question. Duben and Behar published their work about Istanbul households, using a new kind of historical source, the basic rosters *(esas nüfus kayıt defterleri)* of 1885 and 1907, that enabled them to understand the structure of Ottoman households.[6] Duben and Behar were the first researchers who applied methods of the Cambridge Group to the analysis of Middle Eastern households. Their conclusion, in brief, was that Istanbul households were of a "Mediterranean" type, while households of rural Anatolia belonged to the "east" type.[7]

Until now, unfortunately, no one has critiqued their study or compared their data with those from other cities in the Middle East, because it was difficult for researchers to peruse basic rosters for the purpose of study. However basic rosters are now available in a few places,[8] thus providing useful comparison of sources on family and household structures in the Ottoman Empire. In this paper we intend to analyze Damascus households in the late Ottoman period and compare them with Istanbul ones.[9]

The method we use to analyze Damascus households is based on the most widely used criterion of household structure, the Hammel-Laslett classification, i.e., solitaries (singletons in households), no family households (coresidents among whom no conjugal family unit can be discerned), simple family households, extended family households (conjugal family units having kin-linked individuals), and multiple-family households.[10] Using this criterion is essential if we are to compare our results with Istanbul cases. Also, because we do not know enough about how Duben and Behar treated the polygynous family, in this paper we have placed it for the present within the category of multiple-family households.

Historical Setting: Damascus at the Opening of the Twentieth Century

Damascus was incorporated into Ottoman rule in 1516 and, as a provincial capital, played an important political, economic, and cultural role in Syria for nearly four hundred years. In the nineteenth century, the city experienced some serious social disturbances, especially the Egyptian rule (1830–40) and the 1860 massacre of the Christians of Damascus. However, the Ottoman central government in Istanbul then started to reform and strengthen direct control over local provinces. As a result of the reform, Damascus achieved relative political stability and became more closely connected with Istanbul by telegraph, railway, and other means during the reign of Sultan Abd al-Hamid II (1876–1909).[11]

During the nineteenth century, the impact of the West became manifest in Syria. In the 1830s, Syrian commercial relations with European countries increased under Egyptian rule. Establishment of a British consulate in Damascus in 1834 and an Anglo-Ottoman commercial treaty in 1838 opened Damascene markets to European goods. At the same time, European and American Christian missionaries started to open schools and teach European languages and sciences in Damascus and the other inland cities. Due to their activities, European ideas slowly penetrated the region. The visit of the German emperor,

Wilhelm II, to Damascus in 1898 can be considered evidence of the developing interest of European powers in Syria.[12]

Damascus became on good terms with Istanbul in the last two decades of the Hamidian period thanks to two Syrians: Abu al-Huda al-Sayyadi from the Aleppo region, a religious adviser to the sultan, and Ahmad Izzat Pasha al-Abîd of Damascus, the sultan's secretary. The latter played an important role not only in the adoption of a pro-German policy and pan-Islamism, but also in the project of a rail link between Damascus and Mecca. As a result, at the beginning of the twentieth century Damascus witnessed the implementation of many significant public work projects; for example, the construction of a civil hospital, the restoration of the Umayya mosque burned in the fire of 1893, and a new water supply system from Ayn al-Fija.[13] These economic activities reached their climax in the construction of the Hijaz railway.

From the end of the nineteenth century to the beginning of the twentieth century, Damascus saw large-scale Muslim immigration from the Balkans, Crete, and the Caucasus. As a result, the urban population grew rapidly from 154,000 in 1896 to 222,604 in 1911.[14] The census of 1905–6, source of the basic rosters of 1907, was conducted during the aforementioned circumstances and completed without any disturbance. However, this was a was temporary calm before the storm of the Young Turk revolt of 1908, the outbreak of World War I, the upsurge of Arab nationalism, the fall of the Ottoman Empire, and the French occupation.[15]

Basic Rosters as a Source for Ottoman Family History

A modern census was first carried out in 1828–29 in European and Anatolian regions of the Ottoman Empire, but counted only males for the purpose of taxation and military conscription. After this census was completed, the Office of Population Registers (Ceride-i Nüfus Nezareti) was established.[16] However, the first population survey of Arab provinces seems not to have been conducted before 1847.[17] More than thirty years later, in 1877–78, the authorities conducted a census that produced rich information on various aspects of Ottoman population and society.[18]

The Ottoman census system was a de jure census, and the results were recorded in the basic rosters of 1885 and 1907, which recorded individuals as members of residential groups of various types, the most common of which was the household (*hane*). In this paper we use the term to refer to "household," "residence," or simply *hane* according to different periods and places. For each individual name listed, there is information on title or status and occupation (*şöhret, sıfat, sanat ve hizmeti*), relationship to the head of the household, religion, date and place of birth, date of registration, sex, name of father and mother, and marital status, in addition to other information of little sociological value.[19]

As for the 1907 basic rosters of Damascus, on which our study primarily depends, there are two types. One type is an ordinary notebook-style register (size 37 × 24 cm, which we call Type I), a data entry system that seems to have followed the traditional style of registers for vital statistics and population movements (vukuʿat defterleri). Another type is an official-style register (size 43 × 28.5 cm, which we call Type II), whose every page has a formula for population registration.[20] Both types contain quarter name, residence number, first name, family name, father and mother's names, birth year, relation to household head, and some additional data added afterward (birth year of new residents, death, marriage, divorce, conscription, immigration, emigration, and so on). In addition, Type I contains useful information about the occupations of some members of the hane, and Type II includes the religion of every person. Both registers have lost their first pages, so we cannot know how they were officially named. Today, however, they are called basic rosters (sijillat al-nufus) in Arabic.[21]

Type I seems to have been established about 1907, judging by the birth year of infants recorded there, and was used officially longer than Type II; its handwriting has changed several times, ink colors have been changed from black to purple, different calendar systems have been used (from a fiscal [mali or rumi] calendar to Hijri and then to Gregorian), and the language used by officials has also changed from Ottoman to Arabic. These changes indicate transfer of basic rosters from one quarter's headman (mukhtar) to another. Use of Type I seems to have been discontinued after 1930.

We examined dates of census registration, recorded in register Type II, and found that this survey extended from the last ten days of Mayıs 1321 (the first ten days of June 1905) to the first ten days of Temmuz 1321 (the middle ten days of July 1905). Enumerators had walked the round of the hanes one by one at a brisk pace, surveying an average of seven hanes per day. It should be concluded from what has been said above that Types I and II are a product of the last Ottoman population count of 1905-6.[22]

Hane Reconsidered: Some Problems of the Registration System

Hane Reconsidered

Let us now examine the problem of the hane. Hane is a term of Persian origin meaning "a house, dwelling, habitation; a tent, pavilion; a receptacle; a drawer, partition, compartment; department; the arm from the shoulder to the elbow; a field; a woman; a page of letter-paper; a heap of corn; a hillock of sand; verse, poetry."[23] Here, the definition as "house" or "woman," however does not mean "household." According to *The Redhouse Turkish and English Lexicon*, *hane* means "a house, a building; a dwelling; a man's wife; a man's family, his household, especially, the females of the household; a chamber, closet, compartment, etc., set apart to any special purpose; a cell in any substance; a subdivision in a scheme or table, a place of figures in notation; a sign of the zodiac."[24] It is very likely that the original meaning of *hane* changed over time from "house" or "woman" to " household" in the Ottoman period.[25]

Barkan assumed that only when married could a male form one *hane* and be accepted in the category of family heads (*aile reisleri*), and then only if his dependents recognized him as such.[26] If this assumption is true, the Ottoman households appear to show the characteristics of the "west" type indicated by Laslett, in which a household is always formed at the marriage of a household head.[27] Is the Ottoman household composition similar to that of the English household? Barkan's assumption actually had no basis in historical fact. However, many researchers accepted his assumption and translated *hane*, as used between the fifteenth and seventeenth centuries, as "household."[28]

Göyünç criticized Barkan's opinion and defined *hane* between the fifteenth and seventeenth centuries as a taxable household (*avariz hane*), which doesn't mean ordinary household at all. On the other hand, he defined *hane* in the nineteenth and twentieth centuries as a household.[29] Duben defined *hane* as "the word commonly used by Turks," that is, "household," but in the same article said "*hane*, like the old German *hus* or *haus*, retains the older inclusive meaning of the building and the corresponding social group."[30] Thus, we confirm here that *hane* has two basic meanings, "house" and "household."

In Syria, the term has been used until now in an administrative sense, to mean a "permanent domicile" recorded in an identity card (*huwiyya*).[31] To explain the difference between *hane* in Syria and *hane* in Turkey, a comparison between a typical residential plan in intra-muros of Damascus and in Istanbul may be helpful. A typical residence in Damascus was a courtyard-style house. Such houses, if large enough, were often subdivided into several new residences, each with its own courtyard in the center for reasons of inheritance, transaction, and so on.[32] Actually, there are many examples in Damascus basic rosters showing that households unrelated by blood or marriage are registered in one *hane*, as we shall see in the ratio later, in section 5. Thus, it can be assumed that several households live independent family lives in their residences inside one subdivided *hane*. It is doubtful whether the Ottoman authorities could constantly follow up a subdivision of one *hane* into several residences. Viewed in this light, *hane* in Damascus can be regarded primarily as "residence" but cannot be understood as "household" in the case of a *hane* where many households live. This word does not always mean "a single purse and a single pot," as Duben cited in reference to Turkey.[33] On the other hand, the residence of a typical Turk in Istanbul was a two-story wooden structure, and his family consisted of five (e.g., him, his parents, and two younger brothers).[34] This kind of residence seems smaller in size and more difficult to subdivide. If one of its members wanted to set up a new household, he could certainly move to another house. These differences of residential plan between Damascus and Istanbul inevitably affected the meaning of *hane*. Barkan's assumption that a household is always formed at the marriage of a household head is applicable to Istanbul households but not to Damascus ones, because the Turkish *hane* meant interchangeably house and household, while the Damascus *hane* meant residence but not always household.

Registration System of Hane

We will closely examine the Damascus *hane*, analyzing the registration system. In the basic rosters, we find some rules for the population entry system. As mentioned above, the basic unit registered in a basic roster was the *hane*. The priority order among members of the *hane* was basically (1) male prior to female, (2) senior to junior, and (3) upward or downward in terms of the flow on a lineage chart. The order of a simple family household (for example, one couple and their son and daughter) is as shown in (figure 1).

1. *hane* head: male
   (*birinci numara*)

2. his son: male
   (*birinci numara oğlu*)

3. his wife: female
   (*birinci numara zevcesi*)

4. his daughter: female
   (*birinci numara kerimesi*)

Figure 1. Simple Family

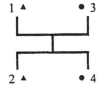

In the case of an extended family household in which the *hane* head forms a simple family and his brother, mother, and sister live with them, (1) male is prior to female, (2) senior to junior, (3) extension upward to extension sideways to extension downward (note: female extension sideways is prior to head's wife). The order is thus as shown in figure 2.

1. *hane* head: male
   (*birinci numara*)

2. his brother: male
   (*birinci numara biraderi*)

3. his son: male
   (*birinci numara oğlu*)

4. his mother: female
   (*birinci numara validesi*)

5. his sister: female
   (*birinci numara hemşiresi*)

6. his wife: female
   (*birinci numara zevcesi*)

7. his daughter: female
   (*birinci numara kerimesi*)

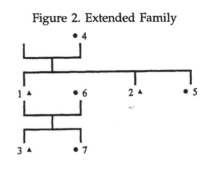

Figure 2. Extended Family

In the case of a multiple-family household in which the head and his brother each form a nucleus, the order is slightly different, (1) head's nucleus is prior to his brother's nucleus, (2) male to female, (3) senior to junior, and (4) upward to downward (see figure 3).

1. *hane* head: male
   (*birinci numara*)

2. his son: male
   (*birinci numara oğlu*)

3. his wife: female
   (*birinci numara zevcesi*)

4. his daughter: female
   (*birinci numara kerimesi*)

5. his brother: male
   (*birinci numara biraderi*),

6. son of no. 5: male
   (*beşinci numara oğlu*)

7. wife of no. 5: female
   (*beşinci numara zevcesi*)

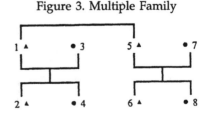

Figure 3. Multiple Family

8. daughter of no. 5: female
    (beşinci numara kerimesi)

Up to here, cases of *hane* in which only one household resides were mentioned. We now move to the most important case, *hane* in which more than two households unrelated by blood or marriage live together (see figure 4).

1. *hane* head: male
    (birinci numara)

2. his son: male
    (birinci numara oğlu)

3. his wife: female
    (birinci numara zevcesi)

4. his daughter: female
    (birinci numara kerimesi)

5. inmate household head: male
    (hanede sakin beşinci numara)

6. son of no. 5: male
    (beţinci numara oďlu)

7. wife of no. 5: female
    (beşinci numara zevcesi)

8. daughter of no. 5: female
    (beşinci numara kerimesi)

9. resident servant:
    male *(hizmetkar)*

10. resident housemaid:
    female *(hademesi)*

Figure 4. Household of *Hane* Head and *Hanede Sakin* Inmate Household

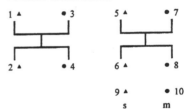

This seems like a multiple-family household. However, it is difficult for Muslim households without any relationship by blood or marriage to live together.[35] It seems reasonable, then, to suppose that actually a residence was divided into two independent households, each of which lived separately. As a matter of course, figures 3 and 4 therefore indicate different *hane* structures. However, since two households were registered as sharing one *hane* in basic rosters, we call the household beginning from no. 5, as indicated in figure 4, an "inmate household." Such an inmate household head was always specified as inmate *(hanede sakin, hanede, sakin or sakin fi al-khana)*, even if the inmate was solitary.

Resident servants do not seem to have been registered as an independent household. They were also always specified by status, male servant as *hizmetkar* or *hadim*, and female housemaid as *hadime* or *hademe*.[36] It is worth noting that the above-mentioned resident servant and housemaid belong to the household of no. 5, not to the household of the *hane* head, because resident servants/housemaids are always recorded just after their master's household.

Household Size and Structure

Household Size

Barkan, a pioneer in the study of *hane* of the sixteenth century, assumed a coefficient of 5 as the mean *hane* size.[37] However, this assumption was also unfounded. After him, many scholars tried to verify the proper number. For example, Cook used 4.5 as a coefficient of *hane* in rural Anatolia between 1450 and 1600.[38] Cohen and Lewis referred to the *hane* (tax-paying household) as one family and used a conjectural coefficient of 6 for a *hane* of Palestinian towns in the sixteenth century.[39] Russell states in his article about the Balkans and Asia Minor population in 1520-34. that "it should be about 3.5" because "the hearth designates a man-wife-child unit with grandparents and other relatives usually living separately."[40] In any case, most of the figures from these studies are little better than guesses. Among them, McGowan's assumption is more solid, because he divided total population by total *hane* number and got as a result an average *hane* size from 3.57 to 6 in the Danubian region in 1568-79.[41] Depending primarily on solid evidence, Stoianovich also figured from 4.6 to 6.5 in the city of Zara on the coast of the Adriatic Sea in 1539-93.[42]

Speculation abounds for estimates of the mean household size of Damascus, although there are few hard facts to build upon. Pascual used 5 for the size of a Damascus *hane* at the end of sixteenth century, based on Barkan's study.[43] Bowring estimated the mean household size in 1840 as 3.5 persons, following the opinion of Werry, the British consul in Damascus.[44] These assumptions also seem to have been unfounded.

From the beginning of the seventeenth to the beginning of the nineteenth century, no land survey was conducted, due to stagnation, relative decentralization, and local autonomy in the empire.[45] Therefore we must use the nineteenth- and twentieth-century censuses to get accurate household sizes. Thanks to published sources and studies, we can use data from six cities, as follows: three cities in the Danubian region (4.5 persons, 1866),[46] the city of Istanbul (4.2 persons, 1907),[47] the city of Aleppo (7.0 persons, ca. 1900, 7.5 persons, ca. 1908),[48] and the city of Tripoli (Lebanon) (5.5 persons, ca. 1905-6).[49] Of these data, only Istanbul can provide enough to be compared with the data of Damascus.[50]

We are now ready to consider Damascus household size and structure. We found in basic rosters of 1907 that many data samples belonged to the last type (figure 3.4), "*hane* in which more than two households with non-kinship lived together." *Hanes* that contain more than one *hanede sakin* inmate household actually amounted to 157 *hanes*, 47.1 percent of the total 333 *hanes*. We should therefore look more closely at those households. If we assume a household of a *hane* head to include only family residents and regard the other inmate household as nonfamily residents, the results are as follows (see table 5).

Table 5. *Hanes* in Damascus 1907, Numbers and Proportions of Types and Residents by Type and Mean Numbers of Residents per *Hane*

| | 1907 | | | | | | |
Hane Type	No. of Type	%	No of Residents	%	Mean Hane Size	Mean No. of Family Residents	Mean No. of Nonfamily Residents
Solitaries	2	0.6%	2	0.1%	1.0	1.0	—
No Family	6	1.8%	38	1.0%	6.3	2.5	3.8
Simple Family	77	23.1%	622	16.6%	8.1	5.1	3.0
Extended Family	69	20.7%	662	17.6%	9.6	5.8	3.8
Multiple Family	179	53.8%	2431	64.7%	13.6	11.1	2.5
All *Hanes*	333	100.0%	3755	100.0%	11.3	8.4	2.9

Source: Damascus basic rosters

Table 6. Households in Istanbul 1907, Numbers and Proportions of Types and Residents by Type and Mean Numbers of Residents per Household

| | 1907 | | | | | | |
Household Type	No. of Type	%	No of Residents	%	Mean Household Size	Mean No. of Family Residents	Mean No. of Nonfamily Residents
Solitaries	152	12.9%	168	3.4%	1.0	1.0	—
No Family	95	8.0%	288	5.8%	3.0	1.6	1.4
Simple Family	470	40.0%	1671	33.8%	3.6	3.4	0.2
Extended Family	188	16.1%	984	20.0%	5.2	4.7	0.5
Multiple Family	141	12.0%	1082	21.9%	7.7	6.9	0.8
Unclassifiable	130	11.1%	739	15.0%	5.7	3.1	2.6
All Households	1176	100.1%	4932	99.9%	4.2	3.6	0.6

Source: Duben and Behar 1991, 49.

In short, the mean size of a Damascus *hane* (11.3 persons) was the largest in comparison with the above-mentioned examples.[51] However, according to this method, one *hane* that actually consisted of 11 households (6 simple family, 3 extended, and 2 multiple) is classified as one extended family, composed of eight family residents with fifty nonfamily residents! It is useful to compare these results with the Istanbul case (see table 6).

At first sight, the Damascus *hane* is much larger than the Istanbul household. Except for solitaries, the mean sizes of all Damascus *hane* types are 3.3 to 5.9 persons more than those of Istanbul. The largest Istanbul household contained 27 persons,[52] while the largest Damascus *hane* contained 58. Another point of interest is the rarity of solitaries and no-family households in Damascus. One of the most characteristic features of the Damascus *hane* was that it was multiple-family (53.8 percent), while Istanbul had many quite small simple-family domestic units (40.0 percent).[53] Thus it would be untrue to say that Damascus *hane* conclusively indicated the social reality of the Damascus household.

Turning our attention to the existence of *hanede sakin* inmate households within *hane*, we tried to define "real" Damascus households. Our restoration work, mainly separating *hanede sakin* inmate households from households of *hane* heads, met with unexpected results (see table 7).

Our data samples have now increased by 234 to 568 as a result. A marked change occurred as the proportion of solitaries dramatically increased from 0.6 percent to 12.5 percent. The increased number of solitaries seemed to be related to the sharp decline of multiple-family *hane*.

Table 7. Households in Damascus 1907, Numbers and Proportions of Types and Residents by Type and Mean Numbers of Residents per Household

	1907						
Household Type	No. of Type	%	No of Residents	%	Mean Household Size	Mean No. of Family Residents	Mean No. of Nonfamily Residents
Solitaries	71	12.5%	72	1.9%	1.0	1.0	0.0
No Family	13	2.3%	41	1.1%	3.2	2.9	0.2
Simple Family	156	27.5%	705	18.8%	4.5	4.4	0.1
Extended Family	100	17.6%	574	15.3%	5.7	5.6	0.1
Multiple Family	228	40.1%	2363	62.9%	10.4	10.3	0.1
All Households	568	100.0%	3755	100.0%	6.6	6.5	0.1

Source: Damascus basic rosters

The slight growth of the proportion of simple-family *hane* also seemed related to the slight decline of extended-family *hane*. The results were then used as criteria in comparison with Istanbul households.

The first point to be compared is household size. The mean household size of Damascus (6.6 persons) is still slightly larger, but acceptable. The mean size of simple-family and multiple-family *hane* points out the difference between Damascus and Istanbul. The mean size of simple-family *hanes* of Damascus is larger than that of Istanbul by 0.9 persons. A modal simple-family *hane* of Damascus is composed of one couple with two or three offspring. The proportion of simple-family *hanes* in Damascus indicated in table 7 is "low" according to Laslett's sets of tendencies in domestic group organization.[54] The mean size of multiple-family *hane* in Damascus is larger than that of Istanbul by 2.7 persons. This considerable difference directly affected the mean household size of all households of Damascus.

Household Structure

In order to understand the difference of the mean size of multiple-family *hane* between Damascus and Istanbul, we have to look at the household structure of Damascus. This is the second point. We suggest a few reasons for Damascus households' trend to form multiple-family *hane*, namely, (1) the Ottoman-Syrian domestic cycle, (2) generational composition, and (3) polygyny.

In Turkey, the fission of the household was in general precipitated by the death of the father,[55] while in Syria, even after the death of the patriarch, *frérèches* (in which no parent or other member of an earlier generation is present and the siblings are connected entirely through the final linkage of each to a conjugal unit no longer represented in the household)[56] live together, and thus fission of the household would not easily take place. Differences in residential structures between Istanbul and Damascus also support this assumption. For example, Najat Qassab Hasan, a Damascene lawyer, wrote in his memoir that at the beginning of the twentieth century, his father and uncle were joint owners of one house, where his father's family, his uncle's family, and his divorced aunt lived together. His father was a carpenter and his uncle was an Ottoman army officer who had participated in the battle of Gallipoli in 1915. At one time, the total number in his house reached twenty-one persons: his parents and seven children, his uncle and aunt and their six children, his aunt and her daughter, and two sons of his maternal uncle.[57] Such a situation is shown in table 7 and supported by the fact that over one-fifth of multiple-family households (21.1 percent) were *frérèches*, and over half of these (50.4 percent) were composed of more than three conjugal family units, the largest one having seven conjugal family units. Such domestic arrangements exhibit a striking contrast to that of Turkish domestic arrangements.

Generational composition also shows a difference between Damascus and Istanbul. In Damascus, 82.6 percent of all households contained two or more generations. Over one-third of all households contained more than three generations. The most multigenerational household consisted of five generations, a *hane* head with his wife and mother and his one male offspring, his nephew and his nephew's wife, and one couple consisting of the nephew and his wife with their male offspring, with the latter's offspring. On the other hand, in Istanbul nearly three-quarters of these households contained two generations only.[58] This multigenerational character of Damascus households seems to have been deeply rooted in the household structure of Damascus.

Polygyny is believed to be one of the most characteristic features of the Muslim family, but the proportion of polygynous husbands in Istanbul in 1907 was only 2.16 percent. Thus polygyny seems not to have affected household structure much in Istanbul.[59] However, at the same time, according to our samples, its proportion in Damascus reached 12.1 percent. Since we placed the polygynous family within the category of multiple-family households, its high proportion directly affects the multiple-family household trend of Damascus.[60]

Now we evaluate resident servants and inmate groups except *hanede sakin* inmate households. Most families in Damascus at that time seem not to have had coresident servants. Only 3.5 percent of all households, twenty households, lived together with servants in 1907. All household types possibly contained coresident servants, with no fixed pattern of hiring servants by household type (see table 8).

Table 8. Servants Resident in Damascus Households by Age Group, 1907

Age groups	1907	
	Number	%
<15	6	25.0%
15–19	5	20.8%
20–29	3	12.5%
30–39	1	4.2%
40–49	3	12.5%
50–59	4	16.7%
60+	2	8.3%
Total female	21	87.5%
Total male	3	12.5%
Total	24	100.0%

Source: Damascus basic rosters

The trend of resident servants themselves was almost similar to the case of Istanbul, and they were predominantly young and female. We observed that the percentage of servants aged between 20 and 39 was slightly smaller than that in Istanbul, while that of those over forty was slightly higher. That most of their fathers' names were recorded as Servant of God (*Abdullah*), and their family names as Ethiopian (Habashi), Negro (*zunji*) or Circassian (*jarkas*) indicates that they came through slave merchants' hands.

Recent research, carried out by the Jinnai group in intramuros of Damascus in 1991, confirms the trend we found in Damascus households: the proportion of the simple-family type in the Muslim population is 34.8 percent and of complex-family (extended-family plus multiple-family) is 65.2 percent. The result suggests that the continuity of the traditional Damascus households has been preserved to this day. However, the Jinnai group did not research households living in the apartments of quarters in the new part of the city. The similarity found simply indicates that residential form and size strongly affect household size.[61] All these findings make clear the "multiple" and "large-size" trend of Damascus households in the late Ottoman period, quite different in character from the "simple" and "small domestic unit" tendency of Istanbul.[62]

Household Headship and Sex Ratio

Household Headship

The purpose here is to explore a little further into household headship. As mentioned above, according to registration rules, the *hane* head should be the senior male with first priority, even if he is an infant. Registration rules of *hanede sakin* inmate households are similar. This means females stood little chance of becoming household heads in an administrative sense.[63] We can confirm this assumption by male headship rates (see figure 5), which indicate male household heads of any given age range from under 15 to over 60 as a proportion of all males of that age range.

In Istanbul, about 60 percent of all males became household heads by their thirties. But the pattern of Damascus indicates that its males rarely attained headship at a young age, since male headship rates did not reach 60 percent until Damascene males were in their forties. The difference between the two cities is about ten years. The curve of Istanbul headship rates gradually declined for males over 60, but that of Damascus reached its highest point at just over 60. This Damascene trend seems more reasonable in conformity with registration rules, that is, the senior having priority over the junior. The headship rates

Figure 5. Male Headship Rates,
Damascus and Istanbul, 1907

Figure 6. Female Headship Rates,
Damascus and Istanbul, 1907

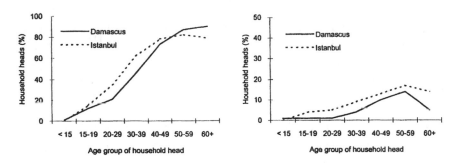

Source: Damascus basic rosters, Duben and Behar 1991, 65–66.

are much lower for Damascene females, as in Istanbul (see figure 6.2).
The curve of female headship reached the top at 50 to 59, but still only
13.6 percent attained headship. In Damascus basic rosters, a female
household head appears only in the case of female solitaries. If we
assume the same for Istanbul, its proportion of female solitaries should
also be higher than that of Damascus.

When we examine the ages of household heads for the various
types of domestic units, a clear age-specific pattern of headship emerges
(see figures 7 and 8).

Figure 7. Headship by Household Type,
Damascus, 1907

Figure 8. Headship by
Household Type,
Istanbul, 1907

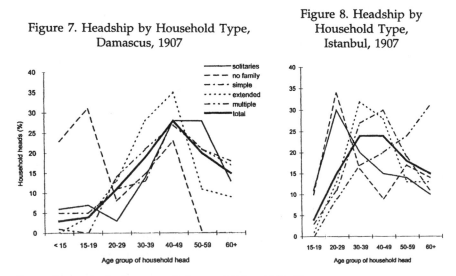

Source: Damascus basic rosters, Duben and Behar 1991, 63.

In Istanbul, the modal age for solitary and no-family household heads is between 20 and 29; for simple- and extended-family household heads, between 30 and 49; and for heads of multiple-family households, over 60.[64] In Damascus, the modal age for all types of household was between 40 and 49 except for no-family households, the modal age of which was between 15 and 19. But these results are also more reasonable in conformity with registration rules. The very low percentage of headship until age 29 shows a sort of stability and unchangeableness for Damascus, also suggested by the high mean age of male solitary head (34.2) and female solitary head (46.2) and the extremely low percentage of no-family households (2.3 percent). The headship pattern of solitaries and no-family households in Istanbul, on the other hand, shows a sort of fluidity and instability.

However, we should not confuse headship recorded in the basic roster with actual control over domestic economy. For example, a *hane* of Damascus consisted of the head (male aged 11), his grandmother (aged 78), his two aunts (aged 39 and 37), and his three female cousins (aged 13, 11, and 10). Though basic rosters keep silent, we assume that headship was not simply patriarch/matriarch. In this *hane*, the grandmother or one of the aunts might act as legal guardian *(wasi)* of the "head." In this case, the household head recorded in the basic roster is apparently "on paper" only; hence, insubstantial. Moreover, Islamic law of inheritance did not allow the *hane* head absolute control over the domestic economy. In order to extend this assumption further, we must use Islamic court records.[65]

Sex Ratio

The last thing left to discuss here is sex ratio. The sex ratio of the city of Damascus population in 1907 shows a problematic imbalance: 78.8 males to 100 females, as the result of a male population of 1,655 to a female population of 2,100. In the city of Istanbul, on the other hand, the sex ratio was 98.9 to 100, quite evenly balanced. One reason for this discrepancy might be problems with the registration system. Since the Ottoman census system was originally introduced for the purpose of taxation and conscription, residents were, in general, reluctant to give full information, especially about males. Early censuses were insufficient, and some high-ranking officials were not counted *(mektum nüfus).*[66] However the census of 1905–6 seems to have been carried out fairly. Thus, the first reason is unsound.

The second possible solution, mortality, can be explained through the population pyramid by five-year age groups (see figure 9). Comparing the sex ratio of age group 0–4 years (107.9) with that of age

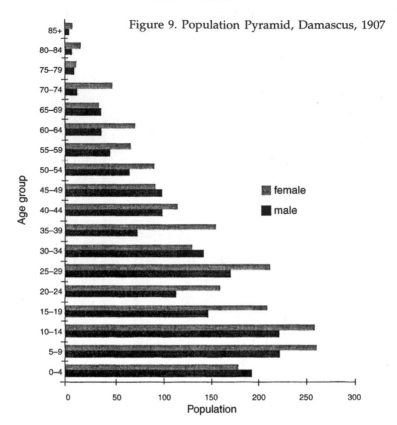

Figure 9. Population Pyramid, Damascus, 1907

Source: Damascus basic rosters

group 5–14 years (85.3), the male child mortality rate seems to have seriously affected the male population. However, this solution is also insufficient to explain the imbalance of sex ratio in Damascus.

The investigation of events hindering male population growth is, in fact, the key to the imbalance. According to yearbooks of the province of Syria *(Salname-i vilayet-i Suriye)* between 1888 and 1900, the sex ratio declined steadily during the period (see figure 10).

These findings indicate a marked decline in the sex ratio of the Muslim population in Damascus, which falls right down to 78.0 in 1900. Since this figure is almost equal to the figure calculated from Damascus basic rosters, the reliability of data used here is confirmed by the result. Male population growth was seriously limited, for Muslim and non-Muslim alike—remarkably more serious for the former. Since the sex ratio of age group 0–4 years is high, it is most likely that events

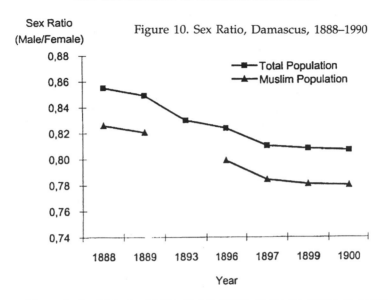

Figure 10. Sex Ratio, Damascus, 1888–1990

Source: *Salname-i vilayet-i Suriye,* 20:134, 21:150, 27:250, 29:324–25, 30:332–33, 31:368–69, 32:364–65

blocking adult male population growth affected the sex ratio of Damascus. Deaths on the battlefield and emigration, rather than epidemics, are most likely, but the former is to be examined here. Soldiers conscripted in Damascus experienced military operations in Mount Lebanon and the Hawran inside the province, and expeditions in the Yemen and a war with Russia outside the province in the 1870s.[67] In the Russo-Ottoman war (1877–78), not only the active duty group (*muvazzaf:* four years from age 20) but also all other groups were called up, including the active reserve group (*ihtiyat:* two years after *muvazzaf),* the inactive reserve (*redif:* fourteen years after *ihtiyat),* and the territorial/local militia (*mustahfaz:* four years after *redif).*[68] The age group 50–54 years experienced all of the above-mentioned wars and was called into *redif* for possible hostilities over the Bulgarian annexation of East Rumelia in 1885.[69] Thus the sex ratio of this group is low (70.8).

Another age group, 35–39 years, also experienced many successive military operations in the 1890s (e.g., Crete in 1889–90, the Yemen in 1891, and Jabal Druze in 1890–96).[70] The sex ratio of this group is only 45.5, the lowest among all male age groups. On the other hand, the sex ratios of age groups 45–49 and 65–69 years, which didn't experience wars as much, are higher than others. Apparently manpower losses during wars of the second half of the nineteenth century affected the sex ratio. We wish to cite the Bowring report, even though it dates from more than sixty years before the time with which we are now concerned: "There can be no doubt, in consequence of the much greater waste of life among men, that the proportion of females is very much greater than that of males, and that this disproportion is increasing by the perpetual draining of the male population."[71]

It may be worth pointing out in passing that the 1905-6 census results curiously show evidence to the contrary. The sex ratio of the province (not the city) of Istanbul was 150.1 and extremely unnatural, while that of the *liwa* (subdivision of a province, not the city) of Damascus was 98.5 and fairly balanced. In the province of Istanbul, a number of unmarried migrant workers affected such an imbalance, while in the *liwa* of Damascus, rural population compensated for the imbalance in urban population to some extent.[72]

Concluding Remarks

On these grounds we have come to the conclusion that Damascus households in the beginning of the twentieth century were large as well as complex in structure. The reasons are primarily (1) the high proportion of multiple-family houses, (2) the large size of a Damascene residence as a courtyard-style house, (3) the relatively high rate of polygyny, and (4) the multigenerational character of Damascus households.

Based on Laslett's classification, Damascus households seem to trend towards the "Mediterranean" type, because in Damascus the proportion of simple-family household is "low" and that of multiple household is "high"; however, the proportion of complex-family household is "very high," which indicates a trend towards the "east" type. Istanbul households, on the other hand, show trends between "west/central or middle" and "Mediterranean," because in the "Mediterranean" type, the proportion of simple-family household is "low," that of extended-family household is "low," and that of multiple-family household is "high," whereas in Istanbul households, proportions of simple, extended, and multiple are all "medium."[73] This indicates a uniqueness of Istanbul, where frequent population movement, birth control, and constant population pressure were all commonplace.

Qassab Hasan writes in his memoir, "[I]n my house, life was relatively better than others thanks to the influence of my uncle—he was an army officer—who saw the civilization in Istanbul and in Russia during war, and brought new ideas back from there." For example, he observed that his uncle introduced the family to the use of a spoon and plate of their own in eating food.[74] Istanbul was the fashion leader, civilized or Europeanized, as viewed by Damascenes. Radical change in Damascus households seems not yet to have begun at that time. Formation of a European-style city outside the old city and the introduction of a Europeanized lifestyle or building are useful explanations for changes in household composition.

The full study of family and household in Damascus lies outside the scope of a brief paper. There is room for further investigation. It is debatable how Damascus households were affected by family strategies, economic stresses, marriage patterns, fertility patterns, modernization, and other factors. We are just at the starting point of family history in the Ottoman Empire.

Notes

The writing of this paper was made possible largely through grants from the Mitsubishi Foundation, and we would like to acknowledge here the generosity of this organization. This paper is also part of a research project, "Family History Study in the Middle East Based on Islamic Court Records: Damascus from the Nineteenth Century to the Beginning of the Twentieth Century," funded by a grant from the Japan Association for Promotion of Science. The archival sources are referred to in the following manner: *Markaz al-Watha'iq al-Tarikhiyya* [MWT] (Center for Historical Documents), Damascus: *al-Awamir al-Sultaniyya* [AS] (Imperial Edicts), Aleppo; *Sijillat al-Nufus* (Damascus Basic Rosters), Private Collection; *Basbakanlık Osmanlı Arşivi* [BOA] (Prime Minister's Archives), Istanbul: *Bab Ali Evrak Odası Sadaret Evrakı Mektubi Kalemi* [A. MKT]

1. For a history of Ottoman demographic studies, see Panzac 1993.

2. Regarding studies of tax registers *(tahrir defterleri)* and their problems as sources, see Faroqhi 1999, 86–95. There are a few exceptions. For example, Elifoglu 1984 reports the existence of some Ottoman *defter*s containing ages of children.

3. For *zadrugha*, see the following articles: Hammel 1972; Laslett and Clarke 1972; and Halpern 1972. Regarding activities and results of the Cambridge Group, see Laslett 1985. Our work owes much to the assistance of the EAP [EurAsian Project on Population and Family History] group, led by Akira Hayami, a member of the Cambridge Group, because the project members always give us helpful suggestions for the application of methods of the Cambridge Group to analyses of households in the Middle East.

4. Regarding the meaning of traditional Europe and four sets of tendencies of domestic group organization, see Laslett 1983.

5. Laslett 1983, 516–33.

6. For their studies and results, see Duben and Behar 1991.

7. Duben and Behar 1991, 8–9, 159–61.

8. For example, basic rosters of Egypt in the nineteenth century are now available for researchers. See Cuno 1995; Alleaume and Fargues 1998a; and Fargues 2000.

9. Regarding the terminology of demography, we generally refer to the International Union for the Scientific Study of Population 1994.

10. Regarding the significance of Laslett's works, see Anderson 1980, 22–49.

11. For the situation until 1860, see Ma'oz 1968. For after 1860, see Gross 1979.

12. Gross 1979, 468–78.

13. Ibid., 498–501.

14. Qassab Hasan 1994, 51–55; Ghazzal 1993, 45. As these refugees *(muhajirun)* formed a new district named after their status within the suburb northwest of Damascus, their immigration did not affect the household structure of our data samples.

15. Gross 1979, 459–540.

16. Karpat 1985, 18, 20, 28.

17. For the first census of the province of Damascus, see BOA. A.MKT. 165/55 (1265 Muharram 14/ 1848 December 10). Regarding the first census of the province of Aleppo, see MWT. AS. Aleppo Register No. 55 Doc. No. 309 (1266 Rabi al-Awwal 26/ 1850 February 9).

18. Duben and Behar 1991, 15. Karpat 1985, 30–35.

19. Duben and Behar 1991, 19–20.

20. Every page of Type II has a formula for population registration: first name and family name *(al-ism wa al-shuhra)*, district and quarter *(al-thumn wa al-mahalla)*, residence number *(numara al-maskan)*, birth year *(tarikh al-wilada)*, and note *(al-mashruhat)*.

21. These basic rosters are now preserved by two families that produced quarter headmen in the late Ottoman period. We regret that, in order to guard privacy, we cannot specify these families.

22. For the 1905–6 census, see Karpat 1985, 35. We would like to add a few supplementary explanations for our data in comparison with Istanbul. Both the Istanbul data studied by Duben and Behar and those of Damascus analyzed here were Muslim. The former is 5 percent from five districts of Istanbul (Duben 1990, 433; Duben and Behar 1991, 18). On the other hand, data here is 30 percent from one district, which belonged to the intramuros districts and did not necessarily reflect trends in Damascus as a whole; however, it is worth mentioning that these samples of Damascus households indicate quite different trends from Istanbul ones. We also add explanations for

some cases in which our data seem to differ from the general trends of Damascus City. Without a doubt, analysis of all districts of Damascus is desirable in the future.

23. Steingass 1973, 444.

24. Redhouse 1890, 827.

25. *The New Redhouse Turkish and English Dictionary* does not give any meaning for *hane* corresponding to "household." Redhouse 1986, 446.

26. Barkan 1953, 12.

27. Laslett named the tendency "neo-localism" (Laslett 1983, 531–33).

28. There are a few exceptions. See Cohen and Lewis 1978, 14–15.

29. As for *avariz hane*, see Sertoglu 1986, 23–24.

30. Duben 1985, 77.

31. Asadi defines *hane* (*khana* in Arabic) as "residence *(manzil)*, particularly permanent domicile *(mawdi sukna sahib sijill al-ahwal al-madaniyya)*." Asadi n.d., 302. We confirmed this from a Syrian identity card *(huwiyya)* in 1997.

32. Suzuki 1993, 47. Arai reported the case of a single residence that was subdivided into three parts thirty-five years ago (ca. 1956) as part of an inheritance arrangement. He regarded this as evidence of a certain breakdown in the extended family as a communal living unit (Arai 1993, 80-81).

33. Duben 1985, 78. Hara pointed out that, in Turkey, the term *aile* now means nuclear type of domestic group and *hane* means extended type of domestic group (Hara 1978, 1–2, 8).

34. Duben and Behar 1991, 48.

35. According to Islamic law, an adult Muslim female *(mar'a)* cannot be seen or touched by an adult Muslim male except by her husband or by a relative prohibited from marrying her. See Qal'aji, Qunaybi, and Sanu 1996, 380. Arai also concluded, based on his field research, that among Muslims, "families unrelated by blood or marriage do not live together" (Arai 1993, 77).

36. We do not find the term *cariye*, which Duben used in his article (Duben 1985, 79).

37. Barkan 1953, 12.

38. In Göyünç 1979, 322.

39. Cohen and Lewis 1978, 14–15.

40. Russell 1960, 265.

41. McGowan figured 3.57 in the case of the *sanjak* of Semendire, 4.59 in the case of Segedin, 5.26 in the case of D'ula, and 6 in the case of Sirem. See Göyünç 1979, 332–33.

42. Stoianovich 1980, 190.

43. Pascual examined the other opinions—4.5 by Cook, 7 by Cohen and Lewis—but did not adopt them (Pascual 1983, 26).

44. Bowring [1840] 1973, 4.

45. Behar 1998.

46. Todorov 1998. These three cities are Hadjioglu Pazardzik, Svistov, and Tarnovo.

47. Duben and Behar 1991, 49.

48. According to the yearbook of the province of Aleppo published in 1900, the urban population of Aleppo was 108,445 and the number of *hane* was 15,467. *Salname-i vilayet-i Haleb*, 28 (1990): 205, 211. Also, according to that of 1908, the urban population of Aleppo was 119,811 and the number of *hane* was 15,890. *Salname-i vilayet-i Haleb* 34 (1908): 217, 224. Ghazzi reported one of the census results in the city of Aleppo quarter by quarter; however, we cannot adopt his data because of some omissions Ghazzi n.d.

49. Sharif (1987), 215.

50. Göyünç figured 4.17 for families of immigrants in the nineteenth century, and Karpat also figured 4.30 for immigrants at the end of the nineteenth century. However their data concerned immigrant families, which is not sufficient to meet our needs (Göyünç 1979, 334-348; Karpat 1987, 137–40).

51. According to the yearbook of the province of Syria (*Salname-i vilayet-i Suriye*) published in 1900, the urban population of Damascus was 143,321 and the number of *hane* was 16,832. Therefore, mean *hane* size was 8.5. Since mean *hane* size calculated here is from data of the intramuros districts, we can recognize that mean *hane* size of intramuros districts was larger than that of extramuros districts (*Salname-i vilayet-i Suriye* 32 [1900]: 364-65, 376).

52. Duben and Behar 1991, 48–49.

53. Ibid.

54. For the meaning of Laslett's sets of tendencies in domestic group organization, see Laslett 1983, 525–31.

55. Duben 1985, 84–85.

56. Such a household is considered typical in southern France and classified as *frèrèche*s in the field of family history studies. See Laslett 1972, 30.

57. Qassab Hasan 1994, 141, 255, 264.

58. Duben and Behar 1991, 56.

59. Ibid., 148–49.

60. In order to study reasons for the high percentage of polygyny in

Damascus, analysis of marriage patterns is required, so this issue cannot be discussed here. However the proportion of polygynous husbands in Damascus in 1907 (12.1 percent) was much higher than that of Syria in 1960 (4.3 percent). See Chamie 1986, 57.

61. The mean household size was 11.9 persons, rather similar to the result of table 5. See Arai 1993, 52–108.

62. Duben and Behar 1991, 55.

63. Istanbul basic rosters provide evidence for this. "Invariably the mother would be listed after her son in the census register. . . . Without her husband, the senior male, her son if she had one, would take over the headship of the household" (Duben and Behar 1991, 56).

64. Ibid., 62.

65. Miura (1998) tried to analyze some cases of *wasi* in Damascus in the nineteenth century.

66. As for hidden population *(mektum nüfus)*, see Aydın 1990, 94.

67. Gross 1979, 197, 199–201, 208–40.

68. Karpat 1985, 6.

69. Gross 1979, 230–40, 395–96.

70. Gross 1979, 398–416, 432–58.

71. Bowring [1840] 1973, 4.

72. Karpat 1985, 162–69.

73. Regarding the criterion of "medium," see Lee, Feng, and Ochiai forthcoming; and Ochiai and Lee 1999.

74. Qassab Hasan 1994, 127.

4

From Warrior-Grandees to Domesticated Bourgeoisie: The Transformation of the Elite Egyptian Household into a Western-style Nuclear Family

Mary Ann Fay

Introduction

In this chapter, I intend to theorize the transformation of the elite eighteenth-century Egyptian household into a Western-style, monogamous nuclear family. The eighteenth-century elite household was characterized by the slave origins of the members of the household, polygamy, concubinage, female seclusion, and a fictive kinship system. The major question that this paper will raise is why elite women like Huda Sha'rawi and others who were instrumental in the creation of the Egyptian Feminist Union (Al-Ittihad Al-Nisa'i Al-Misri) in 1923 became champions of a Western-style nuclear family.

I will argue against teleological approaches to this issue: i.e., that the Western-style nuclear family was the natural outcome of the social and economic transformation that Egypt underwent during the course of the nineteenth century or that the model was adopted as part of a process of westernization by the elite.[1] Rather, I suggest some reasons why a stratum of the female elite represented by the Egyptian Feminist Union (EFU)—some of whom, like Sha'rawi, were born into households such as I have described above—were actively promoting monogamous, companionate marriage along with curbing men's easy access to divorce and raising the age of females at marriage. Or to ask the question in another way, why did women of Sha'rawi's class become dissatisfied with the older model of the household/family? What is the relationship between the political and economic changes of the nineteenth century, and the rise of an explicitly feminist movement that promoted a Western-style nuclear family as a model for a free and independent Egyptian nation?

In order to suggest how these questions might be answered, I propose to do the following: First, describe the older model, that is, the eighteenth-century elite household and women's place within it; second, critique some of the recent literature related to the "woman question" of the nineteenth century; and third, suggest how the political changes of the nineteenth century may have disadvantaged elite women in particular and created the terrain on which a feminist movement could and did flourish.

The Historical Context

The historical background for a discussion of the eighteenth-century elite family/household is the resurgence of Mamluk power in Egypt that occurred at the end of the seventeenth century.[2] This resurgence, which I will refer to as neo-Mamluk, was linked to the rise of the beylicate, whose power was based in their houses (s. bayt). After a series of internecine struggles among the various neo-Mamluk houses, the Qazdughli bayt eventually emerged as the most powerful. Ali Bey al-Kabir, the most powerful bey in Egypt between 1760 and 1772, eventually succeeded in eliminating his rivals and in consolidating power within the Qazdughli bayt. As a result, the neo-Mamluk system changed from one in which the most powerful amir was primus inter pares to a quasi-monarchical system with power consolidated in one house.[3]

Also around mid-century, the process began of fusing the military institution founded on the ojaqs (military regiments) and the neo-Mamluk organization dominated by the beylicate. The result was one system in which service in the ojaqs became a career path within the neo-Mamluk system. As André Raymond has noted, by the end of the century, almost all the positions in the Ottoman hierarchy were held by members of the neo-Mamluk houses.[4] In 1798, Ibrahim Bey described the ruling class as a unique system in which the beys, kashifs (military rank of a provincial governor), mamluks, and officers and soldiers of the ojaqs constituted a socially homogenous and hierarchical group. Piterberg has shown that from the ascendancy of Ali Bey al-Kabir in the 1760s to the French invasion of 1798, the overwhelming majority of beys were manumitted *mamluk*s.[5] Piterberg argues that the eighteenth-century Mamluk system relied primarily on the recruitment of slaves who were primarily Georgian in ethnicity.

I have reached conclusions similar to Piterberg's based on evidence of women's slave origins from their *waqfiyyat* (religious endowment deeds). My analysis of eighteenth-century *waqfiyyat* preserved in Cairo's Ministry of Awqaf as well as the ministry's index to the *waqfiyyat* shows that women made up about 25 percent of the total number of donors. (This figure relates only to the *waqfiyyat* in the ministry. There are additional *waqfiyyat* located in other archives in Cairo, including the Dar al-Watha'iq al-Qawmiyya.) Of the female donors, 49 of 126 can be identified as belonging to the Mamluk elite through their relationship to males belonging either to the military regiments (*ojaqs*) or to one of the beylical households. Of these, 42 can be identified as former slaves and only 7 as freeborn daughters of Mamluks on the basis of their names. Women of slave origin are identifiable by the appellation *bint abd Allah* (Daughter of God's Servant) and the use of the word *ma'tuqa*, or freed. She was called *bint abd Allah* because she did not have a Muslim father, and it was considered shameful to be without a father. On the other hand, the freeborn daughter of a Mamuk grandee would be named this way: al-Sitt A'isha Hanim Bint al-Amir Ridwan Agha Ta'ifat Gamaliyan.[6] A'isha is identified as the daughter of Ridwan, commander of the Gonulluyan military corps known in Egypt as the Gamaliyan or Cameliers.

Of the 42 women who can be identified as former slaves through their names in the *waqfiyyat*, 40 are called *al-bayda* (the white), indicating Circassian or Georgian origin, while one is identified as *al-sawda* (the black) and the other as *al-samra* (the brown), indicating African origin. One of the women of African origin is *al-Hajja* Maryam Khatun *al-samra*, *ma'tuqat* al-Sitt Khadija Khatun *bint* Abd Allah *al-bayda*, *ma'tuqat al-amir* Mustafa Bey Shahin.[7] In this case, Maryam was the freed slave of a woman who was herself the freed slave of an *amir*.

As these figures show, the overwhelming majority of women in this sample had origins as slaves and were Caucasian in ethnicity. These findings for women support the evidence amassed by Piterberg for the slave origins and Caucasian ethnicity of the men in the Mamluk households.[8] As for the freeborn women, it is important to note that they were all daughters of Mamluks; none were Egyptians from the merchant/*ulama* class. This finding is highly suggestive. It indicates that the Mamluk grandees considered concubinage and marriage as part of a political strategy aimed at strengthening the links between the members of the household and thereby consolidating power. It is also clear from a reading of men's and women's *waqfiyyat* that the

Mamluk elite, both male and female, considered itself as a ruling class/
caste. Thus, the importation of slaves and marriage to members of the
same ethnic group should be seen as strategies to mark and preserve
the difference between the elite and the Egyptian population and to
provide internal cohesion.

As power was usurped from the Ottoman establishment by the
beylicate and as beys like Ali Bey al-Kabir and his successors became
the de facto rulers of Egypt, the neo-Mamluk house *(bayt)* became the
foundation of power and the basis for administering the state and
exploiting the resources of the country. The neo-Mamluk *bayt* is the
key to understanding not only the political system of the eighteenth
century but also the position of elite women. This is because the position of these women was linked to their membership in powerful
households and, thus, to their status as part of the ruling class. Women's
membership in these households was buttressed by their economic
rights and property ownership, the importance of alliances created by
marriage and extramarital sexual unions (concubinage) to the reproduction of the system, the role women played in legitimizing the accession of men to power, and to the ability of women to construct
patronage networks of their own. Historically, in periods characterized by fragmented sovereignty and powerful households, elite women
had higher status, more autonomy, and greater influence than in periods characterized by the centralization of power and the development of institutions for the administration of the state. I will argue
later in this paper that women suffered a loss of status in the nineteenth century as the modern bureaucratic Egyptian state arose and
consolidated its power. No longer were the sexual unions created
through concubinage or marriage as important in strengthening the
bonds between men. State institutions such as a national army and a
bureaucracy replaced the households in which women could attain
influence and even some power.

Definitions

For the purposes of analysis and conceptualization, we should attempt to make distinctions among the various components of the neo-
Mamluk system. Let us begin with the overarching entity, the *bayt*, as
a sociopolitical concept and the basis upon which the system was
organized and administered. Relying on al-Jabarti, David Ayalon defined *bayt* as a group or faction whose members were linked by both
Mamluk and family ties.[9] Thus, *bayt* can be understood in the wider
sense, as the Qazdughli *bayt*, for example, and in the narrower sense,
as a group or faction within the *bayt*. Within these houses, factions

emerged, which, following al-Jabarti's lead, we can refer to as *ashira* or *qabila*. Thus, a neo-Mamluk *bayt* would incorporate the households of its followers (beys, amirs, *kashif*s, officers) as well as the various factions that existed within the *bayt*. Ayalon also pointed out that al-Damurdashi and Nicolas Turc used the word *ila* (colloquial for *aʾila* or family) synonymously with *bayt*.[10] Therefore, *bayt* and *ila* have a fluidity of meaning that is not very helpful or useful for an analysis of the neo-Mamluk household.

At this point it is useful to compare the eighteenth-century neo-Mamluk household with the British and French household of the same period in order to distinguish between household and family. Jean-Louis Flandrin researched English and French dictionaries of the early modern period for the meaning of family, which he found was synonymous with household.[11] According to Flandrin, from the sixteenth to the eighteenth centuries, the concept of family straddled the notions of coresidence and kinship, that is, a set of kinsfolk who did not live together as well as an assemblage of coresidents who were not necessarily linked by blood or marriage. For example, Samuel Johnson's 1755 dictionary defined family as those who live in the same house and gave, as a synonym, household.[12] *Le Dictionnaire royal francoys et anglois* of Abel Boyer gave as the definition of *famille* "all those who lived in the same house, under the same head" and listed as English equivalents "family" and "household."[13] The French *Dictionnaire de l'Academie* of 1694 defined *famille* as "Toutes les personnes qui vivent dans une meme maison, sous un meme chef."[14] As Flandrin has written, "It was still the case in the second half of the eighteenth-century, both in France and England, and whatever the social milieu concerned, that the members of the family were held to include both the kinsfolk residing in the house and the domestic servants, in so far as they were all subject to the same head of the family."[15]

Thus, in early modern England and France, the concepts of family and household appeared to be synonymous. The primary issue for historians seems to be whether the persons living under the same roof considered themselves and were considered by society at large as a family. Flandrin suggests that this was indeed the case. We can argue that this was also the case for the eighteenth-century neo-Mamluk household, because of the seeming interchangeability of the words *bayt* and *ila* as suggested by the chroniclers and according to Lane's *Lexicon*.[16] In fact, in the case of the neo-Mamluk household, the evidence is even stronger, because as the various sources attest, the neo-Mamluk system, like the earlier classic Mamluk system of the medieval period, was in fact a fictive kinship system in which descent was traced through the male line. For example, one of the most important horizontal links between men was that of *khushdashiyya*, the tie between comrades who were enslaved and manumitted at the same time. The word *akh* (brother) was used as a synomym for *khushdash*. The most important vertical link was the link between the master and his mamluks that was maintained after their manumission. A master referred to his *mamluks* as *awlad* (sons; s. *walad*) while his *mamluks* referred to him as *walid* (father). A man could refer to the *khushdashun* of his master as his *a^cmam* (uncles; s. *amm*) and the master of his master as *jadd* (grandfather). Earlier generations were regarded as the forefathers or ancestors *(aslaf)* of the present generation.

Where the neo-Mamluk concept of family/household diverges from that of the English and French is, in my opinion, with the notion of coresidence, or that a family or household consists of all those *living under the same roof* whether related by blood or not. I would argue that this is not an adequate definition of the neo-Mamluk household, because it does not include the various members of the fictive kinship system nor the persons who were linked to the master of the household through marriage or concubinage but did not reside with him. For example, it was common for a wealthy amir to construct separate houses for his wives and/or concubines. Al-Jabarti's obituary of Jalila Khatun, concubine of Ali Bey al-Kabir and wife of Murad Bey, related that Ali Bey built her a house at Azbakiyya.[17] Does this mean she was not a member of Ali Bey's household? Ali Bey also built a splendid palace on the shores of Birkat al-Azbakiyya for his wife, Nafisa al-Bayda. Does this mean she was not a member of her husband's household? In addition, a new household formed from the parent household when a freedman established his own residence and purchased his own *mamluks*. However, the freedman remained linked to his master/patron as *walad* to *walid*. Since wives and freed slaves were clearly members of the master's household, the English and French notion that household members had also to be coresidents should be abandoned in the case of the neo-Mamluks.

It is clear that a neo-Mamluk household encompassed more than those persons housed under one roof. Lane's definition of *a^ila* is useful here: "a family or household; a man's *a^ila* are the persons whom he feeds, nourishes, or sustains; or the persons who dwell with him, and whose expenses are incumbent on him, as his young man, or slave, his wife, and his young child."[18] As a working definition of a household, I would submit the following: all those linked to the head of household through slavery, service, marriage, or blood; and all those for whom the master has a financial responsibility or who are dependent on him for sustenance, but who do not necessarily reside with him.

Public vs. Private Space in the Eighteenth-Century

Historically, in societies where power was fragmented and lodged in households rather than centralized and administered through a state-supervised bureaucracy, there were not clear distinctions between public space and private space. This means that although we can speak of a private or family space within the home and a public space outside of the home where economic and social life took place, politics or the exercise of power did not take place exclusively or even predominantly in the public sphere. This is characteristic of many early modern and medieval societies, and it is important for understanding not only how the modern state took shape but also why household politics had clear advantages for women. This appears to be a cross-cultural phenomenon noticed by historians of Islamic societies such as Leslie Peirce and historians of European women such as Sara Maza for prerevolutionary France and Suzanne Wemple for the feudal period.[19] Historically, women benefited from the fact that power was located exclusively or predominantly in households rather than in the more formal mechanisms and structures of the centralized, bureaucratic state. As members of those households, women could achieve influence and possibly even power, as well as rank and high status and access to wealth and property. In short, the distinction between public and private space is not as relevant to elite women's status as whether power was located in a clearly delineated public sphere from which women were excluded.

Some feminist theorists have advanced the distinction between public and private as a way to understand women's lack of power. Power was considered to be located in the public sphere, the domain of males, while females, relegated to the private sphere of the home, were deemed to be disempowered and disadvantaged vis-à-vis men. As Linda Sciama expressed it in her critique of the public/private dichotomy in Mediterranean societies, "women/private/deprived—men/public/privileged."[20]

This public/private dichotomy is not a useful analytical tool for the study of women in eighteenth-century Egypt—or in most premodern societies—or for the allocation of space in the elite Cairene house of the period. This is because power was lodged predominantly in the households of the neo-Mamluk grandees, particularly as the power of the Ottoman establishment in Egypt, expressed through the governor and the regiments, declined. Thus, women had the opportunity to become influential or even to achieve a share of power within their households. Another reason is that clearly demarcated public and private spaces did not exist in the eighteenth century. There has been a tendency to conflate private with the house and domestic space and public with life and events outside the house. Because gender segregation and the seclusion of elite females were practiced in eighteenth-century Egypt, the label private has been placed on the home, and everything outside the home from which women were ostensibly excluded was labeled public. For several reasons, this is a neat but incorrect conceptualization of how space was gendered and of how the gender system functioned to maintain the asymmetry of power between men and women.

First, we know that elite women could and did leave their homes for a variety of reasons, including ritual occasions such as weddings, when they walked in processions accompanying the bride to her new home, and visits connected to the birth of a child. Women also visited the tombs of their family members on Fridays, went to the public baths, attended public festivals such as the opening of the main canal, the Khalij al-Misri, and sailed on the Nile and the *birka*s (lakes or ponds) on richly decorated pleasure boats with enclosed cabins. Second, the concept of private space should be reconceptualized as a space that existed to satisfy the society's need for privacy and a clearly defined familial space. Sciama has given a definition of privacy for Mediterranean society that is useful for understanding eighteenth-century Egypt: "the need for individuals or other social groups to separate themselves from others at various times, or for certain well-defined activities."[21] Thus, in place of private space, I suggest we substitute *familial space*, which was linked to the society's need for privacy.

Third, in eighteenth-century Egypt, the society's need for privacy and familial space was linked to the practices of gender segregation and female seclusion whose aim was to protect marriageable females from men unrelated to them beyond a certain degree of consanguinity. Within the homes of the grandees, the family quarters of the household were known as the *haramlik*. However, we should discard the notion that space(s) in the eighteenth century, whether inside or outside the house, was enclosed with rigid and impermeable borders. On the contrary, space was both flexible and permeable. Although the palaces of the grandees were divided into *haramlik* (women's or family quarters) and *salamlik* (men's quarters), women had access, in some cases indirectly, to all parts of the house through various architectural devices, including screens of turned wood known as *mashrabiyya*.[22] I say "indirect" access because women could not mingle with men in the *salamlik*, including the men's indoor reception room called the *mandara*. However, women had access to it by way of the overhanging gallery enclosed in *mashrabiyya* that allowed them to observe the men and the activities in the *mandara*. *Mashrabiyya* allowed women to observe without being observed and alerted men to the presence of women they were not allowed to see. Thus, women could gain access to male space while maintaining the norms of gender segregation, but there were no devices—architectural or otherwise—that permitted men to penetrate female space.

What further erodes the distinction between private and public space in the eighteenth century is the veiling of elite women, which allowed them to extend familial space and privacy into the streets beyond their homes and palaces. Women in long cloaks and face veils could not be approached or spoken to by men. Indeed, their veils made them socially invisible, which meant that the norms of gender segregation could be upheld while simultaneously giving women access to the streets and social life outside their homes. Thus, instead of the concept of public space, we should use *social space*. I would define social space as that which unrelated men and women shared while observing certain conventions, such as elite women veiling themselves when outside their homes or observing the entertainment in the *mandara* from behind a screen. Finally, the distinction between public and private is not sustainable, because the home of an eighteenth-century neo-Mamluk grandee was not just the domain of the family. While family life was lived in the homes and palaces of the grandees, so, too, was political life, since the home was also a house or *bayt*, and thus a locus of political power.

The neo-Mamluk household should not be conceptualized in terms of public and private spaces for men and women but rather in terms of asymmetries of power between men and women. In other words, gender is a more useful analytical tool to understand the eighteenth-century household than the public-private dichotomy. Michele Rosaldo argued almost twenty years ago that although sexual asymmetry is universal, its form is context dependent. Scholarship, by examining context, must determine how gender acquires meaning through concrete social interactions.[23] Eighteenth-century Mamluks maintained gender hierarchy by making military training and service, from which women were excluded, the primary path to power; by maintaining male control over the most lucrative sources of wealth (i.e., urban and rural tax farms); and by controlling female sexuality and directing it to approved sexual unions, marital and nonmarital. Women, however, could and did exercise agency through their legal right to own property, which allowed them to amass estates of income-producing property, and through their purchase and manumission of slaves to create a network of clients that strengthened their position in the household. In fact, I would argue that women did play a public role when they owned and managed their own property and those of others as *naziras*

(administrators) of *waqfs*, for example; when they served as symbols
of lineage continuity; and when they legitimized the succession of
men to power by marrying their husbands' heirs.

Inside the Eighteenth-Century Household

Religious endowment deeds or *waqfiyyat* are important sources of
information for the history of women and of the household/family.
The documents provide information about the sexual and marital history of women and men, their children, their origins, the size of their
households, their relationships to the members of their households,
and, particularly in the case of women, the extent of their property
holdings. The information supplied by the *waqfiyyat* demonstrates that
the eighteenth-century neo-Mamluk household was characterized by
the slave origins of its members, by concubinage and polygamy, and
by a fictive kinship system.

The *waqfiyyat* of men and women available in the Ministry of Awqaf
demonstrate the features that I believe characterize the elite eighteenth-
century household. An example is the *waqfiyya* of Ammatullah, widow
of Abd al-Rahman al-Kathuda, one of the most important men of the
eighteenth-century Mamluk revival and a builder and restorer of
monuments in the city of Cairo.[24] His widow, Ammatullah, a former
white slave, registered her *waqf* in 1782 when she was the wife of
Muhammad Gawish, also a former slave.[25] Her husband at the time
she registered her *waqf* was named as a witness to the *waqf* and also
as the *nazir* (administrator) of the *waqf* after the death of Ammatullah.
Both he and Ammatullah were slaves of the same master, Abd al-
Rahman al-Katkhuda, who himself was one of the exceptions among
the beys and amirs of the eighteenth century, since he was the actual
son of Hasan Katkhuda al-Qazdughli and not a slave.

Ammatullah's marriage to one of her deceased husband's former
slaves demonstrates how important marriage was as a strategy for
strengthening the links between members of the same household, in
this case the Qazdughli, and the important role women played in
ensuring the stability and continuity of the household. In addition,
when a woman like Ammatullah married and remarried within the
same household, considerable wealth remained within the household
as well. As her *waqf* shows, Ammatullah was a wealthy woman whose
property included a *wakala*, one of the most lucrative investments of
the eighteenth-century commercial economy, a *rab* or apartment building, and twelve shops in Bulaq, the commercial center of Cairo.

The marital history of Ammatullah's mother-in-law, Amina, reveals the importance of women in legitimizing the succession of men

to power. After the death of Amina's husband and Abd al-Rahman's father, Hasan Katkhuda, Amina married his freed slave and successor, Uthman Katkhuda al-Qazdughli; and after Uthman's murder, she married another of Hasan's freed slaves, Sulayman Gawish. Both Uthman Katkhuda and Sulayman Gawish were freed slaves and therefore fictive sons of the deceased Hasan Katkhuda. Acting as one of the leaders of the Qazdughli household as well as a stepfather, Sulayman Gawish was instrumental in restoring Abd al-Rahman al-Katkhuda to his rightful place in the household's hierarchy after the usurpation by one of the former slaves of the deceased Uthman Katkhuda.[26] Fictive fathers, sons, and brothers—or fictive kinship in general—make it clear that within the household system of the period, the personal was political and vice versa.

As for women's position in the eighteenth-century household, it was a paradoxical one, since, on the one hand, it gave women high status and access to wealth but, on the other, denied them autonomy in the marital realm. While arranged marriages were consistent with the political system of the time as well as the social norms, the situation of widows seems to be a departure from the period of the Mamluk sultanate. The women of the neo-Mamluk households were not allowed to remain widows or to assume the position of dowagers but were married off, sometimes very quickly, to their deceased husbands' successors.

The *waqfiyyat* of the eighteenth century illuminate what is otherwise obscure about the lives of men and women—their personal and affective life. Their *waqfiyyat* provide some evidence or documentation about the emotional and familial links between household members. As an example, let's consider the *waqfiyya* of Mahbuba Khatun, wife of Isam'il Bey Kashif.[27] Both Mahbuba and Isam'il were slaves of Ibrahim Bey al-Kabir, who no doubt arranged their marriage. In the stipulations of her *waqfiyya*, which are usually very informative about the donor's sexual and marital history and personal relationships, Mahbuba names herself as the administrator of her *waqf* during her lifetime. After her death, she stipulates that the position should go to her children and then to the children of her husband (*awlad zawjiha*). Thus, while differentiating her children from her husband's, she also recognizes a responsibility and obligation to them as part of her kin or her family.

The stipulation concerning a spouse's children with another woman or women appears also in the *waqf* of Zulaykha Khatun, freed slave of Muhammad Kashif and wife of the Amir Sulayman Agha.[28] Zulaykha names herself as the beneficiary of the income of her *waqf* during her lifetime and, after her death, several heirs including Medina, her female slave; Zabiba, the daughter of her former master, Muhammad Kashif; and her husband, Sulayman Agha, and his children. It seems to have been a common practice for eighteenth-century donors of *ahli* or family *waqfs* to name not only their children but also their husband's children and other relatives such as sisters and brothers as heirs and administrators of the *waqf*. They could also name their slaves. The donor usually stipulates that his or her freed slaves *(utaqa)*, male and female, black and white, share equally in the income from the *waqf* with no distinction made on the basis of gender or race. *Ahli* or family *waqfs* benefit the donor during her lifetime and her stipulated heirs after her death. It is not until her line has been extinguished that the pious or religious causes she named in her *waqf* receive the income. On the other hand, a *khayri waqf* immediately benefits the religious causes and good works stipulated by the donor.

Historians of the early modern Middle East and of the family in particular, like their colleagues in early modern European history, are uncertain how to distinguish between the household and family. However, perhaps we should not try, since it seems that men and women of the eighteenth-century elite household were not making those distinctions themselves. The elite household/family at various times and in certain circumstances appears to have included not just spouses and children, but children of a spouse's other wife or wives as well as brothers and sisters, freed slaves and their children, and even children of former masters. What is clear is that the eighteenth-century elite family was more inclusive than the Western-style nuclear family, which emerged primarily by restricting the designation "family" to the husband and wife in a monogamous relationship and to their children.

Nineteenth-Century Transformations and the Emergence of the Woman Question

During the nineteenth century, Egypt was incorporated into a world capitalist system that was centered in northern and western Europe, and later North America. Its integration into the system came through the production of long-staple cotton. Thus, its economic formation at this time has been described as agrarian capitalism. Wealth in Egypt was derived from ownership of large estates planted in cotton and, secondarily, from trade and investments in urban real estate. Egypt's commercial economy and its manufacturing sector, particularly textiles, declined precipitously.

The destruction of the neo-Mamluk system began with the French invasion of 1798 and was completed by Muhammad Ali in the early nineteenth century. From Muhammad Ali on, a modern, centralized, and bureaucratic state also began to take shape. It grew up around Muhammad Ali and his successors, the khedives, and their court and encompassed government ministries, a state-run bureaucracy that included provincial offices and officials, and a national army. Although the neo-Mamluk system was destroyed, the Turco-Circassians continued to hold power through their relationships to the khedives and their control of government positions. Wealthy, property-owning Egyptians, like Huda Sha`rawi's father, became part of the ruling class after the British invasion and occupation of 1882, as the elite closed ranks in opposition to British imperialism.

Opposition to imperialism and its offspring, a nationalist consciousness, appeared in the 1870s along with a popular press. There was vigorous debate about what kind of state Egypt should construct in the postimperialist era or what kind of state was necessary for the waging of an effective anti-imperialist struggle. Thus, a connection emerged between the nationalist movement and what has been called the "woman question." The question of women's role in an independent and modern Egypt was seen as crucial to the form that the Egyptian state would take. The definition of "modern" and "state" seemed to hinge on the role women were expected to play in the new Egypt. Liberal nationalists, such as Qasim Amin, for example, who spoke against polygamy and for women's education also supported a European notion of the nation-state rather than religion as the basis of community and national identity.[29] As modernists, they also tended to see practices such as veiling and female seclusion as "backward." Thus, they linked the creation of a modern Egypt to ending such practices, allowing women a degree of education so that they could better educate their children, and in general adopting the Western-style nuclear family as a model for Egyptian families. Other nationalists, variously labeled traditionalists, organicists, and eventually, Islamicists, had other ideas, but all of them seemed to be linked to and expressed in terms of the roles that women were expected to play in the new nation-state.

In the literature on women and the state and the emergence of a feminist movement there are two approaches to the Woman Question that I will consider here. The first is concerned with the emergence of a private or domestic sphere for women and a clearly defined public sphere for men associated with the capitalist economy and the apparatus of the modern state.[30] A second approach is one that links the call for monogamy and an end to veiling and seclusion to Western influences.[31] Both approaches seem to agree that the transition to the modern involved in part the construction of a domestic sphere for women and in part a concept of domesticity that included such things as child-rearing, housework, and efficient household management. The debates that have arisen seem to be over the dichotomy between private and public space, whether the boundaries between the two are fluid or fixed, and whether the construction of a domestic space helped or hindered women in their quest for autonomy. Kandiyoti has emphasized the fluidity of private and public boundaries while warning that Mediterranean societies should not be conceptualized as moving cleanly from private to public patriarchies. Kandiyoti defines public patriarchy as women's instrumental subordination within, rather than exclusion from, a public arena.[32] Booth generally agrees with Kandiyoti and argues that although linking women and the domestic was nothing new, "defining women's relationships to the domestic discursively *was* new."[33] In fact, the domestic as a space that claimed attention was new. The need to define how "woman" and "home" overlapped was crucial to (and necessitated by) the shift from a traditional patriarchy to a new public patriarchy inflected by nationalism.[34]

One of the issues that arise is whether the domestic space precluded women from assuming a public role and whether it was an advance or a setback for women. Booth takes a very nuanced position on the issue on the basis of her close readings of women's biographies. As she has written, "When the notion of the domestic as a privileged site is constructed as giving women special powers, foregrounding and then conscripting a moral precedence linked to motherhood, is this a question of enhancing women's place in the home or of displacing the notion of home? Does it confine women's authority or construct a basis for new ways of thinking and acting?"[35] Baron's opinion is that the new ideology of domesticity gave women greater responsibility in the home without challenging its boundaries.[36] Badran in her writings on Huda Shaʿrawi and others connected to the women's movement and particularly the Egyptian Feminist Union clearly links liberation to an end to veiling and female seclusion, and a role for women in the public world of education, work, and politics.[37] In order to accomplish these goals and other reforms, such as increasing the age of women at marriage, a "public feminist movement" was clearly necessary.[38]

I would argue that the discourse of the domestic as a space that claimed attention was not new, and neither was the need to define women's relationship to the domestic. Nationalism may have been responsible for the need to redefine and reconfigure the space and redefine women's position and duties within it, but these spatial considerations were not new. As I have argued earlier in this paper, Islamic society clearly had a need for a private domestic space where family life took place. This not only fulfilled the society's need for privacy but also for maintaining gender segregation and female seclusion. Janet Abu-Lughod and Nelly Hanna have made similar arguments for Cairo and Marcus for Aleppo.[39] Moreover, as Huda Lutfi has shown in her analysis of the treatises of the medieval religious scholar Ibn al-Hajj, "Egyptian Muslim culture viewed the basic role of women to be within the boundaries of the household, caring for the family and managing household matters. Among the middle and upper-middle classes, this view was reinforced by an ideology of strict segregation, where the female was asked not to overstep her spatial boundaries."[40] Marsot makes a convincing argument that harem women were able to take up and succeed in lives of public service because they had learned the necessary skills in managing their households, which were the size of small hotels and which demanded from them a high degree of efficiency and organization to run smoothly.[41]

In contrast to the scholarly arguments advanced above, I would like to propose that the transition to the modern for elite or ruling-class women involved, first, the demise of the household as a locus of power. It was not so much that a new domestic space was created or that a public patriarchy arose—women always were and continue to be subordinated in the public realm—but rather that political power was moved out of the household and relocated in the institutions of the emerging modern state. As long as power was located in households, women as members of those households had rank, high status, access to wealth and property, considerable influence, and even power. The distinction between public and private/domestic is not as relevant to women's status as whether power was located in a clearly demarcated public sphere from which women could be excluded. In the Egyptian case, once power was removed from the household, women were effectively stranded in a space that became almost purely domestic. When this was coupled with a demand that women either should not have a public role at all or only one that was congruent with her primary domestic role and with notions of service to the family, however family was defined, then the options, autonomy, and life choices of upper- and ruling-class women were diminished.

At this point, it would be useful to note the argument advanced by Ahmed—namely, that modernity is equated with an end to veiling, polygamy, female seclusion, and gender segregation was the result of Western influence on reformers like Amin and Huda Shaʿrawi. Ahmed noted the influence that the Frenchwoman Eugenie Le Brun had on Shaʿrawi. Ahmed accuses Le Brun of inducting young Muslim women "into the European understanding of the meaning of the veil and the need to cast it off as the first essential step in the struggle for female liberation."[42] As for Shaʿrawi, Ahmed believes that her perspective was informed "by a Western affiliation and a westernizing outlook and apparently by a valorization of Western ways as more advanced and more civilized than native ways."[43]

It would be pointless to argue that segments of the Egyptian upper class were not influenced by Western or European culture and ideas. However, the positions taken by women like Sha'rawi should not be attributed solely or even predominantly to an appropriation of Western culture and norms. Rather, I think that what happened to upper-class women like Sha'rawi was that the terms of what Kandiyoti has called the "patriarchal bargain" were radically altered by the changes of the nineteenth century. Kandiyoti has defined the "patriarchal bargain" as women's strategies of maneuver and resistance within systems of male dominance.[44] The upper-class household was characterized by polygamy, concubinage, seclusion and veiling and restraints on women's sexual autonomy, but, as I noted above, women also had rank and status as members of powerful households as well as access to wealth, considerable economic autonomy, influence, and even power. The transformation of the warrior grandees of the eighteenth century into the Turco-Circassian ruling elite of the nineteenth, which entailed the relocation of power from the household to the institutions of the modern, centralizing state, had deleterious effects on the status of women. Women were left to face polygamous unions, men's easy access to divorce, and the inability to choose when, at what age, or even whether to marry without the compensating factors of life in the eighteenth-century household that I have described above. In addition, women found their ability to change or ameliorate the material conditions of their lives severely diminished. Their capacity to exercise what social historians and feminist historians call "agency" had been severely curtailed. The reforms called for by Sha'rawi and the EFU should be seen as an effort to rewrite the terms of the patriarchal bargain within the context of the new nation-state that was taking shape in Egypt.

The construction of the new Egyptian nation, which took place in 1923 with Egypt's nominal independence, changed the terrain on which the struggles for women's autonomy had to take place. Since the state defined the community in terms of Egyptian-ness rather than in religious terms and endowed only males with full citizenship rights, it seems to me that women like Sha'rawi had little choice but to struggle for an expanded role for women in the public realm and for citizenship and legal rights that would allow women to change or enact laws for their benefit as well as to represent women in the new public institutions such as the parliament. The battle for rights by women was a struggle for power. In the context of the new nation-state, it was a struggle that could no longer take place within the household or even solely within the Islamic court system but had to be waged in the reconfigured public sphere from which women were largely excluded.

The Demise of the Eighteenth-Century Household/Family

One way to understand the radical nature of the transformation from the warrior-grandee household of the eighteenth century to the Western-style nuclear family is to contrast the households such as those I described earlier in this chapter to that of Huda Sha ʿrawi's natal and marital households.[45] Although her father's household was constructed on the earlier model, Sha ʿrawi clearly preferred, in fact demanded, that her husband give up his concubine in favor of a monogamous marriage with her and, eventually, their children. Both her father and her husband are examples of how the male upper-class Egyptians became part of the Turco-Circassian ruling elite. Members of this elite were part of the political apparatus of the modernizing Egyptian state rather than warrior-grandees in a beylical household.

When Huda Sha ʿrawi was born in 1879, the household of her father, Sultan Pasha, included Huda's mother, Iqbal; her father's wife, Hasiba, known to Huda as Umm (mother of) Kabira; and their children, as well as male and female slaves, nurses and servants. Eventually, it would also include her brother, Umar. It is not clear if Huda's mother was her father's concubine or wife. Badran describes her as a consort, and Ahmed believes that the mother's concern for the welfare of her son, Umar, indicates that she may have been a concubine rather than a wife.[46] In her memoirs, Huda paints a vivid picture of growing up in the family's home in the Cairo neighborhood of Isma ʿiliyya.

In her own married life, Huda departed dramatically from the older household/family style in favor of a monogamous union and a nuclear family. When she was 13, she was married to her cousin and guardian, Ali Sha ʿrawi, in a marriage arranged for her by him and her mother. Sha ʿrawi became Huda's guardian when she was five years old after her father died. After an unhappy year of marriage, Huda discovered that her husband had returned to his concubine, who was pregnant with his child. This event allowed Huda to declare that her husband had violated a clause in the marriage contract that stipulated that he would free his slave concubine after his marriage to Huda and commit himself to a monogamous union with his wife. Consequently, Huda left her husband and moved to her mother's quarters in the family home and lived apart from her husband for seven years.

Clearly, Huda's vision of marriage and family life was radically different from that of the women of her class and background a hundred years earlier and from the women in her own father's household. Unlike Mahbuba and Zulaykha, the eighteenth-century women described above, Huda did not consider her husband's children by his concubine part of her family. Unlike Umm Kabira, her father's wife, Huda refused to accept her husband's concubine as part of her family or household. Huda rejected the model of her father's household, which contained both his wife and Huda's mother living under the same roof with their children, although in separate apartments. She also rejected the example of Umm Kabira who showered Huda, the child of her husband's consort, with love and affection. What Huda wanted was a monogamous union with her husband and a family consisting of herself and her husband and their children. What has been overlooked in discussions and theorizing about the transformation of family life is its effect on the emotional lives of its members. When Huda demanded a monogamous union with her husband within a family defined as nuclear rather than extended, she was also redefining the emotional boundaries of the modern family. The parameters of her emotional life within the family/household would be much narrower than a century before and certainly more constricted than that of Umm Kabira. The children of her husband's concubine would not have either a financial or an emotional claim on her, and unlike her beloved Umm Kabira, she would reserve her affection for her own children.

It is important to note that Huda's demands and her decision to separate from her husband came before she had significant contact with European women like Eugenie Le Brun, wife of Husayn Rushdi Pasha, or before she began educating herself in earnest. Therefore we need to look at factors other than or in addition to Western influence to explain why the household/family model that served Huda's mother and Umm Kabira had become unacceptable to her.

Conclusion

Recent literature on the subject of women and nationalism has enhanced our understanding of women's lives and the women's movement in Egypt. Much of this literature relies on the literary, such as biographies of women, the women's press, and the various writings of women, including memoirs and letters. I want to suggest that as illuminating and important as these studies have been, we also need more studies of the material conditions of women's lives to better understand how the transformations of the nineteenth century affected them. Tucker's book on peasant and lower-class urban women does not yet have its counterpart for elite women, and there has not yet been a full-length study of the women of the new bourgeoisie.[47]

In this chapter, I have attempted to take research and theorizing that I have already done for comparative purposes and use it to place the lives of elite or ruling-class women in an expanded historical context. I have argued that some of the transformations of the nineteenth century, including the reconfiguration of a public sphere from which women were largely excluded, had deleterious effects on women of the upper classes. Although I have focused on the political realm in this chapter, I believe with Marsot that there were economic reasons for the transformation of the Egyptian family in the nineteenth century.[48] My hypothesis is based on my understanding of elite women's economic activity, which in turn is based on a reading and analysis of their *waqfiyyat*. Elite women's *waqfiyyat* demonstrate that they used their positions in rich and powerful households and access to wealth to accumulate assets independently of their husbands or male relatives. Indeed, women used the *waqf* institution as a court-supervised trust to secure an income for themselves during their lifetimes, as well as to ensure their right to manage their own property.

Elite women's economic activity and investments were consistent with the eighteenth-century Egyptian economy when Egypt was the hub of a network of long-distance trading routes extending into Asia, Africa, and Europe. In its commercial economy, the largest fortunes were made in trading coffee, spices, and textiles. Thus, women who invested their capital in khans, the foundation of the country's trading economy, as well as in warehouses, shops, and workshops of various kinds, were behaving like rational economic actors within the context of Egypt's commercial economy and the ways available to men and women to invest their capital productively.

The economic transformation of the nineteenth century eroded Egypt's commercial economy, which had provided women with lucrative investment opportunities and income. The question we must ask is whether women were able to redirect their economic activity to take advantage of the changes that occurred in the nineteenth century or whether the economic transformation disadvantaged them. If the latter was the case, then reforms demanded by women would have both economic and political rationales and implications. The demand for access to the public sphere would be based not only on the criterion of citizenship in the modern state and the right to participate in its political life but also on a need to survive and prosper in the transformed economic realm through access to education and to work outside the home. Therefore, women sought another model for family life and, through movements such as the EFU, struggled to achieve a public role in order press for reforms and to recover some of the influence, power, and economic autonomy that they had lost in the transition to the modern.

Notes

1. This is the argument made by Cole (1981) in his article on the relationship between the changes in the upper-class Egyptian family and the socioeconomic transformation of the late nineteenth and early twentieth century.

2. The classic studies of the Mamluk resurgence in Ottoman Egypt are Shaw 1962; Holt 1968; and Crecelius 1981. Some of the more recent works include Piterberg 1990; Winter 1992; Raymond 1995; Hathaway 1997; and Fay 1993, 1996, 1997, 1998.

3. Mamluk or neo-Mamluk refers to the political and social system that characterized the period of the sultanate and the late seventeenth and eighteenth centuries. The word *mamluk* is the Arabic word for slave.

4. Raymond 1983, 30.

5. Piterberg 1990.

6. Waqf No. 2441, Ministry of Awqaf, Cairo (no page numbers).

7. Waqf No. 2400, Ministry of Awqaf, Cairo (no page numbers).

8. Pieterberg 1990.

9. Ayalon 1977, 291.

10. Ibid, 297.

11. Flandrin 1979, 4

12. Cited in ibid., 4–5.

13. Cited in ibid., 5.

14. Ibid.

15. Ibid.

16. Lane 1955.

17. Al-Jabarti 1967, 382.

18. See Lane's definition of *aʾila* in Lane 1955, 2201.

19. See Peirce 1993; Maza 1993; and Wemple 1987.

20. Sciama 1981, 110

21. Ibid., 89.

22. See Fay 1999.

23. Rosaldo 1980, 389–417.

24. Raymond 1995.

25. Waqf No. 137, Ministry of Awqaf, Cairo (no page numbers).

26. For information concerning the murder of Uthman Katkhuda and the circumstances surrounding the usurpation of power by his freed slave, Sulayman, as well as the interrelationships between Uthman's household and Abd al-Rahman Katkhuda's household, see Al-Jabarti 1967, 2:57–58; Damurdashi 1991, 319–20; and Abd al-Rahim 1989, 211.

27. Waqf No. 3131, Ministry of Awqaf, Cairo.

28. Waqf No. 190, Ministry of Awqaf, Cairo.

29. Amin 1993, 1995.

30. Kandiyoti 1991a, 1991b, 1994; Booth 1991, 1997; Baron 1994, Badran 1987, 1995.

31. Ahmed 1993.

32. Kandiyoti 1994, 377.

33. Booth 1997, 834.

34. Ibid., 861.

35. Ibid., 861–62.

36. Baron 1994, 166.

37. Badran 1987, 1995.

38. Badran 1987, 20.

39. J. Abu-Lughod 1987; Hanna 1992; and Marcus 1989.

40. Lutfi 1991, 103.

41. Marsot 1978.

42. Ahmed 1993, 154.

43. Ibid.

44. See Kandiyoti 1991b.

45. The information on Sha'rawi's household comes from Badran 1987, 1995; Ahmed 1988; and Mursy 1981.

46. Badran 1987, 16; and Ahmed 1988, 163.

47. Tucker 1985.

48. Marsot 1996, 45–46.

II

Family, Gender, and Property

5

Women's Gold: Shifting Styles of Embodying Family Relations

Annelies Moors

Positionings

Although mainstream history remains by and large national history that focuses on the public activities of prominent men, the study of both family history and women's history over the past few decades has rapidly developed into a presence of its own. My contribution on women's gold as the embodiment of family relations stands at the intersection of these two fields, an intersection that is both a source of inspiration and a site of epistemological struggle. Women's history started out to restore women to history, in particular in that area of life where they had been so glaringly absent—that is, the public sphere—and aimed at making the hitherto hidden achievements of women visible. The early generation of feminist scholars was reluctant to deal with the family as a topic of research, as they considered this institution a major source of women's oppression.[1] Much work of family historians, on the other hand, focused on the ways in which households or families developed common strategies to deal with the effects of major socioeconomic transformations. Women's history and family history highlight very different "fields of experience" of women.[2]

More recently, theoretical developments have created a space for greater interaction of family history and women's history. Different notions of person, identity, and power have stimulated a renewed investigation of the concepts "women" and "the family." Rather than taking these as "given" social facts that only need to be discovered, they are seen as socially and culturally constructed. This paradigmatic shift has produced such notions as "the multiple identities of women" and has underlined the importance of taking the diversity in family constructions and relations into account. Concepts of power have also shifted from simple dichotomies of domination versus subordination to more complex notions that point to the ambivalences and contradictions present in particular positions.[3] These developments have inspired those involved in women's history to direct their attention to "the family" and to research the often crucial importance of family relations for women's lives.

At the same time, a focus on gender has evoked some of the most productive critiques of conventional family studies.[4] One central problem of family studies is that the household or family is seen as the unit of analysis and as an actor in its own right. Starting from the dichotomy of the domestic sphere versus that of the market, it is assumed that the circulation of goods and labor that takes place within households is fundamentally different from that between households. Whereas relations within the household are seen as "naturally" based on reciprocity, pooling, sharing, and sacrifice, relations in the public sphere are seen as based on unequal exchange, profit maximization, bureaucratic anonymity, and so on.[5] These assumptions have been criticized along various lines. Relations within households are not necessarily based on reciprocity, but may well be a form of unequal exchange with a sexual division of labor that makes women dependent on men and with rights to consumption that are based on positions of authority rather than on need. An emphasis on separate spheres neglects and negates the crucial connections between the domestic and the public sphere, and the relations of family members with noncoresident kin and nonkin.[6] Furthermore, the notion of the household as the unit of analysis has encouraged a focus on household composition rather than on family relations. This is evident in some historical studies that deal with the shift from extended to nuclear family households and with the ways in which this shift relates to processes of urbanization, industrialization, and state formation.[7] Women's history has convincingly argued for the need to deconstruct the notion of "the family"; women and men (as husbands and wives, brothers and sisters, and so on) are positioned differently within families, and processes of recruiting new members are also gender specific. This is not to say that the notion of "the family" may not be powerful. The point is that instead of taking this as the natural state of affairs, there is a need to investigate at which moments, within which contexts, and under which conditions men and women identify with "the family" and when they see their interests as divergent (or act "as if").

In this contribution I will focus on how gold jewelry works as the embodiment of family relations, a topic for which the intersection of women's history and family history is a highly productive site. In large parts of the Middle East gold is both the most important economic resource women have access to and a highly valued means of display through which people produce and express their various identities. Women acquire most of their gold through kinship (inheritance) and marriage (the dower), while, at the same time, gifts of gold are instrumental in sedimenting and strengthening particular kinship and conjugal relations. In this contribution I will discuss how women's strategies with respect to gold jewelry interact with processes of family formation and shifts in family relations in Jabal Nablus, Palestine, in the course of part of the twentieth century (1920–90). In the first part, I will highlight the specificities of inheriting gold versus inheriting productive property and residential housing. The second part focuses on the meanings of different types of gold in dower payments and gifts.[8]

Inheritance: Differentiating Forms of Property

Legal rules of inheritance are important as a moral frame of reference even if they are not applied in practice. The legal system of inheritance rights in Jabal Nablus, as in other areas once part of the Ottoman Empire, depended on the nature of the property involved. Property held in full ownership (milk)—such as urban real estate, buildings, vineyards, orchards, and movables—is inherited in accordance with the Islamic law of succession. Most agricultural land (but not the plantations) is not milk but miri: land to which individuals could acquire rights of usufruct and possession, but with ultimate ownership vested in the state. This right of possession is also inheritable, but a different law of succession, intiqal law, is employed.[9]

Islamic family law privileges male lineal descendents, but also gives specific rights to women, to spouses, and to lateral kin.[10] For example, if the testator has sons, most of the estate is inherited by the children, with daughters inheriting half a son's share; one-eighth of the estate goes to the widow (if the deceased is a woman, one-fourth goes to the widower). If, however, there are no sons, daughters receive a fixed share: one daughter is entitled to half the estate, two or more sharing two-thirds of it; the remainder goes to the male agnates, often the deceased's brothers.[11] In contrast, the main principle of intiqal law, as codified in 1913 (Ottoman Law of Succession), is the gender-neutral distribution of the estate on the basis of generation. The main heirs are the children of the deceased; compared to Islamic law a greater share of the estate is allocated to spouses and to women, while agnates do not hold special rights.

While the *milk/miri* distinction is the only distinction made in the legal system about the nature of the property involved, social practice has been, and still is, different. When women discuss their inheritance practices they do not differentiate between *milk* and *miri* property; their strategies with respect to inheriting agricultural land, urban commercial real estate, and residential housing are similar.[12] Their inheritance practices with respect to gold, on the other hand, are quite different.

Reproducing the Family

Imm (mother of) Salim, a peasant woman from a small village to the east of Nablus, became a widow in the early 1970s. With most of her sons being adult men with families, it did not take long before the land was divided, so everyone knew what was his. "The land was evenly divided among them, each one receiving about fifteen *dunums* of dry-farming land with some olive trees," Imm Salim said. When I asked her whether her daughters had also taken their share, she laughed, and said, "Why should they? Their brothers have always been good to them." Further elaborating on this, she pointed out that men need the land "because they have to take care of their wives and children; women themselves can do without, as their husbands will provide for them." But she also told me the following tale about one of the few women in the village who had demanded her share: "This woman's husband wanted her to take the land because he had got into a fight with one of her brothers. Pressured by him, she felt forced to do so, and it destroyed her life. Her brothers had always been good to her, and they continued to present many gifts to her sister, who had not claimed her share. But in her case, after her brothers had given her the value of the land in cash, they cut off their relation with her. This affected her so much that she fell ill and never fully recovered. Her husband did not really take care of her; he spent her money, and in the end left her to herself."

Both productive property, such as agricultural land and urban commercial establishments, and residential property are seen as central for the reproduction of the patrilineal family.[13] They constitute the material basis of the family household and embody its continuity in symbolic terms. How this family is defined and bounded becomes visible through the inheritance strategies of daughters. Not only rural women, like Imm Salim, but also urban women generally refrain from claiming their share in the estate if their contending heirs are their brothers. Women strongly identify with their natal family—that is, their father's house—while at the same time they depend on its support for their well-being. This is also the case after marriage. Leaving her share in her father's estate to her brothers, a woman at once enhances her brothers' position and by implication her own, as in this way their obligations to protect and support her are reaffirmed. When explaining why they do not claim their entitlements, women point to men's maintenance obligations. At the same time, they also realize that if a daughter claims her share (perhaps pressed to do so by her husband), she may well have to forgo the support of her kin; this, in turn, would weaken her position with respect to her husband and his kin.

The importance of productive property and residential housing for the reproduction of the patrilineal family is evident in those cases in which women receive something. Thus, amongst the wealthy, giving to daughters is seen as enhancing the status of the family. Thus, women may be "bought out" or receive a share in the income from the property. Productive property itself, however, is usually transmitted in the male line and remains under male family control.[14] Elderly single women also hold particular claims to inherited property, especially usufruct rights to residential houses. In the case of a single woman, however, her brothers are legally obliged to provide for her, and even if such a woman would receive a share in her father's estate, her brothers are her first heirs, so the property stays in the family.

If a daughter does not have brothers, the situation is more complicated. For daughters are less inclined to give up property for the sake of their father's brothers (most often their contending heirs). The strong ties of a woman with her brother do not extend to other patrilineal kin. Her father's brothers are expected to be less concerned about her well-being and less dependable in providing for her. Even if her husband is to profit most from her claiming the estate, it could still be a sensible strategy for a woman without brothers to claim her share. But it may not be easy for her to gain control over this property. If she is already married, her father's brother, usually many years her senior, may well try to ignore her claims, and whether she receives anything also depends on her husband's standing in the community. If the daughter is still young and single, her father's brother is not only her contending heir but also her legal marriage guardian. To forestall further problems about the estate he may try to marry her to his own son, as in that way no property will be lost to strangers. The problematic situation of such a daughter without brothers is socially recognized, and she is not condemned for claiming her share. On the contrary, a man attempting to disinherit his late brother's daughter is often censured. Some fathers without sons actually make premortem arrangements to ensure their daughters' financial security; this may include de facto disinheriting their own brothers.

In short, the notion that productive property and residential houses are to be transmitted to descendents in the male line is hegemonic. Daughters with brothers usually do not claim their legal share in this property; these women by and large agree with or acquiesce in giving up their share for the sake of the reproduction of the family. But "the family" in this case is defined in a specific lineal way; it is their father's house. If the contending heirs are their father's brothers, there is considerable tension and struggle about inheritance claims.[15]

Women's Gold: Weak Matrilineality

Imm Salim was well taken care of by her sons and never considered claiming any land as inheritance from her husband. Yet, she did control the land that she had received as dower. "When the land was divided, they gave me the piece that had been my marriage gift," Imm Salim said. A few years later she handed part of this land over to her youngest son so that he could build a house there. But the gold she owned she spent on her youngest daughter, who at the time was studying at the local university in Nablus. After her father died, her older brothers, already in their forties by then, did not like the idea of their sister traveling every day to Nablus to continue her education. But Imm Salim supported her. "I sold some gold and gave her money for clothing and transport to Nablus," she underlined, "so she did not have to ask them, and they could not say anything about it."

When Imm Muhammad, a refugee from Jaffa living in the old city of Nablus, discussed the division of her father's estate with me, she pointed out that her only brother had been the main beneficiary. It was self-evident that he was to live in her father's house; also, the little money her father had saved was spent on the arrangements for his marriage. But in the case of her mother's gold, things were different. "My mother had a necklace with sixteen small coins that were divided at the same time. As Islamic law prescribes, eight of these were given to my brother, while my sister and I each took four." Some years later Imm Muhammad divided these coins amongst her own daughters; by then she had already sold one of her gold bracelets to help her son with the costs of marriage.

Women stand a better chance to inherit gold than other forms of property. While highly valued, gold is less central in the reproduction of the family household than land and houses. Women inherit gold from their mothers or receive it premortem from them. This does not mean, however, that gold is always transferred to women. Sons may also inherit gold, and a mother may also give gold to her husband and sons during her lifetime, as Imm Muhammad's story indicates.

In general, women feel more comfortable to claim gold jewelry as their share in the estate than other forms of property. The very same woman who parts easily with her share in her father's land in order to secure her kin relations with her brothers may not hesitate to take her mother's gold; she may, in fact, even expect her mother to give this to her premortem. Mothers also are more inclined to present their daughters with premortem gifts of gold jewelry than with other types of property they own. Women, like Imm Salim, who own land or houses tend to transfer these to their sons rather than to their daughters; such forms of property then become the material basis for their sons' households to which they (the mothers) may remain attached. Gold, on the other hand, is a different case. Because of the often close emotional relations between a mother and her daughter, it regularly occurs that a woman will support her daughter with some of her gold jewelry. This support may take a variety of forms. In some cases women sell their gold to help their daughters for some specific aim, such as covering part of the costs of higher education, especially if fathers and brothers are not supportive. In other cases a mother may give her gold jewelry to a daughter she has a particularly close relationship with, such as a daughter who had postponed her own marriage to stay with her mother when she was getting on in age and in need of help, or to a married or widowed daughter who is living in poverty. While these daughters are given gold as a source of financial security, such gold may well have more complex meanings to them; it also embodies the mother-daughter relation, as it were. This then shades into another pattern. Better-off women also present their married daughters with gold jewelry, not so much to provide them with a financial guarantee, but as a memorable gift.

Still, gold does not only travel to daughters but also to sons and, indirectly, to daughters-in-law. In poorer households, such as Imm Muhammad's, women's gold may be an important part of the assets available. Sons, seen as family providers, will often receive at least part of it. If need be, a mother may also decide to give her gold to her son premortem, sometimes in the form of money for education, to help with the initial costs of migration or to defray part of the costs involved in marriage. In the latter case, a mother sells her gold so that her son will be able to buy gold for his wife-to-be. In contrast to the mother-daughter relation, however, in this case it is the economic value of the gold that counts; gold as embodiment of the mother-in-law is not very popular, and brides usually expect newly bought jewelry. Therefore, the mother's gold is often sold, and with the revenue new gold is bought for the new bride, even if this means that in the course of these transactions financial losses are incurred. So, while women sell their gold both to support their daughters and their sons, it is the daughters who may obtain their mother's gold jewelry as it is and who highly appreciate this jewelry as embodying the person of the mother.

Depending on whether one looks at the legal system, at social practices involving land and houses, or at gold jewelry, families are constructed differently and family relations take on a different hue. Islamic inheritance law expresses a preference for male lineal inheritance, but also gives rights to women, lateral kin, and spouses; as such, it provides major resources for the reproduction of the patrilineal family, but also allows part of the property to be siphoned away. In social practice the reproduction of a particular form of patrilineal family is of central importance: a family consisting of lineal descendants. Houses, land, and other forms of productive property are to be inherited by the male descendents of the testator; daughters may hold some forms of use rights, but are not to transfer these to their children. Still, the fact that legal rules are often not followed in practice does not imply that such rules are irrelevant. On the contrary, the existence of such rules, expressing certain moral notions, is central to the way in which "refraining from claiming" works. It is because of the generally acknowledged legal rights of women to the estate that giving up these claims has a strong effect on kin relations, especially in strengthening those of brother and sister. This becomes also visible in the gifts that brothers provide their sisters with, at religious feasts as well as at other occasions. Such gifts may well include gold jewelry. With respect to gold jewelry, daughters are less inclined to give up their shares, and mothers often actively support such matrilineal transfers.

These inheritance patterns have remained quite stable over time. There are no indications that daughters with brothers have more recently started to claim productive property or residential housing significantly more often. Due to demographic developments less women may find themselves "without brothers," and hence, less women may actually be claiming their share in the inheritance. At the same time, the meanings of inheriting property have partially changed. Due to economic transformations in the area, inherited productive property has generally become less important as a source of livelihood. This is particularly visible in the rural areas, where the large majority of households are no longer dependent solely on income generated from agriculture as migratory wage labor has become an important source of income. Related to this development, the ideas about how families ought to organize their housing arrangements have changed. A shift has taken place from the ideal of married sons living in the paternal household for as long as possible to a preference for married sons moving as soon as possible into a dwelling of their own.[16] This ties in with the greater independence of sons, often resulting in fathers supporting their sons' efforts in building a new house or apartment. That is, premortem transfers from fathers to sons also take place at an earlier moment in their life cycle. At the same time, shifts in the ways in which marriages are arranged have an effect on the relations of mothers and daughters. Gradually the marital age of girls has risen. Whereas also in the first half of the twentieth century some women married late (often the ones who would receive their mother's gold), nowadays many more girls stay in the father's house for longer periods of time. This further strengthens the ties between mothers and daughters and increases the likelihood of these being embodied in gold.

Dower Gold: Values and Meanings

In the case of inheritance, gold may well be the minor part of the total assets transferred, but in the case of the dower gold is the central item. According to Islamic family law the (specified) dower is a set amount of money, registered in the marriage contract, which the groom is to transfer to the bride; she is free to use this property as she pleases. Neither her father nor her husband may exert control over it, and marriage does not entail community of goods. Women also receive clothing and household goods, but the value of these items is very different from that of gold. Gold jewelry, especially *baladi* gold, is a highly liquid asset, with a value often more stable than that of local currencies.[17] In the case of inheritance, meanings of inheriting gold jewelry versus inheriting productive property have remained relatively stable, but this is much less true in the case of the dower. Changes in the nature of the jewelry involved and its meaning tie in with different notions about conjugality.

Baladi gold

When she married in the early 1930s Imm Salim had not received any gold; instead, a piece of land was registered in her name. Some ten years later her husband had given her some gold coins, which she sewed onto a ribbon and wore as a necklace (*qilada dhahab*). Later in life she would, at various moments, sell some gold to buy livestock (a cow and a number of goats) and invest the proceeds again in gold. Her oldest daughter followed in her footsteps. When she married in 1958, she received eight Turkish gold coins, some of which she lent out for the use of a piece of land. But by the time that her second daughter married in 1971, the situation had changed substantially. Her husband was not involved in agriculture, but worked as a driver.

She never used the heavy gold *mabruma* (twisted wire) bracelets she had received when marrying to acquire productive property; instead, she sold one of these to help her husband with the costs of building a house. And when Imm Salim's well-educated youngest daughter married an office employee in 1984 she also received a lot of gold jewelry, mainly *baladi* bracelets, earrings, and necklaces, but also a few small items of Italian gold. Still, Italian gold never became very popular in the village; "it has no value," people would say.

Wearing gold has a long history in the Middle East. A number of authors writing on Ottoman times mention gold jewelry.[18] Still, in those days most jewelry was made from silver. In rural Palestine silver jewelry was considerably more common than gold at least until the 1920s.[19] Amongst the wealthy, on the other hand, jewelry did not only consist of gold; diamond-set items were also popular. In the rural areas of Jabal Nablus up to the 1960s the major part of women's gold jewelry was usually made up of Ottoman and British gold coins (*lirat dhahab*), sewn on a cloth ribbon and worn as a necklace. These are not antiques, but facsimiles of official coins ("fake coins"); the price of such a coin is determined by its weight. These twenty-one or twenty-two-carat coins can be seen as a way of holding gold bullion in "small denominations." In the town of Nablus gold jewelry was also commonly worn in other shapes and sizes. In addition to wearing necklaces of various styles, urban women also wore different types of gold bracelets, such as the heavy "twisted wire" (*mabruma*), "pear" (*injasa*), or "snakes" (*hayaya*) bracelets, and the lighter *sahab* (thin, usually purchased in sets of six). Beginning in the later 1960s these gold bracelets also became more popular in the rural areas. The value of individual bracelets—quite standardized, but with small variations in style—was also largely determined by weight; the gold content was invariably twenty-one-carat. For such gold the term *baladi* is used, a complex concept that has come to mean not only local but also indigenous and authentic.

The appearance of gold in the rural areas, first in the form of coins and later also including bracelets, points to a greater availability of cash in the area. Such jewelry was first and foremost a source of economic security; a convenient way of storing value, especially in a location where the value of currency has been far from secure. The price of *baladi* gold is by and large determined by developments on the world gold market; losses due to labor and other costs remain limited. Women themselves were and are highly aware of the economic value of gold jewelry. Whenever they buy gold they always inquire about carat content and the price per gram. Considering gold an economic resource, rather than a memorable gift embodying aspects of the person whom they received it from, women also actively employed gold as such. Up till at the least the 1960s it was not uncommon for a woman, after some years of marriage, to sell her gold and to buy goats, cows, and occasionally a piece of land. This was often the beginning of further transactions, including at times buying gold again.

Still, there is more to *baladi* gold than its monetary value. For women do not only own gold jewelry, they also wear it—some items, such as bracelets, on a daily basis, and other items on special occasions. This public display of gold indicates that the groom (and his family) has been able and willing to spend a large sum as dower for the sake of the bride and her family. It cements the marital tie because it is a major "investment," especially amongst the less well off. At the same time, it is a statement about the relation of the bride and her father. This is so, because in the rural areas until the 1960s the bride's father often kept part of the dower himself, transferring only a portion of it to his daughter as gold jewelry. Women's gold then also expresses her father's willingness to transfer (a considerable part of) the dower to his daughter.

Italian Gold

Imm Salim's youngest daughter received only a few items of Italian gold, but Italian gold was a central part of the jewelry given to young upper-class women in Nablus. When Imm Shakir, who comes from an upper-class family of large traders, married in the late 1940s, both her husband and her own kin presented her with lots of gold jewelry, still predominently *baladi* gold. In response to my question whether she ever sold gold to buy more fashionable items, she aptly pointed out that she never needed to do so, because "whenever there was a new model on the market my husband would buy it for me." Also, she preferred to keep the older items, as they reminded her of the occasions when she had received them. The newer pieces she liked because "they were made of Italian gold, which is much more beautiful and with a much greater variety to choose from." When her daughter married a bank director in 1976 in Amman, her jewelry consisted exclusively of modeled Italian pieces and a three- to four-carat solitaire ring.

Beginning in the 1960s a new type of gold jewelry, "Italian gold," appeared on the market. These were smaller, but more exclusive pieces of jewelry, imported from Italy. They were often referred to as "small pieces" and consisted of a large variety of nicely made necklaces, bracelets, pendants, rings, earrings, and so on. Because it was only eighteen-carat gold and thus had a greater hardness, it could be worked into a much wider variety of models and fashions. This Italian gold was less valuable as a source of economic security and investment, because of high labor costs and import duties; when selling it, women would incur a considerable loss.

Italian gold first became popular amongst the upper classes. For these women gold had always been more a statement about status than a source of economic security. The option of selling their gold did not concern them much; gold jewelry was to them not primarily an economic resource, but represented particular events and embodied specific social relations. In these circles wearing Italian gold coincided with new notions about marriage arrangements and dower registrations. From the early 1960s on, registering only a token amount, such as one Jordanian dinar, rather than a high sum as dower started to become a trend amongst the well-educated middle and upper classes. This did not mean that these brides would receive less in practice, but rather that what they received was no longer a payment to which they were legally entitled; these were "voluntarily" provided gifts. To these women registering a token dower was a statement that they did not need financial guarantees and could afford to place their trust in the groom; it was a sophisticated and modern way of arguing for high status. The jewelry these women would receive—expensive, finely worked pieces of "Italian gold" and diamond-set items—were a means of adornment rather than an economic resource. In fact, it was a sign that these women did not need their marriage gifts as a form of economic security.

Such items of Italian gold were not only an effective statement about wealth, modernity, and refinement. At the same time, because Italian gold is associated with token dower arrangements and, thus, with gifts presented by the groom, such gold is also the embodiment of the conjugal relation—a more personalized relation between bride and groom—and it defines marital relations as companionate and a matter of choice. Still, kin relations are also implicated, because it is amongst the better-off that fathers were also involved in presenting their daughters with gold jewelry. Amongst the wealthy, fathers would not only transfer the whole dower to their daughters, but also usually add numerous gifts, including gold jewelry. In time, the less well off were to do so on a more limited scale and at a more modest level. So, whereas in the rural areas previously one particular piece of gold jewelry may embody at the same time the groom's status and fatherly generosity and protection, amongst the better-off, both the groom and the bride's father would each provide her with their own gifts of jewelry. Thus, conjugality and kinship were separated: that is, the jewelry embodying these relations could be worn separately, and particular pieces of jewelry increasingly became the embodiment of the relation with a particular person.

Forms of Hybridity

Italian gold did not remain the privilege of the upper classes. It did not take long for those of more modest means also to buy some of these items, especially the smaller ones that became more widely affordable. Still, the twenty-one-carat bracelets remained the central element of their dower, for economic security remained important to these women. Simultaneously, the trend towards Italian gold, with all its connotations of modernity and refinement, changed the meaning of *baladi* gold, at least in the eyes of the modern middle and upper classes. If Italian gold is constructed as modern and in good taste, *baladi* gold is no longer seen only as valuable, but also as traditional, in the sense of unpolished and unrefined. Hence, it was self-evident that Imm Shakir's daughter would not wear *baladi* gold.

Still, the shift to Italian gold is far from complete. In fact, only a minority of all gold jewelry has ever been "Italian," and, especially in the rural areas, *baladi* gold has always remained a much more central element of the dower. By the late 1980s Italian gold had lost some of its popularity, as women seemed to realize more and more that Italian gold does not have much economic value. Also, newer and more sophisticated forms of the traditional *qilada* became available on the market, with the coins attached to a heavy gold chain, rather than sewn on a cloth ribbon, and placed in heavy frames. Rather than associating traditionality with "backwardness," some started to link it to notions such as cultural authenticity.

Another development also undermined the position of Italian gold on the market: the increased availability and popularity of gold from the Gulf States. In the 1980s amongst the urban lower-middle classes, the "Indian set" (*taqm hindi*) gained in popularity. It was a set of twenty-one-carat gold, often brought from the Gulf region, in Indian style and consisting of at least a necklace, bracelets, and earrings, elaborately decorated with many small pendants and other attachments. Even if the labor and other costs involved were higher than for the *baladi* bracelets, they still were less than for Italian gold. Such gold, then, seems to strike a balance between brides' yearnings for fashionable jewelry and their interest in some form of economic security.

Women, then, employ multiple strategies with respect to their gold jewelry. The better-off refrain from wearing *baladi* gold, but wear expensive Italian items and obtain rings with a large solitaire. Women from lower-class households not only acquire *baladi* gold but also some small pieces of fashionable Italian gold, and more recently gold from the Gulf States. Many women try to both link themselves to modernity and to hold on to gold jewelry as a source of economic security by acquiring and wearing different types of gold at different occasions and in various combinations.[20]

Reconsidering Women's Agency

In this contribution I have tried to employ a double perspective, as it were, by taking up a position at the crossroads of family history and women's history. This double perspective asks for a particular notion of agency. Women's agency is not only at stake when discussing how women gain access to various forms of property, but also when dealing with the moments at which women first and foremost identify with their families and refrain from claiming their entitlements. Here I will briefly restate the shifts that have become visible in women's strategies with gold and the contexts in which such changes are located, including changes in family relations.

Women received and still receive most gold from their husbands (and his family) as dower, but the meanings of this dower gold and its nature have changed substantially. Through time the conjugal tie has become more central, sons have become less dependent on their fathers, the younger generation has more say in their marriage arrangements, and new couples set up their own households when marrying or as soon as possible after marriage. The nature of the gold they receive is both an effect of and contributes to these changes. In schematic terms, Italian gold is associated with modernity both in terms of an emphasis on conjugal rather than kin relations and on gifts rather than financial obligations, and in terms of a particular style of adornment, while *baladi* gold is linked to tradition, with the dower as financial guarantee and as the embodiment of kin-controlled marriages. Gradually, Italian gold has become more popular, yet *baladi* gold is still more central to dower payments. Many women wear both, or do so selectively at different occasions. Others have turned to types of gold that are neither modern in "Italian" terms, nor traditional in *baladi* terms.

While women increasingly gain access to gold jewelry through their engagement in paid labor, they still often link employment and dower gold, though in different ways depending on their background and position. Professional, (usually upper middle class women) often argue that they do not need a dower, as they have already bought whatever gold they wanted from their own income, usually fashionable Italian gold, a sign of good taste and modernity. Some lower-class women also manage to save from their earnings. While younger women may spend this on small fashionable items, adult women often buy *baladi* gold. For them the economic value is of paramount importance; it is a source of security and may come into good use if they remain single or marry a man with limited means. Actually, a woman may keep this gold hidden and only bring it out at marriage, so that the groom does not need to spend much on gold, but can use his money for the house.[21]

Though there have been major changes in marriage arrangements and preferred styles of dower gold, the inheritance strategies of women have generally remained the same. Dower payments have been a focus of debate both in society at large and in women's organizations; legal changes with respect to inheritance rights (applying Islamic inheritance rules also to *miri* land) have gone largely unnoticed. Also, women's access to paid employment did not bring about a major change in inheritance practices.[22] Ties with nonresident kin, such as brothers, are still crucially important for many women. Here again it is refraining from claiming one's entitlements that provides women with more negotiating space. In other words, women's agency, circumscribed as it may at times be, is also visible in the ways they express their commitments to "the family," that is, the family of origin. In the context of a growing emphasis on conjugality, women's attempts to strengthen their relations with their brothers by giving up property rights do not only reproduce the patrilineal family, but may also be seen as partially balancing women's dependence in conjugal relations.

Notes

Parts of this paper are based on Moors 1995 and Moors 1998b, written after years of fieldwork in Nablus, in Balata refugee camp on the outskirts of the town, and in the village of Al-Balad (a pseudonym) to the east. They are also based on archival research in the Nablus *shari'a* court records of marriage contracts, divorce registrations, and other cases.

1. Tilly (1987) develops this argument in general; Tucker (1993) does so for family history in the Arab world.

2. Doolittle (1999) has argued this in her article on gender and family in English history.

3. In a critical reworking of Gramsci's notion of hegemony, MacLeod 1991 uses the term "accommodating protest." Inspired by Foucault, L. Abu-Lughod 1998 highlights how particular developments may be both disciplining and enabling.

4. This is evident in Cheal 1991.

5. This is the case in a variety of disciplines. For cultural anthropology, see discussions of the domestic or familial mode of production engaged in by Sahlins and Meillassoux. In neoclassical economics, such assumptions form the basis for the statistical use of the household as unit of analysis. See Harris 1981 and Doolittle 1999.

6. These various points have been argued convincingly by Harris 1981 and by some contributors to this edited volume.

7. Some see the development of the nuclear family as the result of processes of industrialization, others as a contributing cause (Doolittle 1999). Also in family studies in the Arab world the shift from extended (or tribal) families to nuclear families is a recurrent theme. For a summary see Mundy 1995.

8. Property here is conceptualized as a social relation between individuals or groups holding rights vis-à-vis each other, which may be expressed in terms of rights of control over things.

9. According to the Jordanian legal system, *intiqal* law was in force until 1984; from then on, the Islamic law of succession was applied to *miri* property. It is not clear whether this change was also applied on the West Bank.

10. Islamic inheritance law needs to be seen within the framework of maintenance rights and obligations. A husband is always responsible for the maintenance of his wife, independent of her own means, while she has no such obligations towards him. A father is to provide for his single, divorced, and widowed daughters if they have no means of their own and for his sons until adulthood. Sons are always responsible for maintaining their impoverished parents, daughters only if they can afford it. And the maintenance of impoverished and disabled kin is to be provided by those who inherit from them and have sufficient means to do so, with their contribution depending on the percentage of their inheritance share.

11. But only after the other categories of heirs entitled to a fixed share have received their share.

12. The argument here is not that we may in general collapse productive property and residential property. Taking the perspective of the testator, there are considerable differences. The strategies of the women concerned, however, are similar.

13. In this contribution I mainly use the term family; the term household is employed when focusing on residential arrangements. I do so, because new members to households are largely recruited through kinship and marriage.

The Arabic term *dar* refers both to the house as a physical structure and to the house as a patrilineal descent group.

14. Another solution could be to only allow a daughter to marry her paternal cousin *(ibn amm)*, so the land would remain in the same lineage; if it was not possible to arrange such a marriage, a daughter would have to remain single.

15. Women's inheritance strategies construct "the family" in remarkably similar ways as did early nineteenth-century *waqf* documents in Nablus (Doumani 1998).

16. Demography has also to be taken into account. High mortality rates may severely hinder the formation of extended family households. Also, even if families look the same in terms of composition, relations of power may have shifted from the older to the younger generation. This is succinctly expressed in the words of an elderly woman who praised her daughter-in-law, saying, "What daughter-in-law would nowadays accept having her mother-in-law living with her?"

17. Whereas the last years have witnessed a dramatic lowering of the price of gold on the international gold market, this has not been the experience common in the period from the 1930s to the 1980s. To evaluate the value of gold, devaluations of the local currencies have to be taken into account. A discussion of household goods and clothing, which during the earlier part of the twentieth century may have been quite valuable, is outside the scope of this paper.

18. See, for instance, Tucker 1988.

19. Weir 1989, 194.

20. Amongst the middle and lower-middle classes dower registrations express similar ambivalences. Registering a token dower became increasingly popular, but for these women it remained a risky thing to do; hence, such a token dower was often accompanied by the registration of household goods.

21. While to these lower-class women owning gold is important, they are more ambivalent about wearing it. They often argue that they work in order to help their families because they are in financial need. Wearing (too much) gold contradicts this.

22. Tracing women's inheritance and dower practices makes clear that this is not a system of divergent devolution. Most property is inherited through the male line, and dower payments are only a temporary divergence. Even gold is not exclusively transferred from mothers to daughters, but also to sons.

6

"Al-Mahr Zaituna": Property and Family in the Hills Facing Palestine, 1880–1940

Martha Mundy and Richard Saumarez Smith

Mahr, the object that the groom gives a bride as a condition of the Muslim marriage contract, would promise to be the epitome of gender-specific property, the object that would "make" the woman a married woman. Women's jewelry, their finery, and the bedroom sets of contemporary marriages all come to mind; the chapter in this volume by Annelies Moors explores such gendered *mahr* in the form of women's gold in the twentieth-century town of Nablus. Yet, as an ancient body of juristic commentary suggests, in Islamic legal tradition *mahr* could be composed of any legally valid property from slaves to land to specie. In legal doctrine and practice *mahr* proved most easily measurable, and hence capable of measuring differences in social status, in the form of money. But unlike its categorical isolation in legal discourse, *mahr* may form part of a series of social exchanges within a network of kin and between households over time. It has thus also to be understood within such a context.

In this chapter we shall begin to explore certain of the forms of such exchanges, and the place within them occupied by *mahr*, in one village, Kufr Awan, of the microregion known as the Kura in what is today northern Jordan. Lying along the hills south of the town of Dair Abu Sa'id, the villages face Palestine, overlooking the Jordan Valley down to which their lands extend. The analysis draws on a small part

119

of a wider body of material concerning the social history of a district in the Southern Hauran, Qada Ajlun, in the late Ottoman and early Mandate periods. Although the material we examine in this chapter is limited, it reveals tensions inherent in women's claims to property in a village society of cultivators. In this way our material contributes to the wider project, common to this volume, of writing the social histories of families defined in time and space—a modest endeavor, but one that alone may sweep away the banalities of earlier generalization concerning "the Arab family" or "the Muslim family."

The period covered by our study is delimited primarily by the source material consulted and by a central interest in the nature of shareholding agrarian systems and late-Ottoman property transformation. The study thus begins with Ottoman Tanzimat property registration (from 1876 onwards in the district and 1884 in the village of Kufr Awan) and concludes with the termination of this system of property certification effected by the cadastral surveys and re-registration of property rights undertaken by the British Mandate government (from 1933 onwards in the district and in 1939–40 in the village in question). The late nineteenth and early twentieth century witnessed the integration of this region of southern Syria within the institutions of government of the modern Ottoman state, the registers of this administration forming the source of much of our documentation. Besides the *tapu* (title deed) and cadastral records, we have drawn on Islamic and civil court records, census records from 1910, and interviews with older inhabitants of the villages.[1]

The centralization of government entailed an administrative uniformization of the categories of the subject and object of government, that is, of political subject and of property. Quite as important as property registration was the census (finally carried out in 1910) and the tying together of the registration of persons and of property in subsequent property transfers.[2] Our study of family history is thus inscribed within this wider change, in which families and households form the first node of government of persons and properties. In registering the shares in open-field land, the Ottoman administration had indeed initiated new forms of property, more individualized and subject to rules of inheritance entailing parity between sons and daughters in succession to *miri* (state) land. The cadastral documentation marks the end of this mode of government and the initiation of another, but for the purposes of our concern in this chapter, it has another virtue: it marked a settlement of right where everyone had then to claim or forever hold their peace. The procedures adopted by the British Department of Lands and Surveys in Trans-Jordan at the cadastre privileged village authority over the *tapu* records of the previous Ottoman administration. Although the *tapu* records were accorded legal status, it was the responsibility of village authorities to draw up the first schedule of claims to property *(jadwal al-iddiᶜaʾat)*. This procedure tended to work against women's interest, but in Kufr Awan women responded by challenging the first schedule of claims in case after case.

The methodological difficulties even in this limited undertaking are so considerable that it would require another chapter to explore them. Hence, beyond the endnotes, the reader is referred to earlier papers published and to a monograph in progress. Only occasionally will reference be made here to the methodological difficulties of reconstructing family history and of situating *mahr* in relation to other transactions. It may be noted, however, that as the reference above to the law's penchant for defining *mahr* in specie suggests, reconstruction of practice in this domain does not appear easy from Islamic court records alone. This is a domain where much is promised but less delivered; where orthodox legal form does not dictate practice, although its terms provide the language for legitimizing practice.

A First Interview and Family Reconstruction

We went to visit Husna Salih Hamdan in December 1992. Husna lived in a house just behind the two olive trees that had formed her *mahr;* together with her were one of her daughters (Arifa), who had married in the village, and her son's wife, Nafal, from the neighboring village of Bait Idis. After we had been presented, the daughter-in-law went out to make tea. Being of the august age of 103, Husna was very hard of hearing and had indeed only faint memories of many things.[3] We asked her of her early life and family.

Before Husna had married, she had lived in a house in the old village site with her mother and father, her brother Hasan, and her two sisters, Hisna and Tamam. (The house was later sold to a Palestinian family, one old lady of which continues to live in the same house in what is today a largely abandoned part of the former village core.) In the 1884 *tapu* registration Husna's father had been recorded as owning twelve *qirat*s of common land in an independent holding, but by the time Husna could remember, he probably farmed only half of that, six *qirat*s.[4] In 1908 her father went to the land registry to effect a transfer of six carats to his half-brother, and the other six to his son, Hasan.[5] Husna remembers that before her marriage, when she was still living at home, they had two plough oxen but no sheep to speak of and no donkeys. In short, they were a family solidly in farming, not in herding. The women present agreed that in their family a woman worked with her husband at all stages of cultivation, be it of wheat or lentils or whatever, and that women and children worked beside men in the winnowing of the harvest. As evidence of the same, Husna explained that she had broken her arm during harvest time when working with the heavy mule-drawn thresher, the *qadim*.

Husna was the third child, born in 1889, after her elder sisters Hisna, born 1884, and Tamam, born 1887, and before her brother Hasan, born in 1890. Hisna married Muhammad Ahmad al-Husain, who belonged to a small family of farmers of much the same social status as her own. Tamam married into a larger and more powerful family, with her brother Hasan marrying a sister of Tamam's husband, Hamda.[6] Whether, as is probable, this marriage was a simultaneous *badal* (exchange) marriage or two sequential marriages, we do not know. In 1911 Hasan's wife Hamda, sister of Tamam's husband, bore Hasan a first son, Muhammad. Hamda was twenty and he a year older, but Hasan had by then already taken a second wife, Khazna, of exactly his age; she was the daughter of his elder sister Hisna's husband's brother. Khazna was later to bear Hasan a second son, Mahmud (see figure 1).

When we asked Husna whom Tamam had married, she did not mention the first marriage of her sister but only Tamam's second marriage to Ibrahim al-Mustafa of the Manasira, a man of Bait Yafa in Palestine, who settled in the village. Husna's silence may reflect a breakdown in both the marriages, perhaps a falling out with that more powerful family in the section. What is clear is that relations between Hasan and Muhammad (his son by Hamda) were distant by 1939–40, the time of Mandate land registration. Muhammad sued his father for an equal part in the land to that of his brother, Mahmud. But Hasan refused, noting that he "had married Muhammad with one and a half carats of land two years earlier."[7] In other words, Hasan had given as *mahr* for his first son's marriage one and a half of the four and a half carats of common land he then held.[8] Although Muhammad had legally challenged his father, the court record notes that he accepted his father's refusal, stating that as the land belonged to his father, he was free to do what he wanted with it. Thus three carats of land were registered in the name of the younger brother, Mahmud, with whom, presumably, his parents continued to live and work.[9]

It was clearly the tradition in this family for a man to arrange the transfer of his land as he wished, so obviating the laws of postmortem succession. Thus, to go back one generation, had Salih not divided his land between his son Hasan and his half-brother Abd al-Karim, the literal application of the law would have led to his half-brother, Abd al-Karim, born the year the land was registered, being entirely excluded. Furthermore, the twelve carats of land would have been divided between Salih's surviving wife, each of his three daughters, and Hasan. Premortem gifts were entirely within the law, and in both cases

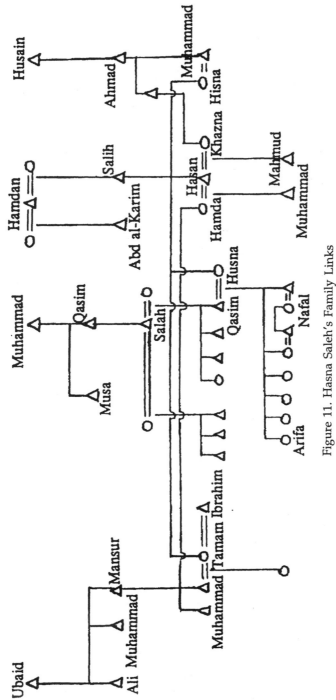

Figure 11. Hasna Saleh's Family Links

permitted fathers in this modest family to transfer land to sons as they wished during their lifetime and to avoid its dispersal to daughters.

But let us return to Husna. She married into another smaller family of the same section of the village, to the oldest son of Salah al-Qasim, a man who at the time of his son Qasim's marriage had two other sons and a daughter from his first wife. He was later to take a second wife, who bore him another three sons. Husna's *mahr* was two *rumi* (literally Roman, but signifying very old) olive trees and the plot of land on which they stood. Doubtless Husna also received a little jewelry and a few clothes, and perhaps the two mattresses and pillows that a father should ideally give his daughter at her marriage. But the *mahr*, which Husna recalled, was neither silver nor clothing but the two olive trees. In 1884 her husband's grandfather Qasim had been registered as owner of three olive trees but not of the land on which they stood.[10] The plot of land appears to have belonged to the owner of another ten trees, a farmer from the family into which Husna's older sister Hisna was to marry. Thus it would seem that Husna's *mahr* of two olive trees, given by her husband's family, was of relative importance to them. The trees and land went first to her father, Husna explained, but after his death reverted to her.

Husna's husband Qasim was some three years older than herself; he was just over twenty when they married. Shortly after the marriage, they established themselves as independent economically from Qasim's father, Salah.[11] Yet the couple continued to live in the same house with Qasim's father for many years until, after Husna's father's death, they finally built a small house on the land at the edge of the village where the two olive trees stood. It was common that a son set up a separate household when he married and that his father give him a separate share of land, either to obtain a wife (as in the case of Muhammad above) or to farm, but also that the donation of land depended on the father's goodwill. When Qasim established his economic independence, his father gave him two carats of land, but as the young couple had very few work animals, he worked more as a ploughman *(harrath)* for others than as a farmer on his own land. In the original registration of 1884, Qasim's grandfather Qasim had farmed jointly with his brother Musa (who was later to predecease Qasim without surviving children, and hence all of whose land was to revert to Salah's line) and with two brothers (Mansur and Muhammad al-Ubaid) of the powerful larger family into which Husna's brother Hasan and sister Tamam were later to marry.[12] This suggests that Qasim's family had earlier worked in conjunction with a family far better endowed with livestock, and hence that Qasim's dependence on the plough animals of others was not novel to his family. Husna's memory of how farming had been organized in former times was that according to the number of animals a person had, so much land did he plough. This statement appears to express both a collective memory of a time when land was abundant but people and animals few and Husna's own appreciation of the importance of livestock, not only of land, in the working capital of a household.

As a woman who had worked in farming, Husna was forthcoming about this domain, whereas several other women interviewed had only faint memories of older cultivation practices. The main arable lands of the village, held jointly by all farmers of the village according to shares, were divided into two blocks, one nearer the village site than the other. Every shareholder was allotted a strip of land in each block whose width (or more generally whose value) was proportional to the size of his share but whose location would be changed every two years at a general reallotment. This meant that each farmer held two plots, one strip a little distance to the west of the village site on the slope down to the Jordan valley and the other closer. In the *araqib*, the distant lands, Husna recalled that they only planted winter *(shitwi)* crops, because the soil was "yellow" and the climate too hot, whereas in the strip nearer home *(watat al-dar)* cultivation was of both winter and summer crops. In the winter season, the strip was divided between wheat, barley, and lentils, the ploughing season extending from the beginning of November to mid-January, depending on the rains. In the summer season the soil was ploughed three times during the winter months, followed by planting after mid-March. Summer crops were more varied: white sorghum *(dhura baida)* from which bread was made, yellow sorghum used as chicken feed, *faqqus* (hairy cucumber), watermelon, tomatoes, okra, and *shammam* (muskmelon). Besides working in the fields, Husna used to go with other women to cut firewood in the woods above the village. And from her two olive trees Husna provided the family with oil and olives. Until today the tradition in Kufr Awan has been to boil the olives briefly and then to dry them on the roof, before taking them to the press, of which there was one in each quarter of the village.

Husna bore five daughters (Arifa, her first child, born when she was 21; Fidda; Fiddiyya; Tamam; and Fatima) and three sons, only one of whom, Mustafa, was to survive. Her daughter Arifa was married in 1934. In those years marriage payments were between ten and thirty *liras*—overall about fifty Jordanian dinars—divided in principle into three parts: grain, livestock, and money *(habb, halal,* and *nuqud)*. But what Arifa actually received was the headband *(urja)* decorated with gold coins. The "cloak" *(aba)* given to the bride's mother's brother was in those days either a *shuwal* of wheat or a quantity of olive oil. The daughter-in-law present at our visit, Nafal, was married in an exchange marriage (*badal*), with another daughter marrying Nafal's brother. But whereas Husna's daughter retained her *urja*, Nafal reported that her headband had only been borrowed for the occasion and had had to be returned.

What has one seen? In the farming families of modest size and middling means from which Husna hailed and into which she married, shares in the common lands of the village were transmitted primarily inter vivos and between men on an understanding of the entitlement of brothers and sons from a father. In neither of the families did a father gift land to a woman and in neither were the laws of inheritance to run their course. In both the father transferred land to sons or brothers before his death. But women appear in relation to agricultural property in two moments here: first, Husna's *mahr* of two olive trees and the land on which they stood, close by the village site, and second, her brother Hasan's alienation of one and a half carats of land to his son Muhammad's bride—or more likely, in the first instance, her family, as her *mahr*. As Husna's account reveals, such productive resources did not generally go directly to the hand of the young bride. But *mahr* was in the bride's name: it was hers both ethically and legally, and hence hers to claim. A young couple was expected to struggle together as the fundamental unit of social production. And sometimes, as in the case of her brother's son, Muhammad, in order to establish such a unit, a young man might have to pledge all of his land as *mahr* to gain a bride and coworker.

Over the century of Husna's life, the village population had grown steadily. The only increase in agricultural resources was in the planting of olive trees, largely in the lands surrounding the village site, although it is impossible to put a figure to this increase.[13] So far as one can tell, other agricultural resources, notably the lands held in shares, appear either to remain fixed or, like pasture lands, to have shrunk markedly over the century. Whereas in the late nineteenth century the Jordan Valley was used extensively for cattle raising, this was less and less possible following land registration and the expansion of irrigated cultivation in the valley over the twentieth century. And the large areas of the village where villagers pastured sheep and goats, both on the hills overlooking the valley and on the steeper, more wooded slopes above the village, were to be declared closed to animals in the 1950s. With population growth, average holdings in the common lands also declined over the years. Thus, we should not be surprised to note that the daughters of Husna did not receive land or trees as part of their dower and that the entire share in common land of Muhammad, son of Hasan, came to one and a half carats.[14] This, as we have seen, was pledged as *mahr* for his bride.

A Second Interview

The family from which Husna came and that into which she married were modest farming families without an elaborate network of marriage exchanges into powerful families of the village. By contrast, the second woman, Yumna, whose family history we shall next consider, came from the same section of the village but from a larger and more prominent family.

Comparing in this way the sets of families to which the two women belong should not lead us to forget just how relatively egalitarian the basic distribution of shares of land had been in 1884. At that first registration, just as Husna's father, Salih, and her husband's grandfather Qasim had both held six carats, so too had Yumna's grandfather and her husband's father. But Yumna's grandfather Nimr was one of five brothers, of two (or perhaps three) mothers, to whom was closely interrelated another family (Abdullah Salih with six carats of land).[15] In short, they formed a largish group, in spite of their holding, as individuals, similar shares in the common land. In 1884 Nimr and three of his brothers were jointly registered as holding a full share (twenty-four carats) of land; this meant that as individuals they held no more than did Husna's ascendants but that collectively the family had greater presence.[16] Furthermore, both Nimr and his brother Abdullah were young at the time—Nimr 20 and Abdullah probably not yet married (see figure 12).[17]

Six carats of land formed the unit termed in the village a *zalama* according to which holdings in the common lands were calculated. In the idiom of the village, which also appears in vernacular documents included in the cadastral documents of 1939-40, the village common land of 1884 was composed of eighty-seven *zalama:* in the property registers of the state these same village lands were described as composed of twenty-one and three-fourths shares (i.e., eighty-seven divided by four). This share was termed a *rub^ca* in local parlance, each *rub^ca* comprising two *faddan* of twelve carats (plough team, or area ploughed by a team in a fixed period of time), and each *faddan* comprising two *zalama* of six carats. Although the higher-order units were used for accounting, it is the *zalama* in which land and farming is most commonly expressed, at least so today when speaking of the past.[18]

In common parlance *zalama* means a young man, but in this village idiom it did not signify an unmarried youth but the holding of a married man, that is, a man and his wife. An unmarried man held only one-half a *zalama* or three carats. A holding of land was thus expressed as a notional male person, but one entailing his female consort. And it was this fundamental pair that mobilized the necessary animal power for

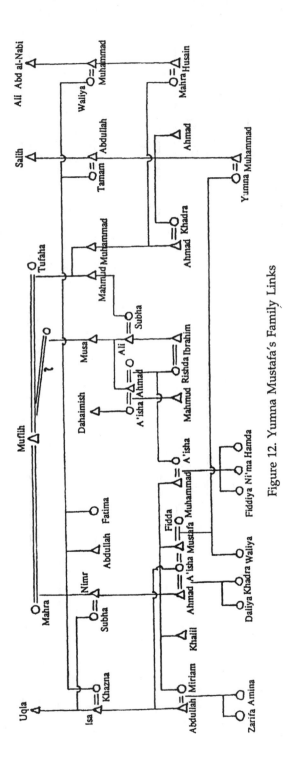

Figure 12. Yumna Mustafa's Family Links

ploughing and whose capacity in production (and in paying the tax imposed on that fraction of the village lands) was translated into two plots of land, a closer and a further strip, in the biennial reallotment. A number of *zulum* (or *zilam*, plural of *zalama*) combined with others, usually along lines of common descent but also along lines of marriage alliance, to form a larger coliable group called a *hamula*. The term *hamula* is used today to designate a group claiming common descent in the Kura as well as more widely in Palestine.

Thus, it was more in numbers (and in the marriage networks that such numbers allow) than in land per adult male that the family to which Yumna belonged might be distinguished from that of Husna's ascendants. To return to the family itself, the 1884 *tapu* registration reveals a complex structure. Of the five brothers the oldest, Musa al-Muflih, perhaps from an earlier first wife, is registered as owning a house, but it is his son Ali whose name appears against all the fifteen carats of family land.[19] Ali's younger brother Ahmad was only about nine years of age when the registration was carried out, and so his share was apparently put in the name of his elder brother.[20] Of Muflih's other four sons, the two sons of the elder wife Tufaha, Muhammad (aged 34 in 1884) and Mahmud (aged 33), had separate houses, but yet another two houses were given in the name of the father, Muflih.[21] His other wife, Mahra, then sixty years of age, mother of Nimr (aged 20) and Abdullah, was to survive until the grand age of 90.[22] In 1889 Nimr and Abdullah registered these two houses in their own names as well as fifteen olive trees inherited from their father, Muflih, who must have died shortly after the *tapu* registration.[23]

In 1910 when the village census was conducted, and Mahra was still alive, the household of Yumna's grandfather Nimr comprised sixteen persons. Nimr's household was one of the three largest households in this village, where average household size was just under six persons. Nimr appears to have taken under his control the share of land that was originally the lot of his younger brother Abdullah, who had died twenty years earlier.[24] In 1910 Nimr's household consisted of himself (aged 46), his mother Mahra (86), his sister Fatima (40), and his wife Subha (39); his eldest son Ahmad (24), and Ahmad's wife A'isha (22) and two young daughters Khadra (3) and Daliya (1); Nimr's second son Mustafa (22) and his wife Fidda (20) and their infant daughter Yumna; Nimr's third son Muhammad (20) and wife A'isha (18) and their two small daughters Ni'ma (2) and Hamda, an infant in arms; and finally, Nimr's fourth son, Khalil, aged 12. Subha was the mother of all four sons. With three young married sons the household thus promised to grow and eventually to divide between the sons and their children. In 1910 the young children of Nimr's sons were as yet all daughters, but surely were to be followed by sons.

This, however, did not happen; the household did not divide. Mahra died five years later in 1915, followed in 1918 by her daughter Fatima. Ahmad al-Nimr was conscripted into the Ottoman army in World War I, never to return. Ahmad's daughter Khadra grew up in the household, her mother A'isha remaining in the household and marrying her deceased husband's brother Mustafa, whose first wife Fidda had died young before the beginning of the World War, leaving her small daughters, Yumna and Waliya. Nimr himself died in 1920 at the age of 56. In 1922, Mustafa al-Nimr died at the age of 34. And then three years later Muhammad al-Nimr died, aged 35, leaving his wife A'isha and daughters N'ima and Fiddiya, his daughter Hamda having died many years earlier.[25]

Thus, by 1925, of the four sons of Nimr only the youngest, Khalil, survived to head the household composed effectively of his own wife and children and of the two widows of three brothers and their young female children. Khalil was then not yet 30. Yumna remembers that she was a little over 3 when her mother died. Her father having remarried, she went to live in her mother's brother's house. As people in the village see it, a mother's care is irreplaceable and a child orphaned on the mother's side will more likely be taken in by a mother's relative than by a stepmother.[26] It was only when she became marriageable that Yumna returned to her uncle Khalil's house. Within two years she was married to a relative on her father's side, who was, more importantly, the son of her paternal great-aunt (FFZ) Tamam. Tamam, Yumna implied, lived as much in Khalil's household as in her marital house during those years, where she would have been the most senior woman.

Yumna stated that her *mahr* was written up in a document (*sanad hujja, wasl al-mahr*) by the imam of the village. It consisted of a carat of common land (*qirat watat*) and twelve old olive trees (*irq zaitun rumi*) lying just below the village on the east in the field called *khallat Hammad*.[27] Yumna noted, however, that as a result of squabbling between the two sides at the time of the wedding only one sheep had been slaughtered for the guests; likewise it turned out that the *urja* headband decorated with gold coins was but a loan.[28]

The household into which Yumna married was small, comprising her husband, Muhammad, and his mother, Tamam. Muhammad's brother, Ahmad, had gone to serve in the Ottoman army during World War I and, like Yumna's uncle, Ahmad al-Nimr, never returned from the war. His sister Khadra had married Nimr's half-brother Muhammad's son Ahmad several years earlier. The household farmed some five carats of land of their own with two working oxen;[29] besides the oxen, they had two milk cows and many chickens, but no sheep or goats. Yumna recalled that all she ever did in farming was to take food out to her husband in the fields; and only with summer crops drill-sown in rows, rather than broadcast, did she or her mother-in-law help her husband with the cultivation.

The house into which Yumna had married was still standing in 1992, on one side of the compound where the modern house in which we were sitting had been built. The house was composed of one very large room, the back part consisting of a raised platform some two and a half feet from the floor. The whole structure had three cross-arches running back to front, between which had been laid branches supporting the mud roof. Across the back wall was a double semi-enclosed whitewashed ledge, with almond-shaped openings, built into the plaster; in it had been stored small jars, glasses, and such like. On all sides there had been storage bins, again built into the structure, with holes at the bottom to release the grain. There was also a much smaller storage container on the right-hand edge of the platform, jutting out of the wall, in which sesame seeds had been stored. On the left-hand wall nearest the entrance was a big storage bin for wheat, constructed against the arch; underneath the bin was a slightly lower area for animals, about two and a half feet deep and four feet across. At the back on the left was a further storage container for barley. In the middle there was yet another storage bin, in front of which jutted out the smaller storage container for sesame. Then on the near right there was a ledge higher up, rather like the one across the back of the house on which small articles had been placed, but on this one stood pigeons. Underneath this was an area for grinding. Cooking had apparently been done outside in the compound, though the timber in the roof looked black with either smoke or age.

This had been a house where persons slept on the raised platform surrounded by storage bins of grain. In good weather animals were kept outside in the compound, but in cold, inclement weather they too were admitted to the lower section of the house. Yumna did not herself grind the grain: like most women in the village she took her grain to the water-powered mills in Wadi al-Yabis, which continued to function until the 1940s, when motor-driven mills were introduced to the village.

Yumna claimed that in a good year one measure of wheat would yield twenty, in both *dar* and *arqub* fields. The nearer fields, the *dar*, were planted with both winter and summer crops. The winter crops were a mixture of wheat, barley (only for animals), and lentils. Of summer crops Yumna mentioned white sorghum and sesame, the latter being primarily a cash crop, and also a few vegetables: hairy cucumber (*faqqus*), onions, and a little garlic. They had made several kinds of bread not only from wheat but also from sorghum.[30]

Yumna's *mahr*, both the land and the trees, together with the document, passed to her uncle Khalil al-Nimr at her marriage. Much later on, after she had had children, Yumna went to the governor *(hakim)* of Ajlun to plead for something to live off of *(rizaq bi-yadi-ha)*. Effectively this made it be known that she and her husband were preparing to go to court. So there was then a meeting of the headmen of the village *(jalsa* of the *shuyukh)* in which Khalil granted her the twelve olive trees but kept the part in the common land *(watat)*. And finally—at the irony of which the women laughed loudly—in the Mandate cadastre in 1939–40, her twelve trees were registered along with her husband's three olive trees in his name.

Yumna bore six sons, of whom only Abdullah survived, the rest having died before they were 2 or 3. Of the five girls to whom she gave birth, four survived: Fatima, Miriam, Fidda, and Amina. The girls married with *mahr* paid in cash, save for Amina, who married in 1956 for ninety dinars and four dunums of land.

A Last Interview and Reconstruction

Ahmad Khalifa Saʿd al-Ahmad, born in 1910, had a grizzled look and proved in good shape for an eighty-two-year-old. He belonged to one of the more prominent families of the village, distinguished by religious status and exceptional endogamy. In 1884 when land was registered, Khalifa had already succeeded his father Saʿd. Thus in 1884, when Khalifa was twelve years old, he was registered as joint holder of an entire share of twenty-four carats along with two of his father's brothers, Id al-Ahmad and Hamd al-Ahmad.[31] A third brother of his father, Saʿid al-Ahmad, had an independent holding of twelve carats.[32] And the fourth brother of his father, Abd al-Rahman, aged 33 at the time, held six carats in a joint holding with the six carats of the brother of his second wife, a man of a smaller family of the same section of the village (see figure 13).[33]

Khalifa married a cousin, Zahiya, daughter of Id al-Ahmad, who was to bear him four surviving sons and three surviving daughters. Only late in life, and after Zahiya's death sometime in WWI, did Khalifa take a second wife. Shaikh Khalifa had been a religious person and had led the prayers, never taking money for it, unlike Muhammad al-Awad "Abu-Khudriya," the village imam, who was said to have led the prayers at noon and sunset but when it came to leading the prayers at any other time would demand payment. Shaikh Khalifa was to live a full span of life, and so was one of the few men to have land registered in his name at both the Ottoman survey in 1884 when he was still only 12, and in 1939–40 when he was about 68 years of age. By the

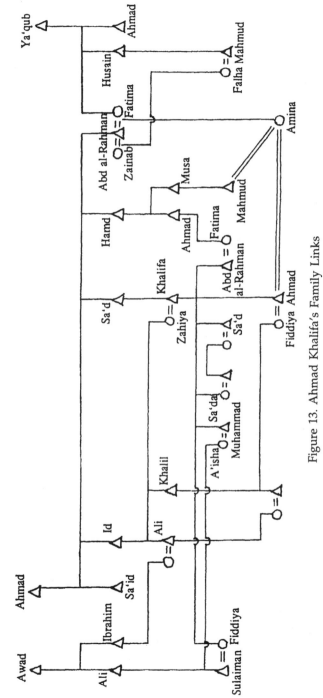

Figure 13. Ahmad Khalifa's Family Links

time of the latter registration, Khalifa had already gone to the *hajj* and on his return had distributed the bulk of his land to his four sons, who each received one and a half carats, while he retained in his name only one sixth of a carat.[34]

Ahmad recalls that when he was young they farmed six carats. They had about one hundred goats, which they grazed up in the hills rather than in Sartaba (a hill overlooking the Jordan Valley), since they had a large cave. At this point of household development, when Ahmad and his younger brother Abd al-Rahman were very small children, they were not cultivating the land that was to be theirs. Rather a man called Muhammad Uthman al-Shihab, of quite another part of the village, took on the land.[35] It was Muhammad Uthman who decided what crops he would sow, but the oxen belonged to their family, so the division of the crop was half and half. A condition of the tenure was that the children would weed, especially his sister Fiddiya, who was six years older than Ahmad, and would help in the harvest. The children would also glean (*ghamar*). This arrangement continued until the time when Ahmad was 5 or 6 and all the males of the family had to leave the village for a period of a year, staying in the nearby village of Ausara, because a distant relative had killed a man of the other half of the village, and it was a year before the *diya* payment (*jamal naum*) was agreed upon and accepted.[36]

In the years just before Ahmad married, the family household had consisted of his father, his father's second wife, his brother Saʿd (who by then was married and took care of the cows), his brother Muhammad (who was married and took care of the sheep and goats), his younger brother Abd al-Rahman, and himself. Saʿd Khalifa had married Khadra al-Ahmad from the village of Ausara in an exchange marriage with his sister Saʿda. Muhammad Khalifa had married Aʾisha Ali al-Awad, an affiliated family of the same half of the village, also of religious status, in an exchange marriage, with his sister Fiddiya marrying Sulaiman Ali al-Awad.

Ahmad noted that he had been a *qarut*, having lost his mother. By the time Ahmad Khalifa was 13 or 14 in the early 1920s, he and his younger brother Abd al-Rahman had come to tend a number of cows and to spend much of their time out of the village grazing them. But there was a plague that decimated the herd, and so for two years when he was 15 and 16 he had gone to Palestine (1925–26) and worked at harvesting in the area of Nazareth and Mulabbas, earning about seven *qirsh* a day in cash.

When he was 19 Ahmad married his cousin (FFBD) Amina Abd al-Rahman al-Ahmad, who was four years older than him.[37] Amina had earlier married another cousin, Mahmud Musa Hamd al-Ahmad (her FBSS), but her first husband appears to have died young.[38] Amina was the only child of the second marriage of Abd al-Rahman, Ahmad's grandfather's brother, who at the time of *tapu* registration had held land jointly with his second wife Fatima's brother, Ahmad Ya'qub. From his first wife, Zainab, Abd al-Rahman had had a daughter, Falha, who was born some thirty-one years before Amina, his daughter by Fatima.[39] Falha married the son of Husain Ya'qub, brother of Ahmad and Fatima. It is not clear whether the two marriages took place as a simultaneous exchange or sequentially, the two families having been interknitted since at least 1884. Amina's mother, Fatima, like Abd al-Rahman's first wife, predeceased her husband. Thus, Amina was, like her husband Ahmad, to grow up without her mother, a *qarut*. In the census of 1910 Abd al-Rahman's household consisted of only himself, aged 59, and little Amina, aged 4, the only household of the village to have such an unusual form.[40] (Presumably Abd al-Rahman's first daughter, Falha, who was married into the family with which her father farmed, helped them at home during these years.) Because Abd al-Rahman had only a daughter and no sons, in 1902 he sold all the six carats he had inherited to the Christian blacksmiths of the village.[41] This did not leave them landless, however, since Abd al-Rahman and Amina had inherited one and a half carats of common land from her mother, Fatima. (It is not clear whether this part was Fatima's *mahr* or inheritance or the result of a double claim concerning both *mahr* and inheritance.)

On Amina's marriage in 1929 Ahmad's family gave as *mahr* two olive trees, a she-goat, and the equivalent of 220 kilograms of wheat.[42] Ahmad Khalifa did not say whether Abd al-Rahman was still alive at the time of Amina's second marriage, by which time he would have been 74, nor whether he took over administration of the one and a half carats of land that Amina had inherited. It seems not, as Ahmad Khalifa stated that he continued to live from raising cattle during these years. Amina bore him a son and daughter, of whom only the first was to survive.

In about 1935 Ahmad took a second wife, again a cousin and again a girl who had already once been married (to a FFBSS), Fiddiya Khalil al-Id al-Ahmad.[43] It appears that Ahmad's father, Khalifa, facilitated a series of exchanges by offering one and a half carats as *mahr* for Fiddiya. Thus, Ahmad married Fiddiya but gave one and a half carats ("ishtara al-zauja wa dafa mahr-ha") to Ibrahim al-Awad, a man of another branch of the family of religious status with whom Ahmad's brother Muhammad and his sister Fiddiya had contracted marriages. Ibrahim al-Awid gave his daughter to Ali al-Id al-Ahmad, who in turn gave his daughter to Khalil al-Id's son, all on the same day. The transfer of this one and a half carats was never formally registered but presumably declared as part of the relevant holdings when the Mandate cadastre took place. At about this time Ahmad's younger brother Abd al-Rahman also married a cousin (FFBSD), Fatima Ahmad al-Hamd al-Ahmad, establishing a separate household.

In the late 1930s, Shaikh Khalifa went to the *hajj* and stayed away for three months. When he returned he divided up the remaining land amongst the four sons, with each son getting one and a half carats. Of the daughters, Fiddiya got a *kail* of wheat and some animals, but if any other daughters survived they seem not to have received anything. Thus it was only after the Mandate cadastre in 1939–40 that Ahmad abandoned raising cattle and took over ploughing his own and Amina's land, each being registered as owning one and a half carats in the cadastral records in a joint holding. Amina was to die before she reached 45, leaving her one son to inherit the two olive trees she had received as *mahr* and the one and a half carats of common land she had owned.

Conclusion

In the family reconstructions sketched above we sense how demography, but also divorce and remarriage, produced a variety and fluidity in household forms over time. The different endowments and fates of individuals in households become evident from such microreconstruction. What then is common to these histories? At a more general level, if marriage exchanges involve both persons and objects, who then are the actors initiating the exchanges, what are the objects of exchange, and how over time does the configuration of agents and objects of exchange shift?

A few basic observations are in order. First, Kufr Awan is a village characterized by a high degree of in-marriage during the period under study. Older people are also proud that little land was alienated to the outside, however hard the times. Second, the primary actors in the exchange known as *mahr* appear in the cases above to be less groom and bride than senior male household heads. The material we have examined does not reveal as large a role for senior women (but consider the role of Tamam in Yumna's marriage), although other cases might in part rectify this. The prominence of senior men in this domain appears to reflect the fact that only they could command the important marriage payments required for the realignment of family relations.[44]

Third, the initial exchange is culturally interpreted as the exchange of a young woman against important objects.[45] Thus Ahmad Khalifa's one and a half carats stand for or release a bride, who in turn releases other brides in a chain ending with a bride for Ahmad Khalifa, the instigator of the multiple exchange. And so here local (male) interpretations appear to share the Levi-Straussian interpretation of marital alliance as woman-exchange.[46] But practice is not without ambiguity, and we may doubt the power of this interpretation to make sense of the reordering of persons and objects effected at marriage. On the one hand, the frequency of *badal* marriages may not be simply for lack of resources with which to endow a bride but may be a preferred model expressing a valued social equality between parties.[47] In many cases, moreover, the marriages renew an entanglement of households (complexes of objects and persons) rather than effect an exchange between unrelated units. In this sense many a marriage appears less an exchange than a matching of junior men with junior women by senior men (and senior women). And, lastly, the interpretation of marriage as pure exchange is difficult to reconcile with the productive quality of the bride for the young groom: she produces not only objects but also persons. A bride is valuable, because she permits the economic individuation of her groom: the bride transforms half a *zalama* into a full *zalama*. It is the productive quality of a bride that lies behind the relatively little systematic variation we remarked in the importance of the *mahr* paid for her, according to whether she is or is not a close relative, or according to whether she is a virgin bride or a young once-divorced bride.[48]

Fourth, there remains an ambiguity in the naming of the "price" of the bride given to her male guardian by the very term, *mahr*, which designates the object that a groom gives his bride as her property.[49] This is all the more so, given that *mahr* entailed not simply cash out of which gendered gifts, notably jewelry, could be purchased, but important agricultural capital difficult to construe as an isolated "object" outside of its mobilization in household production and village-state political relations.[50]

Fifth, this form of women's property, which is in a sense not her property, is doubled by another transformation in women's relations to property during this period. The major transformation related to plough land, which was entirely *miri* land in the village in question. There were two major kinds of agricultural property in the village: olive trees and plough lands. In law and practice ownership rights in the two were not identical. The first were *milk*, subject in principle to *shar'i* rules of inheritance, whereas the land on which the trees stood was usually *miri* in this region. Trees in this village could be seen as more individuated objects of possession.[51] Prior to land registration, plough land had in practice been distributed according to a double principle of anteriority (belonging to an established family) and capacity to plough and assure taxes on a share in the land. A wife was, as in the term *zalama*, conceptually entailed by her husband, although the vagaries of actual household succession meant that the occasional senior widow could become in practice an important manager in cultivation. But from 1884 individual rights were registered and rendered subject to gender-parity between children at inheritance in accordance with the 1847 inheritance regulation and the subsequent 1858 Land Code. (In practice, as we have seen, inter vivos transmission remained critical to ensuring the devolution of plough land between men.) Thus, according to state law, women of the village could acquire the status of ungendered property owners of shares in common land exactly as could men. Until 1910, however, when a full census of the village was made, men often simply did not report women heirs to the land registry in the case of inheritance. But after 1910 rendering such women invisible to the state became far more difficult. From 1914 onwards registration of a devolution of land by inheritance required confirmation of the death by the village *mukhtar*, notification of the civil registry of the death, a clearance from the tax office, and a schedule of the heirs and breakdown of their shares from the *shar'i* court. Hence, increasingly over the period, women, even at the moment of their marriage as young brides, began to carry in their person a potential claim to inheritance of plough land.

Lastly, as the above implies, the change in state law concerning women's rights of inheritance (and hence in women's relation to property) cannot be understood solely in terms of the application of new rules taken in the abstract. Rather, the new laws entailed formal procedures of registration (to which the notes of this chapter refer) that at the same time do not eliminate all vernacular legal documents and transactions outside their kin. Thus the promises made concerning the payment of *mahr* continue to be written in documents drawn up by the village imam. The sphere of exchange expressed in these documents appears only very partially mirrored in the entries made during the formal and costly registration required by the state. This is true in terms both of registration of land transfers in the *tapu* office and of the objects exchanged, grain/*urjas*/trees/animals/land, as against the cash sums appearing in the *shar'i* court registers. One may speak of an articulation of levels of legal expression between the village and the state offices evolving unevenly over time.

Bearing in mind these general points, let us return to our cases. Ahmad Khalifa's first marriage was to a once-divorced, inheriting daughter several years older than himself. Amina was highly individuated by this definition of her person, and there is no doubt that if not the grain, then the two olive trees and the goat that formed her *mahr* went to her hand. In short, Amina was complexly defined by her status within her natal household. But what then of Ahmad Khalifa's second marriage, where he noted that "he bought a wife and paid one and a half carats"? In this case Ahmad, or rather his father, gave the one and a half carats not to the man (Khalil al-Id) who "sold" his daughter to Ahmad, but to a quite different man whose daughter married Khalil's brother Ali at the same time as Khalil's son married Ali's daughter and his daughter married his sister's son Ahmad. The central actors in this exchange appear to have been two senior brothers of Khalifa's first wife, Ahmad's mother: Ali al-Id, who married a third time at the age of 45, and his brother Khalil, who effected the marriage of his recently divorced daughter to Ahmad "in return" for a bride for his son, the daughter, moreover, of his powerful elder brother. The saintly wing of the family, that of Shaikh Khalifa, made this possible by the release of one and a half carats. Yet even here there is ambiguity, as Ahmad noted, since the political act of transfer in the land registry was not carried out; and so—rather like the borrowed *urjas* of several accounts—once the marriages were all sealed, it is not clear whether the outsider really did recoup from that powerful clan, for himself or his daughter, the actual one and a half carats.

And the *mahr* of Yumna? Surely this follows the male ideal, since Yumna's *mahr*, important as it was, was never entered in the registers of the state in her own name. But even here there is ambiguity. Yumna's *mahr* is excessive by the standards of other girls. Yumna was after all a *yatim*, a full orphan, after having been from an early age a *qarut* who had lost her mother, and so we might well ask why her uncle demanded so much. One answer is the acquisitive character of this only surviving son of Nimr, who at the cadastre registered a full eight carats of land, the third-largest holding in the village. Another is that Khalil demanded so large a *mahr* in anticipation of the claim that Yumna held on to land from her father, his older brother, and Nimr's son, as well as against the claim of his aunt Tamam, Yumna's husband's mother. In short, we are in a world of strategy where—and not always to their benefit—the property claims of women are in the back of every player's mind. Recall the howls of women's laughter when Yumna described how her twelve olive trees were eventually registered in the name of her husband—property returning to its source between men. To women the denial of their legal personality as ungendered owners of property—as heirs in the registers of the state—and even more so as gendered owners of *mahr* remains illegitimate.

In the case of Yumna, moreover, it was surely not irrelevant that her husband was by then the sole surviving son of a man who had held six carats of land. Muhammad Abdullah al-Salih still held five carats, not a small holding, even after ceding to Khalil al-Nimr the one

carat of land included in Yumna's *mahr*. In short, this was not a household in dire need, and so we do not see Muhammad Abdullah claiming the part of Abdullah al-Muflih's land due him through his mother,
Tamam, nor do we see Yumna and her husband, Muhammad, taking
on Khalil to claim Yumna's part in her father's inheritance. Regardless
of what she stated before the governor or the village headmen, there
is little evidence that Yumna was in hardship. Rather the point lies
elsewhere: only Yumna could legally claim her *mahr*. If from the point
of view of her husband this simply assured the return of family trees
to where they had originated, it was nevertheless Yumna who had to
mount the claim. And in other cases, such as that of Husna, who was
not up against such a tough opponent as Khalil al-Nimr, her *mahr*,
although earlier integrated into her paternal family's exploitation, was
granted without contest.

By contrast, poorer members of Yumna's family such as the daughters and wife of Muhammad al-Nimr, Khadra (the only surviving
daughter of Ahmad al-Nimr), and the daughters of Khalil's sister
Miriam (who were also granddaughters of Khazna, full sister of Nimr
and Abdullah) all claimed and received small parts in the family land.[52]
The case of the wife of Muhammad al-Nimr, A'isha Ahmad al-Musa,
who quite exceptionally claimed against her own daughters to obtain
a tiny part of her husband's land, deserves a second look. A'isha was
one of three surviving children of Ahmad al-Musa, her full sister Rishda
having married their only cousin, Ibrahim Ali al-Musa.[53] Their half-
brother Mahmud, some ten years younger than they, was from a second younger wife, A'isha Dahaimish.[54] As noted above, in 1884 the
fifteen carats of family plough land had been registered in their uncle
Ali's name, not in that of their father.[55] But unlike the case of Husna's
father, Salih Hamdan, who in 1908 legally transferred land in equal
parts to his half-brother Abd al-Karim and to his son Hasan, Ali died
around 1902–3, perhaps suddenly and in any case at a time when legal
transactions in the land record office were not as yet very common.
Thus A'isha, Rishda, and their younger half-brother Mahmud stood
to obtain no land through their father. In 1910 Mahmud appears as a
qarut living with his mother in his mother's brother's household.[56]
Then in 1918 Ibrahim al-Ali dies issueless with all his plough land
passing by law to his mother, Subha Mahmud al-Muflih, and his wife,
Rishda Ahmad Musa al-Muflih. Rishda and A'isha's half-brother
Mahmud, who would have obtained the lion's part in *milk* property
subject to *shar'i* law, has no legal entitlement to the *miri* land subject
to civil law.[57] In fact, at the time of the cadastre in 1939 Subha al-
Mahmud challenges Mahmud for a part in the land that she states she
inherited from her father (!), but all the village authorities back

Mahmud's claim that she had sold him three carats with a formal sale document and that the document was inadvertently lost during the process of cadastral registration.[58] Hence we find at the cadastre that Mahmud, after payment of a debt worth one and a half carats, is registered as owner of one and a half carats that he then farms alongside the plots of his maternal uncles, sons of Duhaimish;[59] Subha obtains one and a half carats registered in her name (which she farms jointly with her brother Ali Mahmud); and Rishda registers an independent holding of three carats, one of the larger land holdings by women of the village.[60] But Rishda's sister A'isha is left without any land, hence her need to claim through her husband and even against her own daughters.

Here again the accidents of demographic structure at the time of *tapu* registration can be seen to differentiate families one from the next. Unlike Husna's family, where her father Salih re-registered his land giving equal parts to his younger half-brother Abd al-Karim and his son Hasan, here the elder brother failed, while still alive, to rectify before his death the exclusion of his much younger brother Ahmad. Yet Ahmad's son Mahmud, who after his father's early death went to live and work in his mother's brother's house, does in fact come into land by a donation/sale from one of the two legally entitled women: his cousin Ibrahim's mother, Subha Mahmud al-Muflih (who is also his FFBD). In this we again sense the ambiguous relation between what appears in the registers of the state and the practical devolution of land in farming. Given the demographic history of male deaths in this family, some of the fifteen carats registered in the name of Ali Musa al-Muflih appear to have been transferred to other households over time without registration in the *tapu* office, but even so, Subha and Rishda had a legal claim on an important amount of land. So once Subha challenges Mahmud before the committee of registration at the time of the cadastre, as an older widow she manages to extract the basic one and a half carat holding of land, while the younger widow Rishda obtains three carats of land without legal contest.

Between the abstract categories of law and the concrete practices of property and gender stand living persons. The laws of the state recognized an ungendered legal persona, full or usufructuary owner of fundamental agricultural property, a legal status common to women and to men. An individual could accede to this status by receiving property through purchase, gift, *mahr*, or inheritance. But what appears an object in the registers of the state and in legal terminology was inevitably inscribed in the productive and political relations of the village. Hence plough land was not the same as olive trees, as the negotiation over Yumna's *mahr* suggests; it was not so easily untangled or individuated even after *tapu* registration. In the practice of fiscal

administration it was almost entirely men who declared to state officials matters to do with the status of taxpayers for property, and in the
internal village administration of land it was men who oversaw the
redistribution of plots in the common fields every two years. In these
critical spheres of public making or affirming of property, women
were generally invisible. They were not so invisible, however, in the
day-to-day cultivation of plough lands or care of olive trees. And
hence, as so often in cases where women were sole heirs, the combined legal status of heir and ungendered owner were powerful enough
for their claims to property to be honored, even if the disposal of their
person/property in marriage would be jealously controlled. And when,
later in a woman's life, a claim to inherit was redoubled by a claim on
her *mahr*, many a woman proved far more combative than Yumna in
battling for control over some part of what the laws of the state and
their marriage contracts promised them.

In the village during the years under study we may speak of a
series of tensions: between the power of senior men (and to a much
lesser extent senior women) and the economic isolation and individuality of the couple as a fundamental productive unit and household
nucleus; between women's presence in production by the side of their
husbands and their absence from the public moments when productive relations were played out before the view of all, at tax payment
and land redistribution; between the state's recognition of women as
ungendered property owners and the gendered relational definitions
of women in their respective kinship relations to men (daughter, wife,
mother); between women forming in vernacular terms the object of
transaction in marriage and yet the objects of "payment" being legally
framed as property of the women in question. These tensions both
constrict and construct women's agency, a plurality of agency situated
in an arena where three histories intersect: the histories of demography, of family property transmission, and of endowment of marital
alliances over time. This gives individuality to women's histories as it
does to men's in the village. And it means that whereas in 1884 no
women appeared in the list of owners of common land or olive trees
or houses, in 1939–40 (at least in the form of property where we can
draw comparisons, plough land) women represented 18.7 percent of
the owners with 12.3 percent of the land.[61] Compared to villages in the
plains this represents an important admission of women's rights as
ungendered owners. But in the achievement of the claim to that legal
status lies a final ambiguity: women only gained that legal status by
contested negotiation (and a lesser settlement than what the letter of
the law would accord them) of rights legally accruing to them both
through claims to their *mahr* and by claims through inheritance.[62]

The patterns described here were to change in the course of the 1940s and 1950s as agricultural land per head declined with population growth and as men began to find employment in larger numbers in the army and the towns. From then on *mahr* came more to resemble its form in the registry: transfers in cash, translated into gold and other commodities purchased in the market. Thus what we have been observing represents but a moment in a transition from a legal system prior to 1884, when shares in common land could not have been transacted as *mahr* in quite the individuated manner encountered here, and a time after 1940, when cash came increasingly to frame a more uniform understanding of what should be given to make a woman a wife.

Notes

We are most grateful to the following institutions for the permission to consult and copy (by hand) relevant documents: the Jordanian Department of Lands and Surveys, both the Amman and Irbid offices, the Civil Court and Civil Registry in Irbid, and the Department of Historical Documents of Jordan University. Our warmest thanks go to the officials of these institutions and, above all, to the people and officials of the village of Kufr Awan who so generously shared their memories with us. Our reading of their history should be taken as just that: a mere interpretation, even if we have respected our sources and the conventions of historians by employing the real names of persons in this publication. The research initiated in 1988 on which this chapter draws has been supported by the generosity of the following institutions: the Wenner Gren Foundation for Anthropological Research, the Social Science Research Council (NYC), the British Institute for Archaeology and History Amman, the Centre de Recherches sur le Moyen Orient Contemporain Amman, the Kerr Fellowship of UCLA, the Centre National de la Recherche Scientifique (Lyon—MOM/GREMO), and the British Academy. The field and documentary work was carried out thanks to a nonstipendiary Senior Research Fellowship at the Institute of Archaeology and Anthropology of Yarmouk University (1989–92). Lastly, we would like to thank Maisara al-Zu^cbi who helped as research assistant in compiling material from the Irbid Civil Court and the Yarmouk University Research Centre. The spelling of place-names in this paper follows Abd al-Qadir (1973) (see Mundy 1996). If no documentary source is given, the source of information is the relevant interview, all three of which took place in 1992. OM stands for the Ottoman financial year and AH for the *hijri* year. The word *"zaituna"* in the title means "olive tree" in Arabic.

1. See Mundy 1992, 1994, 1996, 2001 for a discussion of these sources.

2. See Mundy forthcoming.

3. According to the 1910 census, she had been born in 1889 CE/1305 OM, Irbid Civil Registry Ottoman List, Kufr Awan M046-06. This information derives from the Irbid Civil Registry Ottoman *nufus* carried out in 1910 (see

Başbakanlik Arşivi, Dahiliye Nezareti Sicil-i Nüfus Tahrirat Kalemi, DH.SN.THR 1805 15\56, 2114 18\51, 3050 27\98 for the orders to carry out the census in the region). The original lists were recopied after the burning of the Civil Registry in 1970. The order of the villages in the recopied lists does not correspond to the original volumes, but in each village list the numbering of households corresponds to the original. Hence in this chapter we refer to the census by village, i.e., Kufr Awan, and household number, C for Christian and M for Muslim, and number of the individual in the household, i.e., M046-06 for Husna, already married and living in her husband's father's household in 1910. There is clearly a tendency to assign an age to the wife about one to three years younger than the husband and to assign too high ages to older women. We have left the ages as reported, however.

4. Jordanian Department of Lands and Survey, Irbid Ottoman *tapu* Registers, August 1300 OM *esas yoklama* register, recopied 1329 OM: 79, entries 688/89–1. Henceforth these registers are simply referred to as Irbid *tapu* registers. *Qirat* is the Arabic term for carats—i.e., one in twenty-four shares—and it is in this form that shares in the common land were calculated. Measures in the common land are discussed in further detail below. In the text we shall use the term carat for *qirat* throughout.

5. Irbid *tapu zabit* register 1323–34 OM: 139, entries 252/55.

6. Kufr Awan *nufus* M045 for Hasan, M053 for Hisna and M078 for Tamam.

7. Jordanian Department of Lands and Survey, Central Cadastral Files, Kufr Awan, court case 7/96, decision 9 May 1939 with reference to article 1817 of the Majalla. Henceforth all reference to these files will be simply as Central Cadastral Files, Kufr Awan. As for how much land Hasan held by 1939, the following appears from the *tapu* registers. Of the six carats, which he had received from his father (see note 4), he sold one and a half carats in 1935 to Khalil al-Id al-Ahmad, leaving him with four and a half carats of land (Irbid *tapu zabit* register 1934-onwards, page 60, entry 1–4, August 1935). And in January 1936 (ibid., 92, entry 18–21) he is registered as selling another one and a half carats to his son Mahmud. There is a problem here, since logically the transfer was to his son Muhammad, not to Mahmud, in whose name his remaining three carats after such an alienation were to be registered (see note 8 below) in 1939. Unfortunately, we also did not ascertain whom Muhammad married and hence cannot see where the one and a half carats may have gone; Muhammad himself has no land registered in his name in the 1939 cadastre.

8. "Common land" is in most respects an incorrect term, especially after land registration in 1884 when individual ownership of shares became not only law but practice. Even before this registration it is not clear that land was truly thought of as common. It appears more accurate to describe the form of holding as a collectivity of rights to land and of responsibility for payment of agricultural tax in which members of the village each held individuated parts, the whole being mobilized from the parts of all the individual holders.

9. Central Cadastral Files, Kufr Awan, *jadwal al-iddiʿaʾat* dated 16 March 1939 (with later corrections from reports *[taqarir]* and court cases and additions from *jadwal al-huquq*), entry number 104.

10. Irbid *tapu* register August 1300 OM (recopied 1329 OM): 84, entry 781. Reading between the lines, it appears that Qasim had cofarmed with the owner of the ten trees, perhaps acquiring ownership of the three trees by his labor. There is not necessarily any discrepancy between the record, which does not record land ownership for Qasim, and Husna's account, whereby she comes to own both the trees and the land on which they stand. The land in question lies close by the original village site. We learn in the general report on the land registration of Kufr Awan (Central Cadastral Files, Kufr Awan, Report to the Director of Lands and Survey, dated 8 July 1940, item 4) that "the area exempted from registration in the block of the village comprises the village site, agricultural lands and olive trees. These lands and trees were not made subject to cadastral registration because their owners did not wish registration to take place. Hence the fiscal distribution of these lands and trees was evaluated and included in the schedules of evaluation for the purpose of tax imposition." The item goes on to explain that the area of the village block registered in the cadastre was only about one-quarter of all the lands of the block. In other words, since the land in question was not registered before the 1990s, the area on which the three trees stood could have become the property of the trees' owner without it appearing so in the registers. In general and in contradiction to plough land, we find no entries in the *tapu* registers concerning transfers of ownership of trees in the village between 1884 and 1940 (apart from the case described in note 22).

11. At the time of the *nufus* in 1910 M046 comprised the following persons in the order they appear in the register: Husna's HF (husband's father), H, HB, HZ, HM, self and D (aged three months). An older HB headed M044 with a second wife and three children by a first wife.

12. Irbid *tapu* register August 1300 OM: 78, entry 658.

13. In 1939–40 land registration was compulsory outside the land forming part of the "village block." Thus, in Kufr Awan villagers chose to register only one stretch of plots in the "village block" (*haud al-balad*) but to exclude the other. This was presumably to spare themselves registration fees, but it did not exempt them from paying the tax on all trees in the village zone (see note 9).

14. By the 1930s one and a half carats, often termed a *watat*, corresponded effectively to the basic unit of land that was transacted and exploited.

15. Irbid *tapu* register August 1300 OM: 79, entry 682/83. In 1884 Abdullah Salih farmed his land together with another farmer, Uthman al-Shihab, who similarly held six carats. Yumna identified her husband's father as Abdullah Salih Hamd al-Muflih.

16. Irbid *tapu* register August 1300 OM: 79, entry 680/81.

17. Kufr Awan *nufus* M083 for Nimr. Abdullah had died by the time of the *nufus*.

18. It is unclear whether in the past, when average landholdings were larger and when, given the link with cattle raising in the Ghor, oxen were more important in farming than in years after the 1930s, the terms for larger units were more common in agriculture in the village.

19. Irbid *tapu* register August 1300 OM: 79, entry 684/5 and p. 81, entry 721. We were long hesitant as to whether Musa al-Muflih was son of the same Muflih al-Musa, father of Muhammad, Mahmud, Nimr, and Abdullah, but we now think that he was almost certainly a much older son, probably from a first wife or perhaps also from Tufaha. In 1884 Musa owns an house but the plough land, a full fifteen carats, is registered in name of his son Ali. This is the structure observable also in the case of the very aged Muflih himself, whose last wife, Mahra, was then sixty years old. The two houses (ibid.: 80, entries 710 & 711) and olive trees (ibid.: 76, entry 595 land: 83, entry 775 trees) were still registered in Muflih's name, whereas the plough lands were in the names of his four sons from Tufaha and Mahra. The only other possibility is that Musa al-Muflih (like Abdullah Salih Hamd al-Muflih), being closely associated by marriage with the "Muflihs," is thus accorded the name "Muflih." But because of the 1884 house registration in the name of Musa al-Muflih and evidence discussed in n. 56 below, we now prefer the interpretation that Musa was a full son of Muflih, although we cannot prove the genealogical relations, since he did not survive to be registered in the 1910 *nufus*.

20. The estimate of Ahmad al-Musa's age is deduced from the age of his son Mahmud and his widow A'isha Duhaimish as given in Kufr Awan *nufus* M011.

21. Irbid *tapu* register August 1300 OM: 81, entries 729 and 730 and 80, entries 710 and 711.

22. These ages are deduced from the *nufus* (Kufr Awan *nufus* M083) and from an account of devolution of property reported to the Islamic court (see following note).

23. It is noteworthy that virtually no transfers of houses, whether by inheritance or by sale, are given in the *tapu* registers, although the first registration of 1884 was of houses as well as land and tree plantings. This registration, which concerns the same two houses, olives trees, and plot that were registered in the name of Muflih, is presented as a new registration in July 1889. We were able to trace this by linking partial information in Irbid *tapu* *yoklama* register 1305–07 OM: 10 or 20 (first three entries missing because page torn) with references to *tahsilat* register of 11/1306 numbers 118–128. In a series of microfilms in the Amman Department of Lands and Surveys of tax registers that had originated from Ajlun, we found entries numbered 115–128 dated 11/1306 register 1: 90. Entry 115 concerns the fifteen olive trees, 116 and 117 concern houses, and 118 concerns the land of the olive trees. These correspond exactly in their borders, value, and description to the properties registered in the name of Muflih (see note 18).

24. Much later in a legal settlement of the early 1930s, Abdullah's land is described as reverting to his mother, Mahra, and thence to his full siblings from Mahra: Nimr, Waliya, Khazna, Tamam, and Fatima (the last also to die without issue): Jordan University, Department of Historical Documents, microfilm copy of Irbid *shar^ci* Court Records, *sijill* 12, *hasr al-irth*, 1929–1931: 163, case 83/177/4, dated 12 November 1930. However the land may actually have passed in farming practice, this report necessarily expresses a later rationalization in line with the letter of the law. This said, it appears that the children of Waliya did inherit land through her, but it is not clear whether those of Khazna did.

25. Ibid.

26. A child orphaned of one parent is termed a *qarut;* a child orphaned of both parents, a *yatim.* Given demographic patterns, of which Nimr's household is an extreme case, the *qarut* was an only too common pattern in the village in the early twentieth century.

27. In the 1884 *tapu* lists, her husband's father was registered as holding twenty olive trees in this plot. Thus Yumna's *mahr* was of importance to the family. Irbid *tapu* register August 1300 OM: 83, entry 765.

28. It would appear that having paid such a big *mahr* to Khalil al-Nimr for his niece, the husband's family held back on the other expenses.

29. Yumna maintained that they had twelve carats, but she had also said of Khalil's household that they had in both cases over twice what either household could have held according to any other source; perhaps she just slipped, using the term *faddan* for *zalama.* Yumna's memory at several points elided generations; the vagueness here may arise from her not having worked much in the fields, unlike Husna.

30. The standard loaf made with yeast was called *karadish;* and Yumna described the making of it with water, in order for it not to break up, and dusted with flour. Another type of loaf was called *tabtabiyat* and made over a griddle *(saj).* A third undesirable, quick kind of bread, mixed only with water without yeast and stuffed into the hot coals, was called *awa'is.*

31. Irbid *tapu* register August 1300 OM: 78, 640/41 and Kufr Awan *nufus* M084.

32. Irbid *tapu* register August 1300 OM: 78, 642/43.

33. Ibid., 636/37.

34. Central Cadastral Files, Kufr Awan, *jadwal al-iddi^ca'at*, 165/69. Khalifa's part was registered in a joint holding with his son Muhammad.

35. See note 14 for Uthman al-Shihab.

36. According to the report found in the Irbid Civil Court Register (untitled) 1918–22, entry 44/60 dated 30/5/1920 charging Isa al-Ali (who had

fled and was not under arrest at the time of the report) with the murder of one man and wounding of his brother, Ahmad Khalifa would have been a few years older than five to six—about nine to ten years of age if the age given in the *nufus* is taken as base.

37. There was an age difference of four years according to the *nufus*. Here again the *nufus* may have slightly underestimated ages of young people. The marriage appears in the marriage registers of the Irbid *sharʿi* court as transcribed onto cards in the Yarmouk University Research Centre, *sijill* 7, number 06016, dated 5 September 1929, where the ages are given as 20 for the groom and 28 for the bride and a *mahr muʿajjal* of three thousand Palestinian *qirsh* (PQ) is specified. The *mahr* recorded for Amina's second marriage compares with a high of nine thousand PQ recorded for one marriage (both parties from the village) in those years.

38. It would appear that Amina was widowed, not divorced, although this is not certain. What is certain is that Mahmud Musa al-Hamd did not survive to be registered with land in 1939.

39. Kufr Awan *nufus* M033.

40. Ibid., M075.

41. Irbid *tapu zabit* register 1315–19 OM: 39, entries 7–10.

42. Compare note 36 above. As always in the marriage registers of these years, the *mahr* is given only in cash terms.

43. Fiddiya had sued her husband, who had taken a second wife in 1932: Jordan University microfilm of Irbid *sharʿi* court registers, *sijill* 11: 163, number 31/21, dated 17 July 1932. In this case Fiddiya stated that she had been married five years earlier and that he had taken a new wife. Four months earlier he had driven her out and left her without maintenance. She demands that he pay what he owes and the legal costs. He agrees that he cohabited with and married his wife for a *mahr* of 4,220 Palestinian *qirsh*, of which 20 PQ is delayed *mahr* and the rest prompt *mahr*. He is willing to have her live in the same house as his second wife or to rent a different house for her, "as I shall furnish it with a mat, two mattresses, covers and three wool embroidered (? *muhashshabin*) pillows, a lamp, a mixing bowl, a water *tanaka*, a jug, a cup for drinking, a cooking pot, a tray and a spoon." He also agrees to pay maintenance of 50 PQ per month and 80 PQ for clothes. Fiddiya agrees to live in the house where he lives on condition that he moves her cowife out. In accordance with clause 51 of *huquq al-aʾila*, he will pay maintenance from that day forward and will settle her in a house. He pays the legal costs of the case. Less than two years later—we have an exact date for the divorce but can no longer trace its source in our notes!—Fiddiya appears to have been (or to have obtained) a divorce. Hence her (and her groom's) second marriage probably took place about 1935 or 1936.

44. Compare Granqvist 1931, 46, 53–60.

45. Compare Granqvist's 1931, 141–42, insightful comments on the idioms of buying of a person.

46. See Lévi-Strauss 1969, 65–68.

47. Compare Granqvist 1931, 118–19.

48. Ibid., 121.

49. Antoun 1972, 169–70 n. 13, remarks on the shift from the use of the term *faid*, the only term that appears in Granqvist's study from Palestine in the mid-1920s, to *mahr* and the fact that in this region only one term appears used to describe the payments, in contrast to some Islamic societies, where one term was used for what was given the bride *(mahr)* and another for what was given her male guardian *(shart)*. Compare Mundy 1995, 131–38 for another example alongside the work of I. Lewis's work on northern Somaliland cited by Antoun, where the two terms are clearly distinguished in marriage transactions. With regard to the structure of *mahr*, Antoun 1972, 123, 170 n. 19 writes that the urban model of delayed *mahr (mahr mu'ajjal)* was not evident in marriage contracts of the nearby village of Kufr al-Ma before the 1960s: "This was the situation up to 1960. By 1966, however, the imam of Kufr al-Ma, who had been appointed ma'thun [*sic*] over four villages in the area, had begun to encourage villagers to stipulate deferred mahr payments as being more in accordance with Islam and as offering more protection to the bride." From the time in the early 1920s when special marriage registers were instituted in the Irbid *shar'i* court, it was not uncommon that a deferred *mahr*, although usually a very small one, would be stipulated in the registers.

50. See Granqvist 1931, 119, where, with regard to land given as *mahr*, she cites the adage that "nothing protects honour like land."

51. It should be noted that this results less from some inherent mystical quality of olive trees than from the manner they enter labor and political relations. Thus, in areas marked by new development of olive cultivation for commercial production, notably in the Kafarat area to the northwest of Irbid, labor relations and ownership patterns were different. But Kufr Awan belonged to a zone where olive cultivation was integrated into household, small-scale strategies of production.

52. The daughters of Muhammad al-Nimr are challenged by their mother A'isha for a part in the inheritance of her husband/their father (Central Cadastral Files, Kufr Awan, Court Cases, No. 1), and hence she is added to the list of holdings as entry 10a with three-fourths of a carat, after entries 9 and 10 with nine-sixteenths of a carat each (ibid., *jadwal al-iddi'a'at*). Khudra is registered as owning three-fourths of a carat farmed in a joint plot with her husband's share (ibid., entry 22). And the two daughters of Miriam al-Nimr claim their inheritance through their mother (Central Cadastral Files, Kufr Awan, Reports, No. 35) obtaining a half carat each, respectively (ibid., *jadwal al-iddi'a'at*, entries 33 and 35, farmed as a joint plot with the holdings of their husbands, two brothers married to the two sisters).

53. Kufr Awan *nufus* M057 referring to Rishda.

54. *Ibid.* M011 referring to A'isha.

55. Compare notes 18 and 19 above.

56. Kufr Awan *nufus* M011.

57. Irbid *shar'i* Court Records, *sijill* 15, *hasr al-irth*, p. 9, case 19, of 24 June 1935 declaring that seventeen years ago Ibrahim Ali al-Musa died, leaving his wife Rishda Ahmad al-Musa, his mother Subha al-Mahmud, and his FBS Mahmud al-Ahmad al-Musa, the *shar'i* inheritance being Rishda three-twelfths, Subha four-twelfths and Mahmud five-twelfths and the *miri* inheritance being Rishda one-half and Subha one-half.

58. Central Cadastral Files, Kufr Awan, *taqarir*, number 10 (a & b). It is something of a mystery as to why Subha claims that her right to land arises from her father, not her husband: perhaps she knew nothing of the registration of rights of succession from her son Ibrahim (see preceding note); but at the same time she notes in her testimony that (a) she had sold one and a half carats only a year earlier and (b) at that time found the three other carats of land registered in her name, which the defendant controls, as documented in the *sanadat al-tamlik* that she possesses. And it is equally anyone's guess whether Subha had in fact drawn up a document dated A.H. 1328, as supported by the testimony of a whole series of important figures in the village to the existence and circumstances of loss of the same, transferring by sale for 90 or 100 *lira faransi* three carats of land to Mahmud.

59. Ibid., *taqarir*, numbers 16a & 19 and *jadwal al-iddi'a'at*, entry 45.

60. Ibid., *jadwal al-iddi'a'at*, entries 14 & 11.

61. Forty-nine women and 213 men held land, with an average holding of 0.6 carats per woman as against an average 1.08 per man.

62. While not entirely absent among the buyers of land, women were distinctly marginal in the land market except as sellers, itself a secondary arena for the acquisition of right to land in this village.

7

Tribal Enterprises and Marriage Issues in Twentieth-Century Iran

Erika Friedl

Methodologically, this chapter is an attempt to understand marriage customs in a tribal area of Iran as a historical process by using ethnographic data. Documents on the topic don't exist. I collected the data by observation, by listening to people remember earlier times, and by eliciting bits and pieces of oral histories. The chapter raises the question of what kinds of historical facts and truths one may recover using memory as a tool for reconstructing history, but given the broad theme of this chapter this question will not be addressed here.[1]

For Iran, the cultural assumptions and social arrangements that the term "marriage" covers are undertheorized and poorly described. In ethnographies they appear mostly in passing.[2] The most insightful treatment of the theme, albeit neither systematic nor analytic, is found in Iranian biographies and fiction.[3] This neglect by social scientists is more the pity, as marriage is a popular topic in Iran, the focus of stories, of newspaper articles, of fiction and films, of fretting and planning and scheming. Moreover, it is said to be the God-willed foundation of a well-ordered society. Social life hinges on marriage as do, to a large degree, the management of property, the reproduction of relations, and the division of labor, especially in pastoral-transhumant communities.[4] This is obvious. Less obvious but no less relevant are the reverse connections in which marital customs emerge as functions of economic relations.

People in Iran see connections between economy and marriage not on a theoretical level, but on the practical level of interactions, expectations, and rationalizations of behavior. This establishes an ethnographic "fit": what the anthropologist sees jibes with what the people themselves realize. For example, elaborate negotiations by the family of a bride-to-be of the size of severance pay in case of divorce were explained in terms of the young woman's economic future, given her near-total economic dependency on her husband. Rural men described their expectations of a wife's duties in terms of labor and production (to keep house, to milk the cow, to bear and raise children), and women described a "good" husband primarily in terms of how good a provider he was. The most valid reason for a wife to initiate divorce is her husband's failure to provide for her economically. Health in both, husband and wife, ranked high on the list of desirable traits because, people explained, a sickly wife cannot work at home and a sickly man cannot feed his family. In the pastoral enterprise, men married to sisters were said to enjoy the advantage of smooth and profitable cooperation in milk processing that sisters are likely to provide for each other. Even character has an economic side: a "good" wife used to be described as one who efficiently and without complaints works well, cooperates with others, and obeys her husband in order to guarantee the economic success as well as the good reputation of the family.

I base this chapter on the assumption that private property and its social relations, the locus of production of economic goods, and control of the distribution of surplus goods shape marital arrangements and customs as well as underlying philosophies. This approach allows for good ethnography, as it comes close to an important indigenous model. It also allows for an explanation of a developing crisis in the local marriage arena as discussed in Iran today. This crisis manifests itself, among other ways, in the recent sharp increase of unmarried young people, but especially of unmarried young women in Iran.[5] Over the past decade membership in this new social category has grown to the point where commonsensical assumptions about marriage as a natural, God-willed calling are being challenged. In popular literature, in gossip, and in daily practice, marriage has come under scrutiny. Again, people overwhelmingly use economic factors to explain the rise of the number of unmarried people and the problems of marriage: the depressed economy forces young men to defer marriage because the men neither can afford the wedding expenses nor afford to provide for a wife and children. And: young women have become very demanding and will refuse a poor suitor. But there is a more complex aspect to this crisis.

For the urban middle and upper classes in Iran, the cognitive frame of marriage started to shift fast in the two generations prior to the revolution of 1979. Members of these classes increasingly structured their social relations within the local Western-style, high-income-producing late capitalist economies. These social relations included emancipatory husband-wife relationships. For the rest of the citizens cognitions of marriage changed with the proliferation of modernist traits such as wage-labor and salaried work for women, the expansion of public transportation, schools, and so-called enlightened attitudes toward children's needs. The marriage age for girls rose most everywhere, leading to the novel phenomenon of what we call (unmarried) teenagers. Later, in the Islamic Republic, certain social programs and economic developments had the unintended effect of weakening parental authority and with it the parents' will or power to impose marriage partners on their children. For example, when the government decided that the postulate of sex segregation necessitated that women be served by women professionals (teachers, physicians), it established a quota system for women's admission to the university. This led to the opening of higher education for some young rural women. Although few of those actually have gone to college, the mere possibility for them to "get out," as they say, to "amount to something," to get a salary and thus some "freedom," has created new outlooks: women can envision a lifestyle that definitely includes some say in marriage choices and some economic independence from a husband. While two generations ago parents who had not arranged a marriage for their children at an early age were charged with neglect by others, now parents who allow their daughters to be spoken for at a young age likely will be criticized for jeopardizing their future well-being.

In the following I will trace the tandem developments of local economies and local marriage practices, down to the marriage crisis, in Boir Ahmad, a tribal/rural area of southwest Iran, mostly as they unfolded in a large village I call Deh Koh. This village can stand as an example for the sociopolitical as well as cultural history of the tribal area.[6]

The Area

The Boir Ahmadi are a Luri-speaking, Shi'ite people of about half a million in the southern Zagros mountains. The environment allows for hunting, pastoralism, and dry and irrigated agriculture.[7] Deh Koh was founded around 1880 as a summer camp of tents and huts for a small transhumant group wintering at a lower altitude. Since then it has grown to about thirty-five hundred people with the mixed economy characteristic of rural Iran today. Reinhold Loeffler and I have studied Deh Koh since 1965, when nearly all people were engaged in transhumant farming. Many developments described in this chapter happened while we were watching.[8] For descriptions of life in earlier times I rely on local people's memories. These are colored by two emotional tints correlating with status: members of the families of tribal chiefs were likely to comment on romantic aspects of tribal life such as wedding parties and feats of bravery, while commoners were likely to comment on hardships and on exploitation by the chiefs.[9]

The basic producing and consuming unit in Boir Ahmad was the extended, nuclear, or composite family embedded in a hierarchically organized tribal network based on lineages.[10] Households comprised patrilineally related men (brothers, a father, and his grown sons) and their wives and children in dwellings that were grouped in courtyards. Locally, the term *famil*, family, covers the nuclear family as well as patrilineal kin. In nuclear families that live neolocally, which in the past happened when an extended family broke up and now is the preferred way of living, "household" and "family" are synonymous.

Over the past 110 years, one can talk about two distinct periods in the development of marriage customs and marriage philosophies: during and after the khans. For the purposes of this chapter, the periodization is somewhat simplified. Suffice it to say that notions of marriage were also very much influenced by coterminous changes in patterns of production, property management, and the flow of surplus.

Marriage in Times of the Khans: 1880–1965

From the beginning the village and its surrounds functioned as a small local tribe whose chief acted as a landlord who controlled land, water, and crops. The chief also siphoned surplus in the form of tributes, taxes, gifts, and rents for land; and acted as link between the village/ tribe and the government. Production (game, grain, legumes, onions; meat, wool, butterfat) was geared toward subsistence. People today remember poverty—the hard work and the cramped living quarters they shared with animals in smoke-filled stone huts and mud brick houses. They also recall violence in the form of raids and fights with other groups. The former chiefs' families assert that without the chiefs the peasants could not have held on to the land or learned to manage fields. In 1963 the last paramount tribal leader *(khan)* of Boir Ahmad was assassinated to end his resistance to the land reform. With his death the power of the chiefs crumbled, wars and raids ceased, and management of property and surplus changed.

In the traditional pastoral economy the strategies to produce a livelihood for oneself and surplus for the chief were segregated by sex. Men produced "status" goods like grain, meat, game, fruits, opium, and occasionally loot from raids. The chief taxed these products. Through his successes in these endeavors a man established his status, just as the khan established his status vis-à-vis other khans by the performance of his tribal peasants in producing goods he could use to feed his retinue and guests, and services for himself and in warfare.

Women created up to 90 percent of all daily necessities—more in times of want, less in times of plenty. They collected acorns and turned them into flour; and they gathered edible plants, berries, nuts, and, occasionally, locusts. They raised chickens; milked sheep, goats, and cows; and processed milk into yogurt, butterfat, and cheese. They spun wool, wove rugs and blankets, and sewed the bedding, as well as most clothes. They tanned hides, wove tent planes and bags (ranging from small toiletry bags to large transport-bags), made ropes, and knit socks. In the 1960s they started to grow tomatoes, corn, and greens. They brought up children and nursed the sick and the aged. A man could do none of these activities without a lot of explaining. There was almost no overlap in the two realms of production. Rather, production was complementary (men worked in the fields, women in the courtyard) or sequential (men managed herds, women milked; men cut wheat, women bundled it) with strong disapproval for transgressing gender lines.[11]

Similarly gendered were the processing and allocation of food. Except for milling wheat and hunting/slaughtering animals, women processed nearly all food. And except for meat and game, women allocated food within a hierarchy of provisioning based on status. Men's dependence on their wives for food even was a motif in folktales: a neglected or cuckolded husband was portrayed as a man whose wife did not feed him well. Processing food was a married woman's foremost everyday duty. It could make or break her reputation.

In this economy no man or woman could make it alone. Even blind or handicapped men "were given a wife," as people say, with the understanding that otherwise their very survival was in jeopardy, although their income was largely furnished through alms. People remembered that even a certain "ugly," pockmarked woman eventually was married to a widower in dire need of a housekeeper. But nobody took a wife without at least the tacit consent of the chiefs. Frequently, a chief arranged the marriage, for example rewarding a man for services by ordering another man to give him a daughter. Like other resources in this culture of scarcity, women were in short supply and were used like other dear commodities to the chiefs' and individual families' advantage. It was quite common to arrange a marriage before a child was born. The future groom's family assumed some expenses for food and clothes for the girl until she was old enough to be transferred to her future husband's household. This could take place as early as at six or seven years of age. A bride-price, negotiated between the boy's and the girl's fathers, "bought," so people said, the bride for the groom.[12]

The marriage contract, a short and routine document, was signed (or thumbprinted) by the bride's father during the wedding feast with the uninformed consent of the bride, who got new clothes, a small gift, and some gold or fake-gold coins sewed in front of her cap. The bride's father gave this with assistance from the groom's people. After the festivity bride and bridewealth were transferred to the groom's father's house. Sometimes the chief furnished the bridewealth for a peasant; sometimes women were exchanged between two families without a bride-price. In any case, the brides had no say in the arrangements, and their grooms had very little say. The chiefs' weddings were lavish feasts lasting several days to the music of local musicians, with guests from far and wide, and with displays of horsemanship and marksmanship. Among the chiefs' families girls were moved for alliance and other political purposes. These were less important for common tribesmen in the star-shaped relations to the chief: the chief's interests came first. In accordance with these economic interdependencies marriage was phrased as a man "acquiring a wife" just as one acquired other goods, and paying for her with the bride-price, and for a woman as consenting through her father to "make a husband" and to provide services for him and his people. In accordance with lineage preference, marriage of father-brother-daughter or else within the father's lineage was preferred, just as property was managed, divided, or fought over within the paternal group.

Most of the rare instances of polygyny among peasants were due to the levirate, a man's obligation to marry his dead brother's widow and to care for his children. Like all other products of a married woman, children were considered to be their father's property, a means to produce goods and services and—if sons—the next generation in his line. Thus they ought to stay in his family should he die. In case of divorce or a widow's exogamous remarriage, a mother lost her children: they stayed with their father's people.

In the times of the khans bride-price demands were small. One reason was that people were poor and nobody had luxury goods. Another was that an unusually high bride-price would attract the chief's attention just as a lavish wedding feast would: occasions were remembered when the chief demanded gifts from both families if he judged them to be "wealthy" by their wedding-related expenses, or else when a girl was given to an outside group. In this case her products and services were lost to her father and thereby to the chief. Wives produced sons for the husband's group and thereby workers for the chiefs. On this count daughters were seen as a loss to their father's group. The bride-price was explained in these terms: it was said to be a compensation for a father's expenses in raising a daughter for another family's ultimate benefit. This also is the explanation given in our textbooks. However, rarely did a father actually use the bride-price this way; rather, he was compelled by local custom to use it to buy the bridewealth for his daughter to enable her to discharge her wifely duties.

Several circumstances (but mostly so-called benign neglect of female infants) led to a numerical male-female imbalance in Boir Ahmadi (as elsewhere in Iran) in favor of males. Marriageable females were scarce. Parents tried to secure a future wife for their son as soon as possible. On the insistence of the groom and his parents, girls often were married off before menarche, and to much older men. Older women talking about their own wedding made the point that they had "no idea" what marriage meant before their wedding, that all they expected was to get new clothes and a necklace, and that there would be a feast; that they were frightened and horrified when they realized that they would not go home any more but live in another house with relative strangers. Under these circumstances there was no point in asking a girl if she agreed to a marriage: girls didn't know what it meant, and so their parents acted on their behalf. A further rationalization for the lack of input into this decision was that the postulated weak rationality in females makes girls poor judges of complex situations such as choosing a husband.

In their in-laws' houses these bride-children worked under the more or less benevolent guidance of their overworked mothers-in-law, as "servants," women said. Most older women remembered their own early marriages as a hardship marked by much work, little food, forced sex, and many pregnancies. Some girls ran away; a few others attempted or committed suicide. To this day there is a term used for young wives who develop an aversion to their husbands that can be overcome only by force or time, or may lead to divorce.

Marriage was taken to be an institution willed by God to make ordered life possible. It was not a choice but a commonsensical, inescapable duty. The local theory of sexuality was used ideologically, i.e., to explain the importance of marriage, to justify arranged marriages for very young people, and to justify women's subordination to men: marriage is needed to harness the potentially destructive sexual urges and powers all people, but especially women, are said to have. Economically as well as socially, an unmarried woman was in a precarious situation unless she had sons assuming responsibility for her material well-being and her conduct. Unmarried men and women were an anomaly unless they were very old. Infatuation outside of marriage was seen as a danger to the whole community. Villagers told the story of a chief punishing a young couple for fornication around 1920 by burning them. Ostensibly he was punishing a moral transgression; but obviously he also was making the point that copulation had to be sanctioned by him just as any other form of transaction leading to production had to be under his ultimate control.

Marriage after Land Reform and in the Post Pastoral Village: 1965–2000

With the land reform in the 1960s the tribal peasants of Deh Koh, who had challenged their chiefs' claim to landlordship for over a decade, became independent farmers, working their land now with full responsibility for the management of all production and distribution of products. The basic productive unit, the extended, composite, or nuclear family, did not change. Land was registered in the name of male heads of households. According to tribal law (and in contrast to Islamic law) daughters did not inherit; land and animals passed from fathers/men to sons/men. Men work herds and land, people explained, and men are responsible for feeding their families; clearly, men ought to be the sole owners.

This first attempt at capitalistic farming was both spurred and hindered by governmental policies such as cheap loans, promotion of cash crops, and price controls on crops. Most farmers lost the economic independence they had won in land reform to urban usurers who soon came to control a substantial part of the surplus produced. At the same time, the population exploded. All available land was put to the plow; pastures were overgrazed, land holdings fragmented; disputes over land and water increased. By 1969 it was painfully clear that the traditional village economy could not support the growing village population despite agricultural development.

By 1975 alternatives for making a living were well established. Seasonal and permanent wage labor inside but especially outside the village, as well as salaried jobs, trading, and crafts, were replacing agriculture. Cash-based transactions had replaced bartered and reciprocal economic arrangements. Farmers started to sell their animals as degraded pastures, rising costs of herding, and low meat prices made traditional animal husbandry unprofitable. The village expanded into former fields and gardens. High-yield apple orchards replaced earlier fruit trees. For the first time in the local history a rural class structure was emerging: few, more or less independent farmers; workers and the wives and children of migrant workers who themselves spent months or even years abroad; shopkeepers and artisans; a growing salaried middle class in governmental bureaucratic positions; a few professionals.

After the revolution of 1979 the incorporation of the tribal area into the state's economic and administrative structures accelerated. It brought outsiders to Deh Koh: teachers, doctors, administrators, shopkeepers. The first salaried people were teachers. With their income and ties to the city they became local opinion leaders for lifestyle, such as for the organization of wedding parties, and also for aspirations of young women. Public education, which in Deh Koh had started in the 1920s, now became seen as the best path to economic well-being in the absence of land and other capital. Like everywhere else in Iran, it produced the category of "unemployed high school graduate," followed, in the 1990s, by "unemployed college graduate": mostly young men who cannot find a suitable job or who try year after year to score high enough on the college entrance examination to be accepted at a university. Living with their families but only marginally participating in their fathers' enterprises, they are in a social and economic limbo.

Population pressure, a depressed economy, easy access to bank loans, increasing social stratification, and ambitions for a middle-class urban lifestyle make for a local economy that conforms to the national pattern of debts, high inflation, and a rapidly widening rift in the standard of living between a rich elite and the rest of the people. While about half of the households in Deh Koh now have a few chickens, goats, sheep, or a cow, and cultivate some land, only few live solely by farming. Surplus is turned into cash to buy ever-increasing varieties of imported goods or to pay back loans or provide necessities. Most villagers are either financially strapped employees or else belong to the rural proletariat. With few exceptions they subscribe to the consumer notion that who you are is what you own. In all social classes aspirations outpace resources.

When the chiefs' interests in marital arrangements of commoners no longer were of consideration, families had the sole responsibility for making reasonable matches. (A popular traditional mourning song says of a woman's untimely death: "Neither have I given my daughter away nor given a wife to my son.") As the locus of most production still was the household, sons and daughters continued to be seen mostly as workers, and the social relations of easy alienation from one's products and of subordination remained and carried over into marriage.

As access to cash rose, brideprice demands rose too, and a father's duty to provision his daughter prior to the wedding became more important for negotiations of status. While in earlier, poorer times all a girl could hope for was that her brideprice would buy a felt mat or a rug, a few pots and pans, bedding, and other domestic tools, now expectations rose to include appliances, fancy clothes, jewelry, and other luxury goods. A father who used most of the brideprice for himself, for example, to help a son to acquire a wife, or to repair his own house, risked being called stingy but also risked his daughter's future well-being—he signaled disinterest in his daughter or a concession of status to her in-laws. His daughter was truly "bought" with all the ownership connotations a purchase implies. But a father who spent more on his daughter's bridewealth than he had received as brideprice showed all and sundry that he valued his daughter and would watch her treatment in her husband's house. Thus, the politics of the brideprice were tied firmly into the economics of gender as well as into status competition between families.

Gifts to the bride and her close kin became more lavish as well. While gifts at weddings mostly were meant to benefit the young household, gifts given to a bride by her groom and his relatives—mostly gold jewelry—were meant to remain the young woman's personal property, an insurance against potential economic crises such as widowhood. In practice, however, a woman eventually passed the valuables on to her daughters, used them as obligatory gifts for her own daughters-in-law, or else was pressed into selling them when the household was in need of cash.[13] A wife who used her jewelry to fulfill one of her husband's obligations toward the family (such as paying for a new roof or a hospital stay) was said to be a "good" wife.

As valuable assets managed by their fathers, children continued to be spoken for, although their age at the time of a betrothal rose, especially for girls. The difference in the male:female ratio shrank as more female children survived due to the spread of modernist ideas about childhood, the sharp increase in the standard of living, and the proliferation of schools and health clinics. Contributions to the future bride's upbringing constituted an investment for a boy's family. A breach of promise on the girl's family's side inevitably led to arguments over the restitution of these contributions. Such breaches occurred more frequently now, sometimes because the girl successfully voiced objections but often because her parents found a better suitor—one with a salaried job, for example. Mainly for this reason, but also to gain another working member for the household, a young man's family would insist on the marriage contract to be written and signed as early as possible, with the wedding feast and the transfer of the bride to follow later. (Earlier, the marriage contract, a simple formality, was written and signed during the wedding feast.) The bride participated in the writing of the contract by saying "Yes" to it when it was read to her. No one ever said "No," although some had to be persuaded or forced to agree. The contracts became more elaborate now. For example, the size of severance pay to the wife in case of a divorce became more of an issue in marriage contract negotiations, although divorce remained rare.[14] High-status, well-off families demanded gold and money; very pious families or those who wanted to demonstrate that they thought the groom's family to be very trustworthy demanded a copy of the Qur'an or a nonsensical item such as a pound of fly-wings. "I don't know why we spend time on negotiating this," said a woman in 1973. "No wife has ever collected any money here!" Indeed, a wife who did not pardon the agreed-upon payment eventually—usually after the birth of the first child—was considered selfish. Yet, in line with the proliferation of economic choices and concomitant changes in the hierarchy positioning of individuals, including a wife's position in her husband's family, spelling out conditions in a contract became important.

Modeled after the grand weddings of the former chiefs, the villagers' wedding parties became larger and costlier, with musicians playing for dances, with ample food, and with target shooting and shows of horsemanship at the parties of the wealthier ones. The groom's family paid for them. Meat came from the family's herds and from game and local chickens; legumes, onions, almonds and walnuts, dried fruit, and wheat bread came from the family's larder; tea, sugar, and rice had to be imported as in earlier times, but now there had to be plenty of it. Relatives volunteered labor for hauling firewood and for cooking and serving food. As in earlier times, brides did not participate in the festivities but waited in their new tribal clothes in their father's house until they were taken away after the feast. The brideprice continued to be seen as an expression of ownership; with it, wives and their labor and products were "bought," as people say. It was unthinkable for people even as late as ten years ago that a man could get a wife for nothing. People argued that surely such a wife was lazy or clumsy, of no use economically, and lax in morals, and probably would refuse to have children.

Households tried to keep daughters-in-law "humble" so as to have docile, cheap workers and willing bearers of many children, especially boys. Yet, for all the hardships, women, especially those with half-grown children or young daughters-in-law who could be pressed into service, remembered the satisfaction their de facto importance brought. A woman who was well established in her in-law's house or lived neolocally (separate from in-laws) potentially had a lot of say at home as she converted her emotional and especially her economic importance into domestic power. Indeed, quite a few men were said to "listen to their wives" and to fare well doing so. A wise husband kept his wife at least satisfied enough to secure her cooperation: a dissatisfied wife could reduce the family's income, for example, by not weaving rugs the husband could sell. She even could leave and take refuge with her father, saddling her husband with the care of children, animals, and the house. The politics of domestic power revolved around a wife's contributions in these gendered economic enterprises.

Compared to the times when families moved with their herds through the pastures around Deh Koh, when women worked hard to keep up with their chores and men spent long hours moving among pastures, fields, and the village, the decades after 1965 meant easy living.[15] The transhumant lifestyle came to an end. Men sold their herds and found other sources of income, which meant that women no longer processed milk and wool. More food, especially rice, became available, although meat became scarcer as game dwindled. Most women stayed in Deh Koh throughout the year. Houses became more solid and spacious, with indoor plumbing and modern kitchens. A pipeline provided water. Electricity replaced kerosene lamps, and gas replaced open fires for cooking. Government loans allowed households to buy machine-woven rugs from the bazaars, kerosene stoves for heating in winter, clothes, and television sets. Gradually women found themselves with little to do at home and nearly no input in production. In most families men became the sole providers, buying food and goods imported from outside the village.

Many more children survived when immunizations and antibiotics became available. The decline of urgent economic tasks in the family economy beyond housekeeping made it possible for children to attend school. It was no longer a sign of good parenting to use children mostly as servants and apprentices or to marry daughters off early. By 1975 nearly all boys and girls in Deh Koh went to school; in 1990, a high school for girls was built in the village, and although the graduating classes still are only about 50 percent the size of those of the boys' high school, the push for higher education as the way to a salaried job led to a rise in marriage age for all. This happened despite the lowering of the legal marriage age for women from 16 to 9 in the Islamic Republic in accordance with the Qur'an. The first two women medical doctors from the village graduated in the mid-1990s, raising hopes, however unrealistic ones, for many schoolgirls. Both physicians married only after they had graduated from medical school, in their late twenties.

With changed aspirations and higher marriage age, young men quite definitely could express their preference for a mate as well as a job, and girls at the very least now were accorded their Qur'anic right to refuse a proposal of marriage. Indeed, quite a few girls acquired the dubious repute of naysayers. A young man no longer could count on marrying one of his father-brother's daughters or another girl relative, neither could a girl count any longer on one of her cousins to "come for her." The competition for spouses spanned a wider network.

In the expanding marriage market, however, local girls started to lose out as more and more young men spent time in towns and cities as workers, employees, students, or visitors, and found wives there. In addition to schooling for girls, this fact contributed to a household composition that, for the first time in the history of these people, included sexually mature but unmarried young women. There is no term for this age group—our term teenager has implications that don't apply. For example, while our teenage girls have considerable financial power and a wide range of movement, teenage girls in Deh Koh are completely dependent on their fathers and brothers financially, and practically confined to their courtyards because of propriety and village etiquette. Yet, at home there is little to do: mother, sisters, and a brother's wife share chores made easy by modern appliances. Before and after the revolution governmental agencies tried to teach local women cottage industry crafts, especially weaving rugs on vertical looms (in contrast to tribal ones), but because of the very low pay only few young women have taken it up.[16]

In tune with rising consumer expectations the brideprice rose even more. Even low-income families demanded enough money to buy "good" housewares, fancy bedding, an electric stove, a refrigerator, and furniture. Parents no longer rationalized it with the compensation theory but explained it as their wish to provide a comfortable house for their daughters' future family. Parental concern with the children's material well-being, with rapidly expanding expectations of what a well-appointed household should have, stood behind the brideprice. While it never had been easy to provide the brideprice, now it started to amount to a major economic burden.

In the near absence of agricultural production involving women, definitions of "good" wife now concentrated on homemaking and on taking care of children physically as well as spiritually. In the pronatal first decade of the Islamic Republic, the birthrate in Deh Koh almost reached a biological maximum. Young women with several young children were overworked in the new neolocal households. Children no longer were presented as an economic asset but as a heavy and costly responsibility, no longer as an inevitable product of married life but, through birth control devices, a choice. This shift in attitude was one of the main factors in the sudden and dramatic drop in the birthrate after 1993.[17]

Women's economic marginalization, the push for higher education, and the drastic drop in the birthrate had startling consequences for the philosophy of marriage. One was that schooling came to be seen as antithetical to marriage, especially for girls. "One either studies or keeps house for a man," said a young woman in eleventh grade. The few married women with jobs complained of the double burden of work and housework. People remembered that the first woman in Deh Koh who fought for a divorce successfully was a teacher. The underlying assumption is that marriage for girls is a confinement, an either-or proposition in regard to study and job. Numerous stories of spoken-for girls who were pressed into marriage by their impatient in-laws before they could finish high school supported, in the minds of the people, the incompatibility of early marriage and education. A young woman with aspirations other than marriage wisely declined entering even an engagement before she graduated. High school girls in the village deliberately kept themselves out of circulation in the streets as well as in the homes of relatives in order not to attract the attention of a young man or his scouts (his mother, sisters, friends) that would result in an unwanted proposal. Avoiding suitors became a strategy to save oneself the premature end to schooling or the embarrassment of rejecting a suitor. Stories of violence in Iran by jilted suitors against the women who had rejected them started to circulate.

Further dilemmas arose. While a young man and his family were eager to secure a wife who would have some income, they usually were too impatient to wait until the young woman finished her studies. The older a girl gets, people said, the greater becomes the likelihood that she will reject her suitor at the last moment, and the more education a girl has and the higher is her salary, the more insubordinate and demanding she will be as a wife. Young women said that holding a job as a married woman was hard, but that being without an income and entirely at the mercy of a husband was not good either. These conflicts were played out in many families: a brother would encourage a sister to study so as to find a job, attract a "good" husband, and thus have an "easier" married life, while for himself insisting on a young wife with too little education to be employable in order to be able to demand obedience and good housekeeping.

A girl whose father refuses suitors to spare her the hardship of household duties while a student will present his refusals as fatherly consideration for her well-being, while earlier everybody would have taken them as undue pride or as neglect of the fatherly duty to arrange a child's timely marriage. Being an unmarried, adult daughter "sitting at home," as people say, has lost much of its earlier social stigma, although it is a financial burden to the household.

As the standard of living rose together with household expenditures in the consumer-oriented new village, the brideprice changed into the "list": the bride and her parents composed a list of desired goods for the groom's family to buy. There was some haggling, compromises were reached, and men (even women) of both families went shopping. Bridewealth goods displayed at the wedding started to fill entire rooms. From the time of the verbal agreement or the drafting of the marriage contract to the actual wedding, the groom was expected to make gifts to the bride and her close family members. In some families, an engagement and the signing of the contract were marked with a party, and gifts were expected then. At the actual wedding the increase in relatives due to the population increase made it necessary to host several large lunch and dinner parties and many overnight guests. Guests at these parties were expected to contribute money to help defray the extraordinary costs of these feasts rather than bring gifts for the young couple.

At the wedding, the bride was dressed in white and made up by a professional beautician, which cost the groom dearly. Indeed, acquiring a wife became so expensive that by 1997 a young man spent well over a year's worth of his salary as a teacher on marriage-related expenses. He was, he said, "in debt for the next ten years." Unemployed and underemployed young men were postponing marriage because they could not afford it, and their fathers and brothers were unable or unwilling to help out. They said that just as a young man became independent financially as soon as he had a job, and just as he more or less chose his own wife, so he was largely responsible for his marriage-related expenses, too.[18] In addition, as his future wife no longer would be integrated into the domestic economy of his extended family, she would be his own responsibility in a neolocal household.

On the basis of these socioeconomic developments a new social phenomenon has emerged in Deh Koh and generally in Iran over the last generation: that of the aging "boy" (an unmarried man of any age) without a "house" of his own, and that of the unmarried mature daughter, i.e., the unmarried girl-student or girl-employee.[19] In most cases the single state only means that marriage is deferred. But this deferment brings with it a new life-cycle stage, especially for women, spanning between five and fifteen years: that of an adolescent female who, in the absence of a husband, continues to be her father's responsibility or else is beholden only to herself. It also changes the cognitive dimensions of marriage.

At puberty girls are considered to be "ripe" like ripe fruit (the same term, *raside*, is used) and thus to be ready for marriage. A girl who doesn't get married then will spoil—become dry and ugly, people say. (For males, this process is less obvious; even old men can sire children.) Thus, and until a generation ago, a girl who was not spoken for by the age of 14 was talked about. "Nobody wants her," people said. This was an indictment of either the parents who reneged on their matchmaking duty or else of unattractive qualities of the family. Well-meaning people likely explained her single state with: "It wasn't her fate yet to get married." This explanation implied the philosophical assumption that a woman's (more so than a man's) quintessential fate is timely marriage—that the conditions of a woman's marriage are "written on her forehead."

In traditional popular cosmology, sexual desires of men and women are a given. These desires and the longing for a spouse and children can be lawfully satisfied only within marriage. Marriage is normal and moral. But with the increasing number of unmarried young people these closely intertwined features have begun to unravel. There is, as yet, no young woman in Deh Koh who has insisted contractually on a childless marriage, but such cases are known to exist elsewhere. Young single women find that they can manage their sexual urges easier than apparently can young men, and that therefore the sexual satisfaction theory is a weak rationalization for marriage. They find that unlike earlier agricultural tasks the modern economic tasks are well within women's abilities, including the management of money. Men complain that their employed wives do not surrender their salaries and resist demands for services. Small wonder that the increasing number of young single people is seen by many as a sign that the God-willed order is breaking down.

As lifestyles no longer have to fit traditional rural economic activities and relations, urban-inspired, middle-class lifestyle expectations are replacing them. As yet, young people cannot articulate very well what they want out of marriage and spouse in the new economy. When I asked them directly, the most frequent answers were, for women regarding marriage: "A house, children, a good life." These were similar to those their grandmothers gave when I asked them two generations ago, but then the question itself was seen as absurd: all a girl could hope for was to be treated reasonably well in her in-laws' house; what she wanted was not an issue at all. Girls now look for a husband who "is good to talk to, pleasant to look at, reasonable and good-tempered, has a good income, and helps with housework." This is markedly different from two generations ago, when no young woman would tell me what she was looking for in a husband—she was not looking at all. Young men in regard to marriage answer like the women; in regard to wife, they say, "She ought to make my life comfortable; she ought to be beautiful; to be either silent or well-spoken and literate so that I can talk to her; to be a good housekeeper." Those with middle-class aspirations also wanted her to have a salary—a middle-class lifestyle necessitates at least two incomes in addition to restricting the number of children to one or two.

Thus a process of individuation has started to separate young men and women from their family's interests and management, which they had come to regard as confining. Indeed, the word "freedom" crept into discussions of marriage frequently, especially by women. By it they meant what we call autonomy—that is, a say in who to marry and in the contractual conditions of marriage, a say in how the household is run and money is spent, the permission to travel and to live without heavy-handed supervision by the husband and his family, and the right to divorce and to severance pay. Young women wanted this freedom, but young men, talking about their future wives, tended to see it as a threat to marital peace. However, as they demanded similar freedom from their own natal families in the course of the economic changes, this gender gap in expectations of marital "freedom" will get smaller. "The times of the oppressive khans are over," said a young woman student from Deh Koh. "Men have to realize this in their own homes, too."

But by the term freedom women also meant a lifting of the severe restrictions placed on them within the village in the name of tradition and morality. Women have come to take these rationalizations of confinement as what we would call an ideology: they are used to enforce the notion of women as the property of a family that claims rights to her loyal services. In this, urban (and ultimately, Western-) inspired relations and lifestyles furnish the most important models, just as the late-capitalist, consumer- and service-oriented Western economy furnishes the models by which the state and individual families try to run their affairs.

Notes

1. For discussions of this topic, see Bertaux and Thompson 1993; Friedl 1998; Leydesdorff 1996; Slyomovics 1998.

2. For example, Beck 1991; Betteridge 2000; Bradburd 1990; Friedl 1991; Hegland 1991; Tapper 1979; Wright 1978. Of the two exceptions, Haeri (1989) writes about a rare form of marriage, and Mir-Hosseini (1993) about court cases. There does not exist a book on Iran like Lindisfarne's (1991) on Afghanistan or Mundy's (1995) on Yemen.

3. For example, Amirshahi 1995; Farman Farmaian 1992; Guppy 1988; Kordi 1991. Sullivan's edited volume (1991) has relevant contributions by several Iranian writers.

4. Transhumant pastoralists are based in a village from which they move with their herds to pastures in season. They also may cultivate some fields.

5. For a discussion of this shift, see Friedl 2001. Tellingly, there does not yet exist a term for a sexually mature, unmarried woman (our "single woman"). The term *dokhtar* is used, but with increasing reluctance: this term implies virginity rather than unmarried status in contrast to *zan*, which implies married status, i.e., a female who, lawfully, is not a virgin.

6. For life in this village, see Friedl 1991, 1997; Loeffler 1988. Within the province of Kohgiluye-Boir Ahmad, Deh Koh always has been taken as being a little ahead of other communities in terms of development, but not as atypical in any way. To what degree the findings from Deh Koh can be generalized for all of Iran only comparative research can establish. My observations during visits in other areas of Iran lead me to suggest that on the level of analysis I employ in this chapter, the similarities outnumber the differences.

7. There are many indications that the pastoral-transhumant Boir Ahmadi replaced earlier sedentary, fully agricultural villages. But these and even earlier settlements are of no concern to us here; they did not influence the lifestyle of the new inhabitants. While hunting was a very important source of food in the past, it all but stopped after 1960, because by then game was hunted almost to extinction. Koelz (1983) describes the rich Zagros environment in 1940.

8. We stayed in Boir Ahmad between 1965 and 2000 twelve times, for altogether some seven years. Various stages of our research were supported by the Wenner Gren Foundation for Anthropological Research, the Oriental Institute of Chicago, the Social Science Research Council, the National Endowment of the Humanities, and Western Michigan University. I am much indebted to their generosity.

9. For the history of local peasant-chief relationships, see Loeffler 1971.

10. "Extended family" refers to married and unmarried brothers and their father, mother, wives, and children living and working together. Until recently, in Boir Ahmad this was seen as an ideal but as practically unstable and problematic. Indeed, the internal dynamics of extended families produces continuous shifts in household compositions as daughters marry out, sons bring in wives, and nuclear families split off to grow into the next generation of extended households. See Friedl and Loeffler 1994 for a description of this process. In the wake of modernization and changes in the local economy, the preferred postmarital residence in Deh Koh over the past forty years shifted from a patrilocal to a neolocal one, but nuclear families always had their own room (or rooms) whenever space was available. At or soon after a wedding, the young couple moved into a separate room, even if farming, food prepa-

ration and consumption, and household chores were shared with other members of the household. For us of interest, because it has to do with marriage, is the most frequent explanation given for breakups of extended families: brothers' wives don't get along with each other and press for separation of the households.

"Composite family" refers to a polygynous household. This always has been a rare arrangement among poor peasants, for economic reasons if no other. Polygyny itself is considered stressful: cowives are said to get along only rarely. A "lineage" comprises people related to each other patrilineally, through men only, and claiming a common ancestor. The most powerful lineages are those of the former paramount chief and, a rung lower, those of the various tribal chiefs and chiefs of tribal subgroups. In Deh Koh, lineages to this day hold the rights to water separate from rights to land. Unless a marriage is endogamous within the patrilineage, wives are outsiders in their husbands' group and give birth to children who belong to their father's group. As the economy drifted away from agriculture, and political relations away from the tribal organization, lineages lost importance in everyday life.

11. By and large women's participation in agricultural production over the past hundred years has increased, while traditional agriculture as such has become of much less importance to individual households' economies. See Friedl 1981.

12. "Bridewealth" refers to the goods a bride brings to the marriage. Usually it is provided by the bride's father with money or goods from the groom or his family—the "bride-price" for the bride.

13. For similar uses of gold in Palestine, see Moors 2000.

14. Islamic as well as tribal law at that time made it nearly impossible for a wife to ask for divorce. Although a man could divorce his wife easily, local custom, family pressure, and the strict division of labor worked against divorce. Childlessness in Deh Koh rarely led to divorce, although this is given as the first reason in the rationalization of the possible necessity of divorce. See also Afshar 1998.

15. I am fully aware of the controversy surrounding these dates: the politically correct opinion is that the 1960s and 1970s were especially bad for rural areas in Iran. This is demonstrably not true for Deh Koh and the tribal area. Deh Koh got water, electricity, health care, an asphalt road, and schools long before the revolution. In the cases I know, rural emigration, which is taken as a sign of governmental neglect of villages by many social scientists, largely was a function of an increase in population reaching the point where agricultural land no longer was available locally; the availability of work in cities; and of the expanding network of public transportation.

16. See Friedl forthcoming.

17. This drop partly was due to the new understanding of children as individuals (rather than as property-wards of their fathers) and to the perceived

need for costly education as the only path to economic well-being. The government's heavy propaganda for birth control played on these concerns, was motivated by sheer economic necessity, and directed children away from serving the productive family unit and toward serving themselves and the state.

18. Young men with an income still have considerable obligations toward their younger siblings and elderly parents. But these obligations no longer are taken for granted, as they were earlier, when fathers, sons, and paternal kinsmen were expected to cooperate closely.

19. See note 5.

III

Family and the Praxis of Islamic Law

8

Adjudicating Family: The Islamic Court and Disputes between Kin in Greater Syria, 1700–1860

Beshara Doumani

It is difficult to overestimate the importance of the Islamic court and its archives to the history of family life in the urban centers of the Ottoman Empire. As the central institution in charge of, among other things, matters relating to personal status and property, the Islamic court constituted the principal legal arena for negotiating and legitimizing the ceaseless reconfiguration of property access rights, kinship relations, and lines of authority both within and between urban families. The voluminous records generated over the centuries by the Islamic courts contain a wealth of information that makes it possible to track specific families and their activities over long periods of time. For the social historian, these archives allow a reading concerned with recovering the role of local agency in the social construction of contemporary notions of kinship, property, and sexual difference that the family, defined as a set of understandings governing relations between kin, is both the crucible for and the product of.[1]

At the same time, any reading for content must take into account that these notions were not simply brought in by litigants and then deposited or reflected in the archives of the Islamic courts. Rather, and in the very process of producing the summaries of the cases that the historian reads, they were reworked and molded to fit into the legal language and scribal codes of an institution that served both as a court based on Islamic law and as a public records office of sorts. Every type of document copied into the records (s. *sijill*) of the Islamic court—whether real-estate transactions, probate inventories, lawsuits, *waqf* (religious trusts) endowments, orders from the imperial capital or numerous others—was precisely that: a type. It was a text with specific form, structure, and set of underlying assumptions that precedes the details of the people and issues brought before the court. Consequently, the social content that the family historian looks for is already discursively embedded in larger discourses of power and authority.[2] This does not mean that these documents can tell us no more than the story of their own production as texts and, by implication, that there is no reality outside of the documents. Rather, one could argue that recovering a fuller sense of the "real" demands attention to both form and content and how they changed over time. Ideally, such a multilayered reading would also build bridges between legal history, social history (broadly defined), and the ethnography of archives as a cultural product.

By way of making a small step in that direction, this chapter tentatively explores the mutually constitutive relationship between kin and court as revealed in lawsuits (s. *da'wa*) between individuals related by blood and/or marriage litigated in the Islamic law courts of Tripoli (Lebanon) and Nablus (Palestine) during the early eighteenth century and the first two-thirds of the nineteenth.[3] The word "adjudicating" in the title is used in a double sense. First, it is used in the same sense that one would describe one's kin as "demanding," "calculating," or "boring." The purpose here is to underscore the fact that kin routinely resorted to the Islamic court as a forum to enact or perform legally sophisticated property consolidation and devolution strategies, often through lawsuits. In so doing, they partially defined the role of the court as a social institution, shaped its archives, and influenced the praxis of Islamic law. At the same time, kin had to take into account, among other things, the legal procedures of the court and its perceived authority (personified by the judge) as a state-sponsored and religiously based institution. Second, therefore, the word "adjudicating" is used in a verb form to highlight the active authority of the judge in rendering legal decisions in lawsuits between kin as well as the discursive authority of Islamic legal norms in setting the parameters for the negotiation of power and property relations between kin, in particular, and in the construction of kinship as a set of legal and cultural understandings, in general. Consequently, the analysis in this chapter, constantly shifts back and forth between what these lawsuits can tell us about family life in these two cities and what they reveal about the stories that are likely to be authorized by the Islamic court records as a specific kind of archive. This is not to say that one can be separated from the other, but for heuristic purposes, the search for connections between the two modes of reading the documents—thus, interpreting the past—must presuppose their distinctiveness.

This double reading is partially enabled by the application of two methodologies of scale. The first is a micro analysis of two sets of lawsuits, both from Nablus, as case studies for raising the following themes: the connections between gender, Islamic legal praxis, and property consolidation and devolution strategies; struggles between kin over the control of domestic space; and the question of authority within families as revealed by the ways that kinship as well as individual kin are legally represented in court. The second is a macro analysis of court records as an archival genre, by way of a comparative examination of the specific characteristics of the Islamic court records of Nablus and Tripoli. The aim here is to locate lawsuits within the overall topography of the Islamic court records, and then to look for patterns in form and content over both space (two urban centers) and time (two periods a century apart).[4]

Locating Lawsuits

The form and content of court records are deeply influenced by the specific political economy of each urban center and by the class, ethnic, and religious composition of its population. A city's particular cultural currents and its degree of integration into the imperial center also mattered, as did the issue of whether the judges were native sons with local knowledge and axes to grind or foreign civil servants rotated on an annual basis. Indeed, how often the court was used, by whom, and for what purpose constantly changed, as did the personnel of the court and the way they perceived and performed their tasks. This held especially true during periods of intense local conflict, foreign invasions, and the implementation of various waves of Ottoman reforms.[5] No safe generalizations can be made prior to a thorough mapping of all the court records, which will inevitably raise still other factors that can affect the historically contingent role of the Islamic court as a sociolegal and administrative institution. Keeping these qualifications in mind, some general methodological notes about the structure of lawsuits and patterns over time and space can be made.

In both Nablus and Tripoli, a typical lawsuit is a brief summary of the relevant legal matter to be decided and its resolution, not a thick description of courtroom drama. The basic narrative structure—which remained virtually the same over the course of the eighteenth and nineteenth centuries—is deceptively simple. After listing the plaintiffs and defendants, a short statement by the former is denied, qualified, or accepted by the latter; then witnesses are called and a decision rendered. It is as if the entire matter was resolved in one short sitting, even though it is fairly certain that lawsuits often spanned several days as witnesses were marshaled and vetted, legal council approved and, in some cases a legal opinion (*fatwa*) by a juris-consult (*mufti*) commissioned. In the absence of detailed protocols describing these stages in the proceedings, one must look for related documents (usually not available) and pay careful attention to subtle clues, silences, and inconsistencies in order to tease out the connections and dynamics between the litigants, witnesses, legal representations, and other individuals involved. Since the outcome of the majority of lawsuits was decided prior to the appearance of the litigants before the judge, precious few clues are provided about the motivation, timing, choice of legal strategies, and how the dispute was actually resolved. One cannot, furthermore, claim that lawsuits reflect the types and frequency of disputes in the society as a whole, for most conflicts did not reach the court and not all court records have survived.

Still, lawsuits do provide a fair amount of information about the relationships between the litigants and about a property's history or genealogy.[6] It is not unusual, moreover, to come across several lawsuits triggered by an unexpected moment of transition, such as the untimely death of a rich merchant without surviving male children in their legal majority. The numerous court appearances that ensue come to involve an ever-widening circle of related individuals over matters such as inheritance, validity of kinship ties, debt, and ownership of residential properties.[7] This information can be used to reconstitute family and business relations and the place of a specific household in the wider community. In addition, when compared to most other types of cases registered in the court records, lawsuits are less rigidly formulaic in structure and broader in scope in terms of the issues introduced than, say, purchase and sale documents. They are also less predictable and involve a larger and more diverse set of individuals than most other types of cases. In relative terms, they are also less successful in completely erasing the voices of the actors.[8] Litigants do have a say on how they are represented in the court and, within limits, in choosing the legal strategies to be pursued. Sometimes litigants who are not satisfied with the results of a lawsuit take the case to a different court, or raise the same issue again but under different legal grounds by hiding some things and foregrounding others, depending on the circumstances.[9] Still others take advantage of the arrival of a new judge to reinitiate legal action.[10]

Lawsuits hold special promise for historians, because there are a large number of them spread over long periods of time. In both Nablus and Tripoli during the 1720s, lawsuits averaged 21 percent and 16 percent, respectively, of the total number of documents registered in the Islamic court records. They are only superseded, in fact, by registrations of purchases and sales of immovable properties (40 percent and 31 percent for Nablus and Tripoli, respectively)—easily the most common type of document in the Islamic court records of almost every urban center in the Ottoman domains. The situation changes markedly by the nineteenth century, especially for Nablus, where the number of lawsuits for the first six decades combined is actually less than the number registered for a six-year period in the 1720s! This decline is even more noticeable when we take into account the fact that the population of Nablus grew significantly during this period. As for Tripoli, a sample based on a volume for the years 1815–16 shows that lawsuits became the fourth most frequent type of case, accounting to about 10 percent of the total: that is, also a decline, albeit a less precipitous one than that of Nablus.[11] The reasons for this change are not clear.[12] In any case, it seems that studies based on lawsuits are more likely to find richer sources in the early as opposed to the late Ottoman centuries.

The Social Uses of Lawsuits

Aside from the Islamic court there were many authorities, official and unofficial, that individuals could turn to for conflict resolution during the early eighteenth century. These range from senior members within families to heads of artisan and merchant guilds, and neighborhood associations. This is not to mention a large body of religious and secular authorities such as Sufi orders and local governors. It is pertinent to ask, therefore, who resorted to the Islamic court for lawsuits and why. Generally speaking, a wide range of propertied urban individuals—male and female, Muslim and non-Muslim, rich and barely scraping by—had occasion to sue each other in court. Merchants, shopkeepers, artisans, and local religious notables tend to be overrepresented, while the two extremes of the social pyramid—unskilled workers and poor migrants on one end and the top political families, on the other—are generally underrepresented. Peasants appear only occasionally, and usually hail either from villages adjacent to the city or from the larger villages that serve as the headquarters for leading rural families.[13]

There is a difference between the two cities when it comes to the sex of the litigants. Women in Tripoli, for example, appeared as litigants in 52 percent of the lawsuits compared to roughly one-third in

Nablus. This difference generally holds true for most types of cases in the court records as well as over time. For example, between 1800 and 1860, 47 percent of all *waqfs* established in Tripoli were endowed by women. The number for Nablus is less than 12 percent. Elsewhere I put forward a partial explanation for this phenomenon based on a political economy perspective, which argued that women in Tripoli had a much more substantive involvement in the productive dimensions of the city's economy, especially in horticulture.[14] This does not mean that women in Tripoli and Nablus went to the court for the same reason and only differed in terms of frequency. In both cities women are disproportionately represented as litigants in lawsuits between kin. Remarkably, the percentage (53 percent) is exactly the same for both. The difference is that women in Tripoli appear more frequently in lawsuits between nonkin.

A very significant pattern, true for both cities, is that women are more likely to appear as plaintiffs than as defendants. This indicates that the court was perceived as an important forum for affirming the legal rights of women, especially to inheritance. That does not mean, necessarily, that women took the lead in initiating lawsuits. Their husband, son(s), brother(s) or other male relatives may have had a stake in pursuing legal action. Still, it is striking that women in Nablus are at least twice as likely to sue men in court than the other way around. In Tripoli, the ratio of female plaintiffs to female defendants is somewhat more balanced (3:2). The general impression is that gender issues were more central to property and inheritance disputes in Nablus than in Tripoli.

As to the kinds of disputes brought before the court, there is little difference between these two cities during the early eighteenth century. The vast majority (55 percent and 51 percent for Nablus and Tripoli, respectively) are disputes over immovable property and *waqf* access rights; and most of those involve at least one set of litigants whose claim rests on inheritance. The remaining lawsuits include commercial disputes, usually over debt; criminal cases, mostly theft but also murder; conflicts over space and claims of *shuf'a* (right of purchase) between neighbors; and litigation concerning divorce or validity of marriage contracts.[15] The only noticeable difference is the change over time, at least in Nablus. It is not clear why, but by the nineteenth century neighbors no longer turned to the court to settle disputes over space. The dramatic descriptions of a judge walking across town accompanied by master builders and a crowd of witnesses and onlookers in order to personally inspect the location of a disputed window, staircase, door, gutter, smokestack, or newly installed wall fade away from the records as one moves forward in time.

Two other types of disputes—rare in the eighteenth century and not appearing at all in the nineteenth century records—are those seeking damages to reputation and person caused by curses and epithets, as well as those claiming that pregnant women suffered a miscarriage due to sudden fright caused by loud threats or other actions by nonfamily members. In any case, it seems that the moral authority of the court when it comes to policing public behavior and public spaces had diminished by the nineteenth century.

Contrary to expectations, kin did not shy away from suing each other publicly in court. In Nablus and Tripoli during the 1720s, the incidence of lawsuits between kin is remarkably similar, averaging exactly 37.5 percent of the total number of lawsuits in both cities. For Nablus during the 1798–1860 period, the rate is roughly the same, at 39 percent. The average for Tripoli during the nineteenth century is yet to be determined, but a small one-year sample (1815–16) yielded a quite large figure of 61 percent. The frequency of lawsuits between kin allow historians to trace several patterns, including who sues whom, over what, and the ways individual kin are represented in court. These patterns make it difficult to distinguish between agency and representation. Perhaps precisely for that reason, they also provide us with clues about the mutually constitutive relationship between kin and court, especially when it comes to the contemporary notions of property and gender. In this respect, the two case studies below, both from 1720s Nablus, point to some issues that may merit further research.

When Two Families Collide

Two lawsuits involving the exact same set of plaintiff's and defendants—three brothers and their two maternal uncles, respectively—were brought before the judge of the Nablus Islamic court a few days apart during the first week of November 1725.[16] In the first case, the plaintiffs (Dawud, Mustafa, and Hamad, sons of the deceased Khalid al-Badawi) claim that over eighteen years earlier, the defendants (Hijazi and Awad, sons of the deceased Musa Za'rur) appropriated properties that they, the plaintiffs, legally inherited from their mother, Hamida (see figure 14). The defendants countered that they purchased these properties almost exactly twenty years earlier on 6 December 1706 from their brother-in-law, the plaintiffs' father, soon after Hamida died. They pointed out that the father sold both his and his children's legal inheritance of these properties for the sum of thirty piasters in order to pay for the expenses (*nafaqa*) of raising his five children, then all in their legal minority. Moreover, they continued, and as plainly stated

in the sales deed that they submitted to the court, it was legally established prior to the sale that the children's shares of the inherited property were of no benefit to them *(baᶜda an thabata anna al-hisas al-marquma
laysa fiha nafᶜun li al-qasirin)*.

The plaintiffs, fully prepared for that line of defense, countered
with a sophisticated and multipronged legal argument. They began by
acknowledging that the sale by their father of his share of the inheritance (one-quarter of the shares of the disputed properties) was law-
ful. But, they continued, the same was not true of his sale of the shares
of his five children, for two reasons. First, they claimed that the sale
constituted *ghubn fahish* (a legal term describing criminal fraud). The
accusation made here is that the price that their maternal uncles paid
for the properties in question was far less than the fair market value.
Second, they argued that there was no legal justification for this sale,
because other properties they inherited from their mother was sufficient to provide for their needs until they attained their legal majority
*(wa anna walidatahum khallafat lahum athathan wa tarikat takfihim li
munatihim wa li-taribiyyatihim ila hina bulughihim)*.

The defendants denied both allegations and demanded proof. In
response, the plaintiffs produced two witnesses who corroborated their
claims.[17] The witnesses, Salim and Ali, sons of Salama al-Badawi, were
agnates of the plaintiffs and could hardly be expected to testify against
them. The judge accepted the credibility and validity of the witnesses
and their testimony. He then ruled that the father's sale of his own
share of the disputed property was legal, but that his sale of his
children's share was invalid in that it constituted criminal fraud *(ghubn
fahish)*. He also noted the absence of a legal justification. He ordered
the defendants to return these shares and not to challenge the plaintiff's
rights in this matter. Finally, he specified the form of the return exchange: the defendants were to deposit the price of the shares into the
inheritance estate of Khalid al-Badawi, the plaintiffs' father, who must
have died shortly prior to these court appearances. In laying out the
legal grounds for his decision, the judge referred to a *fatwa* commissioned by the plaintiffs for this very case.[18]

In the second lawsuit, the same plaintiffs claimed that for more
than eighteen years their maternal uncles illegally withheld from them
the revenues of their mother's share in a joint *waqf* established by their
great maternal grandfather and his brother almost eight decades earlier (i.e., 1648). The value and size of shares under dispute in this case
are far more considerable than the properties involved in the previous
one and constituted a real threat to the material base of the defendants. This time, however, the defendants possessed the strongest
possible legal protection against outside claims to these properties: a

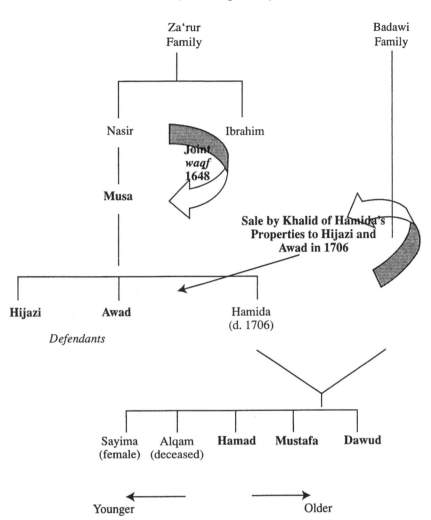

Figure 14. Property Flows: The Zaʿrur and Badawi Families (plaintiffs and defendants in bold)

waqf endowment deed. The defendants countered that the plaintiffs were not entitled to any revenues from these endowed properties, because one of the conditions of the *waqf* was that the children of the endowers' female descendents (*awlad al-butun*) were to be excluded as beneficiaries. In their statement, they noted the exact date of the endowment and the name of the judge that validated it with his seal. These are the two archival keys needed to authenticate their claim in the court's own records and could only be known to those in possession of or having intimate familiarity with the original deed (in Nablus, the judge's name and his seal would only appear on the original deed). When the plaintiffs challenged the existence of this condition, the defendants did not produce the endowment deed, but rather requested that the judge examine the court's records. The judge proceeded to do so and, when he retrieved the court's copy of the *waqf* endowment, he read the entire document aloud word for word. Then, without calling witnesses, he ruled in favor of the defendants.

This case departs from the typical narrative of a lawsuit in two important ways. To begin with, rendering a judgment without resorting to the oral testimony of credible witnesses is puzzling in that written words, standing alone, are not legally sufficient proof. From the perspective of literary analysis, moreover, the strategic location of the judge's oral performance of the written text immediately prior to his ruling *(hukm)* highlights the power of the judge and gives the impression that this power can somehow be a legitimate substitute for a legal requirement.[19] Also unusual is the request by the defendants that the judge consult the official memory of the court. In *waqf* dispute cases, the original deed (or a court-authenticated copy of such a deed, which can be obtained through a legal procedure) is, more often than not, presented by one of the parties as corroboration of claims made. It is not clear why in this instance the defendants chose a different strategy. Perhaps they were no longer in possession of the original deed or did not go through the trouble and expense of the authentication process.[20] Regardless, the combination of these two atypical features, at least when it comes to *waqf* disputes that occasion the most frequent resort to documentation, highlight the importance of access to, as well as the oral performance of, official textual memory to the mutually constitutive relationship between the court and the people who use it.

Patterns

These two lawsuits are typical of five important patterns in legal disputes between kin in Nablus and Tripoli during the early eighteenth century and, perhaps, for the Ottoman period as a whole. First, virtually all disputes between kin are over access rights to immovable property. Second, the vast majority of those revolve around the same two claims of access to property raised in the two lawsuits above: inheritance (56 percent for Nablus and 51 percent for Tripoli) and, to a lesser extent, beneficiary status in *waqf* endowments (14 percent and 25 percent, respectively). The percentages are even higher for the nineteenth century, amounting to 66 percent (inheritance) and 15 percent (*waqf*) for Nablus during the 1798–1860 period, which is almost identical to Tripoli (64 percent and 15 percent, respectively) during the sample year of 1815–16. There can be no clearer evidence that the Islamic court was resorted to by kin primarily as an arbitrator of property devolution.

Third, and most interesting, is the presence of two ingrained narrative structures identical to the two lawsuits in this case study. In roughly half of all inheritance disputes in Nablus (52 percent) and Tripoli (44 percent), the defendants claim that the property in question was already sold to them before or shortly after the death of the person whom the plaintiffs are the legal inheritors of.[21] As to lawsuits about *waqf* revenues, the most common rebuttal (very common in Nablus, less so in Tripoli) is that the *waqf* endowment specifically excludes the descendants of the female children of the endower. This does not mean that reality corresponded to these two patterns in the court records. Rather, these two narratives are so common as to suggest that kin and court have, over the Ottoman centuries, developed a symbiotic relationship to the point that no easy distinction can be made between actual disputes and legal strategy. Indeed, the sheer number of such cases is a strong indication that the existence of the court and its specific role in society are already presupposed as an integral, if not central, part of property devolution strategies as well as litigation over such strategies. This has the effect of making specific actions that short-circuit the normative operations of Islamic law when it comes to inheritance seem natural, familiar, believable, and inevitable. Since no legal documents are required as proof, only the testimony of two credible male witnesses, perceptions about the "normality" of such actions carried tremendous weight.[22]

Fourth, a considerable number of legal disputes between kin are over properties that pass through the female, not male, line (the properties under dispute in the first lawsuit are those of Hamida, a female who married outside her family). One should not jump to the conclusion, however, that the vulnerability of property to conflicting claims is due solely or even primarily to gender. The preponderance of such cases in the court records may be explained by the fact that the Islamic court could be counted on to uphold the right of women and their descendants to property in the face of opposing local customs and cultural ideals. Since the Islamic law court represented the best line of defense for those whose claims rest on access through the female line, it is not surprising that its records would reflect the fact that legal inheritors of females are the most likely to show up in its chambers: a classic example of the mutually constitutive relationship between kin and court.[23]

The fifth and final pattern is that lawsuits between in-laws are the most frequent in both Tripoli (45 percent) and Nablus (34 percent) during the early eighteenth century. The implication here is that marriage strategies produced the most tension between kin, at least the kind of tension amenable to greater involvement by the Islamic law courts. The plaintiffs in the above two lawsuits challenged an established, albeit frequently contested, social practice and cultural ideal in Nablus that defines family in relation to certain types of property as male. That is, access to a family's principal residence and key revenue-producing properties should remain within the male line of that family even if this means excluding individuals who, according to Islamic law, have a legal right to inherit or benefit from these properties. The underlying dynamic operating in these two lawsuits, in other words, is a property reconsolidation strategy by the defendants designed to stem the fragmentation resulting from marriages between (as opposed to within) families as defined by the male line. A key difference between the two cities is that in Nablus we find clear evidence for an additional reconsolidation strategy: namely, the concentration of property within each branch as defined by the male line.[24] The key indication here is the high frequency of disputes in Nablus between agnates, especially between paternal uncles and nephews, between paternal cousins, and between siblings. This is significant, considering that disputes between in-laws are more likely to be litigated in court than disputes between agnates.

The pervasiveness of both strategies is one reason why one must question a rather common assumption about the economic role of women during the Ottoman period: i.e., that the large-scale involvement of women in property transactions is a clear indication of their economic clout. If one makes a distinction on the basis of whether women are the sellers or the buyers, it becomes clear that few women bought property, but many sold it, usually willingly and most often to their agnates.[25] If one were also to trace how these women came to acquire the property being sold, the vast majority of cases would show that they tended to sell property they inherited as opposed to property they received as dowry (*mahr*) or property that they purchased earlier. Finally, the kind of properties being exchanged, as argued in the next section, is of crucial importance.

The Genealogy of Property

It is not surprising that Hamida's widower sold both his and his children's share of those immovable residential and income-producing properties inherited by his wife from her father. After all, he may have fully shared the view that "family property" should stay within the male line and was not willing, therefore, to stand in the way of the reconsolidation efforts of his brothers-in-law. Even if he thought otherwise, the specific character and genealogy of these properties limited his room for maneuver. For one thing, they were in a state of extreme fragmentation: many pieces, each fairly minuscule in size.[26] Worse, if he did not sell, they would have to be further subdivided between six individuals.

But there were other, more formidable limitations. The Zaʿrurs, he must have known, were no strangers to aggressive reconsolidation strategies precipitated by, among other things, this cyclical threat of fragmentation. After all, the disputed properties had passed intact within the male line of the Zaʿrur family for at least three generations, an accomplishment that takes a strong commitment to a particular vision of family and property as well as persistence and skill in maneuvering through the legal terrain. The two brothers who first accumulated these properties and then endowed one-third to over one-half of each as a family *waqf* in 1648 laid a solid foundation. This action proved decisive in keeping key revenue-producing properties within the Zaʿrur male line and in beating back a challenge from the Badawi family seventy-seven years later. Just as important, perhaps, is the fact that many of the agricultural properties were either jointly owned or under long-term lease by commercial partners or tenants of the Zaʿrur family.[27] Thus, these properties were already enmeshed in a web of access rights that would make it very difficult for outsiders who did not enjoy a close relationship with the partners and tenants to establish a foothold.

Finally, the properties under dispute included shares of the principal residence of the defendants: i.e., the property that symbolized and embodied the very possibility of a family's existence and that identified the family as a corporate unit in the social and physical topography of the city.[28] Indeed, principal residences are the sites of the most frequent and hard-fought battles between kin. Khalid Al-Badawi could not hope to move himself and his children into the Zaʿrur family residence nor to embark on a campaign to accumulate enough shares to give him any significant weight in the decision-making process of how this property was used. The extreme importance attached to erecting barriers—legal, political, or otherwise—that can protect a family's principal residence and key productive properties accounts for the defendants' immediate purchase of what their sister had inherited from their father. In fact, it is almost certain that it was at the buyer's insistence that Khalid al-Badawi obtained, before the completion of the sale, a legal authorization from the court affirming both the

justifiability of the sale and the lack of benefit of these properties to
the children. Although ultimately unsuccessful as preemptive strikes
against possible future objections to the 1706 sale, both legal maneuvers illustrate the key importance many families attached to the role
of the Islamic court in the reconfiguration of kinship and property
relations.

Beyond the Material

What is surprising, therefore, is not the sale itself but the fact that its
validity was challenged twenty years later by Khalid al-Badawi's sons,
who, even more brazenly, also challenged the key anchor of the Za'rur
family's property holdings: the *waqf* endowment. True, they stood on
firm legal ground in the first lawsuit, and they were compensated. But
the effort and expense involved in forming a united front, designing
a rather intricate legal strategy, and paying more than a little money
to secure a favorable *fatwa* in advance, not to mention court fees—all
must have amounted to more than what they stood to recover in
proceeds from the minuscule shares that their father had sold. Even
harder to explain is the second lawsuit. While it is conceivable that the
plaintiffs were unaware of the specific condition that excluded them,
they could not be blind to the fact that the overwhelming majority of
waqf endowments in Nablus—before, during, and after the 1720s—
included such a condition. After all, they made it their business to
become acquainted with all the possible legal implications of the sale
that they so effectively invalidated.

    Why did they go through all this trouble? And why did they wait
so long? There is little doubt that it was the death of their father,
Khalid al-Badawi, that determined the timing and made legal action
possible. Even though they reached their legal majority several years
prior to the initiation of the lawsuits, the three brothers, as long as
their father was alive, did not have the legal, moral, or political (in the
wide sense of the word) authority to challenge an injustice they claim
to have been visited upon them. First, it seems that the father had a
legal right to declare that one or more of his children had not reached
the stage of *rushd* or legal maturity that would allow them to press for
certain rights. According to Hanafi law, this prerogative remains in
the father's hand indefinitely.[29] A second possibility is that the brothers were unwilling to press a challenge to the status quo due to the
respect and deference they felt or had to display towards their father
and/or to avoid the public and humiliating spectacle of dragging him
to court and accusing him of criminal fraud and of putting money
ahead of his children's best interests. Finally, it is a fact that the key

to their victory in the first lawsuit was the testimony of two witnesses who happened to be their agnates. It is doubtful that they would have been able to persuade them to testify over their father's objections or to override his testimony about the fairness of the sale.

As to the question of why, I have no answers, though I suspect that their motivation went beyond material gain. Perhaps the death of the father signaled a change in the lines of authority within the Badawi family and created an opportunity to redefine the place of that family in wider social circles. Through these two lawsuits, one could plausibly speculate, the three brothers essentially served notice that they could rise to a challenge, could act in concert, and could marshal both material and political capital to pursue their objectives. In so doing, they would consolidate their position within the Badawi family and make it clear to all, now that the patriarch was dead, that this family was under new management. Whatever the motivation(s), the central point remains: notions of family and property are, as is clear in this case, constituted and transformed in the very process of litigation.

From Brothers to Branches: The Sanunu Family

The male members of the three branches of the Sanunu family—as defined by descent through the male line of a common ancestor two generations removed, Shaykh Abdullah al-Munir Sanunu—gathered in large numbers in the Islamic court of Nablus on three occasions late in 1724.[30] In the first two appearances, they sued each other over ownership of the family's principal residence. In the third they registered a legal agreement (musadaqa shar‘iyya) on how to divide up this jointly owned property among themselves.

Three sons—Shaykh Yasin, Shaykh Taha, and Shaykh Mustafa—who lived together in one large residential structure for at least twenty to thirty years, sharing both income and expenses, survived Shaykh Abdullah al-Munir Sanunu. On 12 October 1724 the legal inheritors of Shaykh Taha and Shaykh Yasin sued the legal inheritors of Shaykh Mustafa over the ownership of the southern apartment (tabaqa) in the upper part of the residence.[31] The plaintiffs claimed that all three brothers jointly and equally paid for the construction of this apartment yet, they continued, members of the Mustafa branch had illegally appropriated it for their own exclusive use. The defendants replied that their father, Mustafa, alone paid for the construction of the southern apartment and that they had proved this on 27 May 1717 when they were sued in court by the three oldest sons of Shaykh Taha over the same issue. When asked for proof, the members of the Mustafa branch called two high-status and eminently credible witnesses who testified

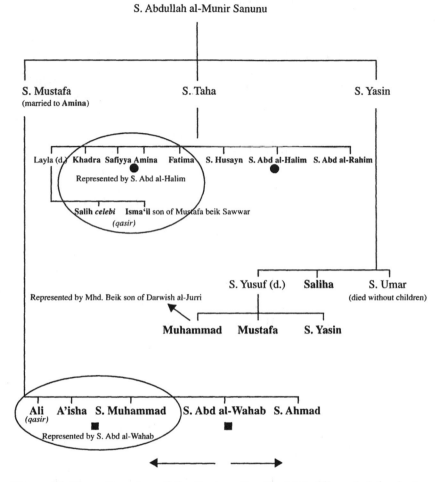

Figure 15. Three Branches of the Sanunu Family (plaintiffs and defendants in bold; S. for *Shaykh*; d. for Deceased)

to this effect. The witnesses—Shaykh Abdullah al-Jawhari and Abd al-Hafiz Tuqan—represented the leading religious and merchant families, respectively, of Nablus. The judge ruled in favor the defendants.

One day later, the legal inheritors of Shaykh Yasin sued the legal inheritors of Shaykh Taha and Shaykh Mustafa for not recognizing their joint ownership of the residential property as a whole. In their testimony, the plaintiffs made several claims. First, forty-eight years earlier, on 30 June 1676, all three brothers jointly and equally purchased the residence for three hundred piasters. Then, sometime later, Shaykh Taha and Shaykh Mustafa built an apartment (*tabaqa*) above the residence known as the "northern." All three brothers, they asserted, paid for the construction of this apartment equally. Thus, they concluded, aside from the apartment known as the "southern," which undisputedly belonged to the Mustafa branch, they legally owned one-third of everything else. The defendants countered that the disputed property belonged only to their two branches and, accordingly, only the names of Shaykh Taha and Shaykh Mustafa appear on the purchase deed of 1676. As further evidence, they added, only the names of these two brothers appear on an *istihkar* (long-term lease of *waqf* property) deed dated 7 October 1683. In this deed, the then supervisor (*nadher*) of the Samadiyya School gave permission to the two brothers to connect their residence to one of the walls of the school and to open two windows that overlooked the school grounds. The defendants did not provide a copy of the title deed, but they did submit the *istihkar* deed to the judge.

The plaintiffs responded to the defendants' version of the property's history by making a very serious and disturbing accusation. They informed the judge that the name of Shaykh Yasin was fraudulently scratched out from both the original purchase contract *and* from the court's copy of that contract. They implored the judge to order the defendants to produce the original deed and requested that he look up the copy of the deed in the records of the court. After carefully examining both pieces of paper, the judge concluded that, indeed, the name of Shaykh Yasin had been scratched out (*mahkuk*) "by the hands of those who do not fear God, the Almighty King." Still defiant, the defendants asked for proof of the plaintiff's claims. In response, the plaintiffs produced three witnesses, who provided a two-layered testimony. First, the same Shaykh Abdullah al-Jawhari that had testified a day earlier (and who must have been a very old man) recalled that the residential structure was indeed purchased by all three brothers jointly. In this testimony he was joined by Ali, known as "al-akrut" (the Bastard). At that point, a third witness, the man known as Husayn son of al-Sharkaji, made an appearance, and together with Ali the Bastard testified that although Mustafa and Taha had built the northern apartment, they did so with money from all three brothers in equal proportion. In light of his discovery of fraud and of the testimony of the witnesses, the judge ruled in favor of the plaintiffs.

The story does not end here. Two months later, on 18 December 1724, the exact same parties to the previous two lawsuits appeared in court along with the legal representative of the wife of Shaykh Mustafa, whose existence is revealed for the first time. The only other difference is the exclusion of one of Layla's sons, Isma ʿil, as a party to the agreement, though his joint ownership of the properties is recognized near the end of the document. All legally acknowledged that, with the exception of the southern apartment, which all reiterated was the sole property of the Mustafa branch, each branch was entitled to privately own one-third of the residence. After the structure of the residence was described in detail, the parties acknowledged a legal agreement as to how to allocate the various rooms among themselves. The actual division, however, retained some areas of the residence, such as a bathroom and the courtyard, as joint property. More important, the division is left intentionally vague in one important respect: rooms are designated as now belonging either to the Mustafa branch or to the Taha and Yasin branches, the latter two treated as a single unit. The document also mentions that the Taha and Yasin branches jointly paid the Mustafa branch a symbolic sum of ten silver coins, or one-quarter of a piaster, in order to "even out" the division. The representatives of the branches then stated that they dropped all rights to use *ghubn fahish* as a legal argument on the basis of which they might challenge this arrangement in the future.

Managing Fission

For over two generations the members of Sanunu family who shared a residence in the Qaryun quarter tried to meet the challenges posed by the unpredictable contingencies of birth and death, by changing economic resources, and by the conflicting interests between the three branches as they grew differentially in size. Decisions about the reallocation of domestic space and about construction projects to enlarge the residence can easily lead to conflicts. This is not to mention the tensions inherent in the transition from joint to divided (by branch) ownership of the family home. Underlying these accumulated decisions were struggles for authority as each of the three brothers nurtured his branch and, ultimately, power and legacy.

The three branches of the Sanunu family did not develop evenly over time. Shaykhs Taha and Mustafa produced numerous children, eight and five of which, respectively, were alive in 1724. Each of these two branches had three adult sons at the time of the lawsuits, and all of these sons possessed the title of Shaykh. One can hardly think of stronger foundations for the continuation of these branches. Meanwhile, the Yasin branch—initially in the strongest position, because Yasin was the oldest son—had become the smallest and weakest. Yasin's first born, Shaykh Umar, died without any surviving children. His second oldest son, Shaykh Yusuf, died relatively early, leaving behind three sons still in their legal minority. The sole surviving off-spring at the time of the lawsuits, his daughter Saliha, remained un-married and continued to reside in the Sanunu family home, perhaps in order to care for her three orphaned nephews and to protect their future rights to a share of the family patrimony (there is no mention of their mother who, most likely, had also died while her children were still in their legal minority).

It is this weakness of the Yasin branch that made it possible for unknown—but well connected, as it required access to the court's archives—member(s) of the other two branches to scratch the name of Yasin from the original sales deed of the residence, in effect cutting off this branch from the family tree in terms of property access rights. No wonder that the Yasin branch was not a party to the original lawsuit (1717) over ownership of the southern apartment. At that time, three grandchildren in their legal minority and their unmarried aunt were hardly in a position to make their voices heard on this matter. This might also explain why even though their private ownership of one-third of the residence was later legally recognized, they were not al-located specific spaces within the residence. Rather, they were literally taken under the wings of the Taha branch.

Can one speak of these three court appearances as orchestrated performances? Three clues suggest that unlike the clash between the Badawi and Za'rur families in the first case study, these lawsuits are not "real," but rather legal maneuvers to enter an already agreed-upon structure of access rights to the family's principal residence into the record. First, the lawsuits are only a day apart and must be seen as a single package. Second, the first lawsuit is a repeat of an exactly similar case seven years earlier between the Taha and Mustafa branches. The only difference is the inclusion of the Yasin branch so as to signal their acquiescence to the already formed consensus that the southern apartment belonged solely to the Mustafa branch. In other words, the purpose of the first lawsuit was to clear the stage for the second law-suit and then the property division summarized above. The third clue is the unusual insertion of an additional element into the normally predictable narrative structure of most lawsuits. This element, found in both lawsuits, is a statement made by the (eventually losing) party immediately after the testimony of the witnesses and just prior to the judge's ruling. The statement begins with the legally binding phrase "let what we say be legally witnessed" (ashhadu ala anfusihim) and goes on to voluntarily (or so it seems) accept the legal validity of the specific configuration of access rights that the judge's decision was just about to formalize. In so doing, the losing parties made it all the more difficult for themselves and for their descendents to mount a future challenge, thus endowing the new arrangement of property access rights with the strongest possible legal and moral foundations.

The above is not conclusive evidence, and it could be just as likely that the Sanunu males, almost all religious scholars, may have had a predilection for resolving their problems in the Islamic court. What is certain is that the leading males of the three Sanunu branches became convinced that it was not enough to privately agree among themselves, nor even enough to voluntarily enter such an agreement into the legal record, as they did in their last appearance before the court. Rather, they went through the trouble of conducting full-fledged lawsuits that raised, disposed of, and preempted all possible future legal challenges to the new arrangement. Indeed, the parties publicly exposed the fact that one of their own committed fraud by tampering with legal deeds, including a document that was part of the official records of the court. Their willingness to mobilize themselves, to air their dirty laundry in public, and to do it at considerable financial expense is also, therefore, a statement about their (common or disparate?) vision(s) of a future. It was a new beginning for each branch to become a site for the rebirth of the type of arrangement, albeit multiplied, that both constituted and threatened to destroy them as a family. Ironically, only by severing the connection of joint property ownership that had symbolized their solidarity for so long could the three branches reinforce and transform the quality of their kinship ties. Towards that end, they devised legal strategies, attached a great deal of importance to documentation, and carefully calculated the timing of legal action. As we shall see below, they also paid close attention to the ways kinship in general and individuals in particular are legally represented in court.

Who Speaks?

The particulars of legal representation in this case study provide us with some hints about contemporary notions of kinship and authority. The first three of the following observations hold generally true for the court records of both Nablus and Tripoli throughout the eighteenth century and most of the nineteenth. First, the name of the father is the key marker in locating every litigant, whether male or female, even if the latter is married. Thus, family is inevitably represented as consisting of a lineage through the male line. Second, individuals are listed according to a ranking based on a combination of sex and age. Male children, for example, are listed first from the oldest to the youngest, followed by the names of the female children, also listed from the oldest to the youngest. If ranking is a measure of the degree of closeness to some mythical kinship core that is the source of authority and object of loyalty, then males, no matter their age ranking, are always closer to that core than females.

Third, the basic distinction in legal representation (as opposed to naming and ranking) is between males in their legal majority, on the one hand, and, on the other, females in their legal majority, as well as children (male and female) in their legal minority. As a general rule— albeit with many exceptions, depending on class, the issues being litigated, and type of property in question—the former appear in court and represent themselves individually, while the latter do not come to court and are represented instead by a variety of legal agents whose standing is validated prior to the hearing of the actual lawsuit. Thus, who represents whom can provide clues about the motivations behind the litigation and the character of relations between the litigants. In this particular case, none of the females or any of the youngest members (even those in their legal majority) legally represented themselves. Rather, the second-oldest male of the Mustafa branch, Shaykh Abd al-Wahab, represented his adult sister A'isha as well as his two youngest brothers, Shaykh Muhammad and Ali, the latter in his legal minority. Similarly, in the Taha branch it was the second-oldest male, Shaykh Abd al-Halim, who represented his four sisters as well as the two sons of his deceased fifth sister, Layla. It is not clear why the second-oldest males in both these branches were chosen for this task. Perhaps the oldest males were seen as too invested in the protracted disputes that led the lawsuits.

A specific positioning is also indicated by whether a female is represented by an unrelated individual who enjoys high status in the community and/or who acts as a professional legal representative; or whether she is represented by her husband (hence, in-laws as a distinct family); or, finally, whether it is her father, paternal uncle, brother, or son (hence, agnates) who speak on her behalf. The liminal role of Saliha, daughter of Shaykh Yasin, is evident from the fact that she appointed (or was persuaded to appoint) a different representative for each of the three cases. In the first lawsuit, which pitted the Yasin and Taha branches against the Mustafa branch, she is represented by Shaykh Abd al-Halim of the Taha branch. In the second lawsuit, in which the Yasin branch sues the other two branches for literally erasing their property rights an outsider, Muhammad Beik, son of Darwish al-Jurri, represents Saliha. Finally, in the *muqasama* (property division) case, her oldest nephew, Shaykh Yasin—who, according to tradition that is still widely practiced, is named after his grandfather—represents her. Who speaks on her behalf is clearly a matter of strategy and depends very much on the specific dynamic of each case.

The dominant form of representation of kinship in this case study is the branch. The large number of litigants grouped themselves into three distinct parties whose legal standing was based on the status of each group as the legal inheritors of one or another of the three deceased brothers. Throughout the documents, the language of branch (though not the actual word) is consistently and emphatically deployed at every transitional point in the narrative. Indeed, after the individual litigants are listed in the beginning of the documents, their names no longer appear. Rather, the arguments and counterarguments only refer to so-and-so's "legal inheritors."

Is this form of representation a product of the legal procedures of the Islamic court concerning matters relating to inheritance, or is it a reflection of a locally pervasive cultural framework that determined how individuals organized and invested their loyalties as family members? It is difficult to draw a line between the two. Initially, the former explanation seems more plausible, since the positioning of litigants as distinct groups of inheritance beneficiaries is legally pertinent in terms of the execution of the judge's decisions. Yet, the official issue before the court in the first two lawsuits is not that of establishing the status of who the legal inheritors are, but rather that of adjudicating conflicting claims about specific financial arrangements between three brothers who are no longer alive. A carefully designed strategy of legal representation is at work here and this is most clearly revealed by silences and omissions: some of the legal inheritors are excluded or kept at arm's length.

For example, an absent presence in the first two lawsuits is Mustafa *Beik* Sawwar, widower of Layla and father of her youngest son, Isma'il, then in his legal minority (we do not know if he is the father of Salih, Layla's older son). Although Mustafa is a legal inheritor through his wife of a portion of the principal residence under dispute, as well as the court-appointed guardian *(wasi)* of Isma'il, he is not a party to the lawsuits in either capacity. In fact, it is specifically stated in the documents that "for the purposes of this case only," Shaykh Abd al-Halim, Isma'il's paternal uncle, is to replace Isma'il's father as the legal guardian as well as to act as his legal representative. As to Isma'il's brother Salih, who is in his legal majority, no explanation is given as to why he is represented by his uncle instead of representing himself. The temporary legal erasure of Layla's husband and the appropriation of the legal standing of her oldest son make the point that only the kin who count (to borrow Meriwether's phrase) are to be in control of this litigation.[32]

The privileging of a culturally specific notion of family over legal norms is made even more obvious by the absence in the two lawsuits of another inheritor with a stake in the outcome: Amina, the wife of the deceased Shaykh Mustafa, matriarch of his branch and probably the oldest surviving member in the Sanunu household. The implication is that as a female from another family her residence in the household, regardless of duration, was understood by all to be a temporary one. This does not mean that she exerted no influence on her sons or on the final arrangement. In fact, and rather dramatically, the *muqasama* document begins with her name, an honor usually accorded to the most senior and important litigant before the court. It is not clear why she officially appears as a player only late in the game. The fact that she was not represented by any of her sons, but rather by a former judge who was also hired to legally represent her youngest daughter, A'isha (formerly represented by her brother Abd al-Wahab), suggests that although (or perhaps because) the ranking males did not perceive her as one of those kin who count, she was taking no chances in protecting her and her daughter's ownership rights in the residence.

Conclusion

Propertied families frequently used the Islamic court as a forum to enact property devolution and consolidation strategies, as well as to deal with the unanticipated consequences of such strategies years and often decades down the line. The crafting of *waqf* endowments, legal acknowledgments deeds, and lawsuits reveals a certain sophistication by most litigants (or their representatives) in the intricacies of Islamic law, the rules of evidence, and forms of legal representation. In using the court for their own purposes, litigants did take into account the institutional and political frameworks within which the court operated and did translate their objectives into the legal language and codes of Islamic law. Indeed, one can go further and argue that the very conceptualization of a property devolution strategy to begin with is already implicated in notions of family, property, and sexual difference produced by the ongoing encounter between kin and court.

I have employed terms such as "enactment," "performance," and "negotiation" to emphasize the mutually constitutive character of this encounter between kin and court, albeit without theoretical elaboration.[33] One of the many issues that need to be addressed is the relationship between the oral and the textual. Truly striking in this respect is the degree of importance the litigants in these two cases studies attached to the issue of documentation, especially in light of the fact that oral testimony by valid witnesses is all that is required under Islamic law. One of the lawsuits discussed, for example, was settled without calling witnesses. Instead, the judge agreed to retrieve the court's copy of the disputed *waqf* endowment, read it publicly word for word, and then rendered judgement. In the second case study, witnesses were called, but not before ringing words of outrage had been expressed in writing by the judge after his personal examination of the original sales document and the court's copy of that document revealed that they had been tampered with.

Over the centuries, the relationship between kin and court must have deepened as the documents generated by the court as well as the court's own copies of the original documents came to constitute the official memory or, phrased more provocatively, the textual memory of kinship and property relations in Ottoman cities and towns. Propertied urban groups were very much aware of the importance of this textual memory. Though when hidden or ignored it stood in mute testimony, its power could be activated at will and sometimes only became stronger over time. *Waqf* endowments and purchase/sale deeds, especially, were kept for generations and waved around during heated arguments at home or submitted in court as corroborating, if not as decisive evidence of, a specific configuration of rights and/or intent. Indeed, the very act of holding a document and deciding when to show it are exercises in power whose significance often goes beyond the actual content. As products of the encounter between kin and court, these pieces of paper came to embody the authority of the court and the will of ancestors. Their very existence and constant reuse made the relationship between kin and court all the more symbiotic as it generated its own dynamic or feedback loop.

There are many possible methodological strategies that family historians and anthropologists can use to partially recover the importance of this textual memory from the surviving Islamic court records. This article has experimented, tentatively and perhaps a little recklessly, with a two-tiered approach: a macroanalysis of patterns in this relationship over time and space, and a microanalysis of two case studies. To take further steps involves a great deal of labor in the massive sets of documents still awaiting interrogation and classification (hence, the violence of the historian). It is also important to look beyond this specific source. One direction worthy of exploration is a study of how the Ottoman state has helped determine the shape and content of these archives by institutionalizing the Islamic court and making it a key instrument of its rule. Were it not for that fact, we would probably not have an archive to work with. In addition to bringing in the state, we need to take into account not just local political economy and social history, but also legal and intellectual history as well as developments in popular culture, all of which helped shape and give meaning to the court-kin matrix.

Notes

I wish to thank Baber Johansen, David Sabean, and Bogac Ergene for commenting on some of the issues raised in this article.

1. For a stimulating discussion on the concepts of family and household, see Netting et al. 1984. Throughout this article, family is used in a general sense as a cultural construct and in a specific one when referring to a particular patrilineal lineage group, depending on the context.

2. Brinkley Messick (1993, 1995) has articulated this position perhaps too forcefully. Concluding his analysis of a 1948 court case in Yemen, he states: "Embodying decisions and agreements, such texts become the reconsultable and reinterpretable inscriptions of an original event, which was nothing than their own production."

3. This study is based on volumes 4 and 5 (1723–26, 1728–30) and volumes 6–12 (1798–1860) of the Nablus Islamic Court Records (hereafter, NICR); and on volumes 4 and 5 (1715–16/1724–25, 1728–30) and volume 44 (1815–16) of the Tripoli Islamic Court Records (hereafter, TICR). Currently, the volume numbers of the Tripoli records are in a state of confusion. The ones above refer to photocopies kept in the Tripoli Municipality Library.

4. This chapter sketches but does not provide an in-depth literary analysis of narrative structures, linguistic styles, and other issues central to the problem of how historians can recover voices, memories, and dialogues from bureaucratic documents that seek to silence them. For an example of such an attempt by a family historian, see Sabean 2001.

5. A preliminary attempt to survey and theorize the differences and similarities in the content and form of court records from nineteen different locales in the Arab, Anatolian, and Eastern European provinces of the Ottoman Empire took place at Harvard, 18–20 May 2001. The results of the Ottoman Qadi Court Records Workshop have not been published, but the program and abstracts of the papers presented can be found on the website of the Middle East Social and Cultural History Association: (http://socrates.berkeley.edu/~mescha).

6. The Tripoli court records usually provide more details about both, probably because Tripoli is a larger city and its judges were "foreigners" who were rotated annually. In Nablus, by contrast, the judges were native sons who had intimate knowledge of their smaller community and usually occupied their posts several years at a time.

7. Particularly fascinating are the court cases precipitated by the death of a rich merchant from the Zamzami family, better known by his nickname "Abi Jaybayn" (Two-Pockets). See for example, NICR 4:278, 280, 285, 289, 289–90, 291, 292, 293, 295; and NICR 5:59, 61, 72–73.

8. For example, TICR 4:142–43.

9. For example, see NICR 4:123–24; 5:169 and NICR 5:7, 63, respectively.

10. In some instances one can notice a rise in the percentage of lawsuits, some of which were litigated previously, soon after a judge is replaced. This is especially true if the new judge is an outsider replacing a native son. See, for example NICR 4:260–270.

11. NICR volumes 4 and 5 contain a total of 1646 cases, 343 of which are lawsuits. The numbers are 861 and 138, respectively for TICR volumes 4 and 5. Out of over ten thousand cases for the 1800–1860 period in Nablus, only 275 are lawsuits. The Nablus and Tripoli records, it should be noted, are not indexed. Space does not permit a full discussion of the taxonomics I have applied in coming up with these figures.

12. One can think of various combinations of factors, such as decline in the authority of the Islamic court, tighter family discipline and centralization, the rise of alternative sites of adjudication such as new secular bodies, and increased fear of intervention by state authorities. It would be useful to find out if this was an empire-wide trend or just specific to certain regions.

13. The population of Tripoli was and still is far more diverse than that of Nablus, and this is reflected in the numerous lawsuits involving Christians and a variety of non-Arab ethnic groups, such as foreign merchants and military officers.

14. Doumani 1998, 31–39.

15. For Nablus between 1800 and 1860, the figure is 60 percent compared to 70 percent for Tripoli during the sample year of 1815–16. These statistics should be treated with great caution due to the somewhat arbitrary nature of the categories used to construct these patterns. For example, the category "space" includes a variety of lawsuits between neighbors about boundaries, privacy, or potentially damaging changes to physical structures. In strict legal terms, these might constitute different types of lawsuits. Also, a single lawsuit sometimes raised several legal issues.

16. NICR 4:277, 281. Both are dated end of Safar, 1138/ Early November, 1725.

17. If a probate inventory of Hamida's property was conducted, the plaintiffs did not produce the original deed, nor did they ask the judge to look it up in the court's own records. This is not unusual, as oral testimony is legally sufficient.

18. The *fatwa* is fairly complex in that it draws on disparate traditions of Islamic law and raises additional legal issues that were obviously argued in court, but which were not mentioned in the official narrative that preceded the judge's decision. A full discussion of what this implies in terms of the way courts produced summaries of legal proceedings, the character and limits of the state's official memory, and the relationship between the heterogeneity of legal discourses in a writing culture and practical strategies by litigants are beyond the scope of this chapter.

19. Messick uses this phrase, albeit in a different context. Messick 1995, 158.

20. Also possible is a motivation to preempt any doubts about the authenticity of the *waqf* deed, the reasoning being that the court's records are less likely to have been tampered with. But, and this is encountered in some similar cases, they could have produced it and still asked the judge to look it up in the court records. Besides, and as we shall see in the second case study, the official memory of the court can and was tampered with. In order to reduce this possibility, scribes left no margins either horizontally or vertically. If, for whatever reason, a substantial empty space was left, almost always it was filled by the word *bayad* (literally "white," signifying empty) written over and over again in large letters. The entire format of record-keeping changes drastically by the late nineteenth century in Greater Syria, but the implications about state authority and relationship between courts and their patrons deserve a separate article. Some of the key issues involved are laid out in Messick 1993.

21. Of the seventy-three lawsuits between kin over inheritance in early-eighteenth-century Nablus, thirty-three (or thirty-eight, depending on whether one also includes those that do not specify when and from whom the property was purchased) follow this pattern. For the former, see NICR 4:13, 15–16, 32, 34, 41, 47, 53, 64, 64, 97, 104, 107, 109, 128, 129, 197, 199, 228, 230, 236–37, 270–71, 277, 290–91, 309–10, 323, 344, 349–50; NICR 5:2, 68–69, 77–78, 90, 122, 162, 165). For the latter, see NICR 4:236, 278, 288, 289–90, 123–24; and 5:3. The same holds true for Tripoli, albeit at a slightly smaller rate (TICR 4:38, 44, 72–73, 175–76, 225; and 5:10–11, 117, 127, 158, 168–69, 171, 172–73). Other common rebuttals include the following: that the property was transferred as a will *(hiba)* (NICR 4:105, 110, 111, 274; and 5:158); endowed as *waqf* (NICR 4:257; and 5:48); or that the plaintiffs had previously made a legal acknowledgment that the property belongs to the defendants (NICR 4:83, 150).

22. It remains to be seen whether these assertions hold true empirewide and, if so, what a satisfactory explanation for the historical development of this phenomenon would look like.

23. Another weak line of property transmission that generated more than its fair share of lawsuits between kin is that of the absence of male children in their legal majority.

24. This additional strategy, also very noticeable in *waqf* endowments, is precipitated in part by the specific ways merchant networks were constructed in Nablus (Doumani 1998, 36–39).

25. For example, over 61 percent of the property purchase/sale deeds registered in Nablus between June 1728 and March 1730 list one or more females as a party to the transaction. Yet, women constitute only 16 percent of the buyers. For the 1723–26 period, the numbers are 62 percent and less than 5 percent, respectively.

26. Hamida inherited shares in thirteen residential, commercial (shops), and agricultural properties. The sizes of the shares ranged from .001 percent to .05 percent.

27. This we know from the description of the properties in the lawsuits. In terms of narrative structure, each property is usually described in the following order: percentage of ownership, genealogy (how acquired, when, and from whom), location, and co-owners or tenants. The property description, in turn, usually comes after the litigants are identified, but before a specific accusation by the plaintiffs is made.

28. Doumani 1998, 14.

29. Baber Johansen alerted me to this legal point.

30. NICR 4:123–24, 129, 153. The dates, respectively, are Muharram 23, 1137/October 12, 1724; Muharram 24, 1137/October 13, 1724; and beginning of Rabi II, 1137/December 18, 1724.

31. A *tabaqa* is a semiattached structure connected to the lower parts of the residence by a short flight of stairs or uneven path.

32. Meriwether 1999.

33. See the chapter by Ferguson in this volume for a more detailed discussion.

9

Text, Court, and Family in
Late-Nineteenth-Century Palestine

Iris Agmon

In this chapter I analyze some of the textual and orthographical features of the *shariʿa* court records in the port cities of Palestine, Jaffa, and Haifa, following the reforms of the Tanzimat. In this analysis these records constitute both source material for and an object of historical investigation. I discuss the late-nineteenth-century innovative recording procedures according to which some of these records were registered, and offer some ideas about their historical context and novelty and how their implementation may have affected the construction of the family in these communities.

I begin by comparing two prototypes of case records, one old and one new, in the court records of Jaffa and Haifa in the late nineteenth century. I then proceed to deal with the implementation of the new recording procedures. This issue is discussed against the background of instructions issued by the central government in Istanbul and certain differences in interpretation between the two courts. I pay particular attention to the novelty of recitation before the parties involved, followed by their signing the final version.

My point of departure in this discussion is that the family as a social practice is discursively constituted in various spheres. It is the family's reconstitution in the legal arena that is considered. I argue that the involvement of the participants in the process of authorizing the documents covering their legal affairs may have resulted in an emphasis on the legal discourse in shaping the construction of the family in Jaffa and Haifa. However, because of the slightly different versions of the new recording procedure that each court adopted, this tendency may have been stronger in Haifa than in Jaffa. I further argue that, following other changes in the courts and communities of these two cities during that period, people of the lower and middle class who attended the court were more exposed than their upper class counterparts to these aspects of the legal culture. Thus, both court and family were undergoing a complicated process of transformation in the communities under discussion.[1]

Two broader themes are demonstrated on a small scale in this chapter. One is empirical—namely, the dynamics by which nineteenth-century legal reforms, which turned the *shariʿa* court into "family court" by default, inadvertently provided this official change with specific social and cultural content, and, how the interaction in court between the lay people and those steeped in *shariʿa* law sustained the reconstruction of both family and court culture in these societies. In the conclusion, I offer some preliminary ideas regarding the significance of these findings for understanding the passage of these societies to modernity. The second theme is the methodology of historical analysis based on court records. The approach used here assumes that orthographical, textual, and other aspects of the records, combined with the analysis of the process of their production and the social background of their producers, are part and parcel of the historical reconstruction they sustain.

The Port Cities and their Shariʿa Court Records

In the course of the nineteenth century, the Ottoman legal institutions underwent a profound change. One of the main institutional consequences of this process was that the *shariʿa* court system, the principal court system of the Ottoman state, lost its exclusivity in favor of a multiple-court structure that followed various legal codes, of which *shariʿa* law was only one. This resulted in considerable reduction of *shariʿa* legal jurisdiction, and family law became its only field of expertise.[2] These reforms also involved the reorganization of the hierarchy of the *shariʿa* courts and their judges, as well as of regulations regarding the court and its procedures. It appears that all these changes forced *shariʿa* courts to redefine their position as representatives of state justice in relation to their legal counterparts and clientele.

At the same time, following the incorporation of the Ottoman Empire into the world economic system and the implications of the

Tanzimat reforms, the growth of Jaffa and Haifa led to increased bureaucracy and legal requirements. These had been small harbor towns at the beginning of the century and emerged as the main port cities on the southern shores of Syria, with a population of about forty thousand and twenty thousand respectively, on the eve of World War I. The growth in the volume of Ottoman foreign trade, the construction of railroads connecting these port cities with the interior, and substantial administrative reforms in the Ottoman Empire were reflected in the growth of economic activity in both Jaffa and Haifa. This in turn attracted immigration and settlement, leading to expansion of the urban areas and a more heterogeneous social structure.[3]

Nineteenth-century immigration to both Jaffa and Haifa resulted in the construction of new neighborhoods outside the city walls, the integration of neighboring villages into the city, and eventually a gradual destruction of city walls altogether. This large-scale expansion occurred in response to the demand for housing and a substantial increase in real estate values. Subsequently, varied housing solutions were adopted. The court records of both cities reflect this change. Most striking are those cases where people were renting out every spare room in their houses and even built extra rooms for sublet, not necessarily to relatives (see, for instance, the case discussed on pp. 208–216 below). This situation must have affected family structures, and at the same time it made the task of the *shari‘a* courts, dealing with the complexities of family matters in a fast-growing population, even harder: as a result of legal reforms, the judges, who were not local and were appointed for short terms, were less familiar with the local scene than previously.

Both Jaffa and Haifa were subdistrict *(kaza)* centers in the hierarchy of the Ottoman provincial administration, with *shari‘a* courts offering legal services to the urban and rural population in their jurisdiction. Jaffa belonged to the district *(liva, sancak)* of Jerusalem, which after the reorganization of the provinces in the 1860s had not formed part of any province *(vilayet)* but had been subordinated directly to the central government *(elviye-i ghyr-ı mülhaka)*. Haifa belonged to the district of Acre, which from the 1880s formed part of the new province of Beirut. Prior to the 1880s, Haifa, as part of the district of Acre, had been governed from Saida, and before that from Damascus. Following the legal reforms, civil *(nizami)* and commercial *(ticaret)* courts of first instance *(bidayet)* also functioned in both Jaffa and Haifa.[4] In the *shari‘a* courts of both cities, several volumes of records have survived and are available for investigation.[5]

Both court records include varied documented legal procedures. These accounts differ from each other in their structure, literary expressions,

legal terminology, and many other features.[6] However, there is a major
division into two types pertinent to almost all the documents in the
Jaffa and Haifa court records. One type is a registration *(sijill)* of a
completed court case or official document, a summary recorded as
one of several forms of legal proceedings, e.g., *hujja* (deed), *i'lam* (notification), *waqfiyya* (endowment), and *wikala* (power of attorney). The
registration was the most common type of document among Ottoman
shari'a court records from various periods that survived throughout
the Ottoman Empire. The other is a detailed protocol of legal proceedings according to court sessions. The development of this type (sing.
dabt, pl. *dubut*) into an authorized official record seems to have been
one of the innovations of the late-nineteenth-century *shari'a* courts,
and it is this form that serves as the focus of the following analysis.[7]

Before discussing the changes that took place in the late nineteenth
century in the court records of Jaffa and Haifa, a general description of
the two types of records and the principal differences between them is
called for. The registration type is a summary of a completed court case
(or an official document that arrived at the court), which was by definition registered after the case was decided, no matter how many court
sessions were conducted or how long the deliberations lasted. Thus,
simple procedures such as giving power of attorney *(wikala)* or the details
of complicated disputes could have been summarized laconically in the
same manner and taken up similar space in the record.

The raison d'être of the registration is clear from the form and
legal narration of documents of this sort: the court decision was their
climax. The aims of the registration were to supply the court with a
legal reference to the decision taken in that case and to supply the
litigants with a formal document that they could use in any future
related business in or out of court.[8] In other words, these documents
ensured the legal work of the court and sustained its function of creating and preserving the public record, and are the most common
among the *shari'a* court records from different Ottoman towns and
periods to have survived to the present day. Recorded after the legal
deliberations were over, these documents obviously leave out many
details, including legal exchanges in the courtroom.[9] Social historians
who read these documents may sometimes feel rather frustrated, for
they are laconic and formulaic, tending to conceal more than they
reveal and mainly covering aspects that may seem trivial and insignificant. However, this only challenges social historians to read between the lines of these legal texts and unfold some fascinating stories
that contribute to a much better understanding of past realities.[10]

The protocol represents a different type of record altogether. A
court case recorded in this way may include an account of each court

session, chronologically listed,[11] and recorded shortly after it was conducted, before the decision was reached and even before any further session took place. The record of a court session includes a full description of its legal content. The participants in the session signed the record under titles stating their legal capacities (plaintiff, defendant, witness, etc.). Sometimes the text of the record was slightly changed, and certain words or lines were erased or missing details were added in a footnote. Below each record the page number of the record of the next session was reported, and the record of that session began with a reference to the record of the previous one. The judge (or the scribe on his behalf) often added a comment regarding the legal agenda of the following session.

The focus of this recording procedure was entirely different from that of the registration. Its climax was not the final decision in the case, but rather the exact details of the deliberations, molded into legal vocabulary and signed by the participants. As mentioned above, this type of record is the focus of this discussion, and its significance is explained in more detail below. Meanwhile, we can conclude, at the risk of stating the obvious, that frequently the details of the legal deliberations recorded in protocols turn these documents into a historical gold mine when compared to some of the registration type of documents, while their textual and orthographical features add further thickness to their description.

The Protocol: From a Draft to an Authorized Record

The first volume of protocols that survived in the court of Jaffa is dated 1293–4/1876–77 and titled Hujaj (deeds, records), like most of the earlier volumes of registrations in that court record. However, on the first page of this volume the scribe explicitly clarified that the volume contained protocols and not registrations by stating that "this register contains protocols of lawsuits . . ." (utukhidhat hadhihi al-jarida li-dabt al-da'awi . . .).[12] The earliest surviving volumes in the shariʿa court of Haifa date from as late as 1870, and several volumes covering a full decade (1874–84) are missing.[13] Thus, the first volume of protocols (Jaridat al-dabt) preserved as part of the court record of Haifa is dated 1308/1890. The first volumes of protocols found in the courts of Damascus and Aleppo date from the late 1880s, and those from Istanbul from somewhat earlier.[14]

Two sets of instructions issued in Istanbul in 1874 and 1879 specify the routine of recording the protocol and preparing the court records.[15] The new recording procedure should be seen as part of the innovations introduced to the shariʿa courts from the 1850s onward, when the Ottomans embarked on reforming the *shari͑a* court system. In 1855 the government issued a set of instructions that organized the *shari'a* judges in a hierarchy of five ranks according to the administrative level of their appointments. The period of service of a judge in one court was limited to eighteen months at the most (twenty-four months in distant places). At the same time, a college for training *shari͑a* judges was founded in Istanbul. More instructions were issued in 1859 and then in 1873. These included a slight extension of the term of judges' service from eighteen to twenty-four months (thirty months in distant places); a list of fixed prices that the courts were to charge litigants in accordance with the legal proceedings; the payment of a judge's salary by the government and not, as earlier, directly from the court income; and the appointment of judges at the lower levels by the Şeyhülislâm, like their higher-level counterparts, and not by their provincial superior, as formerly occurred.[16] In addition to these explicit instructions, the norm of avoiding the appointment of judges to serve in their hometowns was reinforced. Judging by the names and terms of service of the judges in the court records of Jaffa and Haifa in this period, at least there these instructions were implemented more or less strictly.[17]

The logic behind these regulations seems clear: similar to the reforms in other institutions, they aimed at centralizing the *shari͑a* court system and bringing its personnel under tighter state control. Thus, whereas judges were outsiders and changed every second year before they had time to weave ramified networks in the local community, the rest of the court staff appointed by them was usually of local origin and served longer periods. Presumably, this situation put the staff in the position of mediators between the judge and his constituency. This seems to have been the case particularly with regard to the scribes. With the introduction of the protocol, which was accompanied by detailed instructions for authorizing the records by affixing stamps and seals, numbering pages and cases, and maintaining the court records in a way that would allow their supervision by the central authorities, the production of the records became more professional and time-consuming, and hence was considered more important, giving the scribes a relatively stronger position in court.[18]

Furthermore, in towns like Jaffa and Haifa the population grew so fast that even the scribes could not be personally acquainted with all or even most of the litigants, and the judges' dependence on them grew.[19] This may explain why some of the judges brought along a relative, a son or a cousin who had the required professional skills, and nominated him to serve as scribe. Not until 1913 were the instructions on appointing judges for two years in the same court reassessed and the time limit cancelled.[20]

This is the context within which the protocol type of record should be viewed. It clearly would have been most useful in updating the judge, although there is no indication to suggest that this motivated the introduction of this system. In this respect, it should be noted that the protocol very much resembled the *mahdar*, one of the major types of register that the *shariʿa* judge was instructed to maintain in his record *(Diwan al-qadi)* by various pre-Ottoman Islamic manuals. The main purpose of the *diwan*, described by Wael Hallaq, was to ensure the continuity of justice. In the pre-Ottoman court, literally personified in a judge who held his post for many years, the *mahdar* was not intended as a means for updating new judges. Presumably, its purpose was rather similar to that of the Ottoman protocol *(zabt)* before it was reformed in the 1870s. It provided the scribe with accounts of old cases that would serve as a basis for the preparation of summaries to be compiled in the *diwan* in the event that a new judge was appointed.[21]

The protocol record was yet another step toward the further institutionalization of the court. Thus, the problem of continuity was in a way opposite to that described by Hallaq regarding earlier Islamic courts. Whereas in the latter, the continuity represented by *diwan al-qadi* was useful to a judge who held his position for a long period and who had to run the local judiciary system almost single-handedly, in late Ottoman *shariʿa* courts the problem facing judges was a lack of information due to short periods of service in a complicated court system and a fast-growing community. True, at face value, the pre- and late-Ottoman records were rather similar. Nevertheless, the protocol type, whose main feature was that it was an authorized court document registered for preservation and state inspection, does not seem to have been a continuation of the old *mahdar*.

Wael Hallaq has argued that the *shari'a* court records are not a unique Ottoman phenomenon, but rather a more recent link in a much longer chain of Muslim court records. He considers as only circumstantial the fact that they have been preserved while earlier *shariʿa* court records have not survived. However, after examining the concepts behind both the protocol and *diwan al-qadi*, it seems to me that the logic of the former fit the prevailing recording procedures in the Ottoman *shariʿa* courts, but not the logic of the pre-Ottoman court records. In other words, while it is true that the Ottoman court records were a continuation of a Muslim court tradition, the very fact that these court records have been preserved also points to a unique Ottoman contribution to this tradition, namely, the bureaucratic culture of keeping records, which transcended the purpose of continuity. Pre-Ottoman court records were probably not meant to survive for centuries, but merely to aid newly appointed judges during their initial period and to support the work of the current judge until he was replaced. The documents in the Ottoman *shariᶜa* court, on the other hand, served several requirements of the state, local community, and daily work of the courts. Their preservation was both a prerequisite for the fulfillment of these tasks and an indication of the Ottomanization of the *shariᶜa* courts.[22]

While it is true that the protocol, as an official record, was part of a broader concept of state control that was adopted from European legal systems, the way it was implemented and even the name of its recording practice, *zabt* (Arabic: *dabt*), stemmed from both *shariᶜa* court practice and the Ottoman bureaucratic culture. The English lexicon of the Ottoman language published in that period gives six meanings for this noun, the last two being "A taking down in writing" and "A fixing the orthography and vocalization of a word by a verbal description."[23] As I show below, the instructions regarding the recitation of the protocol and their implementation in the courts of Jaffa and Haifa were in keeping with the literal meaning of this term. Moreover, if we look at the period from the 1840s to the 1870s, when the new recording procedure was introduced, a gradual development can be discerned. The scribe's practice of taking notes for the sake of both assisting the judge in the process of decision-making and recording the official verdict evolved into a formalization of these notes into authorized documents that were preserved for the sake of the government's new agenda.[24]

A Domestic Dispute Unpacked: Amina versus Salim

I now turn to a domestic dispute, which was deliberated and recorded in the *shariᶜa* court of Haifa in the course of about four months during the years 1913–14, to illustrate some of the points discussed so far and to raise several other issues. The record of this case includes four legal accounts: two registrations of power of attorney given separately by the disputing husband and wife to their legal representatives; the protocol of the trial; and, finally, the registration of the verdict.[25] The records of this case, like many in these court records, unfold a multilayered story, many aspects of which have bearing on the construction of the family in the context of the changing realities of late Ottoman Haifa.

In the power of attorney given by Amina, an immigrant from Saida, to her attorney (fig. 16), the latter was specifically assigned to represent her in court regarding her marital relations with her husband, Salim, a member of a family that moved to Haifa from Nablus. It took three months before Salim also commissioned an attorney to respond to his wife's claim. The trial began ten days later, on 27 Safar

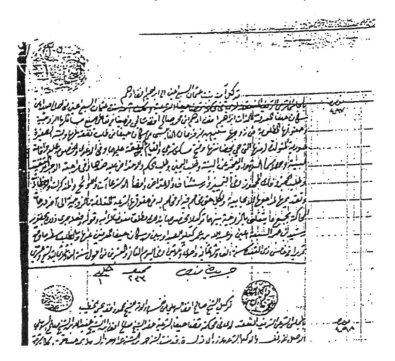

Source: Haifa Court Record, *Sijill* (IX 1913–IV 1914), p. 35, case 497, 5 Za 1331.

Figure 16. The Registration of the Power of Attorney Given by Amina to Ibrahim Efendi

1332 (January 1914), and was decided on 15 Rabi al-Awwal (February 1914) after about three weeks and four court sessions. Amina and Salim did not appear in court until the last session. Salim attended this session and signed the verdict, which looks like a compromise reached out of court and then legally confirmed.

The case was deliberated by Abdülhalim Efendi, an experienced judge of Bulgarian origin with knowledge of both Turkish and Arabic. He was about to complete his two-year term in Haifa when the new instruction for longer terms was issued. Thus, he remained until the region was conquered by the Entente armies, serving as the last Ottoman *shariʿa* judge of Haifa. The recording scribe, Muhammad Hasan al-Badran, who registered the two powers of attorney in this case (fig. 16), recorded most of its protocol sessions (fig. 17, sessions 1, 2, 4), and summarized the verdict, was also a newcomer in Haifa. He was originally from Nablus and had acquired his education at Al-Azhar. One of the session records of this case (fig. 17, session 3) was recorded by yet another immigrant, Muhyi al-Din al-Mallah, the chief scribe, from Tripoli.[26]

According to the protocol, Amina's attorney claimed that Salim had left her and their minor daughter, Huriyya, without support for about a month and demanded that he be forced to pay daily alimony (*nafaqa*) for Amina and to hire a wet nurse for Huriyya. Amina also claimed that Salim had locked up her furniture in his father's house and refused to return it. Salim's attorney stated that, in response to a demand by Amina's attorney, his client had arranged legal accommodation (*maskan shar ͨi*) for both Amina and Huriyya and provided them with their necessities, but that Amina had refused to accept and had expelled him. He was willing to support the two of them, but could not afford to pay alimony. After a dispute between the two attorneys about the meaning of the term *maskan shar ͨi*, in which Amina's attorney stressed that it did not mean that "its resident only dwells within a four-walled room," the burden of proof was left with Salim's attorney.

The latter brought three witnesses: the man who had rented the room to the couple and two of their neighbors. All three of them testified that Amina and Salim had lived peacefully together in that room for four months; then, some twenty-five days before the trial, Amina had borrowed the sum of five *beşlik* from her neighbors. When Salim had come home and brought her bread and meat, she had asked him to return her loan. He had asked her why she had taken the money, and she had said that it was to buy food. He had been furious and had refused to pay. She had reacted by refusing to take the food from him. Since that day, he had not returned, nor did he sleep with her. For the last session, Salim came to court with Amina's attorney and agreed to pay daily alimony and child support of one and a half *beşlik* (a moderate sum, in comparison to other cases), and Amina's attorney agreed. Both of them signed the protocol.

In the summary of this case that is recorded in the volume of registrations, the account of the last session was more or less repeated with the additional condition that Salim was obliged to pay alimony and child support to his wife and daughter until he arranged legal accommodation for them. Meanwhile, Amina was permitted to borrow money up to the total sum of her alimony.[27]

Integrating the Protocol, Inscribing the Family

In this section I examine how this lawsuit developed and was recorded (at a time when the routine of recording protocols was only just evolving in the courts of Jaffa and Haifa), through a synthesis of

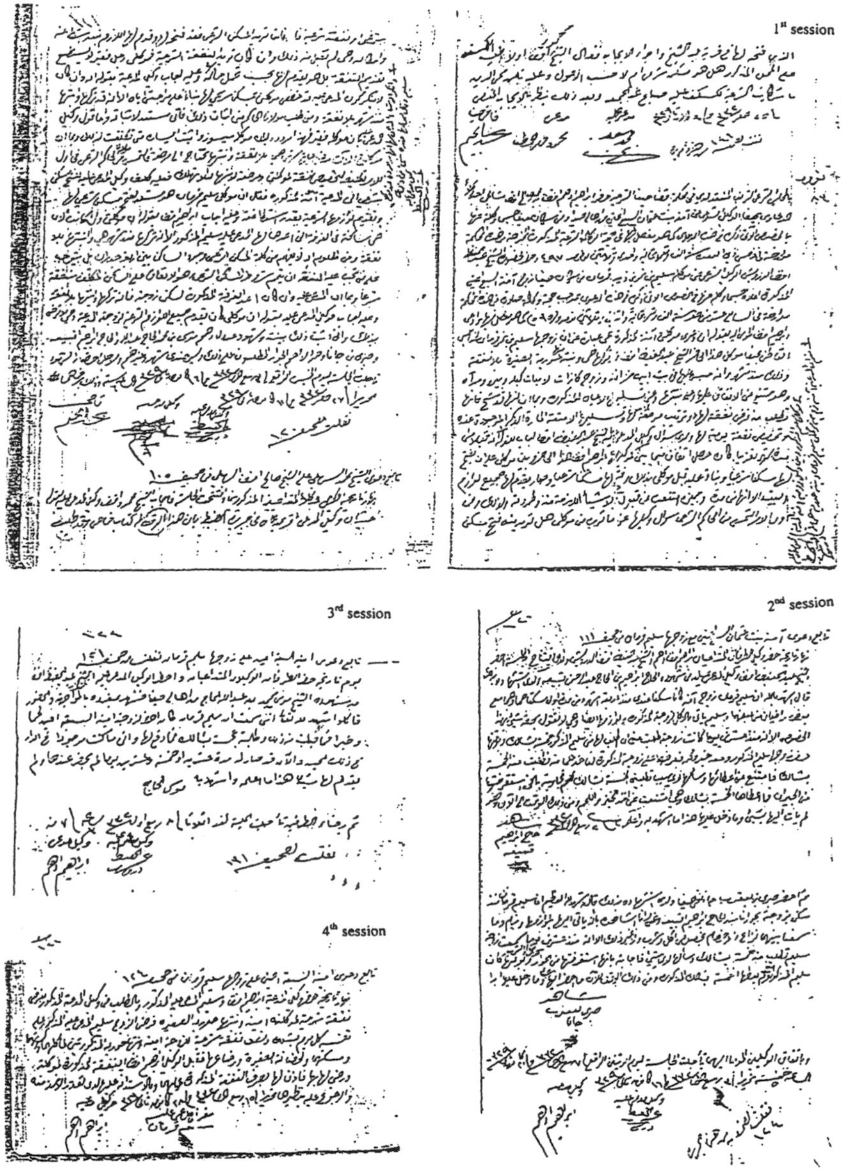

1st session

2nd session

3rd session

4th session

Source: HCR, *Jaridat al-Dabt* 5 (IX 1913–III 1914), pp. 110–11, 120, 124, 131, case 83, 27 S 1332–15 Ra 1332.

Figure 17. The Protocol of the Lawsuit of Amina against Salim (from right to left)

the material presented so far with a discussion of the Ottoman authorities' instructions to the courts.

The Initial Legal Process

Prior to appearing before the judge, litigants had to apply to the court, register, and pay court fees according to the nature of the case. Amina and Salim came separately to the court in Haifa, each with an attorney *(wakil da ʿawi)*, and authorized the attorneys in court to represent them. Amina preceded her husband, while—according to the latter's witnesses—the couple was still living together peacefully in their rented room. Obviously, this was not the case, at least not as far as Amina was concerned, for she authorized Ibrahim Edhem Efendi Ṭalcy to represent her regarding her marital relations at this early stage. It also appears from the record that, sometime after he was hired and before Amina initiated her lawsuit, her attorney had raised the issue of Amina's residence with Salim.

The information provided in the protocol of this case, when compared with the registration, illustrates the substantial gap between these two types of records in terms of the details they provide about the case and their different goals. A study of the registration alone does not give any indication of the rather complicated legal exchange in court (fig. 17), let alone the even more intricate domestic dispute behind this case. In fact, a reading of the registration alone does not lead to the conclusion that the verdict was preceded by a dispute or a lawsuit.[28]

However, while the description given in the protocol is extensive in comparison with the registration, we cannot assume that it provides more than one layer of this multifaceted family affair; more precisely, we are only shown the legal perspective within which the case was deliberated in court, and even these deliberations were not recorded in their entirety.[29] What was behind this dispute between Amina and Salim? Was it really about the limits of her independence in running their tiny household, as the testimonies indicate? Was the complaint from Amina's attorney about her residence connected to its location in a house of nonrelatives, the nature of the neighbors, or the fact that it was small and crowded? Was the difference in origin and perhaps also in social background between Amina and Salim the true reason behind their dispute? Or perhaps it was about an entirely different issue that was not exposed at all by the record, and was molded by the attorneys into one of the most widespread conventions of *shariʿa* family law, namely, legal accommodation? As tempting as it may be to speculate about this affair and to connect it to the family structure in highly populated towns such as Haifa in that period, or to interpret it in terms of a cultural encounter between two immigrants from different backgrounds, there is no way of substantiating any of this without some additional evidence.[30]

What this protocol does illustrate is both the interaction that took place in court between the litigants who brought their family business to court and the legal discourse on the family. In the case of Amina and Salim, they were not part of this interaction, since they authorized legal representatives to take care of their affairs in court, joining a growing group of people in these communities who detached themselves from the court during that period—a phenomenon whose relevance to the current discussion I explain below. Nevertheless, many other people did come to court and participated in the process that remolded their family relations in legal terms.

The recording of protocols was indeed an innovation, and the access historians consequently gain to a detailed account of court cases is also new. However, for the people who came to court and were involved in the interaction this was, to a large extent, not a new experience; in principle, it was typical of hundreds of years of shari'a court work. Historians who have explored court records of varied periods and places have been impressed by the extent to which people who came to court seemed to possess enough knowledge of its concepts and procedures to be able to make rather efficient use of the system to their own benefit.[31] At the same time, this long-standing acquaintance of lay people with legal concepts is in part what leads me to my second and major point, namely, that the new type of record contributed to the intensification of the interaction between lay people and the legal concept of the family.

Rules and Regulations

After the litigants had been legally identified in court and had presented their claims or requests, the scribe prepared a protocol of this preliminary session. When it was their turn to enter, they approached the judge with the scribe. The latter recited their depositions and amended them according to their comments, and the litigants and the judge signed this record. The scribes of the court kept several active volumes of protocols and registrations and recorded the protocol of the preliminary session in the correct volume.[32]

Article 6 of the second set of instructions issued in Istanbul in April 1879 includes specific orders as to how to record protocols. Apparently, most of the volumes of protocols known to historians were registered in shari'a courts after these instructions were issued:[33]

After the protocol of the case [daʿva-ı zabt] has been recorded, the recording clerk comes with the two parties before the official adjunct [müsteşar], in courts that have adjuncts, or before the judge [hakim] or naib, in courts that do not have adjuncts, and reads the protocol [zabt] to him. After the reading, the adjunct (or judge or naib) asks the parties, separately, whether or not their statements conform to the text of the protocol. If each one of the parties so does [the protocol is] immediately recorded in the protocols register. If [however], they do not [so] affirm (either because a mistake or omission has occurred, or because a required question and answer [regarding] some issues has not been recorded by the court), it becomes necessary to correct the protocol. Having been amended, the text of the protocol is to be recorded in the court's protocols register. Once the parties have signed at the bottom [of that protocol] and the seal [affixed to it], no erasing or rubbing is [allowed] to occur.[34]

Articles 4 through 11, including the above, suggest that these specific instructions referred only to the protocols of claims of litigants in a lawsuit (daʿva-ı zabt). Apparently, the record of the first session of Amina's lawsuit against her husband (fig. 17, first session) includes an account of this sort of preliminary session, which was attended by both attorneys, Ibrahim Edhem Efendi Ţalcy and Sheikh Abd al-Hafith Efendi al-Darwish. It was conducted by the scribe Muhammad Hasan al-Badran, who prepared the protocol and then read it out to the attorneys in the presence of the judge, Abdülhalim Efendi. During the recitation, an amendment was requested and made in a footnote, signed by Sheikh Darwish. This footnote indicates that the instructions to recite the record were implemented and also illustrates the role that this recitation played.

In this footnote, Salim's attorney acknowledged that his client was Amina's husband and Huriyya's father. Legally, this sort of acknowledgment should have been included in a husband's response to any claim by his wife relating to their marital relations and offspring. The record of the entire session was seemingly written without interruption. Verbal expressions were omitted and legal formulas were used instead. Either the judge dictated the claims to the scribe or the latter skillfully recorded them this way. The text of the footnote, however, is phrased as the direct speech of Salim's attorney in response to an unrecorded question. He said: "Yes, the plaintiff Amina is my client Salim's wife and his daughter Huriyya is hers." Apparently, when judge ʿAbdülhalim noticed that these basic legal details were missing from the record, he stopped Hasan al-Badran's recitation and asked

Salim's attorney whether he acknowledged his client's marriage to Amina and his fatherhood of Huriyya. When the attorney responded, Badran wrote his exact words in the footnote without rephrasing them, because this took place in the course of the recitation.[35]

In the same volume of protocols, there is one case record that was registered in Ottoman Turkish.[36] This protocol, which also illustrates my point regarding the recitation, uncovers another domestic dispute. Both the husband and the wife, as well as the witnesses and the ad hoc attorney (*wakil musakhkhar*, appointed by the court to represent an absent party), the same Ibrahim Edhem Efendi, were from the Turkish-speaking community in Haifa. The husband was a clerk at the Hijaz railway station; his brother-in-law, who testified as his sister's witness, worked at the customs office, as did her other witness, her brother's colleague. At first I was curious why this record was registered in Ottoman Turkish. Of course, Abdülhalim Efendi, the Bulgarian judge, who had acquired his legal education in Istanbul and served most of his judicial career in Turkish-speaking towns before being appointed to Haifa,[37] and Muhyi al-Din al-Mallah, the chief scribe who recorded this case, knew Turkish, hence most probably the participants were allowed to present their claims in their mother tongue. But why did the judge not dictate the material, molded into legal formulas, in Arabic, as is the case with the other records? Apparently, the answer is that the record was prepared for recitation before the same Turkish-speaking audience.

The second point that the footnote in the case record of Amina versus Salim illustrates is the way the recitation contributed to intensifying the interaction between lay people and the legal discourse. Salim's acknowledgment of his marital relations with Amina and his fatherhood of Huriyya was legally essential. It is true that in this particular case those directly involved, namely, Amina and Salim, were not even in the courtroom when the recitation took place. However, at many trials people did attend the deliberation of their cases. We may also assume that people other than the litigants—such as relatives, witnesses, or litigants awaiting their cases—were among the audience. They heard the legal exchanges, clarifying for them that those details they considered to be so obvious were indeed important in court and therefore required explicit acknowledgment, and they may have reinterpreted their understanding of their own family affairs.

Another such exchange was the debate between the two attorneys about the standard of legal accommodation that Salim was required to provide for Amina. When Amina's attorney claimed that the meaning of legal accommodation (*maskan shar⁽i*) was not just four walls (fig. 17, first session), he presented a much broader interpretation of this otherwise

rather technical term. His interpretation may be understood as stress-
ing the legal obligation of the husband to provide his wife with all her
necessities, not just a roof over her head. At the same time, in this
context *maskan sharʿi* can be understood to mean that a marital residence should not become the wife's prison. However the interpretation is understood (and for the current discussion its importance lies
less in how the attorney defined it and more in what the audience
understood it to mean), the point that it illustrates is the exposure of
the courtroom audience to this type of legal exchange, intensified by
the process of authorizing the protocol record.

The Registration Process in Jaffa and Haifa

From the instructions of the government, it seems that the court scribes
were to keep two sets of protocol registers. One would contain drafts
of the original claims, where the scribes would make the required
amendments and obtain the signatures of the parties and which the
judge would then use during the trial. The other would include the
official register of protocols to which the scribe would copy amended
claims and testimonies and finally add the verdict. All would then be
signed and sealed, authorized by the judge, and kept in a safe place.
The main difference between the actual recording procedure, as inscribed in the court records under observation, and the Ottoman instructions is that both courts kept only one set, which seems to have
been a combination of drafts of protocols and their authorized registrations. Furthermore, although the instructions did not explicitly
mention this, it appears that both courts registered protocols of various types of cases and not only lawsuits.

At this point, the differences rather than the similarities between
the court records of Jaffa and Haifa ought to be discussed. There are
obvious differences between the volumes covering the earlier and later
years, which may reflect the process of adjustment to the new regulations, as well as the stylistic variations between the scribes. But
generally speaking, after about three decades of recording protocols,
the protocol volumes of Jaffa looked more like final records according
to the instructions, whereas those of Haifa were recorded more consistently as a combination of the drafts and the final records.

The instructions did not refer to court sessions. In fact, except for
the above-cited detailed description of the recording of the first session, to be conducted by the scribe before the judge began to deliber-
ate the case,[38] there were no explicit instructions as to how the rest
ought to be recorded. Rather, there were explanations of how their
content should be added later to the authorized protocol. This might

have caused a difference in interpretation between the two courts. Bearing in mind this lacuna in the instructions, it is possible to follow the logic of the two different interpretations. Apparently, in both courts the scribes continued to record draft protocols for the entire proceedings, not just the claims presented in the preliminary session. The reason for this might have been that it was practically impossible to record all in the clean register after the case was over without taking notes during the deliberations. Presumably, taking notes was not even mentioned explicitly in the instructions, since this was standard practice.

However, in Jaffa scribes largely continued with the former method of taking notes, and if they did keep drafts of the claims, these did not survive. In the authorized volume of protocols, the scribe allocated a certain space for each case and registered in it completed session records as the case was pursued (without always mentioning the beginning and end of each session). When the case was over, the scribe completed this protocol, amended it, and obtained the required signatures and seals. If the space allocated in advance to a certain protocol was not sufficient, he continued somewhere else in the volume; if the space was excessive, he crossed out the empty pages.[39]

In Haifa at the same time, the scribes followed the new instructions about recording the claims, which they also applied to the rest of the court sessions. When a session was over the scribe wrote it up in the same volume of protocols where the earlier sessions of this case had been recorded, but not on the same page. He recorded the cases in chronological order (fig. 17). Then he noted the date and the hour of the next session of that trial—if a decision had not yet been reached—and prepared the titles for the signatures of the participants. Later on, perhaps at the beginning of the next session, he read out this protocol. If anyone commented about missing or redundant information in the record, the scribe would correct the text, crossing out words or adding a footnote. The party that had requested the amendment would sign the footnote (fig. 17, first session). Then all the participants, the judge included, signed their names, placed their seals, or put their fingerprints under their respective titles. In the case of Amina versus Salim, two of the witnesses signed their testimonies by fingerprints (fig. 17, second session), as did Salim himself when the compromise reached by the parties finally received the judge's approval (fig. 17, fourth session). It appears that, sometime after a session record was prepared and before the next session, the judge read the new protocols and in the margins added some professional considerations on how to pursue the case. This register became the authorized version, and here, too, if drafts were made, they did not survive.

The difference between the two interpretations may be defined in terms of their focus. In the Jaffa version, the latter part of the procedure, the completion of the protocol record in the official register, was deemed more important. In this respect, this version was closer to the raison d'être of the familiar registration type of records. The form used in Haifa concentrated on the process of amending the protocols according to the comments of the participants and on keeping a record of this process. Its focus represents a more visible departure from the concept of the old registration, perhaps a bigger change than originally demanded by the central government. I will return to the significance of this difference for the construction of the family in the latter part of this chapter.[40]

Finally, when completed case records had accumulated in the volumes of protocols, the scribes would register their summaries twice—in one of the volumes of registrations with reference to the original protocol in the volume of protocols and in a separate authorized document that was handed to those involved. When a volume of protocols came to an end, the chief scribe edited it. The pages were apparently numbered in advance in both the volumes of protocols and registrations, judging by the cross-references and the explicit instructions.[41]

Family and Court Culture

The routine of protocol recording that the courts of Jaffa and Haifa adopted during this period brings to the fore the issue of the reconstitution of the family in the legal arena. I suggest that the entire experience in court, and particularly the recitation and validation of the record in the presence of the parties and other participants—professional jurists together with lay people—should be understood as a significant confrontation of lay people with legal concepts of the family. Lay people, both litigants and witnesses, participated in the deliberations and listened to the exchanges among the judge, the attorneys, and the scribes, exchanges in which their family ties and relations were formulated in legal terms. There was nothing new about being in the audience at these exchanges, but two features of the reformed court intensified this contact. One was the emergence of professional attorneys in the *shariʿa* courts; the other was the recitation and the signing by the participants.

I discuss the emergence of professional attorneys in the post-Tanzimat *shariʿa* courts in my broader research project and here only briefly mention the points that are relevant to this chapter. Unlike the claimant *(wakil)*, a layman who represented one of the parties free of charge in court, the *wakil daʿawi* was a professional attorney. The involvement of such attorneys in court, in the widespread and institutionalized form this took in the late nineteenth century, was a new phenomenon, with economic, social, and cultural implications within as well as outside the courtroom.[42] The involvement of professional attorneys resulted in longer trials and an intensive use of legal terminology, a point illustrated by the above case record. In such cases, lay people in court had more exposure to legal terminology on the family than in earlier periods.

At the same time, the presence and involvement of professional jurists with their own court agenda, in addition to the court personnel, tended to stress the procedural aspects of the court culture. The situation of the port cities and the judges' short terms of service combined to emphasize these aspects, as mentioned above. Thus, while lay people were becoming more involved in the legal culture, that culture was undergoing profound changes and the deliberations were becoming more legalistic. Whereas it is true that litigants who were represented in court by attorneys did not usually come to court themselves, other participants—witnesses of various kinds and sometimes even represented litigants like Salim—did appear. In some instances, only one party was represented by an attorney, whereas the other took part in all sessions. Some litigants would come to court accompanied by their relatives, who also became part of the audience, and, since several legal proceedings were usually scheduled for a single day, some of those who came to court for their own proceedings heard other cases while waiting.

Finally, there was the recitation itself. In addition to the court session, the participants were requested to sign the record soon after it was prepared. Whereas during the session they inadvertently became an audience, the recitation specifically gave them that role. It was not meant to be a lesson in Muslim jurisprudence, and most probably did not become one, but apparently it was a multilayered meeting not only between professional jurists and lay people. In most cases it was also an interaction between educated and illiterate people, elite and lower strata, and, last but not least, the state and its humble subjects. States have many ways of demonstrating their authority in and out of the courtroom, and the Ottomans, like any other rulers, had exhausted most of them during their centuries-long rule. The protocol record with all its symbols of state authority—seals, stamps, and stylized signatures—was clearly one of them. However, involving the people in the process of authorizing these documents by their own signatures, and in this way confirming the symbol of domination, appears to have been a brand-new concept.[43]

The parties and their witnesses certainly held their own ideas about relations within the family, but here they witnessed the scribe reciting their ties in legal terms, interrupted frequently by the judge or the attorneys to demand clarifications or amendments of the record. Presumably in many cases people did not understand most of the terms, yet they were standing there and their cooperation was vital for the completion of the procedure. Some may have taken part more actively, asking for their own amendments, and when the recitation was over signed the record. Some signatures, judging by the handwriting, were clearly of people who could hardly write but insisted on signing their names. Thus, it may be concluded that at least some of the lay people in court were becoming more familiar with the legal jargon and the current court culture and had their own ways of interpreting it. At the end of the day, their understanding of the legal concept of the family must have been strengthened in relation to other perceptions that shaped its construction.

Two points that were mentioned earlier are relevant here. First, there was a slight difference in the application of the novel procedure between the courts of Jaffa and Haifa. If the above analysis of the significance of the recitation for the restructuring of the family makes any sense, then this means that people in Haifa were exposed more intensely to this procedure than those in Jaffa. This is based on the assumption that only in Haifa was the recitation held after each court session. Second, the inclination of litigants to hire professional attorneys suggests another division among the clientele of the court in relation to the new procedure—a division according to class affiliation. Since hiring professional attorneys became particularly widespread among litigants of upper-class or successful and upwardly mobile middle-class families, it was mainly litigants of this social background who were not present in court and hence lacked the sort of exposure experienced by their lower- and mid-lower-level counterparts.

Some Reflections on Court, Family, and Modernity

Dialectically, then, the reforms substantially reduced the jurisdiction of the *shariᶜa* court as well as the *shariᶜa* law as a source of jurisprudence, but at the same time contributed to reshaping and reproducing its notions of the family. The relevance of these notions for the members of the societies under discussion and the interaction engendered with other aspects of the construction of the family are issues that cannot be investigated here. They seem to be extremely significant for the history of the family in these societies. Yet not only do they go well beyond the scope of this chapter, but apparently the *shariᶜa* court records alone are not sufficient as a source, and others must be added for this purpose. Thus, from the methodological point of view, it may be concluded that not only has this chapter illustrated the potential of the *shari*ᶜ*a* court record as a source for family history, but has also outlined some of its limitations.

Nevertheless, some preliminary ideas about the findings of this chapter and how they may contribute to further problematizing the reconstruction of both family and court culture in these societies seem to be in order. The changes that took place in the *shari*ᶜ*a* court were part and parcel of ambitious reforms that the Ottoman state had undertaken in the course of the nineteenth century. The reforms were meant to rationalize the state and equip it with the tools required for a stronger control over its domains. The *shari*ᶜ*a* court, as part of the legal apparatus of the state, was to take part in this project and contribute to the increasing involvement and visibility of the state bureaucracy in social and economic life.

This large-scale modernization process occurred in port cities that were undergoing rapid growth physically, economically, and socially. What kind of change would we then expect in the realms of family households, ties, and relations? If we look at the intensified encounter between lay people in court and the legal notions of the family and we notice that at the same time, the routine of the court tended to stress certain aspects and features of these legal notions—what role would the legal notions play in the reconstitution of the family? What role would the more intrusive state play in it? In other words, what would the passage of these societies to modernity look like when investigated through the prism of the family? What kind of insights about the tensions in these societies can we gain by looking at them from this perspective?

In the broader research that this contribution is part of, I discuss the work of the court in terms of gender and social justice, exploring the role played by the court in implementing *shari*ᶜ*a* rules that forced stronger family members to provide for weaker ones when the latter were in dire straits. I suggest that, in the face of the reduction of their juridical authority and the need to redefine their position as state representatives, the *shari*ᶜ*a* courts in Jaffa and Haifa were quite responsive to the legal demands of their constituencies in family matters, which became their formal field of expertise during this period, and that they made themselves particularly available to people of modest social and economic background. I assume that, following the substantial growth of the two cities and the implementation of the reforms in the nineteenth century, the population's demand for legal services grew. The relatively easy access offered by the *shari*ᶜ*a* courts, which at the outset were more familiar to these people than the new legal institutions, made these people perfect allies for the courts'

user-friendly attitude. Furthermore, we may recall that because middle-
and upper-class people were more likely to be represented by attorneys, it was mainly lay people of modest background who experienced the intensified encounter with legal concepts of the family in
the *shariᶜa* courts. It would seem, then, that various dynamics of change
in the legal arena in the late nineteenth century contributed to reshaping and emphasizing class differentiations within the court and in the
reconstruction of the family out of court.

In conclusion, therefore, I present the following preliminary hypothesis. The urban conditions in the port cities were undermining
multigenerational family households among the urban lower and mid-
lower strata at the same time that the reformed state began to invade
realms of life that had been carried on through the family and other
related social practices. At the same time, the encounter that took
place in the *shariᶜa* court between people from these strata concerning
the legal notions of the family contributed to strengthening the patrilineal family as a unit of social and economic support, while the user-
friendly attitude of the court helped avert the alienation that might be
expected to accompany a bureaucratization process of this sort. This
calls for further research questions: Were these the patterns that reshaped the construction of the family among the urban lower and
mid-lower strata? What happened at the same time among the upper
classes and how did it affect their humbler counterparts? And finally,
to what extent does the interpretation of the responsiveness of the
courts to the needs of people of modest background represent an early
version of the increasing appeal that Islamic frameworks and movements have had for the lower strata in various modern Muslim states?

Notes

This chapter forms part of a broader research project on Family and Court
in Post-Tanzimat Ottoman Palestine. Butrus Abu Manneh, Jun Akiba, Hakan
Erdem, Tomoki Okawara, Tal Shuval, Ehud Toledano, Ursula Wökoeck, and
Mahmoud Yazbak helped in tracing certain sources for this chapter, and I am
very grateful to them for sharing with me their observations on an earlier
draft. I also owe special gratitude to my friend Siham Daud for her invaluable
advice. This article is based on the following Court Records: *Jaffa Sharᶜia Court
Record (JCR)*, 1214–1332/1799–1914, The Library, University of Haifa; *Haifa
Sharᶜia Court Record* (HCR), 1287–1332/1870–1914, The Library, University of
Haifa. It is also based on the following official publications by the Ottoman
government: *Düstur¹* (birinci tertib) (i) 4 vols. (1–4), and 4 supplements, 1289-
1302/1872–85, Istanbul. (ii) 4 additional vols. (5–8), 1937–43, Ankara; *Düstur²*
(ikinci tertib), 12 vols., 1329–1927/1911–27, Istanbul. *Al-Dustur*, 1301/1884,
Beirut [translation of parts of *Dustur1* into Arabic, by Nawfal, Nawfal Efendi
Ni'matulla]; *İlmiyeSalnamesi*, 1334/1916, Istanbul.

1. Obviously, the shari'a courts primarily served the Muslim communities, particularly after the reforms, when they were left with mainly family matters to deal with. However, non-Muslims continued to apply to the shari'a courts—see also Doumani 1985, 160.

2. It should be noted, however, that in practice the shari'a courts sometimes dealt with civil cases as well. It appears that the new division of fields between the various court systems was not so clear-cut in practice.

3. Agmon 1984. See also Keyder, Özveren, and Quataert 1993; and Keyder 1999. The many population estimates for late Ottoman Palestine differ immensely. Justin McCarthy discusses the various Ottoman sources, compares them with other local and European figures and with the first British census conducted in 1922, and arrives at roughly the above-mentioned calculation for the population of Jaffa and Haifa (McCarthy 1990, chart 3, 15–16).

4. As far as I know, the records of the civil courts, which are supposed to be preserved in the Ottoman archives, have not yet been examined. It is my assumption that the foundation and maintaining of the civil courts was rather significant for the changes that took place in the shari'a courts, particularly in towns like Jaffa and Haifa, where the same judge chaired both the shari'a and the civil courts (Al-Dustur 1, 173, "Nidham al-mahakim al-nidhamiyya," 29 L 1288/7 I 1872). However, the specific interaction between the two courts will remain unclear until this source is studied further. See also Deringil (1998, 50–52), about tensions that developed between the two court systems in Yemen.

5. The court record of Ottoman Jaffa includes dozens of volumes from the turn of the nineteenth century onward. The record of Ottoman Haifa starts as late as 1870 and contains some twenty volumes, which include evidence of other volumes of records, both prior to and after 1870, which did not survive. See also Doumani 1985, 165–66. These court records are written in Arabic. Therefore, I use Arabic in transliteration for names and terms mentioned in this chapter, except for terms taken from sources in Ottoman Turkish and names of Turkish-speaking people. All dates not referring to the Christian calendar refer to the Hijri calendar.

6. These differences are discussed in Agmon 1994, 36–56.

7. Whereas these two types of record are to be found in both cities from the mid-1870s on, another difference between them should be noted. The record of Haifa appears to be more systematic and meticulous than that of Jaffa. This may indicate that more differences existed between the work of the two courts, portraying two vernacular court cultures. This issue will be discussed in my broader research project, while here I limit myself to a discussion of those differences between the records that are relevant to the new recording procedure.

8. See references made by the court in one case record to other records in a volume of registrations (fig. 17, first session, lines 4, 7). The aim of the registration type of record is explicitly mentioned in the instructions issued in 1874, requiring the scribes to ensure that the record was legible and written

clearly (*Düstur¹* 4, 83, "Sicillat-ı şer'iye ve zabt-ı da'ava-ı cerideleri hakkında ta'limat," 15 Z 1290/3 II 1874, Art. 3).

9. This assumption relies mainly on ethnographies of contemporary *shari'a* courts in which the legal process as well as the record that documented it were observed. Recording procedures similar in their principles to those described in this chapter seem to have been applied in these courts (Shahar 2000a, 56–57; Shahar 2000b).

10. There are many examples of such fine reconstructions. Here I will mention only "Le dilemme de Fatma" (Peirce 1998a), which I find exceptionally thrilling.

11. See fig. 17.

12. JCR, *Hujaj* 47, 8 M 1293–93 S 1294/1876–77.

13. Scholars who worked at the *shari'a* court of Nablus claimed that these volumes are supposedly kept there. There are also rumors about earlier volumes from Haifa in private possession. So far I have not been able to verify this.

14. HCR, *Jaridat al-dabt* (no number), 1308/1890; Marino and Okawara 1999, 54. Surprisingly, the number of scholarly works drawing on late-nineteenth-century court records that have appeared so far is rather small. I am not aware of the existence of protocols preserved in other court records, but hopefully future research projects will uncover further volumes.

15. *Düstur¹* 4, "Sicillat-ı şer'iye ve zabt-ı da'ava-ı cerideleri hakkında ta'limat," 15 Z 1290/3 II 1874, 83–85; "Bi'la beiyne mazmunuyle 'amel ve hükm ca'iz olabilecek surette senedat-ı şer'iynin tanzimaine da'ir ta'alimat-ı seniye," 4 Ca 1296/26 IV 1879, 78–82.

16. *Düstur¹*1, "Bi'l-'umum mahakim-i ŧer'iye hakkynda müceddeden kaleme alynan nizamname," "Nüvvab hakkynda nizamname," 17 B 1271/5 IV 1855, 301–24; *Al-Dustur* 1, 1310/1883,130–41, "... Umum al-mahakim al-shar'iyya," 16 S 1276/14 IX 1859, 147–49; *Düstur¹* 2, "Hükkam-i şer'iye nizamnamesi," 13 M 1290/12 III 1873, 721-5. See the discussion in Akiba 2000, 3–5.

17. See the discussion of this policy in Yazbak 1998, 46–49. In Nablus, on the other hand, it seems that this policy was not implemented so strictly, apparently because the *ulama* families of Nablus were much more cohesive and deep-rooted in the power elite than their counterparts in Jaffa and Haifa (Yazbak, 1997, 71–91). Doumani portrays a rather different picture for Nablus after 1866, claiming that most of its judges were of Turkish origin (Doumani, 1985, 164). See also Messick 1993, 176–82; İnalcık 1991, 4. The principle of judges not serving in their hometowns is mentioned by several historians as an accepted norm for earlier periods, but it seems that its implementation changed over time. See İnalcık 1965. İnalcık mentions this principle for the sixteenth century, and Özkaya for the eighteenth century, but both without a

specific reference. I am grateful to Jun Akiba, whose ongoing Ph.D. research deals with the Ottoman İlmiye in the nineteenth century, for sharing with me his findings and knowledge of these issues (Akiba, 1998, 185–214).

18. The improved position also involved greater responsibility and mandatory sanctions in cases of irresponsible conduct by scribes (*Düstur*[1] 4, "Sicillat şer'iye . . ." 1874, 83–84, Arts. 7, 9, 10). Doumani presents a similar argument regarding the position of the chief scribe vis-à-vis the judge in the court of Jerusalem in the sixteenth to eighteenth centuries (Doumani 1985, 158). However, he interpreted the changes that took place in the nineteenth-century *shari'a* courts, whereby the responsibility for appointing judges for Nablus was transferred from the judge of Jerusalem to the center, as an indication of the growing importance of Nablus in comparison with Jerusalem (Doumani 1985, 164). This conclusion ignores the fact that the same policy was implemented in the other subdistricts and reflected the efforts to centralize the legal system. His conclusion should be seen in the context of the mid-1980s' research on reforms in the provinces: Doumani studied the Palestinian court records for the above-cited article at a time when many of the prominent provincial histories had not yet been published (including Doumani's own significant book, 1995). For a discussion of the notions behind some of the legal reforms, see Messick 1993, 54–66; Deringil 1998, 44–46, 50–52.

19. See also Messick 1993, 178.

20. According to the amended instructions, a judge would be appointed to serve at a certain court without a terminal date and would then be moved to another court either following his request to the central authorities or at their initiative (*Düstur*[2] 5, "Hükkam-i şer' ve me'murin-i şer'iye hakkynda kanun-y muvakkat," 19 Ca 1331/26 IV 1913, 352–61). In Jaffa, Murtadazade Sayyid Mahmud Nadim Efendi served at the turn of the century as court scribe under the judgeship of his father, Muhammad Darwish Efendi al-Murtada from Damascus (JCR, *Hujaj* 83, 1317–19/1899–1901). Sheikh Ahmad Khayr al-Din al-Mallah, from Tripoli, was appointed judge of Haifa in 1905, and he brought his nephew, Muhyi al-Din, with him to be the chief scribe (*başkatib*). Muhyi al-Din stayed in Haifa and pursued his legal career there. Later, in 1911, under the judgeship of Abdülhalim Efendi (see below, note 26), he became deputy to the judge, conducting legal procedures outside the court, in the town, and in the villages of the subdistrict of Haifa. At the same time, he continued his service as chief scribe and held this position when the case that I discuss in detail below was deliberated and registered. His handwriting can be observed in this case record (fig. 17, third session), and he also edited that volume of protocols and added the references to the following session (HCR, *Jaridat al-dabt* 5, 1331–32/1913–14). See also Yazbak 1998, 52.

21. Hallaq 1998, 418–22.

22. Hallaq's main concern was to show that the recording of legal proceedings was already an institutionalized tradition in the pre-Ottoman *shari'a*

courts and not an Ottoman innovation. He substantiated this claim rather convincingly. However, I detect some confusion over the issue of the preservation of records, which he saw as a mere coincidence, not as an indication of two different kinds of institutionalization. Ibid., 417, 434–35. My argument is that long-range preservation of the record was not part of the institutionalization process typical of the historical circumstances described by Hallaq, whereas it was a typical feature of the institutionalization of the Ottoman court record. See also Findley 1980, 8–12, 51–57, 86–87.

23. Redhouse 1890, 1206.

24. Apparently, the first step in this direction was taken when instructions issued as early as 1840 used the term *zabt* to mean the scribe's note-taking while listening to the litigants' claims at the beginning of a legal proceeding. These instructions were probably based on existing practices of the scribes in the *shariᶜa* courts. Akiba, Ph.D. dissertation (in progress).

25. See figures 16 and 17. The proceedings lasted from October 1913, when Amina bint Othman al-Sabᶜ Aᶜyun gave power of attorney to Ibrahim Edhem Efendi Ṭalcy to represent her in court and sue her husband, until February 1914, when the judge Abdülhalim Efendi decided the case, apparently on the basis of a compromise reached between the parties out of court (HCR, *Sijill*, L 1331-Ca 1332/IX 1913-IV 1914, 35, 79, 99, cases 497, 595, 630; *Jaridat al-Dabt* 5, L 1331-R 1332/IX 1913-III 1914, 110-11, 120, 124, 131, case 83). All four accounts of this case were recorded in two corresponding record volumes of protocols and registrations, which I was fortunate to trace in the court record of Haifa. Both volumes cover about six months, September 1913– March 1914. The volume of protocols *(Jaridat al-Dabt 5)* mainly includes protocols of lawsuits *(dabt al-daᶜawi)*.

26. For the biography of Judge Abdülhalim Efendi, see Albayrak 1996, 1:121–22. On the chief scribe Muhyi al-Din, see note 20 above. When already in Haifa, the recording scribe Hasan al-Badran used to teach another immigrant from Nablus, young Abd al-Raʾuf Karaman, who later married his daughter, Ibriza (privately communicated by members of the Karaman family). The Karaman family became one of the most successful families in Haifa during the Mandate period. It is not clear if and how the defendant in this case, Salim Qaraman, was related to this family.

27. The legal terms mentioned in this case record are rather common in the vocabulary of *shariᶜa* family law. Since the focus of this discussion is not the legal content of this terminology, I mention the meaning of these terms only briefly. According to *shariᶜa* family law, the husband's duty is to provide his wife and minor children with their basic necessities. *Nafaqa* is the sum of money paid by the husband to his wife for buying these necessities. *Maskan sharᶜi* is her residence as a married woman and should meet certain conditions set by *shariᶜa* law.

28. It appears from the protocol that the couple eventually settled the matter out of court. This was then legalized by the judge at the fourth court

session. Several indications in the protocol point in this direction. For instance, after the witnesses were heard there is no record of the procedure of verification of their credibility (*tazkiyya*); the verdict was not based on the content of their testimony, nor was it mentioned in the record explicitly as a decision made by the judge, as in other cases. In fact, there is no continuity between the record of the third and the fourth sessions. But whereas in the protocol of this case the records of all the sessions were kept even after a compromise had been reached, in its registration, due to the nature of this type of record, only the compromise as approved by the judge was deemed important. See also Agmon 1994, 42–43, where I noted several cases of alimony in which the registrations indicate no previous dispute or lawsuit and where I suggested that this does not mean that such a dispute did not precede the verdict. At that point, I was not yet aware of the official difference between the registration and the protocol.

29. See previous note. On the gap between case records and reality and on its implications for historical reconstruction, see Ze'evi 1998.

30. On questions of privacy in densely populated urban areas, see Marcus 1986.

31. See, for example, Marcus 1989, 112–13.

32. It seems that the scribes maintained several protocol volumes, each one containing records of a specific legal procedure, in accordance with the instructions from Istanbul (*Düstur¹* 4, "Sicillat şerʿiye . . . ," 1874, 78, Art. 2).

33. One exception is the first volume of protocols from Jaffa, which was registered after the issuing of the first set of instructions. The second set of instructions was much more detailed than the first (which, apart from its title, mentioned the recording of *zabt* in only one of its articles, no. 16. See note 8 above). We can assume that the first set suffered from a lack of clarity and that a second, more specific set of instructions was then issued and implemented.

34. *Düstur¹* 4, "Biʿla beyine . . . ," 1879, 79, Art. 6.

35. See Peirce 1998b, where she discusses the circumstances under which the litigants and witnesses were recorded in verbatim summaries of divorce cases in the sixteenth-century Anatolian *shariʿa* court records.

36. HCR, *Jaridat al-Dabt* 5, 6–7, case 51.

37. Albayrak 1996, 1:121–22.

38. *Düstur¹* 4, "Biʾla beyine . . . ," 1879, 78–79, Art. 4.

39. As a result, when compared with those of Haifa, these records contain a smaller number of amendments, which were officially allowed in the clean register, provided their number was limited (*Düstur¹* 4, "Sicillat şerʿiye . . . ," 1874, 85, Art. 16: *Düstur¹* 4, "Biʾla beyine . . . ," 1879, 80, Art. 12). In addition, it is not always clear whether a record covered several court sessions or just one. See some examples of crossed-out pages illustrating the method of allocating a

space in advance for each case record, JCR, *Hujaj* 139, Za 1329—R 1332/XII 1911—III 1914, pp. 10, 14, 17, 22, 25–27, 57–58, 110–11, 203, 210, 224.

40. Recently, in the earliest volume of protocols that survived in Haifa (HCR, *Jaridat al-dabt*, 1308/1890), a strange page was found that does not belong there. It contains what seems to be a raw draft of the protocol that is recorded, session by session, in the pages just before and after it. Apparently, it contains the notes that the scribe took during the sessions as a basis for the final protocol and was then forgotten. First, its existence points to the process of preparing a protocol in the first years of the new recording procedures in Haifa. Second, because this draft was prepared at that early stage, it may testify to the tradition of taking notes, which the scribes followed when only summaries of cases were officially registered in the court records. I am grateful to Mahmoud Yazbak, who gave me a copy of this page.

41. *Düstur*[1] 4, "Biʾla beyine . . .," 1879, 83-5, Arts. 1, 16.

42. İnalcık points to evidence of the activities of professional attorneys much earlier on in some Ottoman cities. The authorities objected to this activity and prevented it (İnalcık 1991, 5). About the attorneys in the civil courts, see Özman 2000.

43. This raises the question of the extent to which this involvement represented a change in the concept of the participation of the subjects of the empire in government. This issue will be discussed in my broader research project.

10

Property, Language, and Law: Conventions of Social Discourse in Seventeenth-Century Tarablus al-Sham

Heather Ferguson

Techniques for the writing of history evolve in relation to the sources employed. When new caches of documentation disrupt the historiography of a particular field, they do so by demanding a methodological reassessment. Ottoman historians encountered such a moment upon the addition of documents from local Islamic courts to their repertoire of historical evidence.[1] The strength of the *sijillat* is their potential to render visible aspects of socioeconomic life often obscured in records from the imperial center. Documents, however, do not transparently speak the history of the past. They have their own stories of production and consumption located in particular contexts of "cultural performance"—a phrase I will use in this chapter to mark a dynamic process of social action that both reproduces and transforms the normative structural features of a community. Recognizing this feature of historical documents compels a distinct mode of reading and investigation. Thus, as I engage with a *da'wa*, or case of formal litigation, brought before the Islamic court of seventeenth-century Tarablus al-Sham, I will consider the text as an artifact not of a generalizable past but rather of its own trajectory of operation.

This chapter is an exercise aimed at illuminating a number of general methodological challenges by focusing on the specificities of a single case. Set within the broader scholarship concerning the place of Islamic court records *(sijillat)* in social and cultural analyses of Ottoman history, a case-study approach returns the singularity of these documents to the forefront of the debate. My analysis highlights the temporal nature of the *sijill* as a written trace of social events. By taking seriously the event-centered nature of the document, I draw attention to the shifting constellation of persons and things that constitutes both the "text" and "context" of legal practice in the Islamic court. While focusing on a single case cannot substitute for the meticulous work necessary to craft a microhistorical synthesis of a place or period, it highlights the difference between the court as a site of lived experience and the historian's use of documents to reconstruct a narrative portrait of the past.

Following from the strategy of a case-study approach, and keeping in mind the temporal and contextual issues inherent in the documentary record, I suggest that we read the text as a performance. This mode of reading concentrates on the document as a linguistic act but moves away from a reductive understanding of language either as a transparent medium of communication or, when copied down in summary form by the court scribe, as a mere representation of the judicial process. Instead, I argue that the *sijillat* can be understood as something more than partial summaries of social negotiations taking place outside the documents themselves. Rather, these texts perform a unique social act by labeling and demarcating the very terms of such negotiations.

Setting the Scene

At the close of the first month of Rabi'a, 1078 H. (September 1667), a landholding Janissary named Amr Agha ibn Sha'ban departs Tarablus al-Sham for an extended trip to Istanbul and designates a man of similar status to be his *wakil,* the representative authorized to take charge of his estate.[2] Returning to find that the estate yielded no revenue during his absence, Amr immediately blames the *wakil,* one Ali Amr Basha ibn Abdullah al-Rajul. Angered by Ali's apparent misuse of funds, Amr accuses him of embezzling from the estate. Ali first argues that Amr conferred on him full executive license and that, by implication, he has no right to question how the estate was managed. He attempts to prove this by enumerating the precise nature of the dues and expenses incurred during Amr's absence, including customary taxes on both the land and its products, standing debts owed to various Ottoman officials, general support of the household, and expenses for his own personal maintenance. When Amr refuses to accept the credibility of this delineation of funds, Ali shifts his defense toward an attestation of personal honor and ethical conduct. He takes a vow averring that not one extra *dirham* was withheld for himself from the total proceeds of the estate *(la al-dirham al-fard)* and that he responsibly fulfilled his duties as a temporary executive. Amr does not engage with the issue of morality, however, and demands legitimate proof that he did indeed bestow absolute discretionary authority on Ali before departing for Istanbul.

Ali meets this demand by calling forth two military companions stationed in Tarablus who testify to the occasion of this exchange of authority and to the list of responsibilities assumed by Ali. These include the collection of revenues from agricultural and animal products and the payment of dues and debts, as delineated above. One additional phrase holds greater significance for my later interpretation of this case. Linked to the question of "household support" *(nafaqat beytuhu)*, the witnesses mark the exclusion of Amr's wife from the permissible access and authority granted to Ali in this contract *(ma ada hilaluhu ana fi dhalika zawjatahu)*. The phrasing of this exception marks an explicit set of distinctions between rights, ownership, and responsibilities to which I will return later. Ali displays a *fatwa*, a legal opinion issued by a *mufti* or local religious functionary *(wa abraza min yadihi fatwa sharifa)*, in order to bolster the testimony of the two men by attesting to his veracity and general propriety in matters of commercial contracts. With both the spoken and written evidence of Ali's integrity and moral standing in the community, the judge *(qadi)* lifts the onus of blame from Ali and declares that no further accusations concerning the case should be brought before the court.

My discussion of the court record as a site of performance singles out three "moments" in the narrative sketched above. Most visible are the ways in which the relationship between the two claimants is defined in both legal and social terms. The conditions of the contract, the movement necessitated by Amr's link to Ottoman officialdom, and the choice of the court for determining the possible abuse of a prior agreement all gesture toward a particular constellation of political, socioeconomic, and geographic forces that set the parameters of the case itself. I define the second moment as one that inheres in the various assumptions of land and property operating in the case. These indicate the complexity of ownership in a system where access and obligations incurring from rights to revenue are disassociable from actual possession of the land. The final and perhaps most striking moment is the process whereby Amr's wife comes to literally demarcate the distinction between ownership and proprietary rights. I argue that these three moments in the case are at once textual remnants of fleeting legal negotiations and markers of the social conventions "on trial" in the case. The following sections provide the historiographic and theoretical contexts for my analysis of these moments in regard to their linguistic and performative dimensions.

Objectifying the Record

My reading of the case summarized above has a dual focus. First, in treating the case as a cultural performance, we must ask: what *is* a court record, or better yet, what does the document *do*? I address this question by folding together two modes of social analysis. The first is a cluster of ideas collected under the heading "practice theory,"[3] while the second concentrates specifically on performance as both a historical and interpretive act.[4] For purposes of simplifying what is an otherwise complex literature on discourse analysis and communicative practice, I will use the writings of Bourdieu and Bakhtin as representatives of these respective positions.[5] United by their efforts to interrogate the relationship between symbolic forms or genres and social action, they together articulate a meaningful framework for our analysis of court records.

Bourdieu and Bakhtin's efforts to analyze the relationship between event and structure help me to draw a correspondence between the action that a document records—and often remains the sole record of—and my own acts of analysis and critical intervention. Bourdieu employs the "habitus" as a way of thinking about the interplay between lasting dispositions or rule-governed social forms and emergent, subjective, voluntaristic acts. When Bourdieu addresses issues of language he emphasizes the action-centered, diachronic nature of language use and production. Bourdieu is intent on discursive fields rather than specific moments of utterance. In other words, as in his notion of the habitus, discourse consists of a kind of social interface encompassing speech, writing, and cultural evaluations of each in a specific ethnographic context. Bakhtin's theory of discourse proposes that literary works have a structure of their own not to be conflated with the world they purportedly represent. These formal principles, however, are laden with specific social values that mediate meaning to human consciousness. Each genre or type of discourse emerges as a consequence of this interplay between formal principles, social values, and the situation or object it describes. Furthermore, the formal content of a work is oriented toward "action contexts" and is thus a feature of practical reality. According to this view, ideological creations (documents of any kind) are both the product of historical action and a necessary part of the process that renders this action possible.

The second focus of this essay arises from a specific disciplinary question: how can a historian interested in the materiality of social interaction deploy such records when elaborating her own narrative of the past?[6] I intentionally use the word *elaboration* here because it refers both to the inherent complexity of historical texts and to their careful treatment in the hands of scholars. This term also foregrounds the historian's labor as an issue of practice in the present. In his insightful analysis of the production of historical knowledge, Michel de Certeau separates the writing of history, which he terms the "scriptural function," from other dimensions of "the historiographical operation."[7] He employs the idea of "practice" to refer both to the acts that produce history and to the work of the historian intent on creating a meaningful statement about the past. These comments clarify the "labor" of this essay, where I interrogate the historian's analytical move from the specificity of a document's own criteria of intelligibility to the sociocultural arena that constitutes the site of its production. Analyzing this process as a multilayered cultural performance reminds us that there is a necessary and simultaneous relationship between these two dimensions of the document and that this relationship possesses its own "local history"—an analytic frame that I use to refer to my own synthesis of practice and performance as methodological approaches to documents.

My idiosyncratic use of the phrase "local history" is meant to identify and discuss the series of conjunctures between conventional social and discursive forms and their instantiation in a particular document. These conjunctures include: that of a situated event; the formal dimensions of litigation; the institutional economy of law and morality in the court; the court's active participation in the reproduction of discursive forms of power and value in society; and finally, the ways in which this legal performance is referred to, cited, evaluated, reported, looked back upon, replayed, and otherwise transformed in the generation of social life. These acts of "looking back" and "reevaluating" necessarily encompass my own work with the document. Each interpretive act becomes part of the document's history and cannot be disassociated from the set of relationships that define its production and reproduction. In the case of documents that have been treated by multiple historians in differing historiographical contexts, their local history is in one sense an accumulation of these varied readings.

The Court Historian's Labor and the "Act" of History

Any pronouncement of the skills necessary for historical analysis calls attention to the interpenetration of the document, its field of production, and the historian's labor with the document. Clarifying the particular

ways in which these three moments intersect in historiographical practice constitutes one significant reworking of the relationship between
text, context, and history-writing. To critically understand the implications of this three-way relationship, a student of Islamic court practices needs to take seriously both the particular instantiation of the
record and its role in reproducing an administrative and religio-legal
discourse. The moment of litigation in an Islamic court is a complex
conjuncture of jurisprudential terminology, formulaic references to the
location of the court and the presiding judge, citational references to
clients and witnesses, and the scribal transcription of the event itself.
The technical strategies employed in this chapter both to read and
then discuss the process of reading these documents represent my
current understanding of the *sijillat* as a unique archival source. I first
encountered the material and philosophical detail of the records in the
context of a training seminar with Beshara Doumani, where the sheer
complexity of the documents was palpable. Even as my familiarity
with the texts increased, these initial moments of "awe" cautioned
against any uncomplicated interpretation of the records either as social products or as representatives of a unique societal function.

In one of the more persuasive methodological discussions of court
records as a source for women's history, Iris Agmon identifies three
aspects of legal production that limit a historian's interpretive possibilities.[8] First, she claims that because we do not have a full transcript
of court proceedings we are unable to assess the legal acumen of the
women who represent themselves—and that without a detailed account of their strategies or negotiations we cannot fully assess women's
general knowledge about the law. Second, she notes that there is a
striking lack of detail concerning the events that have led up to a
given court case. The "story" of the case is rarely narrated in conventional form, and we are left with a formulaic recounting of its outcome. Finally, Agmon argues that we cannot determine the overall
social milieu in which the events took place from the records themselves. As a solution to these analytical problems, Agmon proposes
that we concentrate our efforts on elaborating the social function of
the court so as to determine more readily the link between actual
events and court summaries.

The interpretive framework defined in this chapter provides a
counterpoint to Agmon's position. In a previous section I identified
the dual meaning of the "act" as both the historical event and the
historian's interpretive labor with its documentary evidence. This
provides an alternative mode of reading the past—a mode that differs
from any historiographic approach that assumes the separation of a
written record from the "real" of social life. The act of interpretation

in such approaches entails reaching a satisfactory reconciliation between the internal elements *(text)* of the document and the external flux *(context)* of society. If, by contrast, we were to read the court record as an *enunciated event* (i.e., as a temporally defined performance of speech), such an opposition would not singly constitute the problem of historical writing. Avoiding a representational understanding of the document's content, this reading takes seriously human actors and actions in history—as well as the idea that history itself is a continuing performance—and so necessarily interweaves norms, everyday practices, and social reality. Moving in for a more focused reading of the event transcribed in our record, we must attempt to approximate this analytical method to the elaboration of the event itself. Although this requires a close reading of the document, it does not falsely concretize it as an artifact alienated from its social world. Rather, we begin with the assumption that the practice of litigation in effect constitutes this ground of the real. Thus, the position of the Janissaries as a socioeconomic force in the region, the social ties elaborated through exchanges of property, and the gendered dimension of ownership in Islamic law are products of this performance, not its contextual background.

At this point, I will break with the abstract nature of the preceding comments and return to the case of the traveling Janissary. By tacking back and forth between the document itself and the various tools of reading outlined above, I hope to illustrate structurally the kind of historical praxis that I am arguing for in this chapter. In my reading of the document, the focal point of this case is property and the rights and responsibilities incurred in managing it. The economic boundaries of a viable estate are defined with reference to the monetary value of various products and the expected subtraction of funds for taxes, debts, and general maintenance. Property, however, is not defined solely as a material thing situated in an economic field of investigation. The case of Amr and Ali shows how property transactions also play a significant role in forming bounded social relationships— or even how property itself is defined socially. Following David Sabean's critical reflections on the dynamic between material goods, the location and content of culture, and the theatricality of social relations, I suggest that the court is a primary site of cultural performance. If notions of society and property are constituted in the same act, and in the words of Sabean, paraphrasing Rousseau, if "property is not a relationship between people and things but one between people about things,"[9] then the grammar of legal transactions helps to identify how social, political, and economic fields are articulated in specific historical conjunctures. The overlapping sets of relationships—between individuals and families, law and religion, local elites and imperial officials—performed in the court provide a lens through which to identify the simultaneous formation of legal subjects, juridical authority, and the configuration of socioeconomic relations.

The Ethics of Property

In the scribal summary of Amr and Ali's case before the court, we can see how the materiality of property is mobilized through social intercourse. This observation refers us first to the explicit ties between tax collectors, landowners, and a far-flung imperial administration, as well as between lenders and borrowers in more localized transactions. More significantly, however, we see that property is not referenced as a static object but is instead the site where a specific ethical code is elaborated. The returning Amr is convinced that his delegated representative has somehow misused the position conferred on him. With this allegation, the case becomes a moment of social negotiation where the materiality of property is suffused with a set of ethical expectations, and the *qadi*'s ultimate decision rests on a validation of the representative's moral standing. Thus, moving interpretively between the materiality and the sociability of property becomes one of the more productive ways of reading and evaluating court records.[10] At a bare minimum, our case demonstrates the inherent potential of these sources to *perform*, rather than merely to describe, the ambivalences of local administration, communal allegiances, and the gendered nature of ownership. But what is nonetheless central to my argument is that the estate's boundaries and productive capacities are defined socially, a point that emerges most clearly in the distinction made by the defendant between "household" and "estate."

The difference between the two terms is first marked in the testimony of the witnesses summoned by Ali to verify his appointment as full executor of Amr's estate. Having observed the actual event at issue here, their presence in the court initiates a kind of reperformance of the original interaction between Ali and Amr. The witnesses attest to the transaction by enumerating the particular duties Ali was entrusted with: paying the taxes on land, oxen, and cows, administering arrears, and collecting outstanding debts. Their testimony circles back to the initial discussion of whether Ali was entrusted with the full administration of the estate. According to the witnesses' phrasing of the contract, Ali was meant not only to attend to the financial viability of the departing Janissary's property but was accorded the further responsibility of providing for Amr's household (*yanfaqa beytahu*). Through this qualifier the witnesses mark a difference between estate and household, and Ali's role as full executor is legitimated by his relationship to both. Tracing the significance of this contrast explicitly addresses the link between the materiality and sociability of property and suggests that the "household" is both a physical domain and a set of social assumptions concerning marriage and family.

This conception of household stands in contrast to its use in the broader literature on family and economy in the region. The nature of the household as an analytic category is a salient feature of family history within the larger configuration of Middle Eastern Studies. The recent intensification of investigations into the family dovetails with an ever-expanding use of Islamic court records as sources for social history. These documents have provoked numerous questions, many of which address the category of the family as it is constituted or represented in court practice.[11] Unable to ignore the recurring refrain of family names and the obvious linking of kinship, politics, and power, scholars here expressed a growing interest in this conjunction of personal relationships and the larger social order. The products of their analyses include case studies of elite family politics,[12] commentaries on the discursive treatment of women in jurisprudential and theological texts,[13] and investigations of the political and economic life of a community. These various engagements with family history emerge from close readings of *waqf* endowments, marriage and commercial contracts, miscellaneous court proceedings, and the devolution of property through wills.[14]

Most historians of the "Middle Eastern family" are now wary of the previously assumed homogeneity of this phrase and its designated object. In building new approaches to this problem, many attempt to demonstrate the diversity of familial forms in the region and to suggest that scholars should take care to be specific about the period, context, and form of the particular relationships they are describing. Very few respond by addressing the nature of archival sources themselves and the role that particular documents play in shaping our reconstructions of family life in all its multiplicity. A recent article by Beshara Doumani is a good example of an approach that addresses these issues.[15] Doumani employs a social constructivist approach to history that allows him to trace how family, property, and the law are defined and enacted in and through discursive practices.[16] Combining methods of the political economist with concerns of the cultural historian, Doumani is able to capture the flexible system of *waqf* endowments and their role in establishing sexual difference and idealized familial forms. He argues that ideals of the family—which varied dramatically between Tarablus and Nablus, the two cities of his investigation—were articulated and institutionalized through exchanges of property.

Iris Agmon, in her article on gender and class in the court records of late-nineteenth-century Jaffa and Haifa, provides a model for historical investigation that considers both the orthographic features of texts and the specific cultural context of their production.[17] Rather than accepting the household as a predetermined unit of analysis, she stresses the need to individualize our understanding of this concept and to identify those structures of power that define the parameters of men and women's social existence.[18] One of the handful of monographs and articles written within the rubric of a social and cultural history of the family deals explicitly with the "household" as both an experiential and an analytic category. In *Istanbul Households: Marriage, Family, and Fertility, 1880–1940,* Alan Duben and Cem Behar examine household composition in a mode typical of demographic histories of the Western family.[19] Their portrait of the city is based primarily on two empirewide censuses taken in 1885 and 1907. Duben and Behar also successfully employ oral histories as more than archives of memories, sentiments, and beliefs, using them as a way to interrogate the content of the censuses. This methodology generates a text devoted to the problematic tension between normative indices and social practices.

While Agmon's work on the narrative absences in the court record, Doumani's argument for the construction of family through processes of endowment, and Duben and Behar's efforts to define an experiential component for their research methodology all suggest more complex readings of how to understand and analyze "family," their suggestions reinforce an opposition between documents (whether they be written or verbal) and the historical context of their production. In my final return to the case of Amr and Ali, I will argue that a series of relationships exist between an event as history, its reperformance in the court, our access to this cultural performance in the form of a scribal summary, the actual language of the document with its singular relationship to the things and acts it objectifies, and our reobjectification of the case for purposes of analysis. Focusing now on the "household" as both a social process and a category of analysis, let us work back through the links between social and material interactions as they are linguistically inscribed in the dispute between Amr and Ali.

The Materiality of Language

Concerned to publicly account for the apparent lack of revenue accruing during his absence, Amr turns to the court and initiates a sequence of interactions wherein an ethics of socioeconomic responsibility is elaborated. While the ostensible motive for the litigation is financial, I suggested above that the case converges on evidence bearing witness to the defendant's moral standing in the community and on a sense of the household as a social contract of interpersonal obligation. This blending of economic and moral considerations leads me to argue that people negotiate property via the elaboration of an ethical code, with ethics defined as the means whereby individuals relate socially to a particular moral understanding. Morality is necessarily an exclusionary system, in that it normalizes definitions of correct and incorrect behavior. As such, it distinguishes both between social communities and among individuals within specific communal settings. Morality is also a possession, one that can be attested to by witnesses and an affirmation of personal integrity.

Both evidentiary forms are invoked in this case: the first appears with Ali's witnesses and the second is established jointly by the *fatwa*, which provides the *mufti*'s declaration of Ali's upright character, and by Ali's own enactment of the vow. Each of these refers to distinct temporal moments whose combination in the scribal summary embodies a folding-in of several "contexts." First, we have evidence of a contract performed between the two men prior to Amr's departure. This event is "presented" and literally registered as having occurred through the witnesses' testimony. The *fatwa* exhibited during the proceedings inscribes another historical moment of encounter that we infer to have taken place between Ali and the *mufti*. The *mufti*'s position in society as a legal resource and a significant social institution is thus activated within the court and written into the scribal summary. Court performance, then, cannot be read as a unitary event in time, for it consists of multiple temporalities, all of which *are* the case.

These temporal or historical moments are further complicated linguistically in that each of these events is known only through a textual indicator of its prior occurrence. Yet the text itself is also an event, and the scribal summary "acts" by presenting, organizing, and inscribing the written traces of the initial contract, the encounter between Ali and the *mufti*, and the actions and utterances that occurred in the court itself. Language is embodied—it is not separable from its community of users. Neither can it be understood simply as a vehicle that communicates an event or thought, for only in the speaking or writing of a thing is it enacted and rendered socially operable. The contract, for instance, exists in the naming of its details by various participants in the case. In fact, the outcome depends on the description of full executorship. Its social content, or the responsibilities assumed to be a part of the position, are both itemized and actualized in their delineation. This is true for "household" as well: we can't reduce it to a physical structure or even to the site of economic production and reproduction. In the context of this case, the term is suggestive of a complex of duties and responsibilities that transcend its material qualities. It further links Ali's role as executor to social conventions of marital support. The term *nafaqa* refers most consistently to the support expected by a wife from a husband throughout marriage and, in specified conditions, after a divorce. Locating Ali's function as executor of Amr's estate within this framework invokes the structural significance of contracts for modes of social interaction (commercial, religious, familial). The household, we can argue for this case, is identified as a contractual relationship first between husband and wife and then between Amr and his delegated representative.[20]

In reviewing its analytical significance in the literature on the family, I have argued that the household might best be understood as a social relationship embedded in negotiations over property. In this framework property is construed socially and vice versa. The explicit linking of ownership and household to filial obligations renders the organization of property through social relations visible in this case. Thus, gender and its relationship to notions of ownership becomes an important concern. I have waited to engage fully with this aspect of the case for two critical reasons. First, it is important to recognize that social relations, while certainly gendered, cannot be fully understood in these terms. And second, gender as an analytic category serves to mark the role of power and hierarchies of difference in establishing sociocultural forms. As it is not the only way to understand exclusionary mechanisms of community-building, however, I chose first to work through a system of ethics in which social constructions of gender are operationalized. This approach recognizes the importance of difference to the functioning of any community while not narrowly defining it in sexual terms. Further, it signals a constitutive interpenetration of shared systems of values, their investment in material goods, and their enactment in daily practice.

The striking appearance of Amr's wife occurs toward the conclusion of the witnesses' testimony. It follows immediately from the reference to household support as one of the various duties assumed by Ali. The witnesses attest that Amr did not intend for this support to include contact with his wife. We are left to speculate whether Amr himself included this exception or whether the witnesses employ their own interpretive understanding of the limits on Ali's representative authority. The phrase remains in the third person: he did not mean for his wife to be included in the acceptable fulfillment of Ali's duties. We can conclude that while Ali's position as executor allows him to "seize hold and dispose of" a number of Amr's material goods and social responsibilities, the rights and obligations of the marital contract are excluded from his realm of permissible action. The clarity and force of this exception suggests a strong link between notions of household, marriage, and sexuality. In many descriptions of Islamic marriage as a contractual relationship, the woman is said to submit her body in return for the husband's support. Ostensibly, they each have the right to demand full satisfaction of these terms, and, indeed, numerous studies suggest that women used the court to ensure their maintenance rights.[21] In this case, however, the slippage between "full" proprietorship of a household and sexual relations with one's wife illuminates the limits of ownership just as it clarifies the social meaning of *nafaqa*. While the legitimacy of the marriage contract rests on the mutual consent of both partners, and contracts in general entail a relationship between two legally recognized individuals, the use of the term in this case gestures toward another sense of *nafaqa*. The "exception clause" inserted in the case indicates a certain anxiety over boundaries of ownership and entitlement as they are negotiated between the two men.[22]

Nafaqa and its assumed link to both material and marital duties and obligations emerges at an important juncture in Amr and Ali's negotiations over property. Displacing the customary players in negotiating *nafaqa* where the law recognizes the rights of both men and women in a contract of marriage, this case suggests that *nafaqa*'s material and social connotations demand clarification. As we have seen above, a correspondence between household and wife emerges in the case, and both are separable from Ali's position as proprietor of Amr's estate. In a period of land administration where ownership was a fairly uncertain category, linked at most with rights to agricultural surplus, property was by nature configured as a sphere of social relations. Rights and privileges associated with surplus revenue were recognized and registered in legal contracts. These contracts mark a sphere of administrative relations in which proprietary rights were commended and disputed and actual ownership was of less concern than continued access to wealth and status. But the Janissary's household and wife stand in a domain mandated by direct and personal ownership removed from competitive rights to agricultural products. Unlike a common interpretation of *nafaqa*, however, this case demonstrates an internal differentiation in this domain between material assets and a social contract. Ali's substitution for Amr did not sanction any contact with the "household-as-wife," although it did necessitate the continuation of material support for Ali's spouse in his absence. The multiple uses of proprietorship in this case demonstrate that property remains inseparable from the social negotiations that render certain material goods and services meaningful.

In conclusion, while the methodology argued for in this chapter yields significant insight into the dynamic nature of documentary evidence and its intricate relationship to historical analysis, this can only be a partial reading of an otherwise vexed issue. Having identified the problem—the relationship between conventional social structures, be they marriages or court records, and singular events, acts, or instantiations—I resist claiming adequate knowledge of the cultural assumptions performed and reinforced in the linguistic production of the scribal summary. A field of social engagement in Bourdieu's sense cannot be located in a single record; it rather requires an extensive analysis of social practice. This is my future goal as a historian of the ways in which social relationships and cultural conventions are recited and performed in the Islamic courts. By emphasizing the act and its necessary relationship to language in the case of Amr and Ali, I was able to engage in a critical reading of this particular performance. The limited nature of my exposure to the court records prevents me from progressing further to locate this case within a larger field of contractual and ethical relationships. Nevertheless, I have attempted to illustrate how a close reading of a single document need not be alienated from a commentary on the multiple contexts of its production.

Notes

1. The importance of court records for Middle Eastern social history is discussed in Doumani 1985.

2. *Sijillat Tarablus,* 1:75.

3. See for example Bourdieu 1990, 1993; de Certeau 1984.

4. Butler 1993, 1997; Bakhtin 1993; Bakhtin and Medvedev 1978.

5. My work with these theorists began seriously under the guidance of linguistic anthropologist William Hanks at the University of California, Berkeley. Hanks constructs a meaningful synthesis of Bourdieu and Bakhtin in his own attempt to understand the relationship between genres, the "language market," and social context (Hanks 2000). While my analysis of context departs from Hanks's framework, I am indebted to his insightful formulation of the problem.

6. For one of the most helpful book-length treatments of this issue, see Spiegel 1997. Spiegel uses the "social logic of the text" to negotiate the problem of text and context within the epistemological challenges of the so-called linguistic turn in cultural theory. In the end, however, she requires the transparency of some historical texts against which to read critically the primary object of her analysis. Thus, Spiegel's framework can only be a partial solution to the problem of text/context.

7. de Certeau 1988.

8. Agmon 1996, 126-42.

9. Sabean 1990, 17.

10. For additional examples of this approach, see Doumani 1995 and Doumani 1998.

11. See Doumani 1995; Faroqhi 1981; Gerber 1994; Cuno 1992.

12. Meriwether 1999; Schilcher 1985.

13. Sonbol 1996b; Stowasser 1994; and Tucker 1997.

14. For a general introduction to the meaning and function of *awqaf*, see Barnes 1986.

15. Doumani 1998.

16. For an example of this kind of analysis outside the field of Middle Eastern history, see Sabean 1990.

17. Agmon 1998.

18. This intellectual position is clearly articulated in one of the most significant interventions in the field of family history by feminist scholars: Thorne and Yalom 1982. In her review article, Tamara K. Hareven carefully delineates the trajectory of this shift in theoretical perspective; see Hareven 1991a, 253–86.

19. Duben and Behar 1991. Here I mean only to suggest that the authors' notions of the family and their research methodologies are modeled on the work of European and American historians. This may be linked to their period of investigation and emphasis on the processes of westernization at the turn of the century. Their eyes are turned toward "the West" both in terms of the object of study and in regard to their own scholarly assumptions. The fact that they lift Istanbul out of either an Anatolian or Islamic cultural context and argue instead for its "uniqueness" in the sense of its resemblance to Western urban lifeways further underscores this tendency in their work. (Indeed, Duben and Behar claim Istanbul's uniqueness in light of evidence that the modal family was nuclear even prior to their initial census date.) Invoking Michael Anderson's typology of historiographical work on the European family, we could classify Duben and Behar's book as representative of both the "demographic" and "sentiment" approaches. See Anderson 1980. This further substantiates my claim that Duben and Behar straddle a methodological and theoretical divide in the broader literature on the family. It also reveals, incidentally, that one of the salient arguments in their work concerns the relationship between modernity and the nuclear family form.

20. For a general discussion of the significance of marriage contracts, see Tucker 1997.

21. See the articles in Sonbol 1996b.

22. For a discussion of ownership as a legal concept in Hanafite law, see Johansen 1981, 281–303; and Johansen 1995. For a review of Hanafite law as it defines the relationship between material and marital contracts, see Imber 1996.

IV

Family as a Discourse

11

Ambiguous Modernization: The Transition to Monogamy in the Khedival House of Egypt

Kenneth M. Cuno

Introduction

On Thursday, 16 January, 1873, a contract of marriage was agreed to between Tawfiq, the crown prince of Egypt, and Amina Ilhami, granddaughter of the late viceroy Abbas Hilmi I (r. 1849–54). In celebration of the event the reigning khedive, Ismail (r. 1863–79), held a reception at al-Hilmiyya Palace attended by Tawfiq, several ministers of state, and the leading religious dignitaries. Cannons were fired, sweet drinks were had, and the khedive received the congratulations of his guests in order of their rank. Poetry was composed and recited for the occasion by al-Sayyid Ali Abu al-Nasr and Muhammad Qadri Bey. Thus began the celebration of the first of four consecutive weddings of the children of Ismail, each of which entailed a week of receptions, banquets and entertainment, illuminations, and a public procession in which the bride was delivered to her husband's palace.[1]

Like their Ottoman suzerains, the Egyptian khedival (viceregal)[2] family staged celebrations of births, circumcisions and weddings, funerals, and commemorations of religious and dynastic holidays and anniversaries as a way of building popular legitimacy. The month of celebrations accompanying the weddings of Tawfiq and his younger siblings was one such calculatedly lavish display. Yet these weddings were remarkable in another important respect, namely, as marking the beginning of a transition in the pattern of conjugality within the khedival family, from slave concubinage and polygyny to royal endogamy and monogamy.

As members of the Ottoman ruling class, the first five viceroys of the khedival family, beginning with its founder Muhammad Ali Pasha (r. 1805–48), emulated the imperial family in Istanbul by maintaining large households and having multiple consorts of slave origin. From very early in its history the Ottoman line had been reproduced through women of slave origin, very few of whom were elevated from the status of concubine to legal wife between the late sixteenth century and the late nineteenth century. Concubinage and polygyny were features of the imperial household up to the abolition of the caliphate in 1924,[3] some fifty years after their abandonment by the khedival family. Khedive Tawfiq (r. 1879–92) became the first monogamous ruler of Egypt. His wife, Amina, acquired special prominence, at least in part because she was his sole consort and not one of many. She was respectfully referred to in Arabic as "the wife of the khedive" (haram al-khidiwi), and in French and English as the vice-reine, khédiveh, or khediva.

Then and later, some Europeans detected a decline in the practice of polygyny in the Ottoman and Ottoman Egyptian upper classes. In both Istanbul and Cairo in the 1870s, "the now prevailing fashion among the upper class of having only one wife" was reported, and that impression persisted up to the First World War.[4] The retired British consul-general in Egypt, Lord Cromer, opined that "[t]he practice of monogamy has of late years been gaining ground amongst the more enlightened Egyptians," and mentioned as examples the late Khedive Tawfiq, his son Khedive Abbas II (r. 1892–1914), and the state ministers Riyad Pasha and Sharif Pasha.[5]

The concern of Cromer and other, mainly British observers with the evils of polygyny reflected changes in British family culture, one of the most important of which was the rise of the ideal of companionate marriage. This middle-class ideal placed greater emphasis on the affectionate relationship of the conjugal couple than on their economic relationship. According to it, a wife should be her husband's companion and helpmate, managing their household and taking charge of the education of their children.[6] Polygyny was incompatible with a couple-centered notion of family, and as Cromer's remark indicates, the khedives' monogamy was welcomed as both a sign of change and as a positive example for the rest of Egyptian society to follow.

This chapter discusses the meaning of the khedival family's transition to monogamy in the context of late nineteenth- and early-twentieth-century Ottoman Egyptian politics and culture. It argues that the transition to monogamy was not the result of a newfound belief in its virtues, nor of the precocious spread of the ideal of companionate marriage. Rather, it was the consequence of a new marriage strategy of royal endogamy—endogamy within the khedival family—that was implemented by Khedive Ismail. The purpose of this strategy was to consolidate family support for his son and successor, Tawfiq, following a change in the law of succession that limited it to Ismail's male descendants. Endogamy would conciliate and co-opt the collateral lines within the extended khedival family that had been excluded.

In Ottoman culture "monogamy" was a necessary consequence of marriage to a princess. While in theory, Muslim men could have up to four wives and any number of slave concubines, a man who married a woman from a family or household of equal or higher standing than his own would often be constrained from having additional consorts out of deference to her family or household. This contingent aspect of polygyny was so well understood that the khedival palace did not publicize the transition to monogamy as such, even though, as we have seen, it publicized the activities of the family. Nor did the Arabic press in Egypt consider the restriction of most of Ismail's sons and grandsons to a single wife to be something out of the ordinary, and worthy of comment. There does not seem to have been a perception that any significant change in the system of conjugality had taken place.

Europeans, on the other hand, took notice of the transition to monogamy without understanding what was behind it. The khedives themselves helped in this: ever mindful of European opinion, Ismail and, later, Tawfiq professed their belief in the virtues of monogamy and their opposition to harem slavery, which in European eyes were linked. However, they expressed these opinions to Europeans, not to the Egyptian public. Yet, even if the khedival family's abandonment of concubinage and polygyny was a consequence of dynastic politics and not an aim in itself, as I argue, could it have contributed to a trend toward monogamy? This change occurred about a quarter of a century before Egyptian modernist intellectuals mounted an assault against polygyny and the seclusion and veiling of women. The landmark event was the publication of *The Liberation of Women* (*Tahrir al-marʿa*) by Qasim Amin in 1899,[7] which caused a storm of controversy. While Amin was not the first Egyptian to voice such criticisms, the controversy itself indicates that a modernist view of the family had not yet gained widespread acceptance. Yet after the turn of the century the tide quickly began to turn, as modernist writers increasingly upheld a version of the ideal of companionate marriage—a partnership between husband and wife based on respect and affection—which, it was understood, could only be monogamous.[8] After the First World

War polygyny, seclusion and, veiling rapidly came to be regarded as anachronisms.

Whether the way for that was prepared by a late-nineteenth-century trend of monogamy in the upper class, as Europeans perceived, is uncertain. And whether the khedival family contributed to it, even inadvertently, is equally uncertain. Nevertheless, the khedival family's practice of monogamy seems to have acquired importance in Egyptian public opinion with the passage of time, following the prohibition of the slave trade, and as the modernist ideal of companionate marriage took root. Thus Abbas II and the *khédiveh mère* Amina were constrained to cover up their continued acquisition of slaves, and even a polygynous interlude in Abbas's life.

In addition to dynastic politics and European misapprehensions, then, this story evokes some of the complexity and ambiguity of the process by which one style of upper-class domesticity superseded another in late-nineteenth- and early-twentieth-century Egypt. This ambiguity arose from different "readings" of the khedival family's move. European perceptions were grounded in their understanding of the "harem system," which, as they constructed it, was antithetical to monogamy and a sound family life. Hence the apparent adoption of monogamy by the khedival family was regarded as a significant departure from the traditional culture.

The perspective of Ottoman Egyptian culture was different. Within its boundaries a man could practice single or plural marriage, and choose to have concubines or not. Polygyny was contingent on wealth more than anything else, since only those who could afford to support the additional wives were able to practice it. And still another factor inhibiting polygyny, even in the upper class, was the high status of certain wives.

Constructing the Harem System

Europeans understood family life in the Muslim East through the frame of the "harem system"—a term not in use in contemporary Turkish or Arabic—by which they referred to a cluster of practices, the most salient and objectionable of which were slavery, polygyny, and the seclusion and veiling of women. These practices were understood to constitute a "system" in the way in which they were connected. Slavery often was held to be the linchpin. Without a ready supply of slave concubines and domestics, it was believed, polygyny would become impossible and Ottoman domestic culture would be transformed.[9] At other times polygyny was held to be the practice that necessitated the seclusion of women and the employment of domestic slaves.

Notwithstanding their disapproval of the "harem system," the more acute European observers sought to explain it rather than condemn it outright. Although the harem was (and still is) imagined by some to be a site of sexual debauchery, few women writers (who unlike men were able to enter harems) failed to note how far from reality those fantasies were. To be sure, during the first three-quarters of the nineteenth century the Ottoman imperial and Egyptian khedival households contained anywhere from several hundred to over a thousand female slaves. However, all but a few of these women were celibate, and subject to a strict rule of discipline under the master's mother and wives. Harem discipline was comparable to that of a convent; to suggest that harems were like "brothels" was "outrageous."[10]

Hardly any account of harem culture failed to point out that slavery in the Muslim East bore little resemblance to the harsh system known in the Americas. Harem slaves could look forward to manumission and marriage with a trousseau after a period of service. A slave concubine who bore her master's child could not afterward be sold. Her child was free and legitimate, having full rights as an heir on a par with the children of legal wives. It was not unusual for such concubine-mothers to be freed and married by their masters. Slaves were not viewed as "an exploited labour-force, nor merely [as] degraded sexual objects. They had definite legal rights and, most important, they became integrated into the extended Muslim family and the Ottoman political system."[11]

Slavery was ended in Egypt by outlawing the trade rather than the institution itself. Under British pressure, Khedive Ismail banned the importation of African slaves in 1877. Seven years later the ban was extended to apply to the importation of white slaves (by then, mainly Circassian women) as well as to the selling of slaves between households within Egypt. Additionally, beginning in 1877 slaves could apply at the British consulate or at one of four bureaus of manumission and be granted their freedom, and thousands did so.[12]

As for polygyny, it was believed not to be very widespread, if for no other reason than that of the cost of maintaining multiple wives and/or concubines. In Cairo and Istanbul in the first half of the nineteenth century, the number of polygynous men was estimated to be no more than 5 percent. Consistent with the limited extent of polygyny, the harem system was held to be a characteristic of only urban upper-class society.[13] Finally, and as was noted earlier, polygyny, and implicitly the harem system, was said to be in decline in the second half of the nineteenth century.

Outsiders' understanding of harem culture necessarily reflected cultural shifts and debates within their own societies.[14] This is not to say that they failed to see "the reality," but rather that they brought to bear a preformed set of values, assumptions, and interests in their observations, and hence they were more perceptive of some things than of others. Their perceptions represented a certain, contingent reality, but only that. For example, the detailed firsthand accounts we have of harem life by European women are based on access to only the most elite households.[15] There is great attention given to the interior décor, the clothing and jewelry worn by the women, and the elaborate protocol, details that apparently were deemed of interest to readers. The more numerous and modest harems of the remainder of the upper class went unvisited and undescribed, and the existence of harems among the rural notability was hardly noticed.[16] The cruelty of the slave trade, and the sexual exploitation and violence to which female slaves could be subjected, also went largely unremarked.[17] European racial perceptions also permeate these accounts, which tend to read a rigid racial hierarchy into the harem culture. Finally, the existence of a "harem system," in the way that Europeans understood it, is open to doubt. Polygyny, still legal in Egypt, did not disappear with the end of slavery. Nor were female seclusion and veiling *(hijab)* a consequence of slavery and polygyny. Rather, they were grounded in notions of sexual modesty and class respectability, which are historically contingent.

Reframing the Shift to Monogamy

Egyptians began to respond to European criticisms of the harem, and of plural marriage in particular, during the last third of the century. In *Alam al-Din* (Alexandria, 1882), probably written between 1868 and 1872, Ali Mubarak defended polygyny as being sanctioned by divine law, while carefully pointing out that most "Eastern" men had only one wife. He went on to explain the difference between marriage practices in "the West" and "the East" in terms of demography, claiming that while there were more men than women in France, there were more women than men in Egypt.[18] Another defense of polygyny, against claims that it soured marital relations, corrupted mores, and upset the household regime, was published by the chief clerk of the Court of Appeals of Cairo in the newspaper *al-Ahram* in 1881. Like Mubarak, his point of departure was the holy law. After working his way through a juridical argument, he added for good measure that many a man has had only one wife and his relationship with her has soured. If that is to be the criterion for prohibiting plural marriage, then marriage should be prohibited altogether![19]

Writings such as these demonstrate that plural marriage had become a contested issue by that time. Thus, it should not be surprising to hear an echo of the European viewpoint in the words of Khedive Tawfiq, Egypt's first monogamous ruler:

> The great thing . . . is to educate women. They will then not only become true companions to their husbands, but will take an interest in the primary education of the children, which at present is so neglected, and adds so much to our difficulties when they first come to school. Family life is the greatest blessing, and it is impossible unless both men and women are educated. It is the aim of my life to achieve that result; and in time, I trust, we may be able to do away with slaves in the harem. I hate the very idea of slavery, and am doing all I can to put it down: moreover, a harem is only wanted for many wives; with one wife there won't be any necessity for seclusion. It is wrong to imagine that our religion requires us to have more than one wife, or to make the wife our slave instead of our equal. The Hanefite rite [school of law] defines clearly the position of women, and assigns to them almost a leading place; but how can women lead if they are ignorant and uneducated?[20]

Tawfiq often expressed such views, though only (as far as I can tell) to Europeans.[21] Whether he was sincere is not as significant, for our purposes, as his evident familiarity with European criticisms of the "harem system." He followed contemporary thought in linking the education of women to the abolition of slavery, since it was held that upper-class wives would have to take over directly the management of the household and the raising of children. The influence of the ideal of companionate marriage is evident here, in his view that education should prepare women to be "companions to their husbands" and mothers. Finally, he associated polygyny, slavery, and the seclusion of women together with "the harem."

On another occasion, in a more transparently calculated remark, Tawfiq claimed to have married for love.[22] Yet like most royalty, he had not been free to follow his heart in marriage. That decision was made by his father, Ismail, and the new marriage strategy inaugurated with the four princely weddings was presented to Europeans as a decision to impose monogamy on his sons. Ellen Chennells, the governess of one of Ismail's younger daughters, gave this account:

> We were told that four royal marriages were to take place during the winter, and rather a new state of things was to be inaugurated with them. Mohammed Ali had had the same kind of harem as the Sultan, consisting exclusively of slaves, and this custom had

been continued by his successors down to the Khédive. But the latter in mature age wished to adopt the European law of one wife, and direct succession from father to son, instead of the old Mussulman custom of inheritance through the eldest male of the family. The second he succeeded in establishing, by fixing the succession in the person of his eldest son, Mohammed Tewfik Pasha, and the first, by restricting each of his sons to one wife of equal rank with himself.[23]

The self-conscious way in which these weddings were represented is striking: one was told that they represented "a new state of things." The old system was reduced to nothing more than slave-filled harems, consistent with European perceptions, and the khedive was said to be determined to introduce the "European" rule of monogamy and primogeniture, even though primogeniture was by no means universal in Europe. One almost has the sense of reading a press release crafted to present the khedive in the best light and to flatter Europeans at the same time.

Chennells's account hints at what was behind the shift to monogamy by linking it with the change in the law of succession and the princes' marriage to women of equal social standing, namely, princesses from the extended khedival family. A man who married a princess was not permitted to have additional wives or concubines. Not only were Ismail's sons restricted to one wife as a consequence of marrying princesses, but so were the husbands of Ismail's daughters.[24] In spite of what contemporary Europeans were led, and perhaps wished, to believe, the transition to monogamy in the khedival family was not a straightforward case of the adoption of a "modern" or European-derived practice, nor even an end in itself. Nevertheless, Ismail's decision to marry his sons to princesses was an important departure in dynastic marital strategy, one that must be situated in the context of Ottoman Egyptian ruling-class culture in order to be understood.

The Politics of Marriage and Reproduction in the Imperial and Khedival Houses

During most of its history the reproduction of the Ottoman ruling class took place within its elite households. The imperial household in Istanbul was not only the home of the sultan, where he reproduced his dynasty, but also a place where thousands of male and female slaves were trained, the men being prepared for service in the military-administrative elite and the women to become the wives of these state servants in most cases. The military-administrative elite resembled smaller versions of the sultan's household, commensurate in size with their rank and revenues. In much the same way, Muhammad Ali, founder of the khedival dynasty, ruled Egypt through a "household elite" consisting of blood relations, in-laws, freed slaves, and others "who had entered his service by private agreements or were clients by virtue of their household affiliation."[25]

As in the imperial household, in Muhammad Ali's household male and female slaves were prepared for entry into the political elite. The pasha employed male "graduates" of his household (freedmen or mamluks) as military commanders, ministers of state, and provincial governors, as is shown in Imad Ahmad Hilal's important new study of slavery in nineteenth-century Egypt.[26] As in the imperial household, also, most slave women trained in the khedival harem were married to men in the Pasha's service as a way of binding them to him. P. N. Hamont wrote:

> Among Turkish princes it is a very ancient usage, and one that Muhammad Ali has continued in the government of his pashalik, to give female slaves from the harem to the officers of his nation. . . . Each of the functionaries who receives a female slave is given money and a furnished house.[27]

Hamont, a French veterinarian in Muhammad Ali's service, only vaguely understood the culture he was describing. The gift he mentioned was a trousseau that remained the woman's property. Around 1840, or about the time that the pasha was forced to adopt policies of fiscal and political retrenchment, he increased the marrying of his female slaves to state servants. Hamont, apparently believing that the harem was a site of sexual licentiousness, claimed that the pasha was advised to reduce the size of his harem "on account of his age and to conserve his energy"! We may infer instead that his aim was to cement the loyalty of these men and to retain their service. Nearly every female "graduate" of the pasha's harem in Hilal's list was married to an official or officer. The pasha also made grants of land partly for the same reason.[28]

The large slave households maintained by the ruling elite were thus an integral part of the political system. In the age of khedival autocracy the ruler's household, including its harem, was an instrument through which a dependent elite was created and reproduced. By about the middle of the century, the new state-run schools superseded the khedival household in training men to serve in the officer corps and civil service. However, the practice of marrying harem women to state servants, thereby binding them to the ruler, continued through the reign of Khedive Ismail. He, along with princesses and other princes, gave freed slaves in marriage along with houses and grants of land of anywhere from fifty to one thousand feddans (approximately acres). For example, three principals in the Urabi revolution were connected to the palace through marriage. Mahmud Sami al-Barudi married the daughter of Ismail's nurse *(dada)*, and, later, the sister of Mansur Pasha Yakan, a relation of the khedive and the husband of his oldest daughter, Tawhida. Both Ali Fahmi and Muhammad Ubayd married women from Ismail's harem. Such well-connected wives were desired, since they had "influence . . . in pushing husbands to the front."[29]

Despite their slave origin, these women had high status due to their affiliation with the khedival household. They were socially equal or superior to their husbands, even when the latter were freeborn. Hamont attributed the following words to an official "burdened" with such a wife:

> With one of the Pasha's slaves . . . our position is extremely unfavorable. It is a master that the viceroy gives us, and a master that it is extremely difficult to satisfy. At every moment of the day, this woman recalls her origin, she has visits that require expenses, and our monthly salaries are insufficient for the demands of one day. As soon as they leave the [viceroy's] palace, all of these slaves want to command, and henceforth it is we who respectfully kiss the hand of a lady. A woman from the great harem . . . evinces no deference, no respect for her husband, and when he goes to her, the former slave remains sitting, and hardly looks at him! If we show bad humor, if our attitude is not respectful to her taste, the new wife returns to the palace of the viceroy and complains against the man that the master has given her![30]

To Hamont this was a world turned upside down, in which a free man respectfully kissed the hand of a former slave woman. The husbands of elite former slaves such as these most likely were constrained from taking additional wives or concubines, and that could have contributed to the impression of a trend toward monogamy in the upper class. One observer attributed the supposed trend to "wives [who] are jealous of their rights, and—whatever may have been the laxer rule in the good old times—they now-a-days set their faces stoutly and successfully against illegitimate rivals," that is, concubines.[31] In order to be able to do that, however, a woman had to be of equal or higher standing than her husband.

The bankruptcy of 1875 marked the beginning of the obsolescence of this system of marrying harem women to reinforce ties of clientage between the ruler and the elite. In the next several years, which witnessed the Urabi Revolution and the beginning of the British occupation, the foundations of khedival autocracy were undermined. The settlement of the bankruptcy deprived Ismail of his extensive properties as well as of his personal control over state finances. His successors, beginning with Tawfiq, were subject to the financial discipline of a civil list, and lacked the resources with which Ismail had maintained his huge household. At the same time, slaves became more difficult to procure and more costly once the trade was prohibited. Finally, the khedive no longer had exclusive control of government appointments, and one could seek political patronage elsewhere. The impact of these developments on the khedival household is suggested by its shrinkage under Tawfiq, whose harem slaves were reported to number only sixty.[32]

As in the case of Barudi's marriage to the sister of Mansur Yakan, marriage to free, highborn women was another way in which an ambitious man could attach himself to the ruling class. Here also, a man was usually married into a socially equal or superior family and was limited to one wife. Both Sharif Pasha and Riyad Pasha, praised by Cromer for their monogamy, were married to women of high standing. Sharif was married to Nazli, daughter of Sulayman Pasha al-Faransawi (the former Col. Sève), one of Muhammad Ali's top commanders. Riyad was married to the daughter of Husayn Pasha Tapuzada, a Balkan Turk who came to Egypt with Muhammad Ali. Even below the level of the ruling class, a woman of sufficient social standing (or her guardian) could insert a clause in her marriage contract effectively imposing monogamy on her husband, by making his acquisition of a second wife or a concubine subject to her approval. [33]

Finally, Ottoman grand viziers and high commanders often married imperial princesses, and in similar fashion, Muhammad Ali's daughters were wed to top commanders and officials.[34] Plural marriage was out of the question when one married an imperial or khedival princess. Previously wed wives were divorced, and previously acquired concubines were let go.

From Muhammad Ali through Ismail, the khedives emulated still other practices of the imperial household. With the exception of Muhammad Ali's first wife, Amina Hanim (d. 1824), all of the consorts of the first five khedives were of slave origin. Muhammad Ali married Amina long before becoming the viceroy of Egypt. He had only one other legal wife, Mahduran (d. 1880), whom he probably married after the death of Amina.[35] Otherwise he conformed to the Ottoman practice of reproducing through concubines. Hilal's research turned up the names of fifteen of the pasha's consorts, including Amina and

Mahduran. Except for Amina, none had more than one son, an indication that the pasha had also begun to follow the established Ottoman policy "according to which a woman would bear no more than one son to a sultan (or prince)." In addition to the known children of these women, Muhammad Ali had another seven sons who died at an early age, the names of whose mothers have not been preserved. Assuming that the "one-mother-one-son" principle was applied consistently, the pasha would have had no fewer than twenty-two consorts, and there were more than that, since not all gave birth to boys and some had no children at all.[36]

In some other respects the khedival family departed from the imperial model. Khedival princes married and set up their own households, and were employed in political offices and commands, whereas Ottoman princes were confined, denied a public role, and not allowed to father children unless they ascended the throne. The viceroys also married some of their consorts, unlike the sultans. Ibrahim had six consorts, two of whom were legal wives, but none of whom had more than one son. One of the five consorts of Abbas I bore the title hanim, indicating she was a legal wife, while the others were qadins or recognized concubines. None had more than one son.[37]

The famous consort of Said Pasha (r. 1854–63), Inji Hanim (d. 1890), also appears to have been a legal wife. Some otherwise perceptive foreign residents were convinced that she was his sole consort, a measure of the obscurity of Malak Barr Hanim (d. 1890), who bore all of Said's children. Like Muhammad Ali and his grandson Ismail, Said was attuned to international opinion and "courted publicity." Inji Hanim may be an early example of the "diplomatic wife"—the wife that Ottoman statesmen in the later nineteenth century designated as the one to receive the wives of foreign diplomats and other lady visitors. Indeed, she acquired her fame among Europeans mainly due to her willingness to receive visits by foreign women, who admired her beauty and intelligence.[38]

Khedive Ismail assembled the largest household in the khedival family since his grandfather. He had fourteen recognized consorts, each of slave origin, none of whom had more than one son. Four were legal wives. He married the "First" and "Second" princesses, Shahinat Faza Hanim (d. 1895) and Jananyar Hanim (d. 1912), before his accession, and the "Third Princess," Jasham Afit Hanim (d. 1907) sometime afterward. He married Shafaq Nur Hanim (d. 1884) in 1866, elevating her to the position of "Fourth Princess" about fourteen years after she gave birth to his first son, Tawfiq. The sultan, whose firman that year established primogeniture as the law of succession in Egypt, required the khedive to marry the mother of the heir apparent.[39]

Ismail's Dynastic Strategy

In the Ottoman sultanate the rule of succession of the eldest prince became established in the early seventeenth century. As a consequence, father-to-son succession became extremely rare, occurring only three times in twenty-two generations.[40] The principle of succession of the eldest was written into the firman of 1841 that created an autonomous Egyptian province under the hereditary rule of the Muhammad Ali family, and with similar results. Following the brief regency of the pasha's son Ibrahim, the viceroyalty went to the latter's nephew, Abbas Hilmi I. Abbas was succeeded by his uncle, Muhammad Said, and Said was succeeded by his nephew, Ismail. The next two in line were Ismail's half-brother and uncle, Mustafa Fadil and Muhammad Abd al-Halim.

As was mentioned earlier, the khedives never followed the Ottoman practice of confining princes and denying them a public role. Khedival princes were routinely employed in commands and offices. The creation of a pool of princes with experience and a taste for power helped to foster rivalries and factionalism among Muhammad Ali's potential successors. The sharpest cleavage occurred between his son Ibrahim and his grandson Abbas. Ibrahim forced Abbas into exile in the Hijaz, and tried to deny him the succession. As viceroy, Abbas purged many of the Egyptian and French officials who had served his predecessors, and became embroiled in a dispute with the other senior princes over the division of Muhammad Ali's estate.[41] Even after Abbas's death there were rivalries among princes who were presumed or potential successors to the viceroyalty. The idea of changing the law of succession to primogeniture—an idea attributed to each of Muhammad Ali's successors—both derived from and fed these rivalries.

Ismail became the heir apparent when his older half-brother, Ahmad Rif'at, was killed in a railroad accident, and there were persistent rumors that Ismail was somehow behind this tragedy.[42] Additionally, when in 1866 Ismail, as khedive, obtained the change in the rule of succession to primogeniture, it quite understandably caused a rupture with the princes previously next in line, namely, Mustafa Fadil and Abd al-Halim. The latter were obliged to live in exile in Istanbul. Mustafa Fadil, who had served in the imperial government, now began financing Young Ottoman exiles in Europe as a way of pressuring the sultan to restore his right of succession. During the next several years, relations between Cairo and Istanbul worsened to the point of crisis, due in part to the khedive's behavior as an almost independent sovereign. Things were eventually patched up, and a new firman in June 1873 confirmed the new law of succession and other privileges, such as official use of the title khedive, that had been granted earlier.[43] In the intervening years Ismail was concerned lest the sultan change his mind and revise the law of succession once again.

It was in these circumstances that Ismail decided upon a strategy of endogamous marriage within the extended khedival family. Having restricted the succession to his own progeny and denied it to collateral lines, his new marriage strategy seems to have been designed to conciliate those other lines and to consolidate their support for his descendants. We can infer this from the first marriages of his children, nine out of twelve of which were endogamous (table 9). Three spouses were children of Ahmad Rifʿat, and a fourth was his granddaughter, indicating a concern to conciliate that line. Two other spouses were daughters of Ilhami, the son of Abbas I, evidently chosen for the same reason. None of the spouses were the children of Mustafa Fadil or Abd al-Halim, the two princes displaced by the change in the law of succession. The breach with them was irrevocable, and Ismail bought up their properties in Egypt to discourage them from returning.[44] Even after his deposition and exile in 1879, most of Ismail's remaining children married endogamously, which may indicate that the ex-khedive hoped to return to the throne.

In the context of Ottoman Egyptian politics and culture, then, the really significant change heralded by the four princely weddings of 1873 was the shift to royal endogamy. Monogamy was a consequence of this move and not an end in itself, even though Chennells and others were led to believe that it reflected Ismail's conviction "in mature age . . . to adopt the European law of one wife." In its extensive coverage of the four princely weddings, the official gazette, al-Waqaʾi al-Misriyya, never raised the issue of monogamy. The restriction of Ismail's sons to a single wife as a consequence of their marriage to princesses was so obvious and familiar an aspect of Ottoman Egyptian culture that no comment was necessary. In this respect the contrast with discussion of the earlier firman changing the rule of succession is instructive. Not only was it celebrated widely, but it was explained in al-Waqaʾi al-Misriyya as a measure to give the khedivate greater stability. Here the dynasty's rhetoric of progress and advancement was deployed, and it was explicitly stated that primogeniture was something favored by European states.[45]

The Reigns of Tawfiq and Abbas II: Beginning of the End of the Harem System?

During the reign of Tawfiq, his wife, the *khédiveh* Amina, was often present at official events, along with the khedive's mother. Amina's

Table 9. The First Marriages of Khedive Ismail's Children

Prince or Princess	M. Year	Spouse
Tawhida (1850–1888)	1868	Mansur Pasha, son of Ahmad Pasha Yakan[a]
Muhammad Tawfiq (1852–92)	1873	Amina, daughter of Ilhami, son of Abbas I
Fatima (1853–1920)	1873	Muhammad Tusun, son of Said
Husayn Kamil (1853–1917)	1873	Ayn al-Hayat, daughter of Ahmad Rifʾat, son of Ibrahim
Hasan (1854–88)	1873	Khadija, daughter of Muhammad Ali theYounger, son of Muhammad Ali
Zaynab (1859–75)	1874	Ibrahim Fahmi, son of Ahmad Rifʾat
Ibrahim Hilmi (1860–1927)	?	Qamar, Circassian[b]
Mahmud Hamdi (1863–1921)	1878	Zaynab, daughter of Ilhami, son of Abbas I
Ahmad Fuʾad (1868–1936)	1895	Shivakyar, daughter of Ibrahim, son of Ahmad Rifʾat
Jamila Fadila (1869–96)	1879	Ahmad, son of Ahmad Rifʾat
Amina Aziza (1874–1931)	1896	Mustafa Shakib Bey
Niʾmat Allah (1876–1945)	1890	Ibrahim Fahmi, son of Ahmad Rifʾat[c]

Sources: al-Waqaʾi al-Misriyya, 1873–79; Khanki 1938; Tugay 1963; Hilal 1999; *Burke's Royal Families of the World* 1980.

Note: Ismail had at least seventeen children (nine sons and eight daughters). Only those who lived long enough to marry are shown above, and only their first spouses.

[a]Nephew of Muhammad Ali.

[b]Most likely a former slave (no public record of marriage).

[c]Widower of the late Zaynab (above); marriage contracted but not consummated.

unprecedented prominence was due in part to her being the khedive's sole consort, rather than one of many, but there were other contingent factors that favored her emergence as a public personality. She seems to have had a formidable personality, and moreover as a royal princess with a formal education (including French) she was much more capable of asserting herself than her predecessors, who were of slave origin. With the deaths of Tawfiq's mother and paternal grandmother in 1884 and 1886 she became the senior woman in the khedival house, and she retained that seniority afterward as the mother of Khedive Abbas II. Finally, there were the changing needs of the palace. The same demands of protocol that led Ottoman statesmen to designate a "diplomatic wife" required Amina to take up a diplomatic role. As *khédiveh* and *khédiveh mère* she regularly received the wives and daughters of European diplomats and visitors.[46] Now, also, the palace cultivated the popularity of the khedive and his wife through their public presence and activities, and by facilitating press coverage of them. Thus Amina's presence at official events was mentioned regularly, and notices of her and the khedive's movements—attending the opera, traveling from one palace to another—also were published.[47]

Nevertheless, if Amina thereby stretched the conventional boundaries of harem culture, she did not break them. Even more than other secluded women, royal women were protected from the public gaze, traveling in well-guarded carriages with the drapes drawn, or by private train and yacht. When present at state events the *khédiveh* and her entourage would sit behind a screen, and on holidays she would receive the greetings of female guests personally, while those of the male guests were conveyed to her by her *bash agha* (the chief eunuch of the harem).[48] The press usually discreetly avoided mentioning her name. However, Amina's public role as *khédiveh* and *khédiveh mère* may have contributed in the long run to enlarging the space within which upper-class women could be publicly active, for example in charitable and patriotic activities.[49]

As for the khedival household in this period, Tawfiq's was considerably smaller than his father's, if for no other reason than the relative austerity necessitated by the bankruptcy and European control of Egyptian finances, and the prohibition of the slave trade. Moreover, the new political and fiscal realities of the British occupation made khedival autocracy and "household government" a thing of the past, and so a large harem of marriageable women was no longer politically necessary. Tawfiq was genuinely monogamous, often professed opposition to slavery, and even claimed that his personal attendants were paid servants. Amina presided over a harem of some sixty slave women, though none of them were concubines.[50]

The domestic life of Tawfiq's son and successor, Abbas II, shows more clearly the ambiguous nature of the khedival family's relationship with slavery and polygyny. Tawfiq might have opposed slavery and polygyny, but there is no question that Abbas II and Amina, now mother of the khedive, did not. At his accession in 1892 Abbas II was only seventeen years old and unmarried, and Amina took charge of the search for an appropriate princess for him to wed. She passed over his first cousin, and nearly succeeded in arranging a union for him with an Ottoman princess. In the meantime, Abbas began to have sexual relations with Iqbal (1876–1923), one of three Circassian slave women that his mother had assigned to his personal service. On 12 February, 1895, Iqbal gave birth to a girl, named Amina in honor of her grandmother. A contract of marriage between her and the khedive was written seven days later. At the public celebration the *khédiveh mère* hosted the women's reception.[51] Iqbal eventually bore all of Abbas's six children.

By the standards of contemporary Ottoman ruling-class culture, the fathering of a child by a slave concubine was unexceptional, and so too was Abbas's decision to raise Iqbal to the status of legal wife. Both events were duly announced in *al-Waqaʾi al-Misriyya*, which also published some poetry written in honor of the khedival daughter.[52] The announcements did not allude to Iqbal's previous slave status, something that would have been as rude as it was obvious to contemporaries familiar with upper-class harem culture.

Amina may have acquired Iqbal, and almost certainly acquired other slaves, after the importation of slaves into Egypt became completely illegal in 1884. She and Abbas II seem not to have found slavery objectionable in principle, since they kept slaves in their households until the First World War.[53] Even though her husband, Tawfiq, professed opposition to slavery, Amina presided over a harem of slave women, three of whom she gave to Abbas. In spite of breaking with some aspects of traditional harem culture (such as permitting her unveiled portrait to be published in 1923 and later), she continued to conduct herself in accordance with the culture of harem slavery for the rest of her life. She established an extensive endowment (*waqf*), one of the purposes of which was to pay pensions to sixty former slaves, including ten eunuchs.[54] Most of them were women, a slight majority of whom were married or widows, indicating that they had left Amina's service at some earlier date. Others, like her chief servant (*bash qalfa*) Lady Qamar, apparently remained in her service until her death in 1931.

As for Abbas's attitude toward slavery, in Istanbul in 1894 he gave his personal physician, Comanos Pasha, the task of purchasing additional white female slaves "for his harem." The khedive complained that he had but two or three slaves, just enough to serve him personally. He could not procure slaves in Egypt, where the trade was forbidden, so it was necessary to acquire them, discreetly, in Istanbul. Comanos bought six, to serve as domestics and not as concubines.[55] While it was not illegal to own slaves in Egypt at even this late date, their purchase and importation had been prohibited in 1884, a prohibition that the khedive and his mother discreetly violated.

Abbas II also departed from his father's example by practicing polygyny. His second wife was Javidan (Djavidan) Hanim (1877–1968), the former Countess May Torok von Szendro, of Hungarian noble lineage, whom he met during a holiday in Europe. They were married secretly sometime after 1900, and she used to accompany him on trips in disguise. She converted to Islam and she and the khedive were remarried, officially, at the end of February 1910, probably to avoid a scandal. The marriage was dissolved three years later. In her memoirs Javidan mused, "It is curious to think that my husband has two wives."[56]

Unlike the khedive's first marriage to Iqbal, his marriage to Javidan was not publicly announced, even though it was presided over by the grand mufti. There was no notice of the event in *al-Waqa'i al-Misriyya* nor in private newspapers like *al-Ahram*, even though the other activities of the khedive during those days received the usual press attention. In Egypt, knowledge of the khedive's second wife does not seem to have spread beyond palace circles until the 1930s.[57]

To be sure, this polygynous interlude in Abbas's life did not come close to a "return" to the old way of doing things. Whereas it was public knowledge that Ismail had multiple wives and concubines, the secrecy of Abbas's polygyny more closely resembled keeping a mistress in a legally monogamous society. Abbas's polygyny was also contingent. As his former slave, Iqbal was in no position to object to it, but if he had married a cousin or an imperial princess, plural marriage would have been out of the question.

Conclusion

Between the two world wars the "women's awakening" became part of the modernist-nationalist vision of Egypt's historical trajectory, and the ideal of companionate marriage became widely accepted as part of a modern way of life. Reflecting that trend, promonarchy historians in the 1930s emphasized the khedival family's supposed contribution to the advancement of women and the improvement of family life, including an alleged increase in monogamy and a decrease in divorce among the educated.[58] Postrevolutionary historians have abandoned this theme, tending not to associate the khedives of the later nineteenth century with any progressive change at all. My purpose in revisiting the question of the transition to monogamy in the khedival house has been to gain a vantage point on the process of change in late-nineteenth-century domesticity in all its complexity and ambiguity. What European observers saw as a break from traditional practices, and possibly the beginning of the end of the "harem system," was neither intended nor understood within Ottoman Egyptian culture as a departure of radical proportions. Ismail engineered a shift from slave concubinage and polygyny to royal endogamy, which necessarily entailed monogamous marriage. Yet marriage to one wife was understood to be an option, and occasionally a necessity, in a culture that permitted plural marriage.

By the turn of the twentieth century, however, the khedives' supposed choice of monogamous marriage seems to have acquired additional significance, including among Egyptians. After all, in having a second wife Abbas II was exercising what even today is the legal right of Muslim men in Egypt—to have as many as four wives at one time. The only explanation for keeping the khedive's polygyny secret is the scandal it could have caused if it became public. What, then, had changed between 1873, when the transition to monogamy in the khedival house went unremarked by Egyptians, and 1910, when the khedive's polygyny was covered up?

The palace was concerned with public opinion in Europe, as before, but now also with opinion in Egypt. In spite of the difficulties he had with Egypt's British occupiers, British writers generally praised the domestic life of Abbas II as "irreproachable." This meant monogomy: "Following his father's example, he has only one legal wife, to whom he is supposed to be much attached."[59] Such praise appears in British writings up to the time of Abbas's second marriage to Javidan Hanim. Cromer, for example, noted Abbas's monogamy in *Modern Egypt* (1908), but in *Abbas II* (1915) he refrained from comment on the former khedive's domestic life.[60]

British and other Western writers insisted that a sound family life could not be built on polygyny, and that since the family was the basic unit in society, a shift to monogamy was necessary if Oriental societies were to advance toward modern civilization. Hence the palace sought to preserve the "irreproachable" image of the khedive's family life in Britain and other "civilized" countries. Abbas's ambition of ruling Egypt as an independent prince would not be fulfilled unless international opinion was convinced that he was a suitable leader.[61]

The cultivation of European opinion had been a concern of the Muhammad Ali dynasty from its beginning, and, as we have seen, the khedives and their publicists made much of the transition to monogamy during the last quarter of the nineteenth century. What had changed, on the eve of the First World War, was the attitude of Egyptian public opinion—specifically, opinion among the literate middle and upper classes, who consumed the print media and were interested and active in public affairs. While also desiring an end to the British occupation, many leading Egyptian public figures were unenthusiastic about the prospect of returning to strong khedival rule. Abbas's Egyptian opponents favored a constitutional regime that would restrict the power of the monarch and permit them to run things, by means of a representative parliament. Abbas thus needed to cultivate the Egyptian public, among whom an ideal of companionate marriage had begun to be articulated by the turn of the century. And, as in European discourse, in early-twentieth-century Egypt monogamy was held to be an essential element in companionate marriage.[62] By 1910, then, the palace's desire to cover up Abbas's polygyny indicates the extent to which the ideal of companionate marriage had gained ground in Egypt, and perhaps also the extent to which the khedival family had become associated with that ideal.

Notes

Acknowledgements: My interest in the way the khedival family presented itself to the public was aroused several years ago in a conversation with the late Avriel Butovsky. Since in some respects this essay builds upon his ideas, I would like to dedicate it to his memory. I am also indebted to the staffs of Dar al-Kutub and Dar al-Wathaʾiq, the Egyptian National Library and National Archives, respectively, for their kind assistance and permission to use their materials. Thanks are also due to Samir Raafat for sharing his materials and insights, my research assistant Aisha Sobh for her hard work, and Marilyn Booth, Beshara Doumani, Pascale Ghazzala, Leslie Peirce, David Sabean, and my colleagues in the History Workshop at UIUC for their comments on earlier drafts of this paper.

1. *Al-Waqaʾi al-Misriyya*, no. 491 (21 January 1873), no. 492 (28 January 1873), and no. 493 (4 February 1873).

2. During the nineteenth century, Egypt, a province of the Ottoman Empire, became the hereditary viceroyalty of Muhammad Ali Pasha (r. 1805–48) and his descendants. He and his successors used the Persian title *khedive* informally; it was officially conferred on Ismail in 1867.

3. Alderson 1956, 176–77.

4. Quotation from McCoan 1877, 319; Farley 1872, 114–15; Melman 1995, 143.

5. Cromer 1908, 2:158.

6. Lloyd 1999, 87.

7. Amin 1976, 2000.

8. Baron 1991, 278.

9. E.g., St. John 1834, 2:180–81; *Times* (London), 18 December 1880.

10. F. Davis 1986, 7–8; Poole 1851, 74; Duff-Gordon (1983), 112.

11. Melman 1995, 145–47.

12. *Times* (London), 12 January 1884; 1 April 1884 (text of 1877 decree); 7 April 1884.

13. Lane [1842] 1978, 184; F. Davis 1986, 87; Melman 1995, 142.

14. Melman 1995, 99–100, 106.

15. E.g., Poole 1851; Chennels 1893.

16. In the late 1830s an estimated six thousand households in Cairo contained an average of two female slaves (Tucker 1985, 166); slave ownership and polygyny among the rural notability is apparent in census and court records.

17. See Toledano 1998, 57ff.; and also Melman 1995, 106, on Victorian women's understanding of harem seclusion and veiling as offering women autonomy.

18. Dykstra 1977, 405; Mubarak 1979, 2:242–46.

19. *Al-Ahram*, 16 March 1881.

20. De Malortie 1883, 203.

21. A. Butler 1888, 35, 151, 153–54; Dufferin 1917, 248.

22. A. Butler 1888, 204.

23. Chennells 1893, 1:222.

24. Alderson 1956, 19 n. 4; F. Davis 1986, 18; De Leon 1882, 154.

25. Abou-el-Haj 1973, 438; Kunt 1983, 65–67; Hunter 1984, 23.

26. Hilal 1999, 409–12.

27. Hamont 1843, 1:422.

28. Ibid.; Hilal 1999, 412–13; Cuno 1992, 163.

29. Land: Crecelius 1981, 115, and Hilal 1999, 93–94; Urabist officers: Beaman 1929, 27, and Shafiq 1934, 2:155; De Malortie 1883, 210–11 (quotation).

30. Hamont 1843, 1:422–23.

31. Farley 1872, 115.

32. Though no longer the sole source of patronage, the palace retained a central role in politics, and ambitious men still sought to advance themselves through marriage to its women (see, e.g., Djavidan 1931, 107).

33. Sharif and Riyad: Hunter 1984, 153, 158; contract: Hanna 1996.

34. Hunter 1984, 26; Khanki 1938, 45, 47.

35. Muhammad Ali reportedly learned to read at the age of 45, in about 1814 (Clot 1840, 1:lxxx). De Malortie reports that the female slave who taught him to read died two years prior to the writing of his book, which would correspond to the year of Mahduran's death (De Malortie 1883, 65).

36. Khanki 1938, 45–47; I. Hilal 1999, table after 415; Peirce 1993, 42.

37. Ottoman princes: Alderson 1956, 34–35; khedival wives: Khanki 1938, 45–47, and I. Hilal 1999, table after 415.

38. Inji Hamin: Jerrold 1879, 16, De Leon 1882, 60, and De Leon 1890, 174, 202–11, 214–15; Malak Barr Hanim: Khanki 1938, 45–47, and I. Hilal 1999, table after 415; "publicity": De Leon 1882, 61; "diplomatic wives": F. Davis 1986, 93–94.

39. Ismail's consorts: Khanki 1938, 45-47, and I. Hilal 1999, table after 415; Shafaq Nur Hanim: Shafiq 1934, 1:81.

40. The rule of succession of the eldest required a pool of princes to be available but not to pose a threat to the reigning sultan. Hence they were confined during adulthood in an apartment (*kafes,* literally "cage") within the imperial palace. Despite some notable exceptions, the *kafes* system was eased only in the later nineteenth century. See Peirce 1993, 21-22; Alderson 1956, 12.

41. Although Abbas was a conservative, these disputes resulted in his being miscast as a "reactionary" in the standard historical narrative. See Sharubim 1900, 99; Holt 1966, 196; and especially Toledano 1990, 108–48.

42. Raafat 1994b.

43. Shaw 1977, 2:130, 500; Holt 1966, 196–97.

44. Tugay 1963, 142.

45. *Al-Waqaʾi al-Misriyya,* no. 27 (4 June 1866).

46. Caillard 1935, 106–07.

47. Butovsky 1995; Rizq 1994.

48. Rizq 1994; A. Butler 1888, 227, 229; De Leon 1890, 221; Dufferin 1917, 264, 274–75; Caillard 1935, 103, 109–10.

49. See Badran 1995, 47ff.

50. Tawfiq's "paid servants" may actually have been slaves or former slaves, for it was customary to pay them (Djavidan 1931, 103). On Tawfiq's household and his views, see A. Butler 1888, 35, 193; Dufferin 1917, 248; Caillard 1935, 107.

51. Comanos n.d., 48–52, 60–62; Shafiq 1934, 2:155–57, 177–78, 186–87.

52. Al-waqaʾi al-Mistiyya no. 19, (13 Feb. 1895); no. 21 (18 Feb. 1895).

53. Caillard 1935, 110; Djavidan 1931, 103, 110.

54. Al-Ahram, 26 June 1931.

55. Comanos n.d., 50–52; Shafiq 1934, 2:155.

56. Djavidan 1931, 279; for an extensive account of this marriage, see Raafat 1994a.

57. The earliest publications in Arabic containing this information are Shafiq 1934 and Khanki 1938.

58. Al-Rafiʿi 1948, 2:274 (first ed. 1932); Sammarco 1935, 315. Neither author cites any supporting evidence for this interpretation. An earlier monarchist work by Ayyubi (1923), while discussing the four princely weddings at length and crediting Ismail with the introduction of various aspects of European (i.e., modern) culture, does not mention the trend toward monogamy.

59. Dicey 1902, 468.

60. E.g., Cromer 1908, 2:158; and "Khedive Opposes Polygamy. Has Only One Wife—How He Is Rearing Children," Egyptian Gazette, 15 September 1909. On the latter see Raafat 1994a.

61. Family life, and in general the status of women, was one of the indices used by Europeans to measure the backwardness of other societies. See, e.g., Clancy-Smith 1996 and Pollard 1997, 43–88.

62. Baron 1991, 278; Baron 1994, 165.

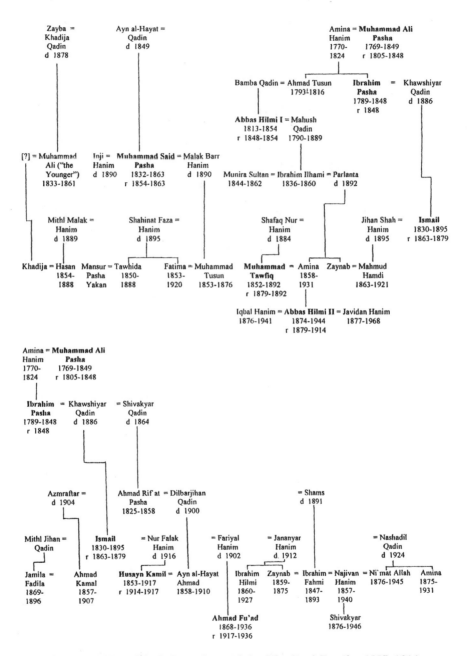

Figure 18. Simplified Genealogy of the Khedival Family, 1805–1914

12

"Queen of the House?" Making Immigrant Lebanese Families in the *Mahjar*

Akram F. Khater

"The woman was created for the house and the man for work, and it is shameful for the man and woman to exchange their jobs."[1] This unequivocal statement was part of an article written by Elias Nasif Elias, a Lebanese emigrant residing in Connecticut, and published in *Al-Huda*, an early Arab-American newspaper. In this, and a host of articles like it, communal and individual identities were being debated, contested, and re-formed within the Lebanese emigrant community.[2] The underlying tensions, which drove this debate, were precipitated by the emigration of over 120,000 villagers from the mountains of Lebanon to the United States between 1890 and 1921. In those thirty years Lebanese emigrants encountered a hegemonic middle-class culture bent on transforming them from Old World peasants to a New World working class. One of the focal points in this effort was a rigid definition of the family in terms of gender roles, parenting, and structure and material surroundings. In opposition, some of these same emigrants also focused on the family as a heightened source of authentic identity. Others, like Nasif, who sought admission into the American middle class, accepted bourgeois notions of family as the defining elements of their own modernity, while attempting to infuse it with an Eastern flavor. Regardless of perspective, all sought to articulate the family in concrete terms that privileged their cultural, socioeconomic, and political values. A look at this moment of intense historical change provides an understanding of the fluid structure and meaning of the Lebanese family.

In order to accomplish this task, I would like to focus on the process rather than on the structure of family. This, of course, is something that American and European historians have been attempting to do for the past two decades.[3] However, I would like to explain more precisely what I mean by the family. I see the family as a set of social relations whose depth and thickness is subject to historical change brought about by internal tensions and external pressures. While at times these social relations are deep, at other times they are stretched to the breaking point and beyond. Alternatively, then, they appear as remarkable in their affectivity amidst a host of other relations (gender, class, etc.), or simply recede to the back as to be insignificant in their relevance to the lives and histories of individuals. If we approach the family in this manner, we may be able to avoid several analytical pitfalls. The family no longer appears as a category with an evolutionary (linear or otherwise) genealogy of structure, size, and lines of kinship. Rather, the family becomes a historical process that unfolds in a multitude of fashions, none of which can be predicted or considered typical. Moreover, as a set of permeable and changeable social relations, we can understand better the contradictions that emanate out of unequal relations of power (whether based on gender or age) inherent in the family. In other words, the family ceases to be a monolithic analytical entity and becomes a complex set of emotions and calculations that at times are coherent, but that are at other times contradictory.

Another critical theoretical underpinning of this work rests with its methodology. In particular, I have tried to understand the relationship between social and cultural history within the context of the story of emigrants. Social history has traditionally focused on retrieving and categorizing facts about subaltern groups in an attempt to reclaim a place in history for these previously marginalized historical actors. However, in the process, the categories became rather stultified and monolithic. Class, gender, and race became ahistorical labels that bundled together disparate people and excluded from our vision the development of these categories over time as well as their complex interplay with each other and other elements. Partly in response to this, cultural history has attempted to reclaim the meaning of history and the contingency of social categories by shifting the emphasis to textuality, in which most everything in life becomes a narrative and power appears to be a conflict between stories told. While this was a very helpful critique of social history, and a new way to look at historical documents, it soon took on a life of its own whereby the only reality was the narrative. More problematic was the slippery nature of "text," any attempt to understand it entailed tools mired in relationships of power. Thus, any meaning extracted was rendered extremely contingent and narrow in its focus. In other words, a minute and fleeting particularity came to replace the previously essentializing universality, thus rendering history almost useless beyond its narrative value, or story.

In this work, I try to resolve some of these tensions by combining historical context with textual meaning. Rather than assume that social and cultural history are irreconcilable, I attempt to create a dialogue between them by juxtaposing my reading of public discourse with statistical information that provides the backdrop for the text. For example, the intense debate about the work of Lebanese immigrant women is presented within the socioeconomic context that necessitated and allowed for this work. I find that the tension between the social and cultural historical approach enables us to better understand the lives we are trying to recapture at the same time that it allows for the extraction of greater meaning from the narrative of those lives. With this in mind I will now tell of the journeys of some peasants from Mount Lebanon to Amirka (America) in order to understand how they changed, or did not change, their concept of the family.

Going to Amirka

Peasants emigrated from Mount Lebanon to the Americas because they thought they needed to and because they could. As with other parts of the nineteenth-century world, this small Eastern Mediterranean Arab area attracted European capitalists seeking markets for their manufactured goods and sources of raw material for their factories. In this instance it was silk that brought merchants from Marseilles and Lyons—through local intermediaries—to the villages that dotted the Mount Lebanon range. Higher prices offered for silk cocoons enticed local producers to sell to the newcomers as well as to increase their production. Typically—as the story usually goes at some point for incorporation into the world capitalist market—after a decade or so the prices started fluctuating. By the 1870s they had definitely stagnated because of the entry of China and Japan into the market, especially as the latter was bent on industrializing through a massive production of higher-quality silk. The opening of the Suez Canal in 1869 and steamboat navigation contributed as well to the saturation of the silk market and to the fall in prices. Finally, the deathblow came from European-manufactured synthetic fibers that, starting in the 1880s, steadily undermined the silk market. For the villagers in Mount Lebanon this historical process had an intimate impact on their daily lives. After two decades of prosperity—in which they experienced a better standard of living that translated into, among other things, a doubling of the population—they saw themselves sliding back into poverty and dispossession of their land. This was effectively making them landless laborers rather than peasants. In an effort to counter this undesirable end, about one-tenth of the peasant population opted to send their daughters to work in silk factories. This family strategy for financial survival strained the gender "contract" to its breaking point.[4] But it did not completely solve the problem, particularly as the factories were underfunded and could not compete with the technological superiority of French factories. Thus, by the early 1890s the decision to emigrate appeared as the most financially viable alternative. At the same time, it was possible for large numbers of families and individuals to implement this decision because of Lebanon's unusual political status within the Ottoman Empire. In 1860 a civil war wracked the Mountain. In the aftermath, European powers bent on increasing their influence in the region worked with some local elites to force the Ottoman government to provide Lebanon a semi-independent status and greater personal freedom of movement for its inhabitants. The peasants in turn used these two elements to their advantage by circumventing intermittent Ottoman regulations against immigration. Combined together, the hard socioeconomic realities and political-administrative loopholes translated into the emigration of over 120,000 individuals and families (in all combinations) from Mount Lebanon to the United States between 1880 and 1920.[5]

Very few of the men and women who left Mount Lebanon for Amirka thought to stay long. They expected to land somewhere, work for a while to gather money, and return home to live as financially comfortable landowning peasants. Focused as they were on these straightforward goals, it was only the most clairvoyant amongst the emigrants who could have anticipated the voyage to be far more complex. Even fewer could have foretold that the days spent peddling lace and buttons, shopping for food and clothes, and strolling in the streets of their temporary communities would be transformative. Almost none would have expected that their experiences in the *mahjar* (the lands where emigrants traveled) would entail social and cultural contacts that necessitated a self-conscious examination of their individual and collective identities.

Yet, all these things did happen. Emigrants from Mount Lebanon arrived in the United States at a time when a predominantly white,

Anglo-Saxon, and Protestant middle class was ascendant in all matters of life. Through a cult of domesticity, hierarchical notions of race and ethnicity, and physical distance from the working class and cities, members of this class had come to ascribe to themselves a positivist modernity. As this social class became more isolated from the tumult of the cities in their suburban retreats, they grew increasingly suspicious and alienated from social and ethnic groups that they deemed foreign, including immigrants. Directly through philanthropic works and public schooling and indirectly through their insistence that they represented America, this middle-class projected disdain and patronizing attitudes towards immigrants in general. Within this context, Lebanese emigrants came to be regarded as part of an East depicted as irrational, emotional, unclean, and suspicious by a hegemonic middle-class culture. These characterizations were part of a process of dividing the world neatly and absurdly into two irreconcilable categories of a modern and positive "us" and a negative and traditional "them." Such a dichotomy forced emigrants to articulate and defend a sense of self in the midst of a larger society that contradictorily sought to Americanize them while shunning them.

There was not a single overriding notion of what that self was to be. Opinions ranged widely between those few who sought to emulate middle-class America in every facet, and those who considered any departure from tradition a disaster. This effort, carried out in community newspapers and private conversations, left little untouched. At the intersection of many of its inquiries was the family. Inside and outside the physical house people argued, got upset, compromised, and stomped out of rooms in search of a surety that they thought they had with regard to marriage, parenting, women's work, and other defining social traditions. In other words, their new and demanding environment compelled them to make concrete that which was fluid— to freeze outside history, however fleetingly, that which had always been transformed and to call these Traditions. While that fixed sense of family was never—and, really, could not be—attained, the search gave rise to a tentative new class with a hybrid cultural ideology and social structure that challenged the very precept of modern and traditional, East and West.[6]

Family and Identity

To understand this process we need first look at how the lives of emigrants changed. A majority of Lebanese women—like their Chinese, Jewish, and Italian counterparts[7]—who came to the United States worked outside the physical boundaries of their residences. Their desire for work as well as their need and reasons for employment were hardly uniform, but the fact that most worked at one time or another outside the house is the common thread running through their varying experiences. Leaving the private space of the house and sallying forth on a daily basis into the public world of city streets was a new experience for most of these women—even when work was not. It was made so by the fact that these spaces were being articulated into a gendered division of American society even as they arrived at Ellis Island or other ports of entry into the United States. Social workers and the burgeoning middle class of America did not expect women—the proposed repository of morality in society—to work in the sullied world outside the door of the home.[8] Thus, these women were not only transgressing their own imported gender boundaries; they were also trampling across the terrain of a middle-class world rising all around them. Their work was implicitly and explicitly questioning both the traditional and the modern notion of women's role in society. Equally, the crisscrossing between private and public spaces was wreaking havoc upon the lines that were being drawn between the two by the emerging middle class. Lebanese emigrant women, then, were challenging the simplifying division of the world surrounding them, making the ideas of modern and traditional largely irrelevant and presenting an alternative notion of America.

Elements of the American middle class responded to this by seeking to civilize the emigrants even as they shunned them.[9] In the words of one social worker, "Old standards must be changed if we are sincere in our desire to attain a higher form of civilization. The strangers from across the water must be taught to discard un-American habits and conventions, and to accept new ideals."[10] Or as M. A. Howe wrote in 1903, "To cope with these new conditions [the influx of immigrants] the same efforts are being made in Boston as elsewhere in America. The attempt to amalgamate the diverse elements into a common citizenship goes forward through hundreds of agencies—the public schools, the social settlements, the organization of charities, secular and religious, designed to meet every conceivable need of the unfortunate, but in such a way as to create citizens instead of paupers."[11] Immigrants could not be allowed to hover indeterminately between the modern and traditional, for such a position would expose the absurdity of these ideal types and their irrelevance as either historical devices or symbols of the present world. Immigrants were expected to choose . . . and choose to be American.

This was not a vague and diffused sense of citizenship. Rather, most social workers attempted to universalize the particular social relation of modern middle-class life.[12] Domesticity for women, leisured children, and working fathers were the norms of the middle class. These same values were projected as the ideal to which immigrants must aspire because it was culturally superior. Such sentiments were not the reserve of only conservatives—who were more likely to demand the deportation of immigrants—but the primary goal of the more liberal of the "Settlement Houses." One writer in the *Survey*—a progressive social reform magazine—noted: "The social and moral life of a smaller family where the father earns enough to support wife and children, and where the mother can devote her time to the care of them, and where neither she nor the children go out and help in the support of the family, is superior to that of a family with a large number of children where the wife and often the older children must slave."[13]

Even those settlement workers who struggled to protect the right of the immigrants to retain control over their identity and values inadvertently undermined that same goal. This was most evident in their approach to children and adolescents. Settlement workers were "shocked to discover the number of parents who regarded offspring as potential sources of revenue."[14] Horrified by the "abuse" of children, these workers called for the enactment of better labor laws and for more rigorous enforcement. As Gwendolyn Mink shows in her study *Wages of Motherhood*, progressive social reformers believed that Americanization would emancipate immigrant women and their children.[15] Far more radically, reformers like Robert Hunter, Florence E. Kelley, and Lillian Wald argued that the state should intervene on behalf of the children by "taking them off the street." In blunter terms, one social worker by the name of Philip Davis argued that the unprotected street child was "public property of which the community is trustee."[16] The obvious irony of intruding public policy into the private lives of the working class in order to ascertain that they led private lives appears to have eluded Mr. Davis and other such reformers.

Public schools were equally active in assimilating the children of immigrants to an American life that was imbued with middle-class values. As their numbers increased from 160 in 1870 to 6,000 by the end of the century, the reach of these schools grew.[17] And their purpose was specific. In the words of one New York high school principal, "[E]ducation will solve every problem of our national life, even that of assimilating our foreign element."[18] Or, as the Cleveland Americanization Committee advertised in one 1917 poster, public schools were to draw immigrant children from their parents' "Peasantry" to "American City life."[19] In this fashion many children were exposed to the narratives of American modernity, and learned to feel that their own languages, dress, and customs were stigmas in an intolerant environment.

As all of these forces pulled and tugged at the social fabric of their existence, emigrants became aware of the need to reweave that cloth even as its threads frayed at the edges. In other words, they had to self-consciously (re)discover who they were, and reconstruct their home as a container of their identities. Home, as it emerged, was a concoction of romanticized memories stoked by distance, new realities that required a place in this collective abode, and plenty of gaps in between. In apartments, on the street, in coffeehouses, at churches, and in various social gatherings questions about tradition were argued and not always resolved.

At moments in the history of these emigrants the debate centered around whether they were Ottoman, Syrian, or Lebanese—with the latter two being the more popular, albeit not more meaningful. Other times witnessed an intensification in religious identity—at least by a few who found in it security and power. Village associations and secular organizations also worked to draw fences around their members, which would strengthen what they feared was being diluted in the mass urban society of Amirka. Yet, despite their importance, these identities were not a constant in the daily existence of emigrants in the *mahjar*—at least from within the emigrant community. Referring to one's Syrianness or church or association was rarely necessary when talking to other emigrants. A far more immediately relevant set of social signifiers was embodied in the family. And at that level the discussion about identities and social traditions was more pronounced and tendentious. Evidence of this is to be found in the articles and debates that appeared in the Syrian press. Rarely would one have encountered articles about national identity, associations, or even religion—except for a good number of critiques of the "corrupt clergy." Far more common were essays that dealt directly and indirectly with the establishment of a new social space with clearly defined roles for individuals and traditions for families—albeit that clarity could never be attained in real life. At the turn of the century, when some emigrants had become financially successful, the text of these articles centered on a search for a way to establish an *emigrant middle class*. As one author put it, "It is time for everyone to know his or her place. . . . Not everyone who gathers some money becomes a member of the middle classes and not everyone who has dressed his wife in a twenty-dollar hat becomes a notable; rather, social status in our days is the status of knowledge and manners."[20]

A host of articles appeared in the Lebanese-American press that was meant to articulate the outlines of these new manners and to map the horizons of this new knowledge. One such article was published in the "Social Conventions for the Man and the Woman" section of *Al-Huda*, under the title "Knocking on the Door." Salim Mukarzel, the author, brought to the attention of his readers that "amongst the public in Lebanon, [entering a house] without asking for permission is not considered a failure but a sign of sincere friendship . . . but here in the United States . . . entering upon [the private space] of a person without asking for permission is considered a fault." Mukarzel went on to provide an inventory of the "modern norms for entering [the workspace of] . . . a friend or a stranger."[21]

These recommendations were an attempt to redefine the social working space of the emigrants. In essence, Mukarzel was concerned with establishing a modern etiquette that he believed should govern the social relations of individuals. He began his essay by establishing that Lebanon and the United States represent two social environments that sit on opposite sides of the modern/traditional divide. After essentializing both spaces in such a manner, Mukarzel clearly delineated the boundaries of the modern social space. In this conception—which he invites his fellow emigrants to subscribe to—social space is centered on the individual and not the community. Gaining access to such space ceases to be a privilege of belonging to a community and becomes dependent on invitation into that privatized territory.

If men's visits were in the eyes of many writers a waste of time, women's socialization was "the great disaster . . . for [the visit of the Syrian woman] is also heavier than a mountain," because it is spent discussing "trivial" subjects, eating, drinking, and smoking. The writer shows his absolute disdain for such frivolity by counseling that "visits in the absolute should be short because work is a duty . . . and the woman also has duties, some of which are managing her house by preparing food, sweeping rooms, and cleaning the furniture; and she is also entrusted with . . . raising children and other many things. If she wastes time, how can she do all of this?"[22] Thus, not only were men expected to be more focused on isolated tasks than on building social relations within a community, but women were to be equally attentive to "their tasks." Only, in their case, women were to work alone at home, emulating the domesticity of the middle class. In this fashion, a new division of labor was being assigned to a social space that both authors were anxious for their compatriots to adopt, and which they regarded as an absolute staple of modernity, and as a way to merge into the mainstream of American society.

Mothering

The tension pulling at the lives of emigrants transcended the issue of physical space of the family. Parenting was another arena that some emigrant authors sought to rationalize and modernize. One treatise with that goal was written by Elias Qirqmaz, who argued that emigrant parents, but particularly mothers, were not rearing their children in a proper manner. (This was an accusation that was also being leveled against women in Egypt, Iran, and provinces of the Ottoman Empire during this same period.) In his article, which he wrote for *Al-Huda* in 1899, Elias summarized all the "ills" that beset Syrian children under the title: "The Misery of the Syrian Child in the Crib, and in the House, and in the Market."[23] He began his argument by marveling at the "health and vigor" so apparent among children of the "civilized foreign *millal* [plural of *millet*]," especially when compared to the "weak" Syrian child. Then he noted that "Arab newspapers [in the *mahjar*] have long dedicated substantial space for doctors and researchers to show the great mistakes that mothers commit in raising their children." These mistakes begin at infancy when "the mother throws the baby in the crib and begins to tie him up [swaddle him] to the point where he cannot breathe at times. . . ." From there things only get worse as "she places the baby in the kitchen or in a room where the air is spoiled . . . or cigarette smoke hovers above the room like clouds." If a child makes it to the age of 4, Elias mused, then his digestive system is assaulted by all manner of foods that "his weak stomach cannot digest." But the greatest mistake that parents were committing, according to our author, is in the moral upbringing of their children. He wrote, "[W]e would like to bring [your] attention to the ugly habit that the people of our country have grown accustomed to, which is the habit of hitting a child. . . . [It is ugly] because it makes him like an animal who is not afraid of anything but the stick. And if he grows up, then he stays this way, not doing anything except with fear, and not saying anything except while shaking [from fear]."

His solution to this problem was to morally educate the child and "to habituate him to respect the words of his parents."[24] He then proceeded to criticize parents (but, again, mainly mothers "upon whom rests the advancement of the world in the future or its destruction") for letting their children spend so much time "on the streets." Such laxity, he complained, only brought the children to a lower level of "lying, cheating, and general sleaziness."[25] Finally, Elias concluded this essay with the grave pronouncement that "it is better for parents not to have children born to them if they are going to disregard them like most Syrians disregard their children in the big cities."[26]

In 1903 another writer, Nasrallah Faris, concurred with this judgment in the course of his essay entitled "Syrians and Schools." He began his article in much the same way as Elias Qirqmaz—namely, by drawing an unfavorable comparison between American and Syrian children. He wrote, "The Syrian does not care to send his children to school, as opposed to the American whose child grows and becomes ready to accept the principles of science and moral education."[27] On one hand, the "American sends his little one [to school] to learn the sciences because he considers learning and morality the best inheritance he can leave for his children." Juxtaposed with such an "enlightened" attitude toward education is the Syrian who—per Nasrallah—could care less about his child's education, and who lets him "roam the streets and alleys and pick up insolent language." In fact, things had gotten so "bad" in Bangor that the "government [has] sent two of its officials to the Syrians to threaten the fathers with penalties and punishment if they do not send their children to the public schools."[28]

Through these representations of ideal types of families there emerged a new proposed meaning of childhood and adolescence. Modern children were to be isolated from the community and constrained within the walls of the private home and the schoolroom in order to protect them from the "bad influences" of the larger society. They were to be sheltered from work and not required to contribute to the family's income. All these elements were obviously the hallmarks of a child-centered middle-class life in America. While well-meaning and sensible in some ways, they also engendered their own problems—despite their positivist claims. This advice narrowed the focus of daily life to singular households rather than an integrated community, and shifted a far greater deal of the burden to the shoulders of the mother. Economically, it also meant that the family as a whole would have to make do with less by losing the income they derived from their children's work. In turn, this implied that they were that much further from attaining their goal of returning to their villages and living the comfortable life they desired. In other words, the tension between "individual time and family time" was exacerbated through this vision of an idealized middle-class life.

Standing in the path of these attempts to impose a middle-class view of modernity on the emigrant community was the fact that most Lebanese women worked outside the home. Consequently, the desired cult of domesticity could not be achieved without the construction of a new concept of woman and gender roles. Hence, we find—beginning with the earliest appearance of Lebanese newspapers (circa 1892)—articles dealing passionately and vociferously with the topics of women's work, status, education, and comportment, as well as marital relations. By the turn of the twentieth century a few newspapers (like *Al-Sa'ih, Mira'at al-Gharb,* and *Al-Huda*) were even dedicating regular columns to gender issues. Under the title "Womanly Topics of Discussion" there appeared in *Al-Huda* one or two (and sometimes three) articles on womanhood at least every other day. And while in the late 1890s one only read the writings of a couple of women authors, by 1905 the number of such contributors had surpassed ten. On one hand, most of these essays were attempting to deal with the contradictions in the traditional patriarchal contracts brought to light by women's work. On the other hand, this labor transgressed across the public/private divide that was coming to define middle-class life in America—a life that, as noted earlier, some observers were anxious for the community to join.

Elias Nassif Elias, a regular early contributor to *Al-Huda,* was one of those. He argued that women's work tarnished the honor of the Syrians. To make his point, Elias told of an experience he had while sitting in the lobby of the Central House hotel in Bridgewater, Maine. "While talking with some men about various matters," he wrote, "[we heard] a light knock on the door, so one of us got up to open it, only to find a Syrian woman weighed down by her heavy load . . . and she sighed saying: I will sell [my things] to those men for the amount of 4 or 5 dollars and I do not care if they laugh at, or make fun of, me." With the stage set, Elias proceeded to describe a scene in which the American men ask the Syrian woman to do various "humiliating things" (such as letting one of the men tie her shoes), and are patently making fun of her. Elias could not stand the situation anymore, so . . . he left without identifying himself as a compatriot of the woman. Without reflecting on the irony inherent in his lack of intervention in the "degrading" affair, Elias proceeded—in his composition—to reproach the Syrians for letting "their" women work. He scathingly asked, "Oh, you dear Syrians who claim honor . . . is it honorable to send your women to meander and encounter such insults?"[29] As more of the emigrants made the move from itinerant peddling to a respectable settled life, the tone of opposition to women's work grew more strident. A local merchant by the name of Yusuf al-Za'ini was far more explicit about the nature of the danger facing this honor. In his tract "The Female Qashé Sellers," he proclaimed women's work as "a disease whose microbes have infested healthy and sick bodies alike," and said it leads women to "lewd, filthy, and wanton behavior."[30] Five years later, in 1908, Yusuf Wakim wrote with concern about this same matter of women's unabated work and its effects on their honor, and that of the Syrian community.

But the concern was not just about protecting an honor grounded in the traditional construct of patriarchy. Many of those objecting to women's work saw it as a departure not only from village norms, but more importantly from the standards of the middle class in America, into whose ranks they were trying to gain entry. Using clinical terms, women's work was identified as the "disease" that was "infecting" the communal body, and simultaneously destroying traditional honor and modern morality. In a singular turn of phrase, then, these authors collapsed women's economic independence with sexual freedom, and termed both as detrimental. Part of the cure for these problems was to subjugate women to male authority and confine them to the home. This recommendation echoed the fears of the larger American middle class of sexuality and the restrictions that its members applied to confine female sexuality within the house.[31] And like the Anglo-Saxon bourgeois moralists who surrounded them, these authors sought then to universalize the true gender identity that derived from middle-class history and sensibilities. In fact, other authors argued that the only way to avoid the fall of women into ruin was to mix with the "middle classes of America" and not the lower classes "with whom we the Syrians mingle."[32]

The criticism leveled against women's work was met with mild objections from more liberal elements within the emigrant community. These contrarian views did not advocate women's work as inherently good, but rather as a necessary evil. Speaking from an equally modernist and middle-class perspective, these latter writers tended to emphasize that the fault lay not with the women but with their "lazy" or "incapacitated" husbands or fathers. Read, for example, the following rejoinder by Nasrallah Faris. Reacting to Nassif Elias's story of the woman peddler in Bridgewater, Maine, Nasrallah wrote, "[W]e agree with the writer that [a woman] should not travel to sell if her husband is capable of properly taking care of her needs and the needs of her house, but if that woman had emigrated and left in the country a sick man . . . or one heavily indebted, then is it not permissible for her to sell? Or if her husband is with her and he is sick, then who will take care of him, or if he is a gambling drunkard, then how can she depend on him?"[33] Afifa Karam, one of the earliest and most prolific women writers in the *mahjar*, took up the same theme in a later article.[34] In addressing those writers who were maligning the "honor" of women peddlers, she said, "[Y]ou ascribe licentiousness, depravity, and immorality only to the [female] *qashé* sellers, but you are wrong, because an immoral woman is not constrained from committing bad acts simply because she is living in palaces, or because she is imprisoned there."[35] Elaborating further on her defense of women peddlers, she emphasized that

> There are many [female] *qashé* sellers who are chaste in soul and
> body . . . and they may be forced to sell neither because of poverty
> nor because they have no one to support them, but rather because
> they have someone they have to support and he is like the useless
> beast. You probably know that there are many poor widows or
> orphaned girls in the country [Lebanon] who are suffering from
> the pain of hunger . . . they and their children. Those, therefore,
> were driven by circumstances and came to these lands [the United
> States to make a living].[36]

In this construction, women's work is dissociated from morality and
honor, while maintaining its connection to class. Karam and Nasrallah
make it clear that only poor women work, and by extension that work
is a necessary evil and not a right for the woman.

Yet, even as they defended poor women's work as a necessity, these
writers converged with their conservative counterparts in constructing
an ideal of womanhood that is distinct in its modernity from the life
experiences of most emigrant women and from the lives of peasant
women. Thus we find the editor of *Al-Huda* addressing the issue of
gender roles with a lengthy article—replete with historical "evidence,"
fables, and imagery from American life—that contended that men and
women should occupy separate but equal places in society. Waxing
poetic, he wrote, "Jules Simon, the famous French philosopher said,
'The improvement of human society is by the improvement of women,'
and others have said, 'she who rocks the cradle with her left [hand]
shakes the world with her right.' There is no doubt that the education
of the woman and her elevation in status is an education and elevation
of ourselves, because the woman is the nurturer of children, and children are the men and women of tomorrow. . . ."[37]

Afifa Karam went further in elucidating the notion of womanhood by creating four mutually exclusive categories of woman. Seeking to dispel the mirage that the American Woman is perfect, she
submits to her readers that sublime womanhood does not reside in
appearances or external beauty but in deeds. Accordingly, a woman is
either "good," "deceitful," "working," or "ignorant." The "good"
woman is the one who attends to her duties and helps her mother,
and who later as a bride makes her husband happy and makes her
house a paradise." "Working" women on the other hand are not—
"God Forbid"—necessarily without morals, but they do exist in an
environment that is filled "with dangers" that could compromise their
honor. However, for Karam, the worst two kinds of women are the
"ignorant," one who is "the disease of civilization and the curse of
modernization," and the "deceitful" woman who pretends to be "good"

but is in reality a "snake that poisons the honey of life."[38] Beauty, powdering the face, and wearing corsets to make thin waists were all considered frivolous affairs by Karam. They were wasting money on external beauty while ignoring the need for an inner beauty that the "good" woman maintains through proper manners and morals, as well as the knowledge necessary to run her household efficiently and effectively.

Education was a critical element in this imagining of the new "good" woman. Education would allow the woman to fulfill her natural duty of being the "queen of her house and her small following: her little children," a role deemed critical by these writers for the modernization of their community.[39] The editor of one Lebanese-American newspaper approvingly quoted an American magazine on this point. He wrote that the "educated, wise, gentle, hardworking and pure woman lifts her husband and brother and friend [to a better status] while the ignorant, frivolous, mean, and idiotic woman lowers them."[40] Mariam al-Zammar, who saw women as "queens of [their] house," illustrated this point through the juxtaposition of two types of mothers: one is educated to manage her house while the other is illiterate and incapable of taking control of matters inside her kingdom. The first mother plants good seeds and reaps good fruit, while the latter produces wayward children.

Yet, a serious obstacle stood in the way of attaining this level of civilized existence: men's recalcitrance. One author noted, "[T]he [Syrian] man demeans curses and hits the woman."[41] Carrying this refrain, Afifa Karam noted in one of her earliest essays that the Syrian woman is among the most pathetic of women in the world, and "that she is not of the same status as Western women."[42] Asking rhetorically of her opponents in the debate (in this case with Iskandar Hatem), "[W]hat is the cause of this inferiority?" she quickly added:

> If he [Hatem] tells me that the whole fault does not lie with the man, then I will answer him: with who then? Isn't it he [Hatem] who said that he [the man] is the manager of her affairs . . . so if he respected . . . and dwelt on educating her does he not think that she will learn and acquire [better] status, and in fact become a complete woman?"[43]

Thus, Karam created a circular relationship between gender roles and status. A man cannot climb the social ladder of respectability without the woman on his side. Yet for the woman to help in this process she must be educated and made complete, and this is the responsibility of the man.

Later articles expanded on this theme, coupling rise in social status with the notion of "equal but separate" gender roles. Both Mariam
al-Zammar and Karam argued that marital harmony must suffuse the
household, creating an environment suitable for nurturing children
and keeping them from vices like "drunkenness and gambling." Such
a state of being can only come about, according to these moralists, if
the roles of the man are revised as well as those of the women. "When
a man marries," one woman wrote, "it becomes parts of his primary
duties to provide happiness to his wife and his children."[44] Such happiness will not be attained unless he spends his free time with his
family rather than in the coffeehouses or at the homes of people.
Furthermore, and in exchange for the hard work that a woman puts
into the house and its management, the husband should provide love,
gentleness, and guidance rather than consider himself the "boss and
the lawgiver within the family."[45] Although the woman must "of
course" obey the man, this obedience would be voluntary rather than
forced, and deriving out of love rather than fear.

True love was located at the heart of this marital bliss. Thus, it too
had to be defined for the consumption of the readers of the press. The
first step in this process was to depict previous marital relationships
as barbaric and devoid of compassion, in order to make the contrast
with romantic love all the more compelling. For this purpose, many
serialized novels, poems, essays, and articles attacked the tradition of
arranged marriage and exalted the ideal of romantic and free love. As
one writer put it, "Love is one of the necessities of this universe and
it is given to all."[46] This sentiment was dramatized in many novels,
one of which was named *Layla*. In one particularly saccharine passage,
the father of Layla has the following exchange with his daughter: "Do
you not know that I am planning to marry you to your paternal cousin,
Yusuf, for he is the best man in our city and he has asked for your
hand, so what do you say to that? So Layla cried deeply then sighed
and said: Oh Father, do you not take pity on your daughter whose
heart has been seared by love, do you not take pity on my youth, do
you not take pity on my sorrows? If you insist on marrying me to
Yusuf then I will die. I do not want any other than Farid as lover and
husband."[47]

Sprawled across the pages of Lebanese-American newspapers were
articles that questioned more directly what Layla's father was attempting to do. *Al-Huda* launched this attack in a series of articles starting
in 1899 and continuing through 1908. Throughout, new and modern
rules for marriage were laid out to enlighten the readers. For instance,
in an article dated 5 March, 1899 one writer emphasized that marriage
is not only desirable but economically sound, since single men tend to

waste their money on "immoral" behavior in "clubs, theaters and houses of ill-repute." Approaching the issue "scientifically," the author stated that men should marry between the ages of 22 and 30, and "should choose their mates not for their wealth but for their education."[48] A little over a year later, these modern ways of marriage were expanded upon by another author, who declared that marriage should be based on "individual preference" and not be arranged or forced choices. A. Hakim, who decried the "pathetic" custom of arranged marriage in an article in the *Syrian World*, expounded further on the reasons for modern marriage. Just like other authors who linked the progress of society to the cult of domesticity and to new relations between husband and wife, Hakim contended that modern marriage "is the basis of happy family life, which in turn is the basis of the property and progress of the nation." Borrowing from the racial theories that abounded in the United States at the time, he went on to argue that "the improvement of the status of the race or its deterioration will depend upon the outcome of our efforts along this direction."[49]

In all these ways, a new family was being proposed as the signifier of the modernization of emigrants. It was a family that begins with a love that develops between a young man and a young woman without the interference of their families. The purity of this love (juxtaposed with the oppressive "horror" of arranged marriages) was expected to spawn a new and separate household made up of wife, husband, and children. Furthermore, the members of this family were to close their front door and turn towards each other in affection and support. The father was expected to work outside the house long enough each day to support the family financially, while the mother tended to raising morally and physically clean children within the confines of the house. Reunification at the end of the day behind closed doors and windows would reaffirm the singularity of these connections through edifying activities. In this manner, society, race, and nation would be improved.

Complications

This composite vision of the ideal family certainly filtered into the community, but hardly in a complete or unchanged fashion. The realities of daily life and the breadth of experiences were far too complex to be contained and ordered within the flat boundaries of the categories of woman, man, and family. For example, as Christine Stansell noted concerning the working class of New York in the 1860s, "the . . . culture of [working class] mothers [was] antithetical to the terms of home life and womanhood developed and championed by urban ladies."[50] In other words, women's work outside the home did not disappear because of the articles and speeches of middle-class moralists—emigrant or indigenous.

Women's work continued to be an economic necessity for many, and for some women it served as a way out of the house. For example, for Sultana al-Khazin work was a necessity of survival for her and her children. Sultana traveled to Philadelphia in 1901 to join her husband. However, upon arrival she discovered, much to her dismay, that he was living with another woman, named Nazira. His plan was for all of them to live together in the same house as one family. Sultana was not quite so cavalier—to say the least—in her approach to marriage, so she packed up the three children and moved out on her own. Soon she was selling linens door to door.[51] Some women lost their husbands not to infidelity but to death. They, equally, had to contend with raising a family on their own. Budelia Malooley recounted how "Mother arrived and started to peddle in Spring Valley . . . must have been in her mid-teens at the time. She resumed peddling on her return to Spring Valley from Lebanon after my father died and I was born [about the first part of 1904]. She'd make $5 to $10/week. She'd have to send money back to Rachaya to support my sister and brother."[52] Alice Assaley was also widowed when she was only in her twenties. In order to raise her son and daughter without her husband or any other male relatives, Alice was left to fend for herself by working first as a janitor and later as a peddler in Springfield, Illinois.[53]

Some women found in the *mahjar* a way out of the house. Mayme Faris remembers arguments between her father and mother about the latter's peddling activities.

> My mother peddled when my father had the [supplier's] store. It was a controversy between them; he didn't like her to; he didn't like her independence. Once my father got mad and destroyed her satchel—in front of the other peddlers and the women who lived around there too. No, she wasn't disgraced. . . . She stopped it for a while and when she felt they needed more money, she would go. But independence was a big thing in their [women's] lives.[54]

Sophia Mussallem was equally persistent and restless in seeking financial independence. Starting in 1885, when she first immigrated to the United States at the age of 14, she worked. From Milwaukee, Wisconsin, to Greenbay and Watertown, then across to the Oklahoma Territory, she peddled all the way to Muskogee. Throughout her expeditions she stashed away money for the dream of owning a store, which she finally accomplished in Muskogee.[55] And Oscar Alwan's mother made more money as a peddler than did his father. "She was a strong woman. . . . She was never afraid, people [in upstate New York] loved her and waited for her to arrive. She knew how to deal with people, she was a good saleswoman."[56]

This multifaceted reality of women's lives made the idealized middle-class family life either untenable or undesirable, or both to varying degrees at different times. That women continued to work through the 1920s, and that authors kept writing to complain about this, is perhaps the best indication that the project of middle-class domesticity was never completed. But more interestingly, women's work forced a constant negotiation about the meanings and practices of the family. A husband who had to negotiate with his wife about her desire to work, or a woman who accumulated more money than her husband, created a complexity that made the proposed gender roles within the modern family irrelevant—however partially. Clearly, these contradictions were not all lost on the children in such families.

Women's work was but one obstacle that stood in the way of the emergence of the modern family. Emigrant families do not seem to have taken well to the idea of isolating themselves from the larger community. Two things kept many from adopting the isolating existence being proposed by fellow emigrants and reformers alike: money and sociability. Since emigrants had left their homes in Lebanon on an errand of gathering some modicum of wealth, most were loath to spend their hard-earned money on what they considered "frivolities." Thus, when faced with the abhorrent novelty of paying large sums of money for monthly rents, emigrants balked. If they could not refuse, then at least they could shrink this constant drain by crowding together into small apartments or houses. Counting emigrant families and apartments in New York, one observer found that over 70 percent of the families lived in apartments that rented for less than $14 per month, and that were made up of two rooms or one.[57] On average, the same observer calculated methodically, four to five people lived in these apartments. Sleeping under those conditions meant a spread of mattresses across the whole floor. The scientific tone of these characterizations becomes slightly more impassioned when the report states, "[T]he number of baths in the Syrian homes . . . can be counted on the fingers of one hand, and there are very few private closets . . . many [of which] are constructed in the illegal sink fashion."[58] Taking baths "on Saturdays" meant a galvanized steel tub sitting in the middle of the kitchen with traffic of relatives and neighbors swirling around the lone bather. In winter the discomfort was accentuated by the bitter cold, which was barely staved off by a single wood or coal-burning stove (piped heat was a luxury that only those paying upwards from \$360 in 1909 annual rent could afford).[59]

In outlying areas crowding was even more intense. In an article titled (in a straightforward racist fashion) "Don't Like Arabs," which appeared in the 16 July, 1901 edition of the *Cedar Rapids Evening Gazette*, neighbors complained of "the deportment of fifty Arabians who represent the colony [of Lebanese emigrants] living in a building . . . at 1220 South Third Street."[60] The building included only two apartments and a store below them, which made for very dense living conditions. Squeezing together for warmth and frugality was also common amongst emigrants in Fort Wayne, Indiana. By sleeping ten, twelve, or even twenty souls to a room in the hotel of Salem Beshara, emigrants limited their rent to five or ten dollars a month.[61] Cramming into an apartment meant that there were strangers in the midst of families. Boarders were a necessary part of the formula of cutting cost. Many families took in boarders because the dollar or two they paid reduced rent costs by 10 to 20 percent. For those desperate to save money this was nothing to scoff at. Out of a total population of 1,891 emigrants in Brooklyn, some 464 were boarders—men and women who were not directly related to the family with whom they were staying.[62]

But it was not just money that kept emigrants from retreating into a more solitary existence. Their desire for social company was not abated by the refrains from social reformers. Recalling the "time of the emigrants," the daughters of George Abdelnour described the peddlers' house on Minnesota Street. "It was used by all the peddlers when they were in town. It had one kitchen and often about two dozens at a time—both men and women, husbands and wives, single men and single women—slept there on the floor, two or three families in one room. A man and his wife maybe partitioned off with a drape or something."[63] In addition to the discomfort of such a tight existence, emigrants held *haflat* (parties) in the evenings at which food, drink, and song would be their entertainment. Without tinting their experience with an unfounded sentimentality or even harmony, one could still find amidst the many stories they left behind a sociability that they erected around themselves. Within this context, the family became any group of people living in the same quarters and sharing their daily lives. Some of the members of these transient families were related by blood, many were from the same village, and few were strangers. In fact, many emigrants were consciously aware of these new social dynamics in their language and action. For example, the new arrivals would call the more established emigrants by the name of *ammi* (my paternal uncle) and *khalti* (my maternal aunt).[64] Salem Beshara became the godfather to countless children, many of whom were not his direct relatives. Those who were blood relatives would leave the house for weeks and months as they sought their fortunes in outlying regions of the country. Thus, the boundaries of family were spread beyond the nuclear or extended household to include a constantly changing group of individuals.

Marriage patterns also remained far from the ideals of the social reformers. Many emigrant men returned to Mount Lebanon specifically to marry their cousin, or someone else from their natal village.[65] And those marriages were neither perfect nor horrifying. Some women had to suffer through life with an abusive or demanding husband. Others simply took the opportunity offered in the anonymous world of Amirka to leave an unhappy environment. There were those who recounted their initial horror at their arranged marriage, only to develop a loving relationship with their husband. Some wrote in their memoirs of weak husbands who were incapable of sustaining the family economically or emotionally, while others fondly recollected husbands who were a positive force in their lives.[66] In other words, arranged marriage was no more a uniformly negative experience than romantic love was a positive one. In practical measures, these arranged marriages maintained a link to a larger number of relatives, thus creating a network of support that was mobilized to cope with life's various crises. As the numbers of relatives, children, and boarders changed over time, the nature of the relationship between husband and wife also fluctuated in the levels of intimacy and affectivity that were possible.

The relationship between parents and children was as complicated and diverse as that between spouses. One emigrant recalled her father's refusal to allow her to continue her education, and her joy when her aunts—who had greater influence, since they were the main breadwinners in the family—successfully intervened. Then, she proceeded to describe her dislike for the regimented school system in America.[67] Some married the man or woman that their parents chose for them, while others insisted on marrying the one they loved. Some told stories about sacrificing their lives for the sake of their parents, while others insisted that the parents sacrificed all on their behalf. Compromises between the demands of the state and the demands of the family were also constantly negotiated. For example, in Gibran Khalil Gibran's family, his sisters continued to work as peddlers and seamstresses while he—being the youngest—went to school. In other families, the children would attend school intermittently while continuing to help with the family's financial needs. And certainly, many emigrants recalled their childhoods with fondness that derives from memories of parental love and affection. Others found in the *mahjar* a means to escape from an unpleasant family life, and some went as far as Alaska to be rid of haunting memories.[68]

Ultimately, we know many emigrants rejected the idealized vision of middle-class life in America, because anywhere between a third to a half of them went back to Mount Lebanon permanently.[69] Reasons for return were many. Some had failed to achieve wealth, while others had saved what they deemed to be enough money to return. And many returned because that was their plan from the start. Yet, in returning they provide us with examples of emigrants who did not consider the modernity of America enticing enough to stay. In fact, some wrote of their dislike for what they saw as the loneliness, materialism, and emotional emptiness of American life. The following words, written by a Russian Jewish emigrant to the Yiddish newspaper *Forverts*, echoed the sentiments of many other emigrants, including some of those from Mount Lebanon:

> Where is the golden land, where are the golden people? What has happened to human feeling in such a great wide world, in such a land which is, as it is said, a land flowing with milk and honey? When in such a rich city like New York on 88 Clinton Street a woman is dying of hunger, of loneliness, and need—that can only say: "Cursed be Columbus, cursed be he for discovering America."[70]

In turning their back on America and its positivist modernity, many did so because they feared that its influence was corrupting their families and their values. Without accepting the presumed authenticity—inherent in these statements—we can still see in it a rejection, complete or partial, of the modernization project. And yet, even as we do so we are kept from arriving at a definitive conclusion in this matter, because many of those who went back proceeded to build houses whose internal architecture emulated the middle-class spaces that they had encountered in the *mahjar*.

"In-Betweeness"[71]

Like other emigrant communities, then, the Lebanese came face-to-face with a new and politically charged map of the world that divided it into traditional and modern.[72] They experienced criticism and derision of their way of life in the words, social mores, and material culture of a powerful middle class in the United States. This compelled some emigrants to seek a modernization of their community that would bring them close to the idealized middle-class life in America. Yet, others—and even the ones just noted—did not want to forgo the native identities that distinguished them as Lebanese, Syrian, Arab, Easterners. In those they saw a set of identities that were satisfying

emotionally and that allowed them a sense of uniqueness and individuality that modernity was threatening to immerse in its sea of
middle-class uniformity.

As a result of this tension, emigrants were not assimilated, nor did
they remain insulated in a cocoon of tradition. New hairstyles—including short hair for a few brave souls—lipstick, and other imple-
ments of modern self-decoration became the tools of young emigrants
for burrowing underneath the foundations of patriarchal control. Yet,
fathers and mothers still kept a tight rein over the movements, labor,
and actions of their daughters. Romantic love was propounded as the
ideal of individual liberty that would lead to social progress, even as
many emigrants continued to travel to Lebanon to marry their paternal cousins. A woman was expected to become a queen of her house,
at the same time as most women were outside their home working to
make a living. A man was counseled to stay home and embrace the
middle-class norm of isolated domesticity even as more coffeehouses
opened in the larger emigrant communities. Emigrants attended the
nickelodeon, where they were supposed to passively see America and
learn to be American, yet these theaters were the sites of self-expres-
sive commentary and antics.

Because of these dizzying circumstances the construction of new
set of identities was a tumultuous affair that produced many variations on similar themes. Most notably, however, the family as the
locale of intense social relations was subjected to the severest pressures of modernization. There were constant calls to shrink the scope
of these familial relations to an idealized nuclear family living a pro-
totypical middle-class life. However, this ideal could not be realized.
The relations that defined the family were never isolated behind closed
doors, but continued to extend—albeit in a revised form—into the
neighborhood and even across the ocean. Relations between husband
and wife may have grown more intimate, but that did not exclude
either of them from their gendered spheres. Daughters and sons gained
more independence, but many still had to work to satisfy familial
obligations. In short, then, between 1890 and 1920 the Lebanese emigrant community constructed a new set of relations that were neither
modern nor traditional, neither Eastern nor Western. Rather, these
new identities were peculiar to their individual, familial, and communal historical experiences. And as much as "hybridity" differentiated
them from middle-class America, it would also come to distinguish
them—upon the temporary or permanent return of many of them to
their villages—from peasant Lebanon.

Such an inconclusive conclusion is not only a reflection of the history of these emigrants, but also brings to the fore my own ambivalence

about the category of family and the way I—and many others—have gone about telling its history. Clearly, we have come a long way from the time (only few decades ago) when the family was pigeonholed in certain well-defined categories.[73] Tamara Hareven summarizes the most current approach to the history of the family as "An effort to understand interrelationship between individual time, family and historical time."[74] While this represents a far more fluid and sophisticated approach to the retelling of people's lives, it remains embroiled in defining and articulating an analytical category. Regardless of how well nuanced our categories may be, they remain a means to generalize, and generalizations are a discourse of power. As Lila Abu-Lughod put it, this discourse "is the language of those who seem to stand apart from and outside what they are describing."[75] This linguistic distance—from which we as historians derive our authority—facilitates the construction of others, and our alienation (along with our readers) from their experience. This is ironic, given that we write these histories to make them relevant to our human present and future. In other words, it would seem that we are dehumanizing history by constructing categories—however contingent we make them. And family is not an exception.

How would our histories be if we focused on the particular? How would this paper appear if I wrote it about the specific experiences of individual emigrants? Would there be a difference if instead of speaking about emigrants, I told the story of Sultana al-Khazin, her travels to Philadelphia to find her husband living with another woman, and her subsequent departure with her children? Typicality cannot be sustained in such a story, and particulars become critical to the making of historical experience. Furthermore, we can begin to see how—as Bourdieu put it—"people live their lives." It would show people feeling pain and joy, arguing and contesting interpretations of what is happening, and struggling to shape their own destiny through a myriad of daily small decisions. These paths—which are twisted, divergent, and convergent, as we should know from own lives—become parts of the histories of families. While we can still read from within these texts the larger forces that made them possible, we are restrained from totalizing the particular into an essentializing narrative. We would narrate lives instead of categories, and we would do so from a far more humble vantage point that would place us at the same level of unpredictability as those whose stories we wish to tell.

Yet, I recognize the limitations of this approach—mechanical (paucity of sources) and theoretical (inability to draw large historical patterns). Moreover, I am not willing to throw out the use of larger narratives in history, because I believe that they are profoundly critical in constructing collective memories, an essential element of our human existence. While generalizations do imbed within their text a discourse of power, they do not necessarily have to create a hegemonic of the Subject. Rather, what I hope my work shows is the need to use the tension between the general and the particular, between the metanarrative and the life story, between facts and meaning, and between social and cultural history in writing our stories. This tension allows us to present our categories as contingent even as we highlight their boundaries to illustrate a point. It clearly shows our intellectual vantage point as authors of the narratives without disregarding the factual premises of the stories we tell. In other words, without assuming that this tension resolves all the contradictions inherent in writing our narratives, it still allows us the intellectual space to infuse our reconstruction of events with a meaning that is indeed relevant, even if it is limited. Thus, the story of Sultana al-Khazin is meaningful on its own as the story of a woman struggling to retain her dignity and to take care of her family. But it is also meaningful in what it has to tell us about the stresses that brought about changes in gender roles and the construct of the family. Without placing hers, and the rest of the emigrant stories, as a coherent and contained point on a linear historical progression, we can still read them as stories that have something to tell us about how people dealt with changes at a particular time and space. In short, we can still read these stories as history.

Notes

1. *Al-Huda*, 6, no. 75 (26 May 1903): 2.

2. I do not use terms such as modern, traditional, East, West, family, woman, public, private, Lebanon, or Syria as set definitions of a state of being, or even as words that designate clearly defined and "real" historical ideas or structures. Rather, I consider all of these terms to be contingent, contestable, and ever changing in their meaning and their historical implication. Thus, the term "family" does not denote for me a particular form or structure, but is a term that I loosely use to speak of groups of individuals who come together in various changing configurations on the premise of a blood-relation or prolonged occupancy of the same physical space. This is even more the case for the politically loaded and value-laden terms like "modern" and "traditional." These are, in my opinion, constructed terms that obfuscate more than they delineate. Thus, I use them, as well as the other terms, as indicators of a mindframe that we need to question and not simply accept as valid.

3. Hareven 1996; Tilly 1988; and Stone 1981.

4. Khater 1996.

5. Another 120,000 to 180,000 emigrated to South America during this same period. Statistics on this matter are rather difficult to assess accurately. For the latest numbers on this subject, see Hourani and Shehadi 1992.

6. This process also thoroughly undermines the notion of a typical Mediterranean family, a notion that still lingers despite the multitude of works that have successfully debunked its counterpart in the artificial dualism of West/Other.

7. Ewen 1985; Friedman-Kasaba 1996; and Yung 1995.

8. For excellent studies of the middle class in America, see Ryan 1981 and Blumin 1989.

9. American reactions to immigrants ranged greatly over the social and economic map of the United States. There were the nativists, who rejected immigration as "mongrelizing" the species. (See, for example, J. Higham 1988). There were also the elitist romantics who imagined a "pure and noble East" that should not be sullied by modern industrialism (R. Waterfield 1998, in her biography of Gibran Khalil Gibran, has a very interesting section about this group, particularly with regard to those residing in Boston). Then there were the social workers, who tried hard to assimilate immigrants into the mainstream of American life.

10. Razovki 1917, 117.

11. Howe 1903, 382.

12. It is important to note that some social workers had a more critical approach to the ideal of middle-class life. For example, Mary Simkhovitch noted that immigrant women had a stronger position within the family than "often obtains in families of a higher economic level" (M. Simkhovitch 1938, 136; also see J. Addams 1902, 40–41). And young charity workers like Jane Addams came to recognize that the "tidiness" of the middle-class charity worker is hardly a claim to cultural superiority; in fact, she says, it represents "parasitic cleanliness and a social standing attained only through status" (Addams 1902, 18).

13. Knoph 1916, 161.

14. Woods and Kennedy 1922, 185.

15. Mink 1995; See also Boris 1995.

16. P. Davis 1915, 227–29.

17. New York City, which had the most extensive public school system, was teaching 1,376 foreign students in 1879 and 36,000 in 1905 (Straubenmueller 1906, 177).

18. Buchanan 1902, 691.

19. Juliani 1978, 119.

20. *Al-Huda* 8, no. 39 (8 April 1905): 4.

21. *Al-Huda* 1, no. 25 (22 March 1898): 9.

22. At least one article on visits and time ran in several Arabic newspapers every year through World War I.

23. *Al-Huda* 2, no. 8 (18 April 1899): 13.

24. Ibid., 14

25. Ibid., 15.

26. Ibid.

27. *Al-Huda* 6, no. 42 (17 April 1903): 2.

28. Ibid.

29. *Al-Huda* 6, no. 75 (26 May 1903): 2.

30. *Al-Huda* 6, no. 103 (12 July 1903): 2

31. In the 1860s American writers on sexuality such as Dr. R. T. Trall argued that women controlled the "passional expression of love." While admitting the possibility that women can experience sexual pleasure, he and other writers either subordinated female sexual desire, or lust, "to the passive, loving faculties of feminine character or denied [it] entirely" (Ryan 1981, 105).

32. *Al-Huda* 7, no. 261 (12 January 1905): 3.

33. *Al-Huda* 6, no. 88 (11 June 1903): 3.

34. *Al-Huda* 6, no. 105 (14 July 1903): 2.

35. At the beginning of this article, Afifa Karam wrote, without the slightest hint of sarcasm, "I read above the article [of Yusuf al-Zaʾini titled "Women *Qashé* Sellers] words from *al-Huda* asking 'educated men to respond and criticize' without including educated women. But I ask *al-Huda* to excuse this action of mine [writing in response]." At the end of the article, the editor of *al-Huda* wrote: "We wish more educated women were like the writer of this article, not afraid to appear in a literary setting nor of the objections against them by foolish people. . . ." Both comments were indications that the entry of women writers into this field was a fairly novel event.

36. Ibid.

37. *Al-Huda* 3, no. 53 (8 April 1900): 2.

38. *Al-Huda* 1, no. 37 (23 August 1898): 3.

39. *Al-Huda* 11, no. 92 (10 June 1908): 2. In 1903 Afifa Karam noted that only 5 percent of emigrant women were educated. This is a difficult statistic to verify. Our other source of information is immigration records that stipulate a slightly higher figure of literacy among Syrian emigrant women.

40. *Al-Huda* 4, no. 153 (1 September 1900): 2.

41. Ibid.

42. *Al-Huda* 6, no. 146 (21 August 1903): 3.

43. *Al-Huda* 6, no. 156 (2 September 1903): 2.

44. *Al-Huda* 7, no. 266 (1905): 2.

45. Naff Arab-American Collection; Smithsonian Institute; Series 4-B-5. Interview with Maryam A., 1980.

46. *Al-Huda* 7, no. 261 (12 January 1905): 2.

47. *Al-Huda* 2, no. 4 (2 March 1899): 19.

48. *Al-Huda* 2, no. 5 (5 March 1899): 15.

49. *Syrian World* 3, no. 13 (October 1928): 51.

50. Stansell 1986, 219.

51. Naff Arab-American Collection; Smithsonian Institute; Series 4-B. Interview with Dorothy Lee Andrache (granddaughter of Sultana), 18 January, 1991.

52. Naff Arab-American Collection; Smithsonian Institute; Series 4-C-5. Interview with Budelia Malooley, 1980.

53. Naff Arab-American Collection; Smithsonian Institute; Series 4-C-5.

54. Ibid. Interview with Mayme Faris, 1980.

55. Ibid. Interview with Eva Frenn, 18 November, 1980.

56. Ibid. Interview with Oscar Alwan, 16 July, 1980.

57. Miller 1969, 16.

58. Ibid., 9.

59. Ewen 1985, 150–52.

60. *Cedar Rapids Evening Gazette,* 1901: 8.

61. Naff Arab-American Collection; Smithsonian Institute; Series 4-C-1. Interview with Tafeda Beshara, Spring 1968.

62. Miller 1969, 46. Of this group, 164 were women, while the rest were men.

63. Naff Arab-American Collection; Smithsonian Institute; Series 4-C-5. Interview with Amelia and Haseby Abdelnour, Spring 1968.

64. Ibid.

65. Naff, 1985.

66. Many of these stories are to be found at the Smithsonian Institute, Naff Arab-American Collection, Series 4-C-1, 2, 3, 4, and 5.

67. Naff Arab-American Collection; Smithsonian Institute; Series 4-C-1. Interview with Tafeda Beshara, Spring 1968.

68. Naff Arab-American Collection; Smithsonian Institute; Series 4-C-5. Interview with Hisham Abdel-massih, Spring 1966

69. Numbers are very difficult to ascertain because of the confusion of sources and statistics. However, I have arrived at this estimate by looking at French, Ottoman, and American sources.

70. Szajkowski 1978, 305. Similar sentiments were echoed in various essays by emigrant writers in the Lebanese-American press. See *Mira 'at al-Gharb* and *al-Huda* for examples of such pieces.

71. This is a term that was employed by Southern nativists to indicate the threat that Italian immigration posed not only to the purity of the white race but also to its solidarity. I am using it here in this sense, but also from the other perspective whereby the Lebanese emigrants were in between the spaces of America and Lebanon.

72. There is a multitude of books on this subject for other ethnic communities in the United States. For the Italian community see, for example, Donna Gabaccia (1984), and Michael La Sorte (1985).

73. Here, I am thinking of the early work of Peter Laslett (1972, 1983), as well as Jack Goody's various essays on the "Evolution of the Family" (1969, 1983).

74. Hareven 1991a, 95.

75. L. Abu-Lughod 1993, 8.

Bibliography

Abd al-Hakim, Muhammad Subhi. 1968. *Al-Watan al-Arabi, arduhu wa-sukkanuhu wa-mawariduh:* (The Arab homeland: Territory, inhabitants, resources). Maktabat al-Anjlu al-Misriyah. Cairo.

Abd al-Qadir, H., et al. 1973. *Asma al-mawaqi al-jughrafiyah fi-l-urdunn wa-falastin.* Amman.

Abd al-Rahim, Abd al-Rahman Abd al-Rahim. 1989. *Kitab al-durra al-musana ta'lif al-amir Ahmad al-Katkhuda Al-Damurdsashi Katkhuda Azaban.* Cairo.

———. 1996. "The Family and Gender Laws in Egypt during the Ottoman Period." In *Women, the Family, and Divorce Laws in Islamic History,* edited by A. Sonbol. Syracuse.

Abou-el-Haj, Rifaat Ali. 1973. "The Ottoman Vezir and Pasa Households, 1683–1703: A Preliminary Report." *Journal of the American Oriental Society,* 94:438–47.

———. 1984. *The 1703 Rebellion and the Structure of Ottoman Politics.* İstanbul.

Abu Jaber, Kamal S. 1967. "The Millet System in the Nineteenth-Century Ottoman Empire." *Muslim World* 57 (3): 212–23.

Abu-Lughod, Janet. 1971. *Cairo: 1001 Years of the City Victorious.* Princeton.

———. 1987. "The Islamic City—Historic Myth, Islamic Essence, and Contemporary Relevance." *International Journal of Middle East Studies* 19:155–76.

Abu-Lughod, Lila. 1990. "Anthropology's Orient: The Boundaries of Theory on the Arab World." In *Theory, Politics and the Arab World: Critical Responses,* edited by Hisham Sharabi, New York and London.

———. 1993. *Writing Women's Worlds: Bedouin Stories.* Berkeley.

———, ed. 1998. *Remaking Women: Feminism and Modernity in the Middle East.* Princeton.

Addams, Jane. 1902. *Democracy and Social Ethics.* New York.

Afshar, Haleh. 1998. *Islam and Feminism: An Iranian Case Study.* New York.

Agmon, Iris. 1984. "The Development of Palestine's Foreign Trade, 1879–1914: Economic and Social Aspects" (in Hebrew), Master's thesis, University of Haifa.

———. 1994. "Women and Society: Muslim Women, the Shariʿa Court, and the Society of Jaffa and Haifa under Late Ottoman Rule, 1900–1914" (in Hebrew). Ph.D. diss., The Hebrew University of Jerusalem.

———. 1996. "Muslim Women in Court According to the Sijill of Late Ottoman Jaffa and Haifa: Some Methodological Notes." In *Women, the Family, and Divorce Laws in Islamic History,* edited by Amira El Azhary Sonbol. New York.

———. 1998. "Women, Class, and Gender: Muslim Jaffa and Haifa at the Turn of the Twentieth Century." *International Journal of Middle East Studies* 30:477–500.

Ahmed, Leila. 1988. "Between Two Worlds: The Formation of a Turn-of-the-Century Egyptian Feminist." In *Life/Lines: Theorizing Women's Autobiography,* edited by Bella Brodzki and Celeste Schenk. Ithaca.

———. 1993. *Women and Gender in Islam.* Cairo.

Ahram, Al-. 1876–81, 1910, 1931. Alexandria and Cairo.

Akiba, Jun. 1998. "Reforms in the Organization of the Late Ottoman Ilmiye, 1826–1914" (in Japanese). *Annals of Japan Association for Middle East Studies,* 13:185–214.

———. 2000. "The Making of a Judge in the Late Ottoman Empire: Some Observations on Social Mobility and Integration." Working paper for MESA Annual Meeting, Orlando.

Albayrak, Sadyk. 1996. *Son Devir Osmanly Ulemasy (Ylmiye ricalinin Teracim-i Ahavîli).* Vols. 1–5. Istanbul.

Alderson, A. D. 1956. *The Structure of the Ottoman Dynasty.* Oxford.

Alleaume, Ghislaine, and Philippe Fargues. 1998a. "La naissance d'une statistique d'État: Le recensement de 1846 en Égypte." *Histoire et mesure* 13 (1/2): 147–93.

———. 1998b. "Voisinage et frontière: Résider au Caire en 1846." In *Urbanité arabe,* edited by J. Dakhlia. Paris.

Amin, Qasim. 1976. *Qasim Amin: Al-aʿmal al-kamila.* Edited and translated by Muhammad Amara. Beirut.

————. 1993. *The Liberation of Women: A Document in the History of Egyptian Feminism.* Translated by Samiha S. Peterson. New York.

————. 1995. *The New Woman: A Document in the History of Egyptian Feminism.* Translated by Samiha S. Peterson. Cairo.

————. 2000. *The Liberation of Women and The New Woman. Two Documents in the History of Egyptian Feminism.* Translated by Samiha Sidhom Peterson. Cairo.

Amirshahi, Mahshid. 1995. *Suri & Co.: Tales of a Persian Teenage Girl.* Austin.

Anderson, Benedict. 1983. *Imagined Communities: Reflections on the Origin and Spread of Nationalism.* London.

Anderson, Michael. 1980. *Approaches to the History of the Western Family, 1500–1914.* Cambridge.

Anker, Richard, and Martha Anker. 1995. "Measuring Female Labour Force with Emphasis on Egypt." In *Gender and Development in the Arab World*, edited by Nabil Khoury and Valentine Moghadam. London.

Antoun, Richard. 1967. "Social Organization and the Life Cycle of an Arab Village." *Ethnology* 6.

————. 1972. *Arab Village: A Social Structural Study of a Trans-Jordanian Peasant Community.* Bloomington.

Appadurai, Arjun. 1986. "Theory in Anthropology: Center and Periphery." *Comparative Studies in Society and History* 28, (2): 356–61.

Arai, Y. 1993. "Separate Residences and District Study," *Iichiko, Journal of Intercultural and Transdisciplinary Studies* 26: 49–114. (Special issue: Damascus).

Ariès, Philippe. 1962. *Centuries of Childhood: A Social History of Family Life.* New York.

Ariès, Philippe, and George Duby, general eds. 1987. *A History of Private Life: From Pagan Rome to Byzantium.* Edited by P. Veyne. Cambridge, Mass.

Artan, Tülay. 1993. "From Charismatic Rulership to Collective Rule: Introducing Materials on Wealth and Power of Ottoman Princesses in the Eighteenth Century." *Toplum ve Ekonomi* 4: 53–94.

————. 2000. "Aspects of Ottoman Elite's Food Consumption: Looking for 'Staples,' 'Luxuries,' and 'Delicacies' in a Changing Century." In *Consumption Studies and the History of the Ottoman Empire, 1550–1922: An Introduction*, edited by Donald Quataert. Albany.

Asadi, Kh. n.d. *Mawsuʿat Halab al-muqarana* (Comparative encyclopedia of Aleppo). Vol 3. Halab.

Ata, Ibrahim W. 1986. *The West Bank Palestinian Family.* London.

Atran, Scott. 1986. "Hamula Organization and Musha ʿa Tenure in Palestine." *Man* 21:271–95.

Ayalon, David. 1977. *Studies on the Mamluks of Egypt, 1250–1517*. London.

Aydyn, M. 1990. "Sultan II: Mahmud döneminde yapylan nüfus tahrirleri." In İstanbul Üniversitesi Edebiyat Fakültesi, Tarih Araştirma Merkezi, *Sultan II. Mahmud ve reformlary semineri*, 81–97 İstanbul.

Ayyubi, Ilyas. 1923. *Tarikh misr fi asr ismaʿil*. 2 vols. Cairo.

Badran, Margot. 1987. *Harem Years: The Memoirs of an Egyptian Feminist*. New York.

———. 1995. *Feminists, Islam, and Nation: Gender and the Making of Modern Egypt*. Princeton.

Baer, Gabriel. 1969. In *Studies in the Social History of Modern Egypt*. Chicago.

———. 1983. "Women and Waqf: An Analysis of the Istanbul Tahrir of 1546." *Asian and African Studies* 17: 9–28.

Baker, Hugh D. R. 1979. *Chinese Family and Kinship*. New York.

Bakhit, Muhammad Adnan. 1982. "The Christian Population of the Province of Damascus in the Sixteenth Century." In vol. 2 of *Christian and Jews in the Ottoman Empire*, edited by Benjamin Braude and Bernard Lewis. New York.

Bakhtin, M. M. 1993. *Toward a Philosophy of the Act*. Translated by Vadim Liapunov. Austin.

Bakhtin, M. M., and P. N. Medvedev. 1978. *The Formal Method in Literary Scholarship: A Critical Introduction to Sociological Poetics*. Translated by Albert J. Wehrle. Baltimore.

Barakat, Halim. 1985. "The Arab Family and the Challenge of Social Transformation." In *Women and the Family in the Middle East*, edited by Elizabeth Warnock Fernea. Austin.

Barkan, Ömer Lütfi. 1953. "Tarihi Demografi Aratyrmalary ve Osmanly Tarihi." *Türkiyat Mecmuasy* 10:1–26.

———. 1978. "Research on Ottoman Fiscal Surveys." In *Studies in the Economic History of the Middle East: From the Rise of Islam to the Present Day*, edited by M. A. Cook. 2d ed. Oxford.

Barnes, John Robert. 1986. *An Introduction to Religious Foundations in the Ottoman Empire*. Leiden.

Baron, Beth. 1991. "The Making and Breaking of Marital Bonds in Modern Egypt." In *Women in Middle Eastern History: Shifting Boundaries in Sex and Gender*, edited by Nikki Keddie and Beth Baron. New Haven.

———. 1994. *The Women's Awakening in Egypt: Culture, Society, and the Press.* New Haven.

Barth, Frederick. 1954. "Father's Brother's Daughter's Marriage in Kurdistan." *Southwestern Journal of Anthropology* 10:164–71.

Batu, Selahattin. 1938. *Türk Atlary ve At Yetiştirme Bilgisi.* Ankara.

Beaman, Arden Hulme. 1929. *The Dethronement of the Khedive.* London.

Beck, D. F. 1957. "The Changing Moslem Family in the Middle East." *Marriage and Family Living* 19.

Beck, Lois. 1991. *Nomad: A Year in the Life of a Qashqaʾi Tribesman in Iran.* Berkeley.

Behar, C. 1998. "Qui compte? 'Recensements' et statistiques démographiques dans l'Empire ottoman, du XVIe au XXe siècle." *Histoire et Mesure* 135–46.

Bertaux, Daniel, and Paul Thompson, eds. 1993. *Between Generations: Family Models, Myths, and Memories.* Oxford.

Betteridge, Anne H. 2000. "The Controversial Vows of Urban Muslim Women in Iran." In *Unspoken Worlds: Women's Religious Lives in Non-Western Cultures*, edited by Nancy Auer Falk and Rita M. Gross. San Francisco.

Binder, Leonard, ed. 1966. *Politics in Lebanon.* New York.

Bizri, Dalal. 1997. "Authority and Society in Family Law: The President's Independence Day Initiative and the Reaction to It." Paper delivered at the Conference on Gender and Citizenship in Lebanon. March. American University in Beirut.

Blumin, Stuart. 1989. *The Emergence of the Middle Class: Social Experience in the American City, 1760–1900.* New York.

Boinet, Antoine. 1886. "L'Accroissement de la population en Égypte." *Bulletin de l'Institut Égyptien* (Cairo), 7:272–305.

Booth, Marilyn. 1991. "Biography and Feminist Rhetoric in Early-Twentieth-Century Egypt: Mayy Ziyada's Studies of Three Women's Lives." *Journal of Women's History* 3 (1): 38–64.

———. 1997. "May Her Likes Be Multiplied: 'Famous Women' Biography and Gendered Prescription in Egypt, 1892–1935." *Signs: Journal of Women in Culture and Society* 22 (4): 827–90.

Boris, Eileen. 1995. "The Radicalized Gendered State: Constructions of Citizenship in the United States." *Social Politics* 2:160–80.

Bourdieu, Pierre. 1990. *The Logic of Practice.* Translated by Richard Nice. Stanford.

———. 1993. *The Field of Cultural Production: Essays on Art and Literature*. New York.

Bowring, J. [1840] 1973. *Report on the Commercial Statistics of Syria*. New York.

Bradburd, Daniel. 1990. *Ambiguous Relations: Kin, Class, and Conflict among the Komachi Pastoralists*. Washington.

Bradbury, Bettina. 2000. "Feminist Historians and Family History in Canada in the 1990s." *Journal of Family History* 25 (3): 362–83.

Brink, J. 1987. "Changing Extended Family Relationships in an Egyptian Village." *Urban Anthropology* 16.

Buchanan, John. 1902. "How to Assimilate the Foreign Element in Our Population." *Forum* 32:687–94.

Burke's Royal Families of the World. 1980. Vol. 2, *Africa and the Middle East*. London.

Butler, Alfred J. 1888. *Court Life in Egypt*. London.

Butler, Judith. 1993. *Bodies That Matter: On the Discursive Limits of "Sex."* New York.

———. 1997. *Excitable Speech: A Politics of the Performative*. New York.

Butovsky, Avriel. 1995. "Images of Monarchy: The Khedivate of Tawfiq Pasha and Reform." In *The Languages of History: Selected Writings on the Middle East*. Cambridge, Mass.

Butros, Gabriel M., trans. 1973. *The Lebanese Constitution*. Beirut.

Caillard, Mabel. 1935. *A Lifetime in Egypt, 1876–1935*. London.

Censer, Jane Turner. 1991. "Whatever Happened to Family History? A Review Article." *Comparative Studies in Society and History* 33 (3): 528–38.

———. 1988. *The Writing of History*. Translated by Tom Conley. New York.

Chaichian, Mohammed. 1988. "The Effects of World Capitalist Economy on Urbanization in Egypt, 1800–1970." *International Journal of Middle Eastern Studies* 20:23–43.

Chamie, J. 1986. "Polygyny among Arabs." *Population Studies* 40:55–81.

Chao, Paul. 1983. *Chinese Kinship*. London.

Chatila, Khaled. 1934. *Le Mariage chez les Musulmans en Syria*. Paris.

Cheal, David. 1991. *Family and the State of Theory*. New York.

Chennells, Ellen. 1893. *Recollections of an Egyptian Princess by her English governess, Being a Record of Five Years' Residence at the Court of Ismael Pasha, Khédive*. 2 vols. London.

Çynar, Ali Abbas. 1993. *Türklerde At ve Ondokuzuncu Yüzyyla Ait Bir Baytarnamede At Kültürü (Yazyly ve Basyly Kaynaklarla Karşilaşrma)*. Ankara.

Clancy-Smith, Julia. 1966. "La Femme Arabe: Women and Sexuality in France's North African Empire." In *Women, the Family, and Divorce Laws in Islamic History*, edited by Amira El Azhary Sonbol. Syracuse.

Clark, Hugh. 1890. *An Introduction to Heraldy, with Nearly One Thousand Illustrations (Including the Arms of About Five Hundred Different Families)*. London and New York.

Clot Bey, A.-B. 1840. *Aperçu général sur l'Égypte*. 2 vols. Paris.

Cohen, A., and B. Lewis. 1978. *Population and Revenue in the Towns of Palestine in the Sixteenth Century*. Princeton.

Cole, Juan Ricardo. 1981. "Feminism, Class, and Islam in Turn-of-the-Century Egypt." *International Journal of Middle East Studies* 13:387–407.

Comanos. n.d. *Mémoires du Dr. Comanos Pacha publiés à l'occasion de son jubilé de 40 ans d'exercise médical*. N.p.

Cosson, André. 1917. *Armorial des cardinaux, archevêques et évêques, français actuels résidentiels et titulaires au 1er janvier 1917*. Ouvrage orné de 190 blasons et sceaux et de 182 portraits hors texte. Paris.

Courbage, Youssef, and Philippe Fargues. 1997. *Christians and Jews under Islam*. London and New York.

Crecelius, Daniel. 1981. *The Roots of Modern Egypt: A Study of the Regimes of Ali Bey al-Kabir and Muhammad Bey Abu al-Dhahab, 1760–1775*. Minneapolis.

Cromer, Earl of. 1908. *Modern Egypt*. 2 vols. New York.

———. 1915. *Abbas II*. London.

Cuno, Kenneth M. 1992. *The Pasha's Peasants: Land, Society, and Economy in Lower Egypt, 1740–1858*. Cambridge.

———. 1995. "Joint Family Households and Rural Notables in Nineteenth-Century Egypt," *International Journal of Middle Eastern Studies* 27:485–502.

Daghestani, Kazem. 1932. *Etude sociologique sur la famille musulmane contemporaine de Syrie*. Paris.

———. 1953. "The Evolution of the Moslem Family in the Middle Eastern Countries." *International Social Science Bulletin* 5:681–91.

Damurdashi, Ahmad. 1991. *Al-Damurdashi's Chronicle of Egypt: al-Durra al-musanah fi akhbar al-Kinana*. Translated and annotated by Daniel Crecilius and Abd al-Wahhab Bakr. Leiden, New York.

Davis, Fanny. 1986. *The Ottoman Lady: A Social History from 1718 to 1918.* Westport, Conn.

Davis, Philip. 1915. *Street-land, Its Little People and Big Problems.* New York.

Davis, Ralph. H. C. 1989. *The Medieval Warhorse.* London.

de Certeau, Michel de. 1984. *The Practice of Everyday Life.* Translated by Steven Rendall. Berkeley.

Delanoue, Gilbert. 1982. *Moralistes et politiques musulmans dans l'Egypte du XIXe siècle (1798–1882).* Cairo.

De Leon, Edwin. 1882. *Egypt under Its Khedives; or, The Old House of Bondage under New Masters.* London.

———. 1890. *Thirty Years of My Life on Three Continents. With a Chapter on the Life of Women in the East, by Mrs. De Leon.* 2 vols. London.

De Malortie, Baron. 1883. *Egypt: Native Rulers and Foreign Interference.* London.

Deringil, Selim. 1998. *The Well-Protected Domains: Ideology and the Legitimation of Power in the Ottoman Empire, 1876–1909.* London.

Dewald, Jonathan. 1993. *Aristocratic Experience and the Origins of Modern Culture, France, 1570–1715.* Berkeley.

Dib, George M. 1975. "Law and Population in Lebanon." *Law and Population Monograph* 29. Medford, Mass.

Dicey, Edward. 1902. *The Story of the Khedivate.* London.

Djavidan Hanim. 1931. *Harem Life.* New York.

Doolittle, Megan. 1999. "Close Relations? Bringing Together Gender and Family in English History." *Gender and History* 11 (3): 542–54.

Doumani, Beshara. 1985. "Palestinian Islamic Court Records: A Source for Socioeconomic History." *Middle Eastern Studies Association Bulletin* 19:155–72.

———. 1994. "The Political Economy of Population Counts in Ottoman Palestine: Nablus circa 1850." *International Journal of Middle Eastern Studies* 26:1–17.

———. 1995. *Rediscovering Palestine: Merchants and Peasants in Jabal Nablus, 1700–1900.* Berkeley.

———. 1998. "Endowing Family: Waqf, Property Devolution, and Gender in Greater Syria, 1800 to 1860." *Comparative Study of Society and History* 40 (1): 3–41.

Duben, Alan. 1985. "Turkish Families and Households in Historical Perspective." *Journal of Family History* 10:75–97.

———. 1990. "Household Formation in Late Ottoman Istanbul." *International Journal of Middle East Studies* 22:419–35.

Duben, Alan, and Cem Behar. 1991. *Istanbul Households: Marriage, Family, and Fertility, 1880–1940*. Cambridge.

Duff, Gordon, Lucie. 1983. *Letters from Egypt*. London.

Dufferin and Ava, H. 1917. *My Russian and Turkish Journals*. New York.

Dykstra, Darrell I. 1977. "A Biographical Study of Egyptian Modernization: Ali Mubarak (1823/4–1893)." Ph. D. diss., University of Michigan at Ann Arbor.

Egyptian Gazette. 1909–10. (Alexandria)

Elifoglu, E. 1984. "Ottoman Defters Containing Ages of Children: A New Source for Demographic Research." *Archivum Ottomanicum* 9:321–28.

Erder, Türköz, ed. 1985. *Family in Turkish Society*. Ankara.

Ewen, Elizabeth. 1985. *Immigrant Women in the Land of the Dollars*. New York.

Fargues, Ph. 2000. "The Stage of the Family Life Cycle in Cairo at the End of the Reign of Muhammad Ali, according to the 1848 census." *Harvard Middle Eastern and Islamic Review* 5:1–39.

Farley, J. Lewis. 1872. *Modern Turkey*. London.

Farman Farmaian, Sattareh. 1992. *Daughter of Persia*. New York.

Farouqhi, Suraiya. 1981. *Men of Modest Substance: House Owners and House Property in Seventeenth Century Ankara and Kayseri*. Cambridge.

———. 1999. *Approaching Ottoman History*. Cambridge.

Farsoun, Samih. 1970. "Family Structure and Society in Modern Lebanon." In *Peoples and Cultures of the Middle East: An Anthropological Reader*, edited by Louise Sweet. New York.

Fathi, A., ed. 1985. *Women and the Family in Iran*. Leiden.

Faubion, James D. 1996. "Kinship is Dead. Long Live Kinship." *Comparative Studies in Society and History* 38 (1): 67–91.

Fay, Mary Ann. 1993. "Women and Households: Gender, Power, and Culture in Eighteenth-Century Egypt." Ph.D. diss., Georgetown University.

———. 1996. "The Ties That Bound: Women and Households in Eighteenth-Century Egypt." In *Women, the Family, and Divorce Laws in Islamic History*, edited by Amira Sonbol. Syracuse.

———. 1997. "Women and Waqf: Property, Power, and the Domain of Gender in Eighteenth-Century Egypt." In *Women in the Ottoman Empire: Middle Eastern Women in the Early Modern Era*, edited by Madeline Zilfi. Leiden.

———. 1998. "From Concubines to Capitalists: Women, Property, and Power in Eighteenth-Century Cairo." *Journal of Women's History* 10 (3): 118–40.

———. 1999. "In Search of the Harem: Gender, Space, and the Body in the Upper-Class Egyptian Household." Unpublished paper presented at the Eleventh Berkshire Conference on the History of Women, University of Rochester.

Ferchiou, Sophie, ed. 1992. *Hasab wa Nasab: Parenté, alliance, et patrimoine en Tunisie*. Paris.

Fernea, Elizabeth Warnock, ed. 1985. *Women and the Family in the Middle East*. Austin.

———. 1995. *Children in the Muslim Middle East*. Austin.

Findley, Carter V. 1980. *Bureaucratic Reform in the Ottoman Empire: The Sublime Porte, 1789–1922*. Princeton.

Flandrin, Jean-Louis. 1979. *Families in Former Times: Kinship, Household, and Sexuality*. Translated by Richard Southern. Cambridge.

Friedl, Erika. 1981. "Division of Labor in an Iranian Village." *MERIP Report* 95.

———. 1991. *Women of Deh Koh*. New York.

———. 1997. *Children of Deh Koh*. Syracuse.

———. 1998. "Telling the Stories of Iranian Women: Memory as Ethnographic Dilemma." Paper delivered at Rutgers University, New Brunswick, N.J.

———. 2001. "A Thorny Side of Marriage in Iran." In *Everyday Life in the Muslim Middle East*, edited by Donna L. Bowen and E. A. Early. Bloomington.

———. Forthcoming. "Rural Women's History." In *Women in Iran from Medieval Times to the Islamic Republic*, edited by G. Nashat. Urbana.

Friedl, Erika, and Agnes Loeffler. 1994. "The Ups and Downs of Dwellings in Iran." *Archiv für Völkerkunde* 48.

Friedman-Kasaba, Kathie. 1996. *Memories of Migration: Gender, Ethnicity, and Work in the Lives of Jewish and Italian Women in New York, 1870–1924*. New York.

Gabaccia, Donna. 1984. *From Sicily to Elizabeth Street: Housing and Social Change among Italian Immigrants, 1880–1930*. Albany.

Geertz, C., L. Geertz, and L. Rosen. 1979. *Meaning and Order in Moroccan Society*. Cambridge.

Gellner, Ernest. 1981. *Muslim Society*. Cambridge.

Gerber, Haim. 1989. "Anthropology and Family History: The Ottoman and Turkish Families." *Journal of Family History* 14 (4): 409–21.

———. 1994. *State, Society, and Law in Islam*. Albany.

Ghazzal, Z. 1993. *L'economie politique de Damas durant le XIXe siècle, structures traditionnelles et capitalisme.* Damas.

Ghazzi, K. N.d. *Kitab nahr al-dhahab fi tarikh Halab.* Vol. 2. 1st ed. Halab.

Giladi, Avner. 1990. "Some Observations on Infanticide in Medieval Muslim Society." *International Journal of Middle East Studies* 22.

Goody, Jack. 1969. *Comparative Studies in Kinship.* London.

———. 1983. *The Development of Family and Marriage in Europe.* Cambridge.

———. 1990. *The Oriental, the Ancient, and the Primitive: Systems of Marriage and the Family in Pre-Industrial Societies of Euroasia.* Cambridge.

Goody, Jack, Joan Thirsk, and E. P. Thompson. 1976. *Family and Inheritance: Rural Society in Western Europe, 1200–1800.* Cambridge.

Göyünç, N. 1979. "Hane deyimi hakkynda." *Tarih Dergisi* 32:331–48.

Gran, Peter. 1996. "Organization of Culture and the Construction of Family in the Modern Middle East." In *Women, the Family, and Divorce Laws in Islamic History,* edited by Amira El-Azhary Sonbol. Syracuse.

Granqvist, Hilda. 1931. *Marriage Conditions in a Palestinian Village.* Helsingfors, Finland.

Gray, John N., and David J. Mearns, eds. 1989. *Society from the Inside Out: Anthropological Perspectives on the South Asian Household.* New Delhi.

Green, Arnold H. 1981. "Family History in the Arab World: Archival History as a Complement to Ethnography." *International Journal of Sociology of the Family* 11 (July–December): 327–46.

Gross, M. L. 1979. *Ottoman Rule in the Province of Damascus, 1860–1909.* Ph.D. diss., Georgetown University.

Guppy, Shusha. 1988. *The Blindfold Horse.* Boston.

Haeri, Shahla. 1989. *Law of Desire: Temporary Marriage in Shiʾi Iran.* Syracuse.

Halaçoğlu, Yusuf. 1991. "At." In *Türkiye Diyanet Vakfy İslâm Ansiklopedisi.* İstanbul.

Hallaq, Wael. 1998. "The Qadi's Diwan (sijill) before the Ottomans." *Bulletin of the School of Oriental and Asian Studies* 61:415–36.

Halpern, J. M. 1972. "Town and Countryside in Serbia in the Nineteenth Century: Social and Household Structure as Reflected in the Census of 1863." In *Household and Family in Past Time,* edited by P. Laslett and R. Wall. Cambridge.

Hammel, E. A. 1972. "The Zadruga in Process." In *Household and Family in Past Time,* edited by P. Laslett and R. Wall. Cambridge.

Hamont, P. N. 1843. *L'Égypte sous Méhémet-Ali*. 2 vols. Paris.

Hanks, William. 2000. *Intertexts: Writings on Language, Utterance, and Context*. Lanham, Md.

Hanna, Nelly. 1992. *Habiter au Caire: La Maison moyenne et ses habitants aux XVIIe et XVIIIe siècles*. Cairo.

———. 1996. "Marriage among Merchant Families in Seventeenth-Century Cairo." In *Women, the Family, and Divorce Laws in Islamic History*, edited by Amira El Azhary Sonbol. Syracuse.

———. 1998. *Making Big Money in 1600: The Life and Times of Isma'il Taqiyya, Egyptian Merchant*. Syracuse.

Hara, T. 1978. "Two Levels of a Domestic Group: An Islamic Case and Its Applications" (in Japanese). *Journal of Asian and African Studies* 15:1–14.

Hareven, Tamara K. and Andrejs Plakans, eds. Family History at the Crossroads: A Journal of Family History Reader, Princeton.

Hareven, Tamara K. 1991a. "The History of the Family and the Complexity of Social Change." *American Historical Review* 96(1): 95–124.

———. 1991b. "The Home and Family in Historical Perspective." *Social Research* 58 (1): 253–86.

———. 1996. "History and the Family: The Discovery of Complexity." *Journal of Marriage and the Family* 43:489–529.

Harik, Iliya. 1968. *Politics and Change in a Traditional Society*. Princeton.

Harris, Barbara J. 1976. "Recent Work on the History of the Family: A Review Article." *Feminist Studies* 3:159–72.

Harris, Olivia. 1981. "Households as Natural Units." In *Of Marriage and the Market*, edited by Kate Young, Carol Wolkowitz, and Roslyn McCullagh. London.

Hatem, Mervat. 1986. "The Enduring Alliance of Nationalism and Patriarchy in Muslim Personal Status Laws: The Case of Modern Egypt." *Feminist Issues* 6.

Hathaway, Jane. 1995. "Marriage Alliances among the Military Households of Ottoman Egypt." *Annales Islamologiques* 29.

———. 1997. *The Politics of Households in Ottoman Egypt: The Rise of the Qazdaghlis*. Cambridge.

Hegland, Mary Elaine. 1991. "Political Roles of Aliabad Women: The Public-Private Dichotomy Transcended." In *Women in Middle Eastern History*, edited by N. R. Keddie and B. Baron. New Haven.

Hibbert, Christopher. 1980. *The House of Medici: Its Rise and Fall*. New York.

Higham, John. 1988. *Strangers in the Land: Patterns of American Nativism (1860–1925)*. New Brunswick, N.J.

Hilal, Imad Ahmad. 1999. *Al-Raqiq fi misr fi al-qarn al-tasi ashar*. Cairo.

Hilal, J. 1970. "Father's Brother's Daughter Marriage in Arab Communities: A Problem for Sociological Explanation." *Middle East Forum* 46 (2): 73–84.

Hodges, Sarah. 1999. "Conjugality, Progeny, and Progress: Family and Modernity in Twentieth-Century India." Ph.D. diss., University of Chicago.

Holt, Peter M. 1966. *Egypt and the Fertile Crescent, 1517–1922*. Ithaca.

———. 1968. *Political and Social Change in Modern Egypt*. Oxford.

Holy, Ladislavn. 1989. *Kinship, Honour, and Solidarity: Cousin Marriage in the Middle East*. Manchester.

Hourani, Albert, and Nadim Shehadi. 1992. *The Lebanese in the World: A Century of Emigration*. London.

Howe, H. A. 1903. *Boston: The Place and the People*. New York.

Hudson, Michael. 1968. *The Precarious Republic: Political Modernization in Lebanon*. New York.

Hunter, F. Robert. 1984. *Egypt under the Khedives, 1805–1879: From Household Government to Modern Bureaucracy*. Pittsburgh.

———. 1998. "Egypt under the Successors of Muhammad Ali." In *The Cambridge History of Egypt*, vol. 2, *Modern Egypt from 1517 to the End of the Twentieth Century*, edited by M. W. Daly. Cambridge.

Hyland, Ann. 1994. *The Medieval Warhorse: From Byzantium to the Crusades*. Dover, N.H.

Imber, Colin. 1996. "Women, Marriage, and Property: Mahr in the Behçet ül-Fetava of Yeniehirli Abdullah." In *Studies in Ottoman History and Law*. Istanbul.

İnalcık, Halil. 1965. "Adaletnameler." *Belgeler* 2:77.

———. 1980. "Military and Fiscal Transformation in the Ottoman Empire, 1600–1700." *Archivium Ottomanicum* 6. The Hague.

———. 1991. "Mahkama: The Ottoman Empire (the Earlier Centuries)." In *Encyclopedia of Islam*, 3–5. New ed.

Inhorn, Marcia C. 1996. *Infertility and Patriarchy: The Cultural Politics of Gender and Family Life in Egypt*. Philadelphia.

International Union for the Scientific Study of Population, ed. 1994. *Multilingual Demographic Dictionary*. Translated into Japanese by Nihon Jinko-Gakkai (Japan Association of Demographers), Tokyo.

al-Jabarti, Abd al-Rahman. 1967. *Aja'ib al-atharfi al-tarajim wa al-akhbar*. Cairo.

Jaussen, J. A. 1927. *Coutumes palestiniennes: Naplulouse et son district*. Paris.

Jerrold, Blanchard. 1879. *Egypt under Ismail Pacha: Being Some Chapters of Contemporary History.* London.

Johansen, Baber. 1981. "Sacred and Religious Elements in Hanafite Law: Function and Limits of the Absolute Character of Government Authority." In *Islam et politique au Maghreb,* edited by Ernest Gellner et al. Paris.

———. 1995. "Casuistry: Between Legal Concept and Social Praxis." *Islamic Law and Society* 2(2).

———. 1996. "The Valorization of the Human Body in Muslim Sunni Law." *Princeton Papers: Interdisciplinary Journal of Middle Eastern Studies* 4:71–112.

———. 1999. *Contingency in a Sacred Law: Legal and Ethical Norms in the Muslim Fiqh.* Leiden.

Johnson, Kay Ann. 1983. *Women, the Family, and Peasant Revolution in China.* Chicago.

Joseph, Suad. 1978. "Muslim-Christian Conflict in Lebanon: A Perspective on the Evolution of Sectarianism." In *Muslim-Christian Conflicts: Economic, Political, and Social Origins,* edited by S. Joseph, and B.L.K. Pillsbury. Boulder.

———. 1983. "Working Class Women's Networks in a Sectarian State: A Political Paradox." *American Ethnologist* 10 (1): 1–22.

———. 1988. "Family, Religion, and State: Middle Eastern Models." In *Dialectics and Gender: Anthropological Approaches,* edited by Richard R. Randolph et al. Boulder.

Juliani, Richard N. 1978. "The Settlement House and the Italian Family." In *The Italian Immigrant Woman in North America,* edited by Betty Boyd Caroli, Robert Harvey, and Lydia Tomasi. Ont.

Kandiyoti, Deniz. 1985. "Continuity and Change in the Family: A Comparative Approach." In *Family in Turkish Society: Sociological and Legal Studies,* edited by Türköz Erder. Ankara.

———. 1988. "Bargaining with Patriarchy." *Gender and Society* 2 (3): 274–90.

———. 1991a. Introduction to *Women, Islam, and the State.* Edited by Deniz Kandiyoti. Philadelphia.

———. 1991b. "Islam and Patriarchy." In *Women in Middle Eastern History: Shifting Boundaries in Sex and Gender,* edited by Nikki Keddie and Beth Baron. New Haven.

———. 1994. "Identity and Its Discontents: Women and the Nation." In *Colonial Discourse and Post-Colonial Theory: A Reader,* edited by Patrick Williams and Laura Chrisman. New York.

Karpat, K. 1985. *Ottoman Population, 1830–1914: Demographic and Social Characteristics.* Madison.

————. 1987. "The Ottoman Family: Documents Pertaining to Its Size," *International Journal of Turkish Studies* 4:137–45.

Keddie, Nikkie, and Beth Baron, eds. 1991. *Women in Middle Eastern History: Shifting Boundaries in Sex and Gender.* New Haven.

Kertzer, David I. 1984. "Anthropology and Family History." *Journal of Family History* 9:201–16.

Keyder, Çağlar. 1999. "Peripheral Port-Cities and Politics on the Eve of the Great War." *New Perspectives on Turkey* 20:27–46.

Keyder, Çağlar, Y. Eyup Özveren, and Donald Quataert. 1993. "Port-Cities in the Ottoman Empire: Some Theoretical and Historical Perspectives." *Review* 16 (4): 519–58. Special issue entitled *Port Cities in the Eastern Mediterranean*, edited by Çağlar Keyder, Y. Eyup Özveren, and Donald Quataert.

Khalaf, Sulayman Najm. 1981. *Family, Village, and the Political Party: Articulation of Social Change in Contemporary Rural Syria.* Los Angeles.

Khanki, Aziz. 1938. "Zawjat hukkam misr min muhammad ali basha al-kabir ila jalalat al-malik faruq al-awwal," Special issue of *al-Musawwar* on the occasion of the royal wedding (King Faruq and Farida). Reprinted in idem, *Nafahat Tarikhiyya.* Cairo, n.d.

Khater, Akram. 1996. "House to Goddess of the House." *International Journal of Middle East Studies* 28:325–48.

Khuri, Fuad. 1970. "Parallel Cousin Marriage Reconsidered: A Middle Eastern Practice That Nullifies the Effects of Marriage on the Intensity of Family Relationships." *Man* 5:597–618.

Knoph, S. Andolphus. 1916. *Survey* 37:154–69.

Koelz, Walter. 1983. *Persian Diary, 1939–1941.* Ann Arbor.

Kolenda, Pauline. 1996. "Religion, Caste, and Family Structure: A Comparative Study of the Indian 'Joint' Family." In *Structure and Change in Indian Society*, edited by Milton Singer and Bernard Cohn. Jaipur.

Kordi, Gohar. 1991. *An Iranian Odyssey.* London.

Kunt, Metin. 1983. *The Sultan's Servants: The Transformation of Ottoman Provincial Government, 1550–1650.* New York.

Lane, Edward W. 1955. *Arabic-English Lexicon.* Book 1, part 5. New York.

Lansing, John B. and Leslie Kish. 1957. "Family Life Cycle as an Independent Variable." *American Sociological Review* 22(5):512–19.

————. [1812] 1978. *An Account of the Manners and Customs of the Modern Egyptians, Written in Egypt during the Years 1833–1835.* London.

Laslett, Peter. 1972. "Introduction: The History of the Family." In *Household and Family in Past Time*, edited by P. Laslett and R. Wall. Cambridge.

———. 1977. *Family Life and Illicit Love in Earlier Generations.* Cambridge.

———. 1983. "Family and Households as Work Group and Kin Group: Areas of Traditional Europe Compared." In *Family Forms in Historic Europe,* edited by P. Laslett, J. Robin, and R. Wall. Cambridge.

Laslett, Peter, and Eugene A. Hammel. 1974. "Comparing Household Structure over Time and between Cultures." *Comparative Studies in Society and History* 16.

Laslett, Peter, and Karla Oosterveen. 1973. "Long-term Trends in Bastardy in England: A Study of Illegitimacy Figures in the Parish Registers and in the Reports of the Registrar General, 1561–1960." *Population Studies* 27.

Laslett, Peter, and M. Clarke. 1972. "Houseful and Household in an Eighteenth-Century Balkan City: A Tabular Analysis of the Listing of the Serbian Sector of Belgrade in 1733–4." In *Household and Family in Past Time,* edited by P. Laslett and Richard Wall. Cambridge.

Laslett, Peter, and Richard Wall, eds. 1972. *Household and Family in Past Time; Comparative Studies in the Size and Structure of the Domestic Group over the Last Three Centuries.* Cambridge.

Laslett, Peter, Richard Wall, and Jean Robin, eds. 1983. *Family Forms in Historic Europe.* Cambridge.

La Sorte, Michael. 1985. *La Merica: Images of Italian Greenhorn Experience.* Philadelphia.

Lee, J., W. Feng, and E. Ochiai. Forthcoming. "Domestic Group Organization and Demographic Behavior in Eurasia, 1750–1900: A Reassessment of Metageography." In *Prices, Households, and Death in Eurasian Societies,* edited by T. Bengtsson, and C. Campbell. Cambridge.

Le Play, Frédéric. 1982. *On Family, Work, and Social Change.* Chicago and London.

Lévi-Strauss, Claude. 1969. *The Elementary Structures of Kinship.* Translated by J. H. Bell, J. R. von Sturmer, and R. Needham. London.

Leydesdorff, Selma, et al., eds. 1996. *Gender and Memory.* Oxford.

Lindisfarne, Nancy. 1991. *Bartered Brides: Politics, Gender, and Marriage in an Afghan Tribal Society.* Cambridge.

Lloyd, Jennifer M. 1999. "Conflicting Expectations in Nineteenth-Century British Matrimony: The Failed Companionate Marriage of Effie Gray and John Ruskin." *Journal of Women's History* 11(2).

Loeffler, Reinhold. 1971. "The Representative Mediator and the New Peasant." *American Anthropologist* 73(5).

———. 1988. *Islam in Practice.* Albany.

Lutfi, Huda. 1991. "Manners and Customs of Fourteenth-Century Cairene Women: Female Anarchy versus Male Shar`i Order in Muslim Prescriptive Treatises." In *Women in Middle Eastern History: Shifting Boundaries in Sex and Gender*, edited by Nikki Keddie and Beth Baron. New Haven.

Macleod, Arlene Elowe. 1991. *Accommodating Protest: Working Women, the New Veiling, and Change in Cairo*. New York.

Maher, Vanessa. 1974. *Women and Property in Morocco*. Cambridge.

Makdisi, Ussama. 1997. "Gender, Citizenship, and the Nation." Conference on Gender and Citizenship in Lebanon. March. American University in Beirut.

Ma׳oz, M. 1968. *Ottoman Reform in Syria and Palestine, 1840–1861*. Oxford.

Marcus, Abraham. 1986. "Privacy in Eighteenth-Century Aleppo: The Limits of Cultural Ideals." *International Journal of Middle East Studies* 18/19:165–84.

———. 1989. *The Middle East on the Eve of Modernity: Aleppo in the Eighteenth Century*. New York.

Marino, Brigitte, and Tomoki Okawara, eds. 1999. *Catalogue des Registres des Tribunaux Ottomans conservés au centre des archives de Damas*. Damascus.

Marsot, Afaf Lutfi al-Sayyid. 1978. "The Revolutionary Gentlewomen in Egypt." In *Women in the Muslim World*, edited by Lois Beck and Nikki Keddie. Cambridge, Mass.

———. 1984. *Egypt in the Reign of Muhamad Ali*. Cambridge.

———. 1995. *Women and Men in Late-Eighteenth-Century Egypt*. Austin.

———. 1996. "Women and Modernization: A Reevaluation." In *Women, the Family, and Divorce Laws in Islamic History*, edited by Amira El Azhary Sonbol. Syracuse.

Maza, Sarah. 1993. *Private Lives and Public Affairs: The Causes Celebres of Prerevolutionary France*. Berkeley.

McCarthy, Justin. 1990. *The Population of Palestine: Population History and Statistics of the Late Ottoman Period and the Mandate*. New York.

McCoan, J. C. 1877. *Egypt as It Is*. London.

Medick, Hans, and David Warren Sabean. 1984. "Interest and Emotion in Family and Kinship Studies: A Critique of Social History and Anthropology." In *Interest and Emotion: Essays on the Study of Family and Kinship*, edited by Hans Medick, and David Warren Sabean. Cambridge.

Melman, Billie. 1995. *Women's Orients: English Women and the Middle East, 1718–1918*. Ann Arbor.

Meriwether, Margaret. 1999. *The Kin Who Count: Family and Society in Ottoman Aleppo*. Austin.

Messick, Brinkley. 1993. *The Calligraphic State: Textual Domination and History in a Muslim Society.* Berkeley.

———. 1995. "Textual Properties: Writing and Wealth in a Shariᶜa Case." *Anthropological Quarterly* 68 (3): 157–70.

Mettam, Roger. 1995. "The French Nobility, 1610–1715." In *The European Nobilities in the Seventeenth and Eighteenth Centuries,* vol. 1: *Western Europe,* edited by H. M. Scott. London and New York.

Midlefort, H. C. Erik. 1994. *Mad Princes of Renaissance Germany.* Charlottsville and London.

Miller, Lucius Hopkins. 1969. *Our Syrian Population: A Study of the Syrian Communities of Greater New York.* San Francisco.

Minault, Gail, ed. 1981. *The Extended Family: Women and Political Participation in India and Pakistan.* Delhi.

Mink, Gwendolyn. 1995. *The Wages of Motherhood: Inequality in the Welfare State, 1917–1942.* New York.

Mir-Hosseini, Ziba. 1993. *Marriage on Trial.* London.

Mitchell, Timothy. 1990. "The Invention and Reinvention of the Egyptian Peasant." *International Journal of Middle East Studies* 22:129–50.

Miura, T. 1998. "Personal Networks Surrounding the Salihiyya Court in Nineteenth Century Damascus." Document dactylographie, table-ronde *"Espace et société dans les villes* arabes du *Machreq à l'epoque ottomane,"* May 1998, IFEAD, Damas.

Molho, Anthony. 1994. *Marriage Alliance in Late Medieval Florence.* Cambridge, Mass. and London.

Moors, Annelies. 1995. *Women, Property, and Islam: Palestinian Experiences, 1920–1990.* Cambridge.

———. 1998a. "Debating Islamic Family Law: Legal Texts and Social Practices." In *A Social History of Women and the Family in the Middle East,* edited by Judith Tucker and Margaret Meriwether Tucker. Boulder.

———. 1998b. "Wearing Gold." In *Border Fetishisms: Material Objects in Unstable Spaces,* edited by Patricia Spyer. New York and London.

———. 2000. "Women's Gold: Shifting Styles of Embodying Family Relations." Paper delivered at the Conference on Family History in Middle Eastern Studies, University of California at Berkeley.

Mubarak, Ali. 1979. *Ali mubarak al-aᶜmal al-kamila.* Edited and introduced by Muhammad Amara. 3 vols. Cairo.

Mundy, Martha. 1988. "The Family, Inheritance, and Islam: A Re-examination of the Sociology of Faraʾid Law." In *Islamic Law: Social and Historical Contexts,* edited by Aziz al-Azmeh. New York.

———. 1992. "Shareholders and the State: Representing the Village in the Late-19th Century Land Registers of the Southern Hawran." In *The Syrian Land in the 18th and 19th Centuries*, vol. 5: *Berliner Islamstudien*, edited by T. Philipp. Stuttgart.

———. 1994. "Village Land and Individual Title: Musha and Ottoman Land Registration in the Ajlun District." In *Village, Steppe, and State: The Social Origins of Modern Jordan*, edited by E. Rogan and T. Tell. London.

———. 1995. *Domestic Government: Kinship, Community, and Polity in North Yemen.* London.

———. 1996. "Qada Ajlun in the Late nineteenth Century: Interpreting a Region from the Ottoman Land Registers," *Levant* 28:79–97.

———. 2001. "Village Authority and the Legal Order of Property (the Southern Hawran, 1876–1922)." In *New Perspectives on Property and Land in the Middle East*, edited by R. Owen. Cambridge, Mass.

———. Forthcoming. "The State of Property: Late Ottoman Southern Syria (the Kaza Aclun, 1875–1918)." In *Constitutions of Property in Comparative Perspective*, edited by H. Islamoğlu. London.

Murphy, Robert F., and Leonard Kasdan. 1959. "The Structure of Parallel Cousin Marriage." *American Anthropologist* 61:17–29.

Mursy, Abdel Hamid Fahmy, ed. 1981. *Mudhakirat Huda Sha'rawi.* Cairo.

Musallam, Basim F. 1983. *Sex and Society in Islam.* Cambridge.

Naff, Alixa. 1985. *Becoming American: the Early Arab Immigrant Experience.* Carbondale.

Netting, Robert McC., et al., eds. 1984. *Households: Comparative and Historical Studies of the Domestic Group.* Berkeley.

Newton, Sarah. N.d. Senior honors thesis, University of California, Davis.

Nuran, İnci. 1966. "XVIII. Yüzyilda Ystanbul Camilerine Baty Etkisiyle Gelen Yenilikler." *Vakyflar Dergisi* 19.

Ochiai, E., and J. Lee. 1999. "Household and Domestic Group Organization in Eurasian Populations." Paper distributed in the EAP Meeting in The Hague, 17 June 1999.

Ofeish, Sami Adeeb. 1996. "Sectarianism and Change in Lebanon: 1843–1975." Ph.D. diss., University of Southern California.

———. 1999. "Muslim Feminism: Citizenship in the Shelter of Corporatist Islam." *Citizenship Studies* 3 (2).

Ortayly, İlber. 1985. "The Family in Ottoman Society." In *Family in Turkish Society*, edited by Türköz Erder. Ankara.

Owen, Roger. 1996. "The Population Census of 1917 and Its Relationship to Egypt's Three Nineteenth-Century Statistical Regimes." *Journal of Historical Sociology* (Oxford) 9 (4): 457–72.

Özman, Aylin. 2000. "The Portrait of the Ottoman Attorney and Bar Associations: State, Secularization, and Institutionalization of Professional Interests." *Der Islam* 77 (2): 319–37.

Panzac, D. 1993. *La population de l'Empire ottoman: Cinquante ans (1941–1990) de publications et de recherches.* Aix-en-Province.

Pascual, J.-P. 1983. *Damas à la fin du XVIe siècle.* Damas.

Pateman, Carole. 1988. *The Sexual Contract.* Stanford.

Peirce, Leslie P. 1993. *The Imperial Harem: Women and Sovereignty in the Ottoman Empire.* Oxford.

———. 1998a. "Le dilemme de Fatma: Crime sexuel et culture juridique dans une cour ottomane au début de temps modernes." *Annales: Histoire, Sciences Sociales* 53 (2): 291–320.

———. 1998b. "'She is trouble . . . and I will divorce her': Orality, Honor, and Representation in the Ottoman Court of ʿAintab." In *Women in the Medieval Islamic World: Power, Patronage, and Piety,* edited by Gavin R. G. Hambly. New York.

Peristiany, Jean G., ed. 1976. *Mediterranean Family Structures.* Cambridge.

Pine, Leslie Gilbert. 1963. *The Story of Heraldry.* London.

Piterberg, Gabriel. 1990. "The Formation of an Ottoman Egyptian Elite in the Eighteenth Century." *International Journal of Middle East Studies* 22:275–89.

Plakans, Andrejs. 1984. *Kinship in the Past: An Anthropology of European Family Life, 1500–1900.* London.

Pollard, Clarissa. 1997. "Nurturing the Nation: The Family Politics of the 1919 Egyptian Revolution." Ph. D. diss., University of California at Berkeley.

Poole, Sophia Lane. 1851. *The Englishwoman in Egypt.* 3 vols. London.

Powers, David. 1993a. "The Islamic Inheritance System: A Sociohistorical Approach." In *Islamic Family Law,* edited by Chibli Mallat and Jane Conners. London.

———. 1993b. "The Maliki Family Endowment: Legal Norms and Social Practices." *International Journal of Middle East Studies* 25 (3): 379–406.

———. 1994. "*Kadijustiz* or *Qadi*-Justice? A Paternity Dispute from Fourteenth-Century Morocco." *Islamic Law and Society* 1 (3): 332–66.

Prothro, Edwin Terry, and Lutfy Najib Diab. 1974. *Changing Family Patterns in the Arab East.* Beirut.

Qal ʿaji, M. R., H. S. Qunaybi, and Q. M. Sanu. 1996. *Mu ʿjam lugha al-fukaha*. Beirut.

Qassab Hasan, N. 1994. *Hadith Dimashqi, 1884–1983*. 4th ed. Damascus.

Qattan, Najwa. 1994. "Discriminating Texts: Orthographic Marking and Social Differentiation in the Court Records of Ottoman Damascus." In *Arabic Sociolinguistics: Issues and Perspectives*, edited by Yasir Suleiman. London.

———. 1996. "Textual Differentiation in the Damascus Sijill: Religious Discrimination—or Politics of Gender?" In *Women, the Family, and Divorce Laws in Islamic History*, edited by Amira Sonbol. Syracuse.

Raafat, Samir. 1994a. "Queen for a Day." *Al-Ahram Weekly*, 6 October. http://www.egy.com/historica

———. 1994b. "The Much Debated Royal Death on the Nile." *Egyptian Mail*, 11 June. http://www.egy.com/historica

al-Rafi ʿi, Abd al-Rahman. 1948. *Asr Isma ʿil*. 2 vols. Cairo.

Raymond, André. 1974. *Artisans et commercants au Caire au XVIIIe siècle*. 2 vols. Damascus.

———. 1983. "Le Caire sous les Ottomans (1517–1798)." In *Palais et maisons du Caire*, vol. 2: *Epoque ottomane (XVI-XVIIIe siècles)*, edited by Jacques Revault and Bernard Maury. Paris.

———. 1993. *Le Caire*. Paris.

———. 1995. *Le Caire des janissaires: L'Apogee de la ville ottomane sous Abd al-Rahman Katkhuda*. Paris.

Razovki, Cecilia. 1917. "The Eternal Masculine." *Survey* 39:112–19.

Redhouse, Sir James W. 1890. *A Turkish and English Lexicon*. Constantinople.

———. 1986. *New Redhouse Turkish-English Dictionary*. Istanbul.

Reimer, Michael J. 1996. "Demographic Statistics of the Arab World in the Ottoman Period." Paper delivered at the Arab Regional Population Conference, International Union for the Scientific Study of Population, Cairo.

Rizq, Yunan Labib. 1994. "Al-Ahram: A Diwan of Contemporary Life." *Al-Ahram Weekly*, 22–28 September Summary translation of "Al-Ahram diwan al-haya al-mu ʿasira" no. 61, *Al-Ahram*, 22 September.

Rosaldo, Michelle. 1980. "The Use and Abuse of Anthropology." *Signs* 5:389–417.

Rosen, Lawrence. 1990. *The Anthropology of Justice*. Cambridge.

Rosenfeld, Henry. 1958. "Processes of Structural Change within the Arab Village Extended Family." *American Anthropologist* 60:1127–39.

———. 1968a. "Change, Barriers to Change, and Contradictions within the Arab Village Family." *American Anthropologist* 79 (4): 732–52.

———. 1968b. "The Contradictions between Property, Kinship, and Power, as Reflected in the Marriage System of an Arab Village." In *Contributions to Mediterranean Sociology: Mediterranean Rural Communities and Social Change*, edited by J. G. Peristiany. The Hague.

———.1976. "Social and Economic Patterns in Explanation of the Increased Rate of Patrilineal Endogamy in the Arab Village in Israel." In *Mediterranean Family Structures*, edited by J. Peristiany. Cambridge.

Rudolph, Richard L. 1992. "The European Peasant Family and Economy: Central Themes and Issues." *Journal of Family History* 17 (2): 119–38.

Rugh, Andrea B. 1984. *Family in Contemporary Egypt.* Syracuse.

———. 1997. *Within the Circle: Parents and Children in an Arab Village.* New York.

Russell, J. C. 1960. "Late Medieval Balkan and Asia Minor Population." *Journal of Economic and Social History of Orient* 3:265–74.

Ryan, Mary. 1981. *Cradle of the Middle Class: The Family in Oneida County, New York, 1790–1865.* New York.

Ryder, Norman. 1987. "Reconsideration of a Model of Family Demography." In *Family Demography: Methods and Their Application*, edited by John Bongaarts, Thomas K. Burch, and Kenneth W. Wachter. New York.

Sabean, David Warren. 1990. *Property, Production, and Family in Neckarhausen, 1700–1870.* Cambridge.

———. 1998. *Kinship in Neckarhausen, 1700–1870.* Cambridge.

———. 2001. "Peasant Voices and Bureaucratic Texts: Narrative Structure in Early Modern German Protocols." In *Little Tools of Knowledge: Historical Essays on Academic and Bureaucratic Practices*, edited by Peter Becker and William Clark. Ann Arbor.

Sacks, Karen. 1975. "Engels Revisited: Women, the Organization of Production, and Private Property." In *Towards an Anthropology of Women*, edited by Rayna Reiter. New York.

Salem, Paul, K. Shehade, and M. Young, with Z. Majed. 1996. "Preliminary Draft of Report on Associational Life and Public Space in Beirut: Dialects of Unity and Diversity." Beirut, Lebanese Center for Policy Studies.

Salname-i vilayet-i Haleb (Halab). 1900, 1908. Vols. 28, 34.

Salname-i vilayet-i Suriye (Damascus). 1888–89, 1895–1900. Vols. 20–21, 27, 29–32.

Sammarco, Angelo. 1935. *Précis de l'histoire d'Égypte.* Vol. 4, *Les Règnes de abbas, de Saʾid et dʾIsmaʿil (1848–1879).* Rome.

Sandrow, Nahma. 1977. *Vagabond Stars: A World History of Yiddish Theater*. New York.

Schilcher, Linda. 1985. *Families in Politics: Damascene Factions and Estates of the Eighteenth and Nineteenth Centuries*. Stuttgart.

Schneider, David. M. 1984. *A Critique of the Study of Kinship*. Ann Arbor.

Schneider, Jane. 1984. "Review of Jack Goody, *The Development of the Family and Marriage in Europe*." *Man* 19 (4): 686–88.

Sciama, Lidia. 1981. "The Problem of Privacy in Mediterranean Anthropology." In *Women and Space*, edited by Shirley Ardener. New York.

Scott, H. M., and Christopher Storrs. 1995. "Introduction : The Consolidation of Noble Power in Europe, 1600–1800." In *The European Nobilities in the Seventeenth and Eighteenth Centuries, vol. 1: Western Europe*, edited by H. M. Scott. London and New York.

Sertoğlu, Mithat. 1986. *Osmanly tarih luğaty*. Istanbul.

———. 1994. *Tarihden Sohbetler*. İstanbul.

Shafiq, Ahmad. 1934. *Mudhakkirati fi nisf qarn*. 3 vols. Cairo.

Shah, A. M. 1974. *The Household Dimension of the Family in India*. Berkeley.

———. 1998. *The Family in India: Critical Essays*. London.

Shahar, Ido. 2000a. "Palestinians in an Israeli Court: Culture, Control, and Resistance in the Shariʾa Court of West Jerusalem" (in Hebrew). Master's thesis, [Hebrew], Hebrew University of Jerusalem.

———. 2000b. "The Dabt (Protocol), the Sijill (Verdict), and Their Context: The Politics of Court Record Production." Working paper presented at the International Workshop on Text, Context and the Constitution of Difference, Ben-Gurion University of the Negev, Beer-Sheva.

Sharabi, Hisham. 1988. *Neopatriarchy: A Theory of Distorted Change in Arab Society*. New York and Oxford.

Sharafeddine, Fahmiyyi. 1997. "The Constitution and Gendered Punishment: Discussion." Paper delivered at the Conference on Gender and Citizenship in Lebanon. March. American University in Beirut.

Sharara, Yolla P. 1978. "Women and Politics in Lebanon." *Khamsin* 6:6–32.

Sharif, H. 1987. *Tarikh Tarabulus al-Sham min aqdam azmaniha ila hadhihi al-ayyam*. Tripoli.

Sharubim, Mikhail. 1900. *Al-Kafi fi tarikh misr al-qadim wa al-hadith*. 4 vols. Bulaq.

Shaw, Standord J. 1962. *The Financial and Administrative Organization and Development of Modern Egypt, 1517–1798*. Princeton.

———. 1977. *History of the Ottoman Empire and Modern Turkey.* 2 vols. Cambridge.

Shorter, Edward. 1975. *The Making of the Modern Family.* New York.

Shuʿaysha, Mustafa. 1984. "Tiʿdad al-nufus fi Misr am 1262H/1846 A.D." (Le recensement de la population d'Égypte de 1846). *Alam al-Kutub* (Cairo), 7 (3): 313–24.

Simkhovitch, Mary. 1938. *Neighborhood: My Story of Greenwich House.* Boston.

Singerman, Diane, and Homa Hoofdar, eds. 1996. *Development, Change, and Gender in Cairo: A View from the Household.* Indiana Series in Arab and Islamic Studies. Bloomington.

Slyomovics, Susan. 1998. *The Object of Memory: Arabs and Jews Narrate the Palestinian Village.* Philadelphia.

Sonbol, Amira al-Azhary. 1995. "Adoption in Islamic Society: A Historical Survey." In *Children in the Muslim Middle East,* edited by Elizabeth Warnock Fernea. Austin.

———.1996a. "Adults and Minors in Ottoman Shariʾa Courts and Modern Law." In *Women, the Family, and Divorce Laws in Islamic History,* edited by A. Sonbol. Syracuse.

———, ed. 1996b. *Women, the Family, and Divorce Laws in Islamic History.* Syracuse.

Spiegel, Gabrielle M. 1997. *The Past as Text: The Theory and Practice of Medieval Historiography.* Baltimore.

Springborg, Robert. 1982. *Family, Power, and Politics in Egypt: Sayed Bey Marei— His Clan, Clients, and Cohorts.* Philadelphia.

Stack, Carol. 1974. *All Our Kin: Strategies for Survival in a Black Community.* New York.

Stansell, Christine. 1986. *City of Women: Sex and Class in New York, 1789–1860.* New York.

Steingass, F. 1973. *A Comprehensive Persian-English Dictionary.* New Delhi.

St. John, J. A. 1834. *Egypt and Mohammed Ali.* 2 vols. London.

Stoianovich, Trajan. 1980. "Family and Household in the Western Balkans, 1500–1870." In *Memorial Ömer Lutfi Barkan.* Paris.

Stone, Lawrence. 1979. *The Family, Sex, and Marriage in England, 1500–1800.* New York.

———. 1981. "Family History in the 1980s: Past Achievements and Future Trends." *Journal of Interdisciplinary History* 12 (1): 51–87.

Stowasser, Barbara. 1994. *Women in the Qurʾan: Traditions and Interpretation.* New York.

Straubenmueller, Gustave. 1906. "The Work of the New York Public Schools for the Immigrant Class." *Journal of Social Science* 44:165–83.

Suleiman, Michael. 1967. *Political Parties in Lebanon: The Challenge of a Fragmented Political Culture.* New York.

Sullivan, Soraya, trans. 1991. *Stories by Iranian Women.* Austin.

Sümer, Faruk. 1983. *Türklerde Atçylyk ve Binicilik.* İstanbul.

Suzuki, Sh. 1993. "General Discussion and Analysis of the Islamic Residence." *Iichiko, Journal of Intercultural and Transdisciplinary Studies* 26 31–48. Special Issue: Damascus.

Szajkowski, Zosa. 1978. "Deportation of Jewish Immigrants and Returnees before World War I." *American Jewish Historical Quarterly* 67:291–313.

Tapper, Richard. 1979. *Pasture and Politics: Economics, Conflict, and Ritual among Shahsavan Nomads of Northwestern Iran.* London.

Times. (London). 1854, 1880–84.

Thomas, A. 1620. *Illustrations sur l'histoire de Chalcondille.* Paris.

Thompson, I. A. A. 1995. "The Nobility in Spain, 1600–1800." In *The European Nobilities in the Seventeenth and Eighteenth Centuries,* vol. 1: *Western Europe,* edited by H. M. Scott. London and New York.

Thorne, Barrie, and Marilyn Yalom, eds. 1982. *Rethinking the Family: Some Feminist Questions.* New York.

Thornton, Thomas D. 1807. *The Present State of Turkey, or a Description of the Political, Civil, and Religious, Constitution, Government, and Laws of the Ottoman Empire.* London.

Tilly, Charles, ed. 1978. *Historical Studies of Changing Fertility.* Princeton.

———. 1988. "Family History and Social Change." *Journal of Family History* 12:319–30.

Tilly, Louise. 1987. "Women's History and Family History: Fruitful Collaboration or Missed Connection?" *Journal of Family History* 12 (1–3): 303–15.

Todorov, N. 1998. "Données démographiques sur la population urbaine de la province danubienne (Tuna Vilayeti) en 1866." In *Society, the City, and Industry in the Balkans, Fifteenth to Nineteenth Centuries,* edited by N. Todorov. Aldershot, U.K.

Todorova, Maria. 1983. "Population Structure, Marriage Patterns, Family, and Household (according to Ottoman Documentary Material from Northeastern Bulgaria in the 1860s)." *Etudes balkaniques* 1. Sofia.

———. 1988. "Myth-Making in European Family History: The Zadruga Revisited." *Etudes balkaniques* 2. Sofia.

———. 1993. *Balkan Family Structure and the European Pattern: Demographic Developments in Ottoman Bulgaria*. Washington, D.C.

Toledano, Ehud R. 1990. *State and Society in Mid-Nineteenth-Century Egypt*. Cambridge.

———. 1998. *Slavery and Abolition in the Ottoman Middle East*. Seattle and London.

Tucker, Judith E. 1985. *Women in Nineteenth-Century Egypt*. Cambridge.

———. 1988. "Marriage and Family in Nablus, 1720–1856: Towards a History of Arab Marriage." *Journal of Family History* 13 (2): 165–79.

———. 1993. "The Arab Family in History." In *Arab Women: Old Boundaries, New Frontiers*, edited by Judith E. Tucker. Bloomington and Indianapolis.

———. 1998. *In the House of the Law: Gender and Islamic Law in Syria and Palestine, Seventeenth-Eighteenth Centuries*. Berkeley.

Tugay, Emine Foat. 1963. *Three Centuries: Family Chronicles of Turkey and Egypt*. Oxford.

Turner, Byran S. 1993a. Preface to *Citizenship and Social Theory*. Edited by Bryan S. Turner. London.

———. 1993b. "Contemporary Problems in the Theory of Citizenship." In *Citizenship and Social Theory*, edited by Byran S. Turner. London.

Tutel, Eser. 1998. *At ve Atçlk*. İstanbul.

Uberoi, Patricia, ed. 1993. *Family, Kinship, and Marriage in India*. Delhi.

Vatuk, Sylvia. 1990. "The Cultural Construction of Shared Identity: A South Indian Muslim Family History." *Social Analysis* 28:114–31.

Waqa'i al-Misriyya, Al–. 1866–95 (selected years). Cairo.

Waterfield, Robin. 1998. *Prophet: The Life and Times of Kahlil Gibran*. New York.

Weir, Shelagh. 1989. *Palestinian Costume*. London.

Wemple, Suzanne. 1987. "Sanctity and Power: The Dual Pursuit of Early Medieval Women." In *Becoming Visible: Women in European History*, edited by Renate Bridenthal, Claudia Koonz, and Susan Stuard. 2d ed. Boston.

Wills, Howel. 1901. *Florentine Heraldry. A Supplement to the Guide Books*. London.

Winter, Michael. 1992. *Egyptian Society under Ottoman Rule, 1517–1798*. New York.

Woods, Robert Arhcery, and Albert J. Kennedy. 1922. *The Settlement Horizon: A National Estimate*. New York.

Wright, Susan. 1978. "Prattle and Politics: The Position of Women in Doshman-Ziari." *Journal of the Anthropological Society of Oxford* 9(2).

Yanagisako, Sylvia. 1979. "Family and Household: The Analysis of Domestic Groups." *Annual Review of Anthropology* 8:161–205.

Yanagisako, Sylvia J., and Carol Delaney, eds. 1995. *Naturalizing Power: Essays in Feminist Cultural Analysis*. New York.

Yanagisako, Sylvia J., and Jane Fishburne Collier, eds. 1987. *Gender and Kinship: Essays toward a Unified Analysis*. Stanford.

Yazbak, Mahmoud. 1997. "Nabulsi Ulama in the Late Ottoman Period, 1864–1914." *International Journal of Middle East Studies* 29:71–91.

―――. 1998. *Haifa in the Late Ottoman Period, 1864–1914: A Muslim Town in Transition*. Leiden.

Young, William and Seteney Shami. 1993. *Anthropological Approaches to the Arab Family: An Introduction*. Proceedings of a UNICEF Conference: Seminar on the Arab Family. Amman.

Yung, Judy. 1995. *Unbound Feet: A Social History of Chinese Women in San Francisco*. Berkeley.

Yuval-Davis, Nira. 1997 "Women, Citizenship and Difference." *Feminist Review* 57:4–27.

Zalzal, Marie Rose. 1997. "Personal Status and Sectarian Laws." Paper delivered at the Conference on Gender and Citizenship in Lebanon. March. American University in Beirut.

Ze'evi, Dror. 1998. "The Use of Ottoman Shari'a Court Records as a Source for Middle Eastern Social History: A Reappraisal." *Islamic Law and Society* 5 (1): 35–56.

Contributors

Iris Agmon is a lecturer in the Department of Middle East Studies at Ben-Gurion University. She is currently writing a book on family and court culture in nineteenth-century Palestine.

Kenneth M. Cuno is Associate Professor of History at the University of Illinois at Urbana-Champaign. He researches and writes on the social and cultural history of the Middle East since 1500. His first book, *The Pasha's Peasants: Land, Society, and Economy in Lower Egypt, 1740–1858*, received "honorable mention" in the Albert Hourani book prize competition of the Middle East Studies Association in 1993. He is currently writing a book on the history of the family in nineteenth-century Egypt.

Beshara Doumani is Associate Professor of History at the University of California, Berkeley. He is currently working on a comparative study of family history in Tripoli (Lebanon) and Nablus (Palestine) during the eighteenth and nineteenth centuries that focuses on the relationship between property, gender, kinship, and the praxis of Islamic law.

Philippe Fargues is senior fellow at Institut National d'Etudes Démographiques (Paris) and scientific director of the French journal of Middle Eastern studies *Maghreb-Machrek*. He has been director of the French research center in Cairo, visiting professor at Harvard, and research fellow in Beirut. He is the author of several books and articles on population issues in the Arab countries, methods of demography, minorities in the Middle East, geography, and current political economy.

Mary Ann Fay is Assistant Professor of History, American University of Sharjah, United Arab Emirates. Her research interests include women in eighteenth-century Egypt, family and households in the early modern period, gender and space, and the representation of women in European travel writing. She is the editor of *Auto/Biography and the Creation of Identity and Community in the Middle East from the Early Modern to the Modern Period* (Palgrave Press, 2001).

Heather Ferguson is a graduate student in history at the University of California, Berkeley. Her project—based on a combination of historical analysis of court records and the *fiqh*, *fatawa*, and *adab* literatures of Syria and Turkey in the sixteenth to eighteenth centuries with more contemporary anthropological fieldwork—explores the significance of boundaries in both religious law and in everyday practice.

Erika Friedl is the Emerita E. E. Meader Professor of Anthropology at Western Michigan University, where she taught for twenty-nine years. Her research, started in 1965, concentrates on Iran, especially on family issues in a tribal area. Her most recent book is *Children of Deh Koh* (1997). She lives in Michigan and continues to travel to the Middle East regularly.

Akram F. Khater is Associate Professor of Middle Eastern History at North Carolina State University. His recent book, *Inventing Home: Emigration, Gender, and the Middle Class in Lebanon, 1870–1920* (University of California Press, 2001) traces the lives of peasants from Mount Lebanon across the Atlantic and back, and highlights the transformations that they wrought through their voyages. He is currently working on the history of gender and religion in eighteenth century Lebanon.

Annelies Moors teaches in the Department of Anthropology and Sociology and is director of the Institute of the Study of Islam in the Modern World (ISIM) at the University of Amsterdam. She is at present writing about gender in Islamic family law and the body politics of photography in Palestine, and she is involved in research projects on dressing styles and wearing gold and on migrant domestic workers.

Martha Mundy is Senior Lecturer in the anthropology department of the London School of Economics. She studied Greek, Latin, Arabic, and geography before completing doctoral work under the supervision of Jack Goody at the University of Cambridge. She has taught history at UCLA and anthropology at Yarmouk University, the American University of Beirut, Université Lyon 2 Lumière, and the London School of Economics. Her research has concerned kinship, agrarian sociology, and the anthropology of law and the state. The article published in this volume forms part of a research project entitled "Property, Family and Administration: A Historical Anthropology of Islamic Jurisprudence and the Modern Ottoman State."

Tomoki Okawara is Lecturer of History at Keio University in Tokyo, Japan. He does research on the social and family history of the Middle East. He is currently finishing a book on family history in the Middle East, using Islamic court records as a historical source. He is the co-editor of *Catalogue des registres des tribunaux ottomans, conservés au centre des archives de Damas* (1999).

Richard Saumerez Smith is Associate Professor, Social and Behavioral Studies Department & Cultural Studies Program, American University of Beirut. He studied mathematics and anthropology at the Universities of Cambridge and Delhi. He has worked on techniques of governance developed by the British in India (census, land registration, mapping) and their relation to the colonial sociology and historiography of India. This background allows him to bring a comparative perspective to joint work with Martha Mundy on late Ottoman systems of land administration and the village sociology of what is today north Jordan.

Index

∽

SUNY Series in the Social and Economic History
of the Middle East

Donald Quataert, editor

341

Printed in the United States
25941LVS00003B/155